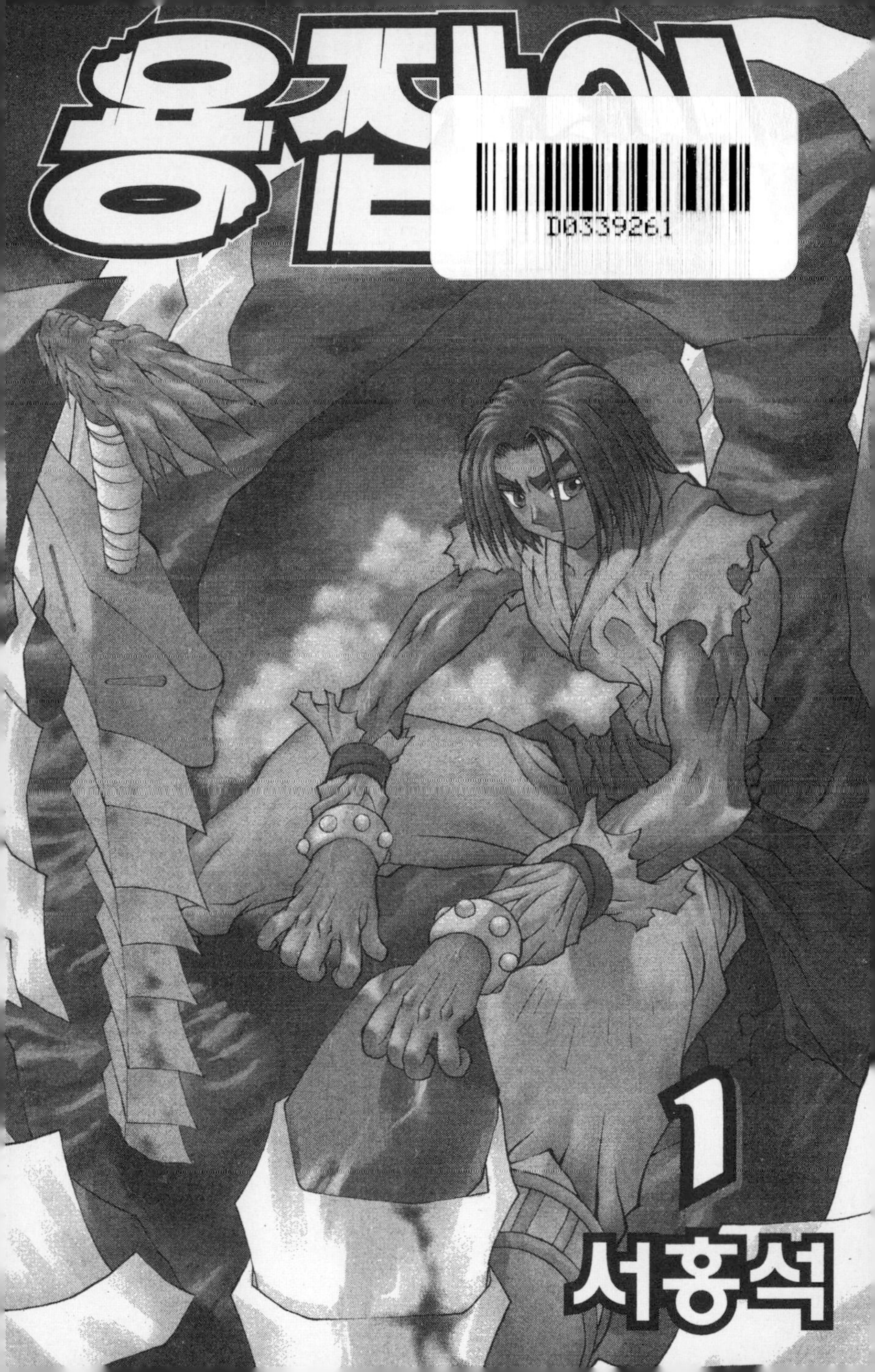

용
1
서홍석

ALSO AVAILABLE FROM TOKYOPOP®

MANGA

@LARGE (August 2003)
ANGELIC LAYER*
BABY BIRTH* (September 2003)
BATTLE ROYALE*
BRAIN POWERED*
BRIGADOON* (August 2003)
CARDCAPTOR SAKURA
CARDCAPTOR SAKURA: MASTER OF THE CLOW*
CHOBITS*
CHRONICLES OF THE CURSED SWORD
CLAMP SCHOOL DETECTIVES*
CLOVER
CONFIDENTIAL CONFESSIONS* (July 2003)
CORRECTOR YUI
COWBOY BEBOP*
COWBOY BEBOP: SHOOTING STAR*
DEMON DIARY
DIGIMON*
DRAGON HUNTER
DRAGON KNIGHTS*
DUKLYON: CLAMP SCHOOL DEFENDERS*
ERICA SAKURAZAWA*
ESCAFLOWNE* (July 2003)
FAKE*
FLCL* (September 2003)
FORBIDDEN DANCE* (August 2003)
GATE KEEPERS*
G GUNDAM*
GRAVITATION*
GTO*
GUNDAM WING
GUNDAM WING: BATTLEFIELD OF PACIFISTS
GUNDAM WING: ENDLESS WALTZ*
GUNDAM WING: THE LAST OUTPOST*
HAPPY MANIA*
HARLEM BEAT
I.N.V.U.
INITIAL D*
ISLAND
JING: KING OF BANDITS*
JULINE
KARE KANO*
KINDAICHI CASE FILES, THE*
KING OF HELL
KODOCHA: SANA'S STAGE*
LOVE HINA*
LUPIN III*
MAGIC KNIGHT RAYEARTH* (August 2003)

MAGIC KNIGHT RAYEARTH II* (COMING SOON)
MAN OF MANY FACES*
MARMALADE BOY*
MARS*
MIRACLE GIRLS
MIYUKI-CHAN IN WONDERLAND* (October 2003)
MONSTERS, INC.
NIEA_7* (August 2003)
PARADISE KISS*
PARASYTE
PEACH GIRL
PEACH GIRL: CHANGE OF HEART*
PET SHOP OF HORRORS*
PLANET LADDER*
PLANETES* (October 2003)
PRIEST
RAGNAROK
RAVE MASTER*
REALITY CHECK
REBIRTH
REBOUND*
RISING STARS OF MANGA
SABER MARIONETTE J* (July 2003)
SAILOR MOON
SAINT TAIL
SAMURAI DEEPER KYO* (August 2003)
SAMURAI GIRL: REAL BOUT HIGH SCHOOL*
SCRYED*
SHAOLIN SISTERS*
SHIRAHIME-SYO: SNOW GODDESS TALES* (Dec. 2003)
SHUTTERBOX (November 2003)
SORCERER HUNTERS
THE SKULL MAN*
TOKYO MEW MEW*
UNDER THE GLASS MOON
VAMPIRE GAME
WILD ACT* (July 2003)
WISH*
WORLD OF HARTZ (August 2003)
X-DAY* (August 2003)
ZODIAC P.I. * (July 2003)

*INDICATES 100% AUTHENTIC MANGA (RIGHT-TO-LEFT FORMAT)

CINE-MANGA™

CARDCAPTORS
JACKIE CHAN ADVENTURES (COMING SOON)
JIMMY NEUTRON (September 2003)
KIM POSSIBLE
LIZZIE MCGUIRE
POWER RANGERS: NINJA STORM (August 2003)
SPONGEBOB SQUAREPANTS (September 2003)
SPY KIDS 2

NOVELS

KARMA CLUB (July 2003)
SAILOR MOON

TOKYOPOP KIDS

STRAY SHEEP (September 2003)

ART BOOKS

CARDCAPTOR SAKURA*
MAGIC KNIGHT RAYEARTH*

ANIME GUIDES

COWBOY BEBOP ANIME GUIDES
GUNDAM TECHNICAL MANUALS
SAILOR MOON SCOUT GUIDES

Dragon Hunter

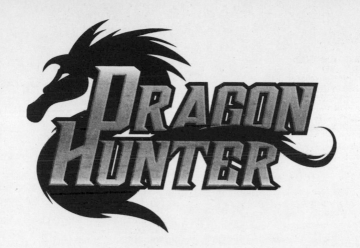

Volume 1

by

Hong-Seock Seo

with

Studio Redstone

TOKYOPOP®

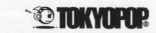

Los Angeles • London • Tokyo

Translator - Hye-Young Im
English Adaption - J. Torres
Associate Editor - Bryce P. Coleman
Retouch and Lettering - James Lee
Cover Artist - Puddnhead
Logo Design - Patrick Hook
Additional Design - Mark Paniccia

Editor - Mark Paniccia
Managing Editor - Jill Freshney
Production Coordinator - Antonio DePietro
Production Manager - Jennifer Miller
Art Director - Matthew Alford
Director of Editorial - Jeremy Ross
VP of Production & Manufacturing - Ron Klamert
President & C.O.O. - John Parker
Publisher & C.E.O. - Stuart Levy

Email: editor@TOKYOPOP.com
Come visit us online at www.TOKYOPOP.com

A 🐭 TOKYOPOP® Manga
TOKYOPOP® is an imprint of Mixx Entertainment, Inc.
5900 Wilshire Blvd. Suite 2000, Los Angeles, CA 90036

Dragon Hunter © 2000 by Hong-Seock Seo
All rights reserved. First published in Korea in 2000 by SEOUL CULTURAL PUBLISHERS Inc., Seoul.
English translation rights arranged by SEOUL CULTURAL PUBLISHERS Inc.

English text © 2003 by Mixx Entertainment, Inc.
TOKYOPOP is a registered trademark of Mixx Entertainment, Inc.

All rights reserved. No portion of this book may be reproduced or
transmitted in any form or by any means without written permission
from the copyright holders. This manga is a work of fiction.
Any resemblance to actual events or locales or persons,
living or dead, is entirely coincidental.

ISBN: 1-59182-161-4

First TOKYOPOP® printing:June 2003

10 9 8 7 6 5 4 3 2 1
Printed in USA

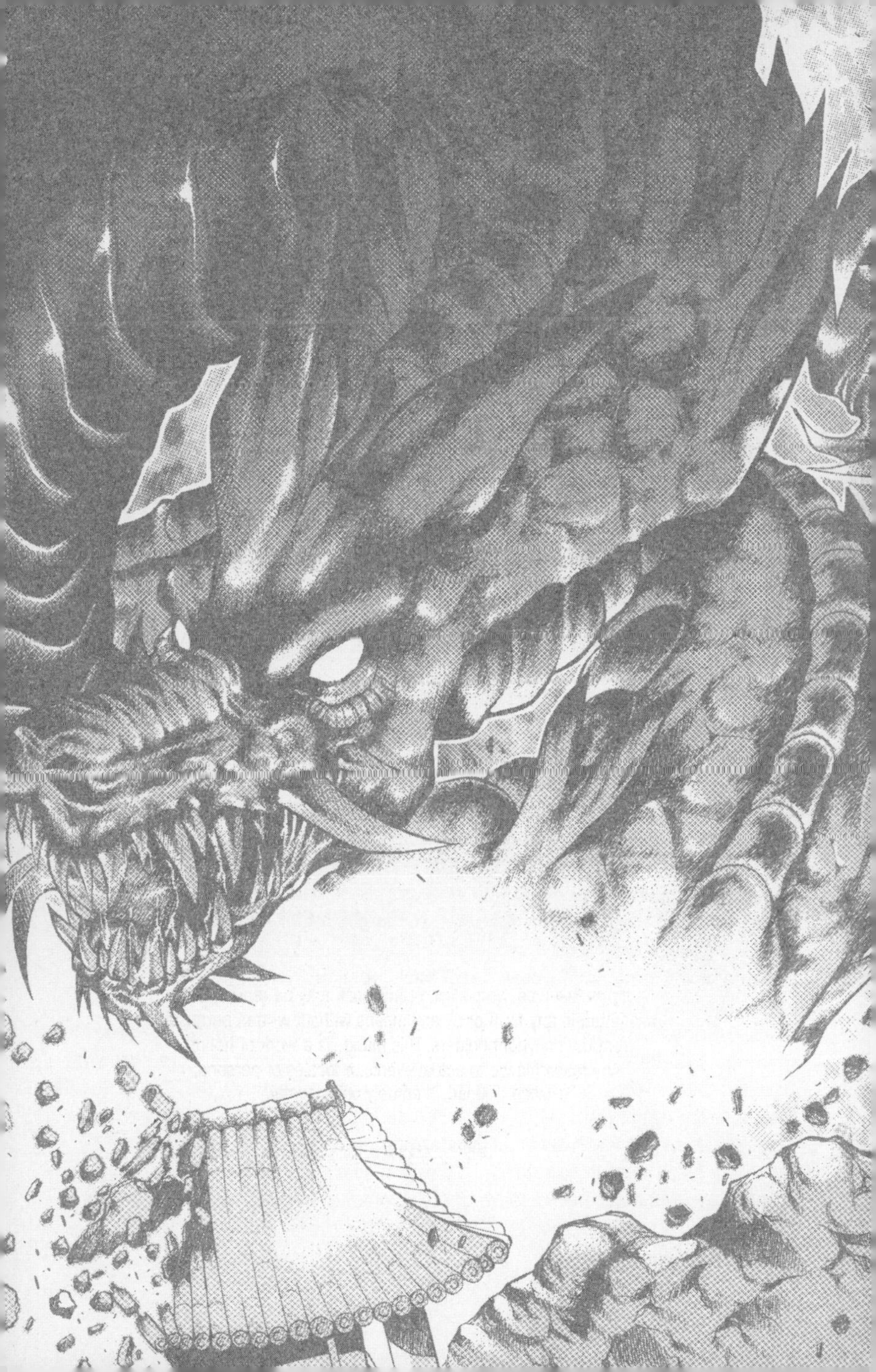

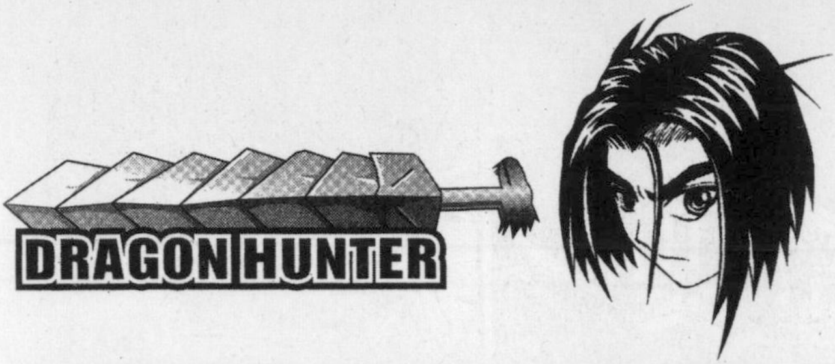
DRAGON HUNTER

ABOUT DRAGON HUNTER PART 1

As the title says, *Dragon Hunter* is about people who hunt dragons. I was reading a book with a subplot about tiger hunters and I thought, "That's it!" However, I figured tigers were too ordinary and wanted something more imaginative. I was also looking for something iconic and Korean, and what I came up with was dragons! That was my inspiration for creating *Dragon Hunter*. "I'll work on this later for sure," I told myself after making some notes. That was three years ago while I was working on another series.

Anyway, allow me to clarify a few things about the concept.

Dragons are not the main characters in the story and you will quickly come to understand how they appear to form the relationships between Dragon Hunters.

The story is set during a time before the Three States of Korea (editor's note: circa 500 A.D.) when the country consisted of many different smaller countries and kingdoms. However, I did not really do my research and I just chose to create a world based on an image of Korea that I liked. More than anything, Studio Redstone created this world. That's why you see houses on wheels we call "mobile units." These houses appear at the beginning of this volume and don't have a big part. I was a bit disappointed that I couldn't describe the mobile unit properly in the story, but I guess it will have a bigger role soon.

In Asia, dragons are holy animals that exist in the imaginary world. But dragons really exist in the world of this comic book. The Asian dragon is a creature with tiger-like eyes, deer-like antlers on its head, a snake-like body, etc. The common design of the dragon in Asia is a fantastic combination of different real animals. However, there are many types of Western dragons. So, for this comic book I fused the Asian dragon and different Western species. I did a lot of research on dragons but will leave you readers to discover what I found and put in the story.

Hong-Seock Seo

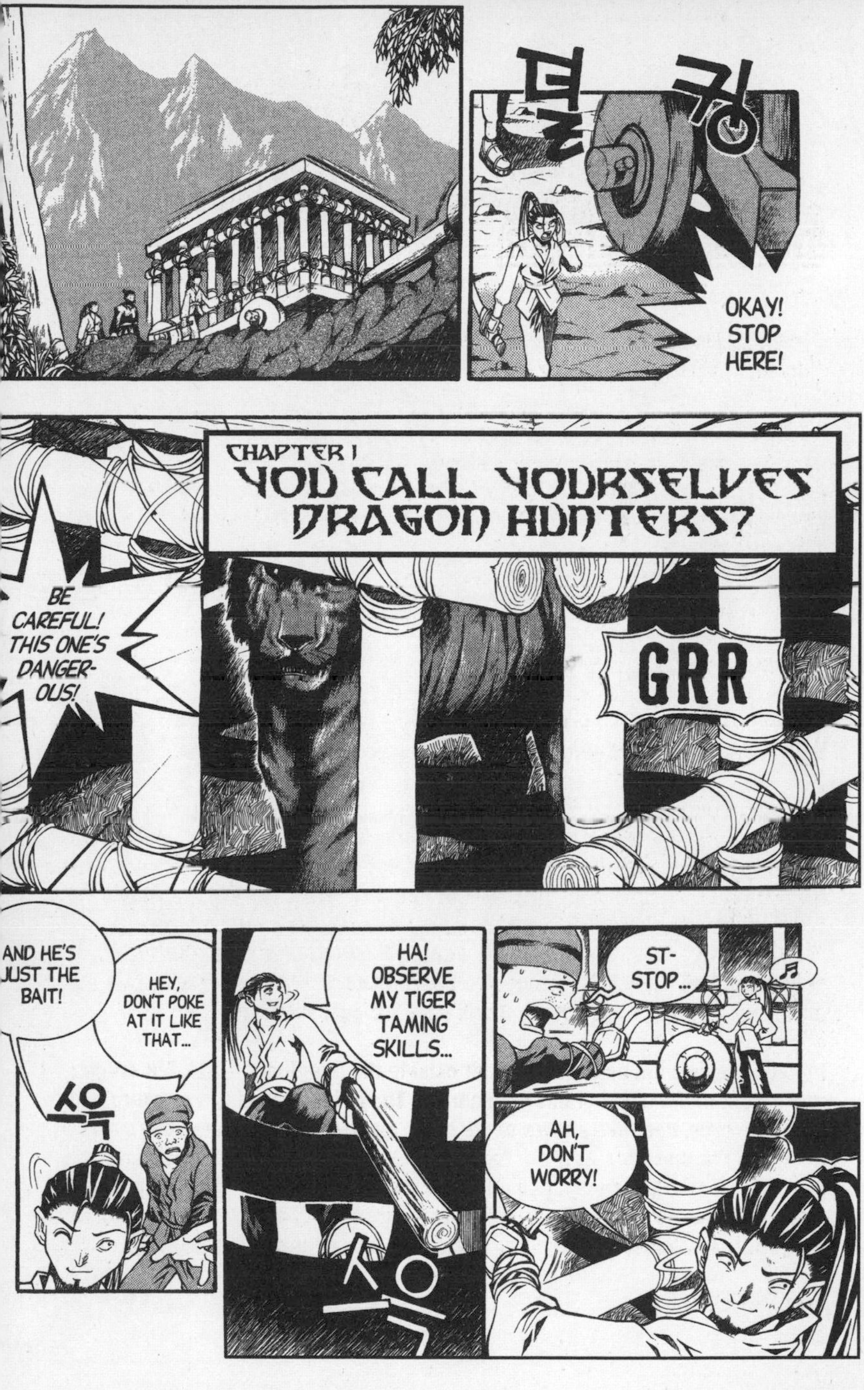

덜컹
OKAY! STOP HERE!
CHAPTER 1
YOU CALL YOURSELVES DRAGON HUNTERS?
BE CAREFUL! THIS ONE'S DANGER-OUS!
GRR
AND HE'S JUST THE BAIT!
HEY, DON'T POKE AT IT LIKE THAT...
HA! OBSERVE MY TIGER TAMING SKILLS...
ST-STOP...
AH, DON'T WORRY!

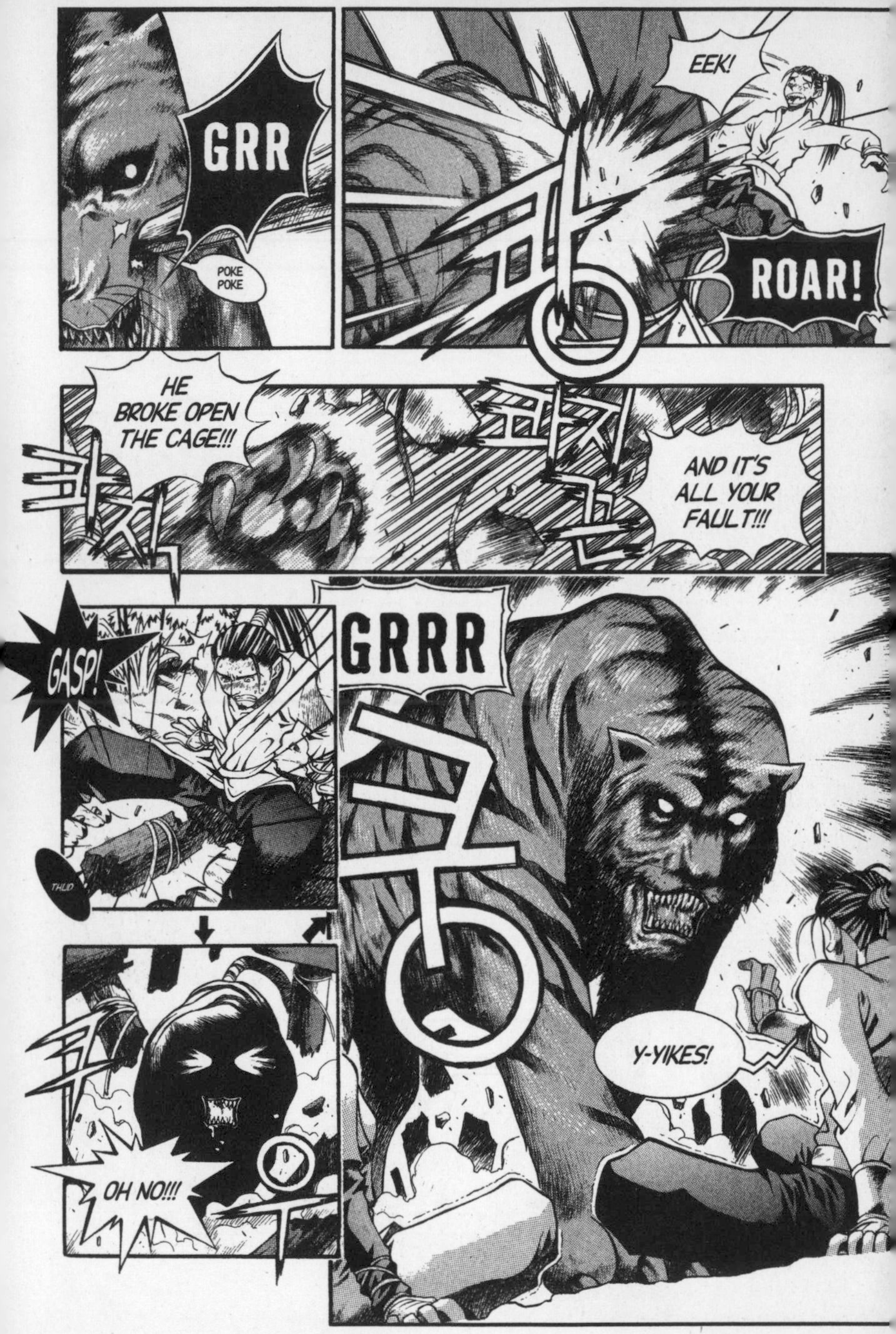
GRR
POKE POKE
EEK!
ROAR!
HE BROKE OPEN THE CAGE!!!
AND IT'S ALL YOUR FAULT!!!
GASP!
THUD
OH NO!!!
GRRR
Y-YIKES!

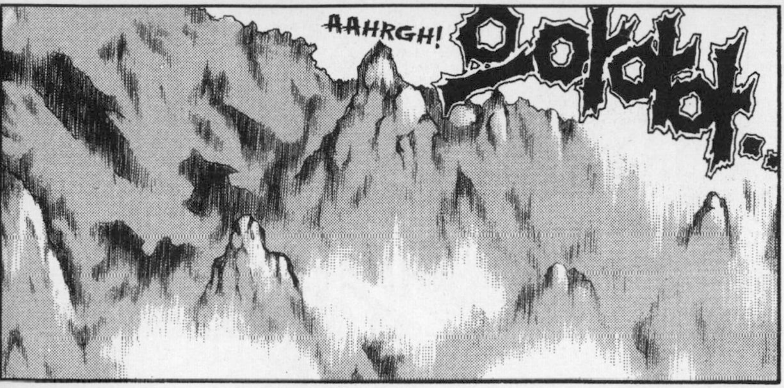
AAHRGH!
으아악..
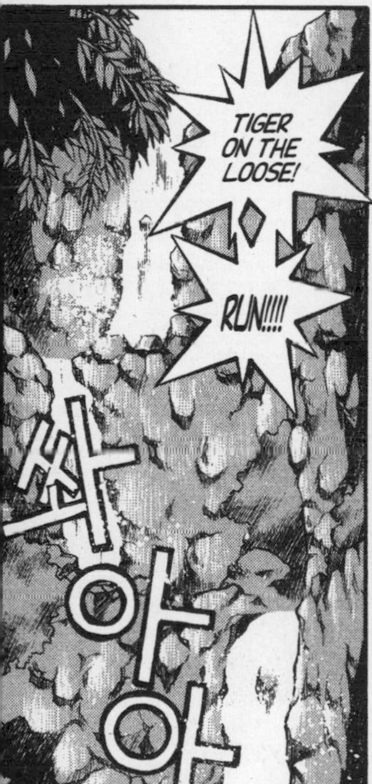
TIGER ON THE LOOSE!
RUN!!!!
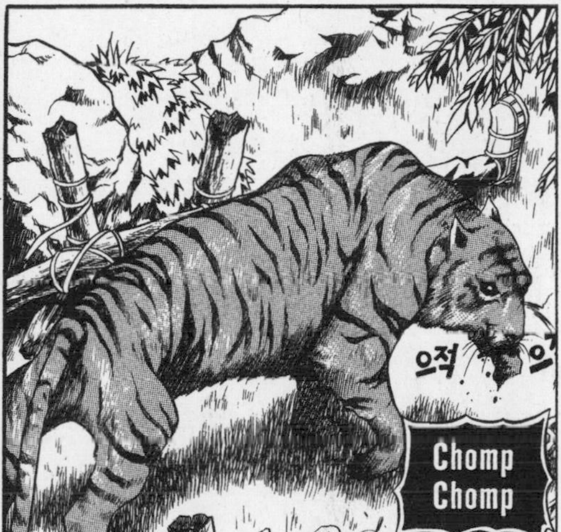
으적 으적
Chomp Chomp
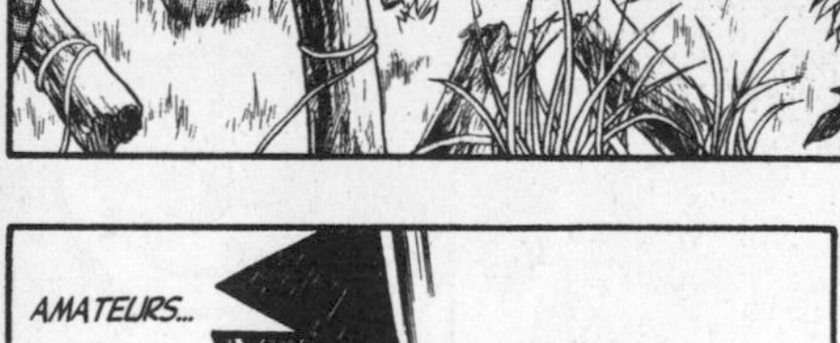
AMATEURS...
CRUNCH

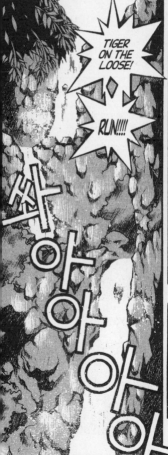

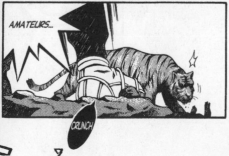

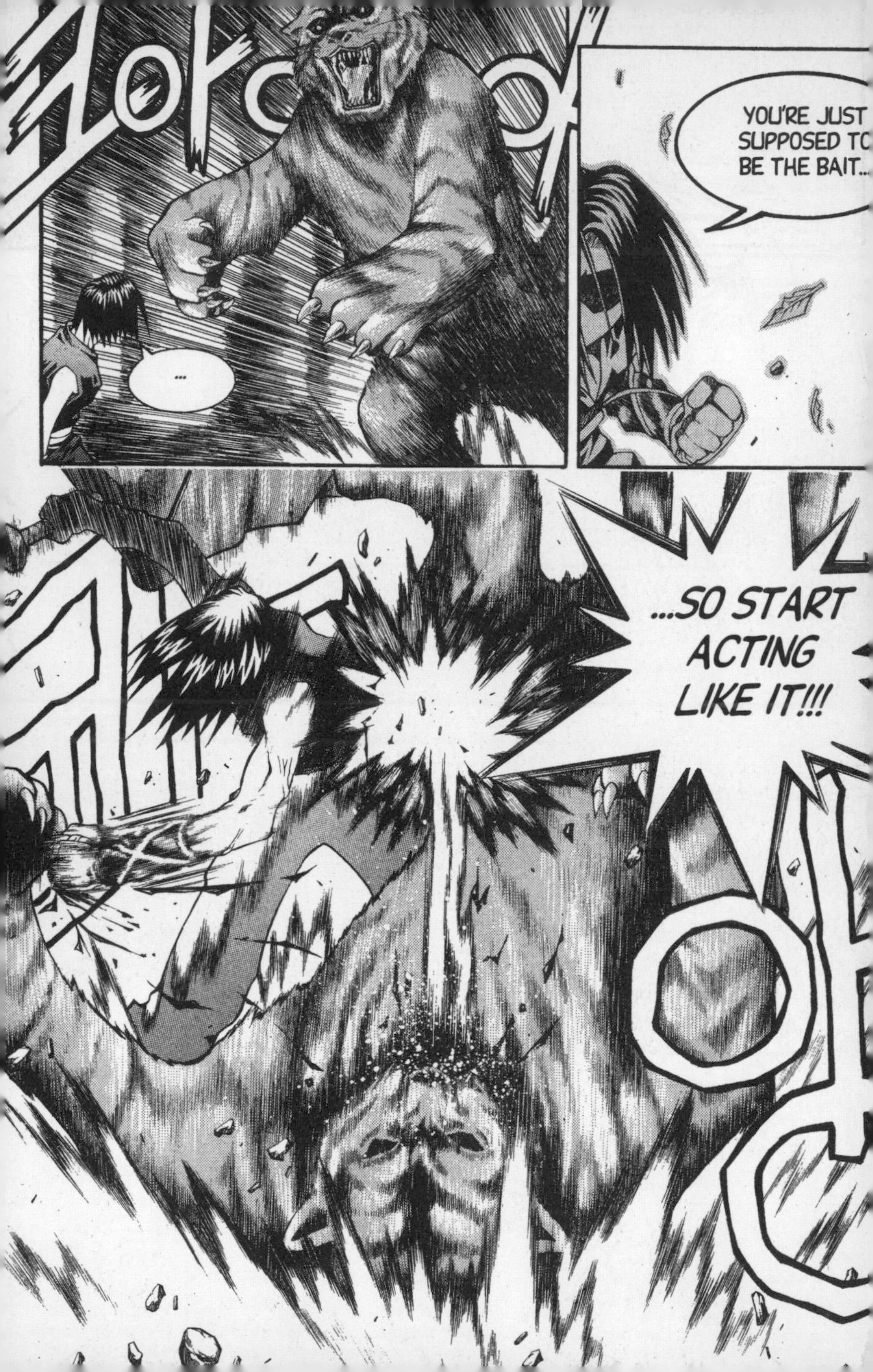
...
YOU'RE JUST SUPPOSED TO BE THE BAIT...
...SO START ACTING LIKE IT!!!

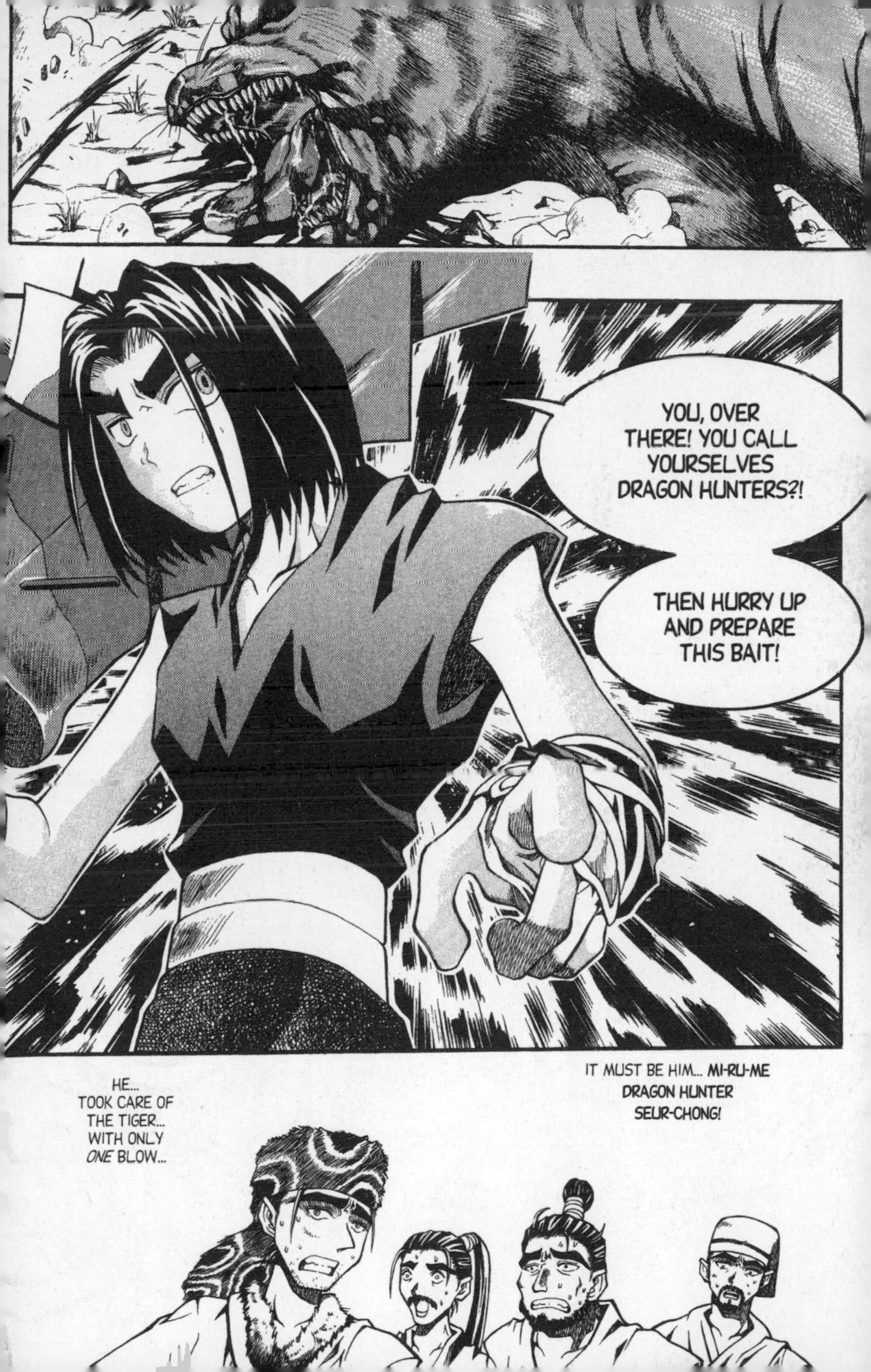
YOU, OVER THERE! YOU CALL YOURSELVES DRAGON HUNTERS?!
THEN HURRY UP AND PREPARE THIS BAIT!
HE... TOOK CARE OF THE TIGER... WITH ONLY *ONE* BLOW...
IT MUST BE HIM... MI-RU-ME DRAGON HUNTER SEUR-CHONG!

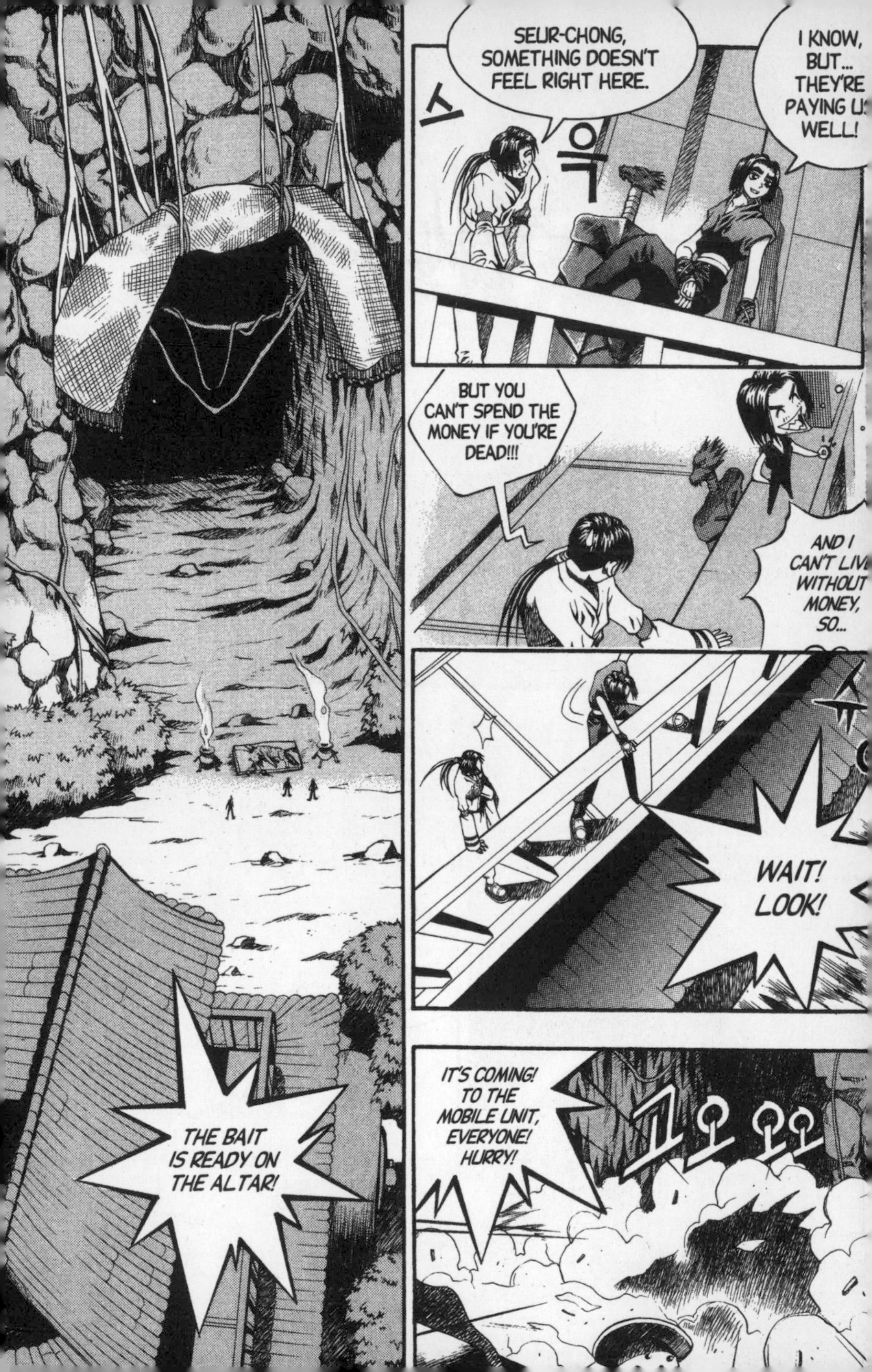
THE BAIT IS READY ON THE ALTAR!
SEUR-CHONG, SOMETHING DOESN'T FEEL RIGHT HERE.
I KNOW, BUT... THEY'RE PAYING U WELL!
BUT YOU CAN'T SPEND THE MONEY IF YOU'RE DEAD!!!
AND I CAN'T LIV WITHOUT MONEY, SO...
WAIT! LOOK!
IT'S COMING! TO THE MOBILE UNIT, EVERYONE! HURRY!

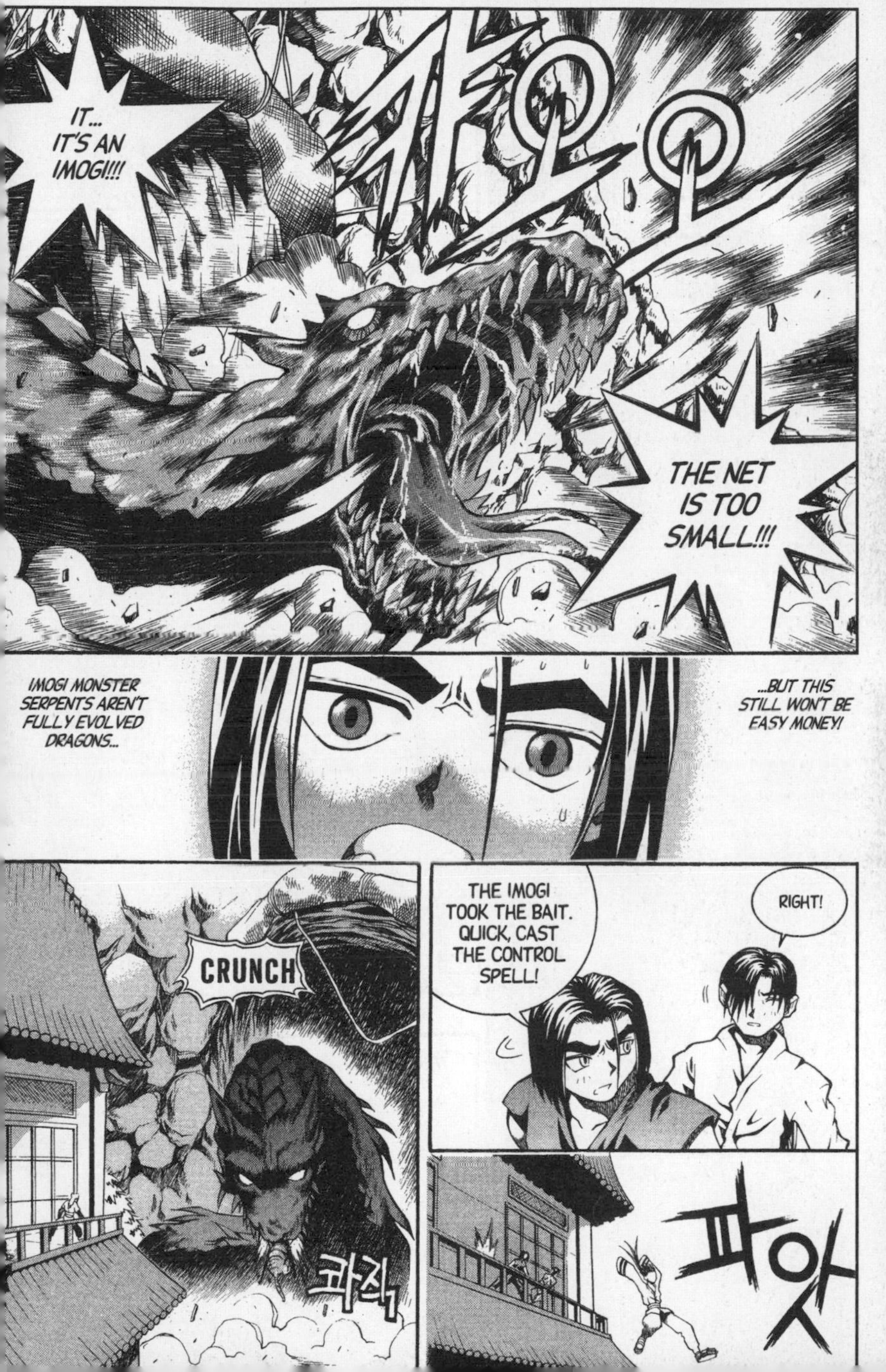
IT... IT'S AN IMOGI!!!
THE NET IS TOO SMALL!!!
IMOGI MONSTER SERPENTS AREN'T FULLY EVOLVED DRAGONS...
...BUT THIS STILL WON'T BE EASY MONEY!
CRUNCH
THE IMOGI TOOK THE BAIT. QUICK, CAST THE CONTROL SPELL!
RIGHT!

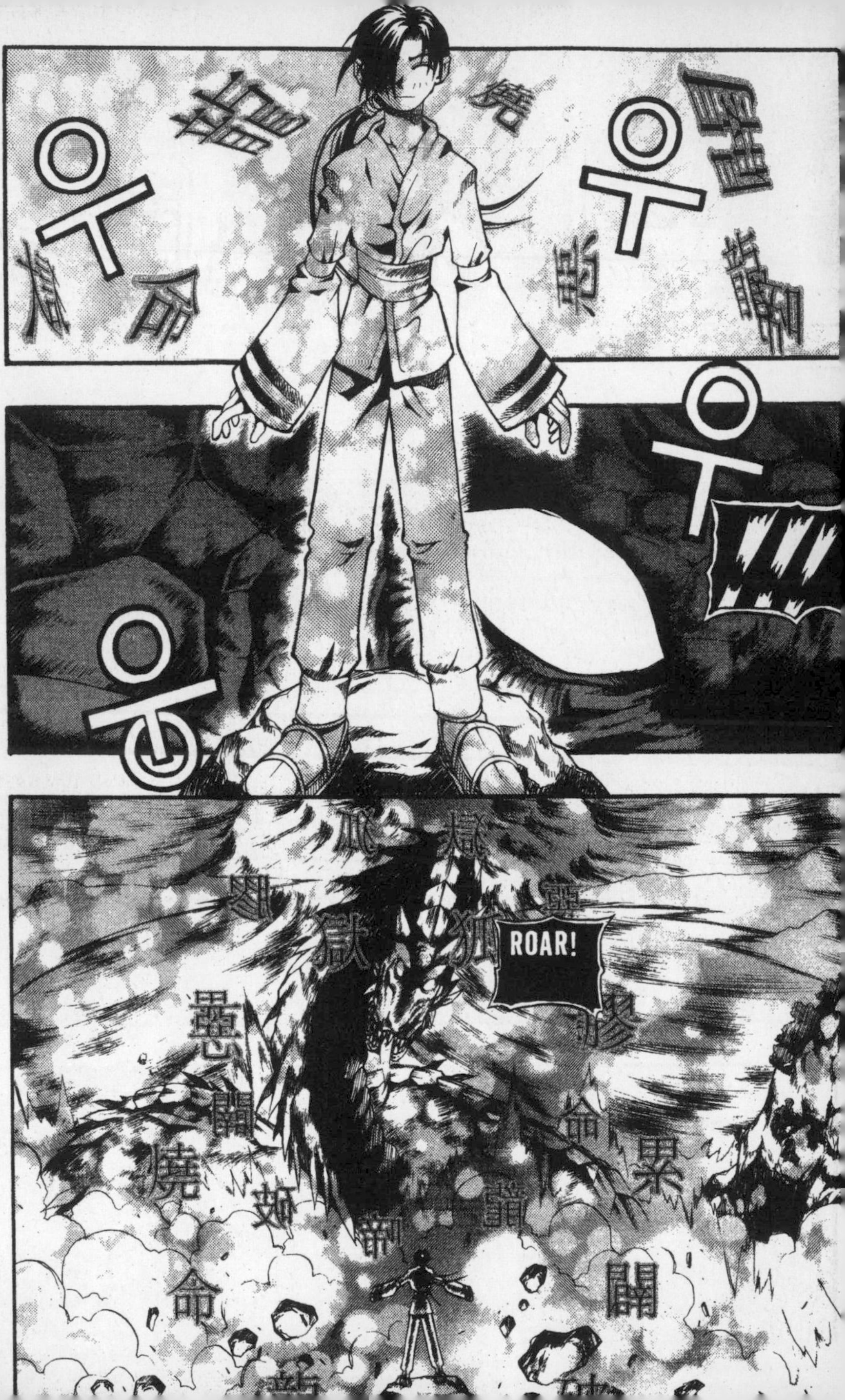
ROAR!

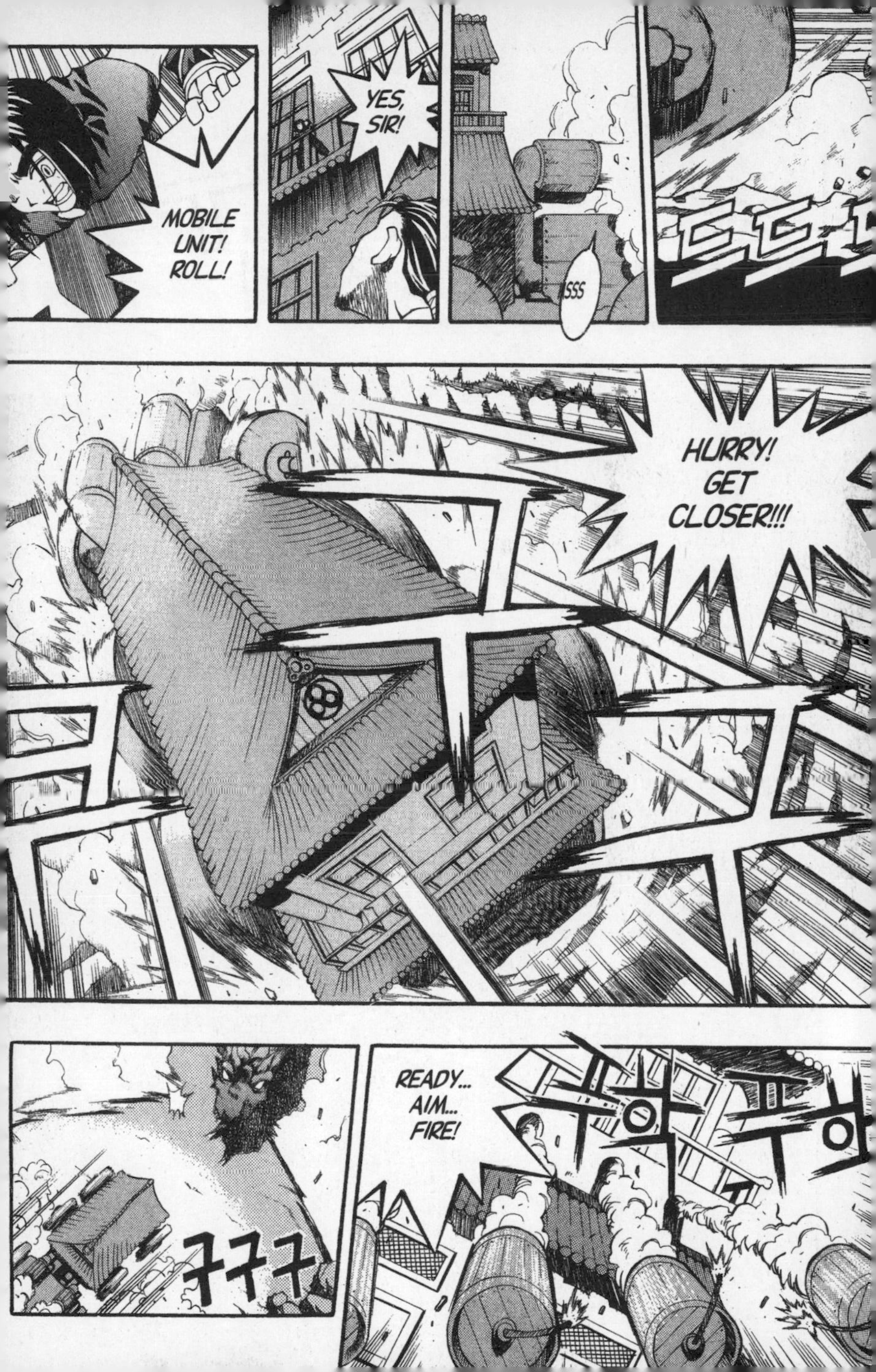
MOBILE UNIT! ROLL!
YES, SIR!
SSS
HURRY! GET CLOSER!!!
READY... AIM... FIRE!

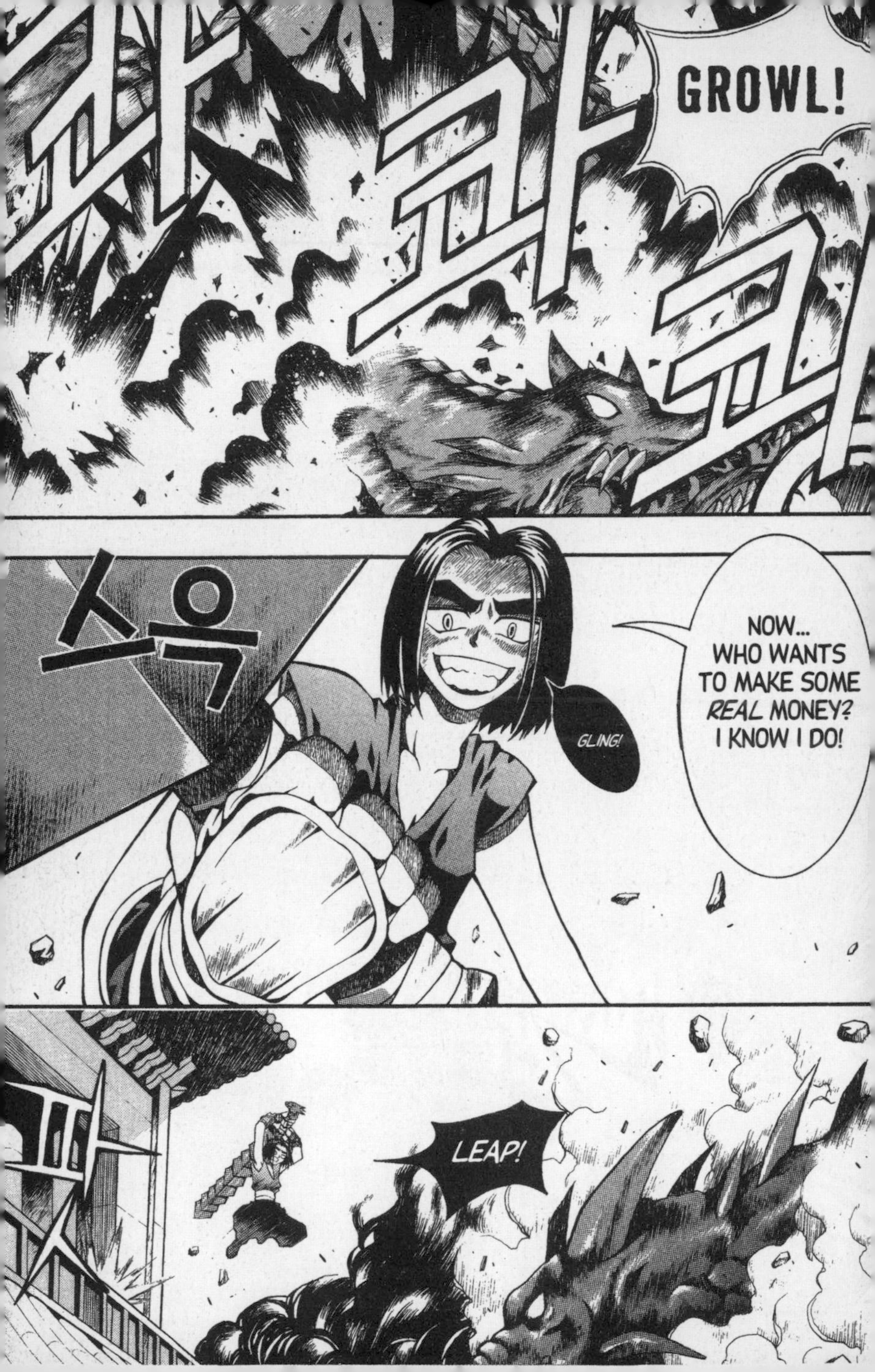
GROWL!
NOW... WHO WANTS TO MAKE SOME *REAL* MONEY? I KNOW I DO!
GLING!
LEAP!

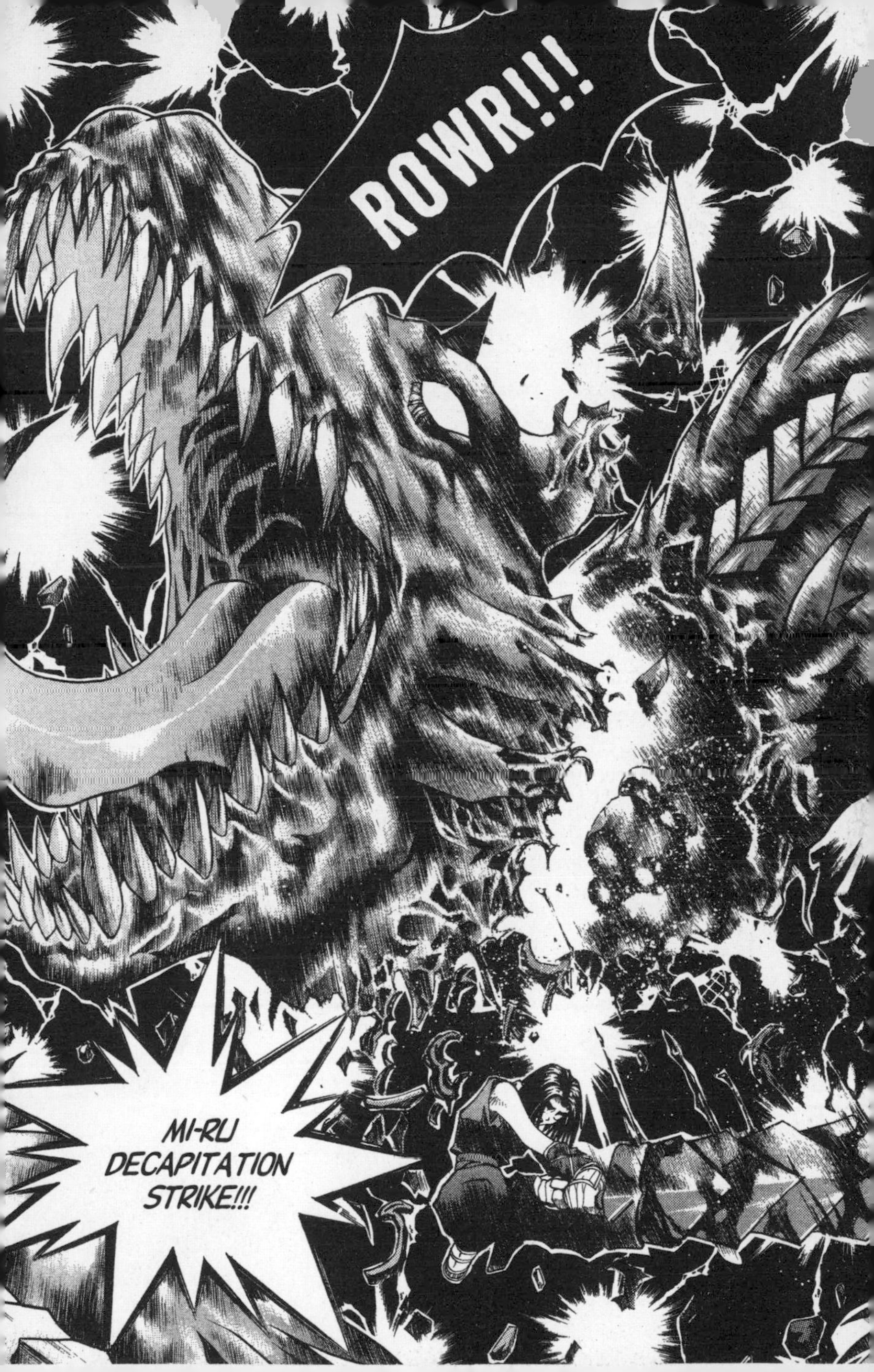
ROWR!!!
MI-RU DECAPITATION STRIKE!!!

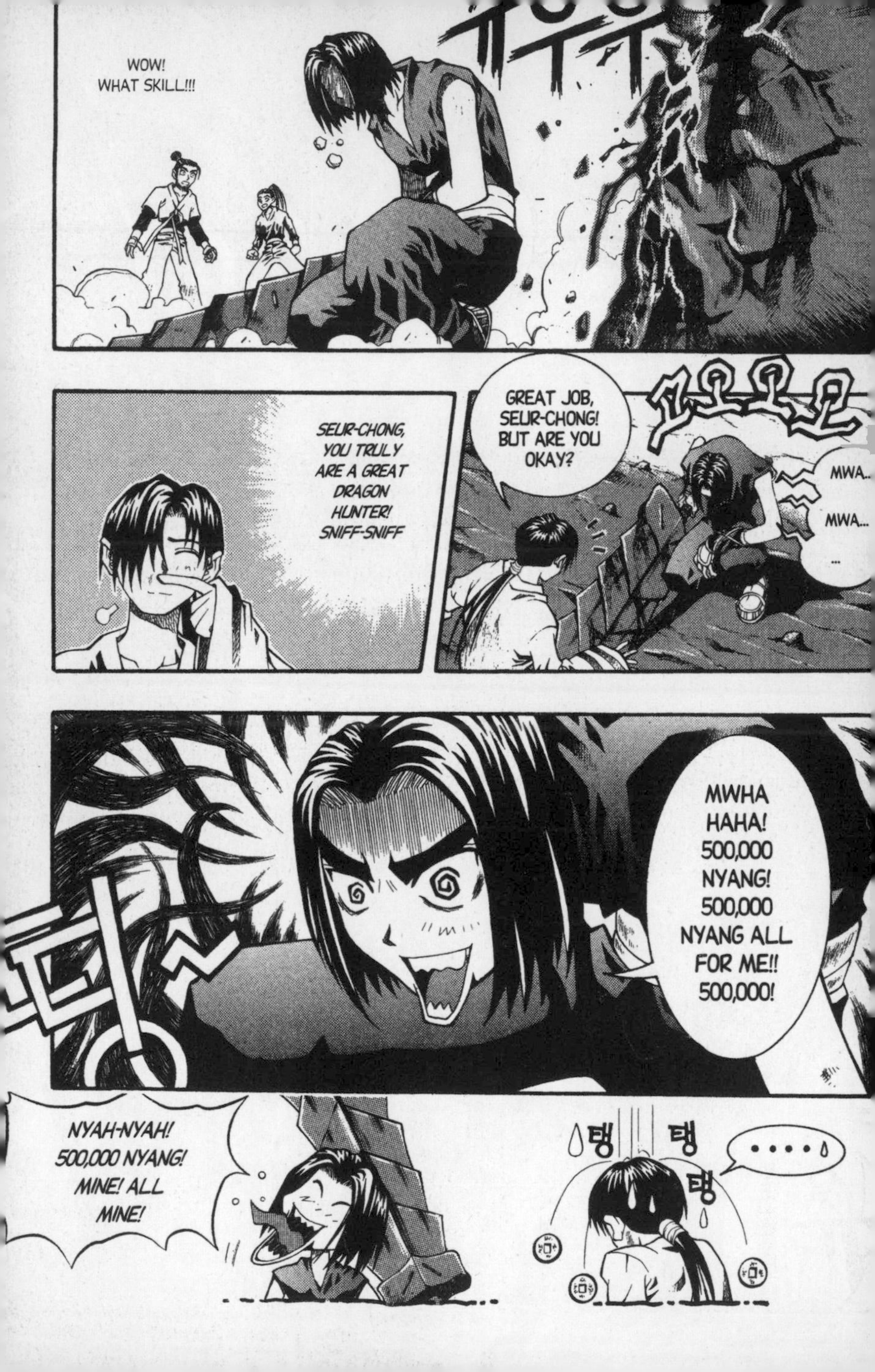
WOW! WHAT SKILL!!!
SEUR-CHONG, YOU TRULY ARE A GREAT DRAGON HUNTER! SNIFF-SNIFF
GREAT JOB, SEUR-CHONG! BUT ARE YOU OKAY?
MWA... MWA... ...
MWHA HAHA! 500,000 NYANG! 500,000 NYANG ALL FOR ME!! 500,000!
NYAH-NYAH! 500,000 NYANG! MINE! ALL MINE!
탱 탱 탱
.....

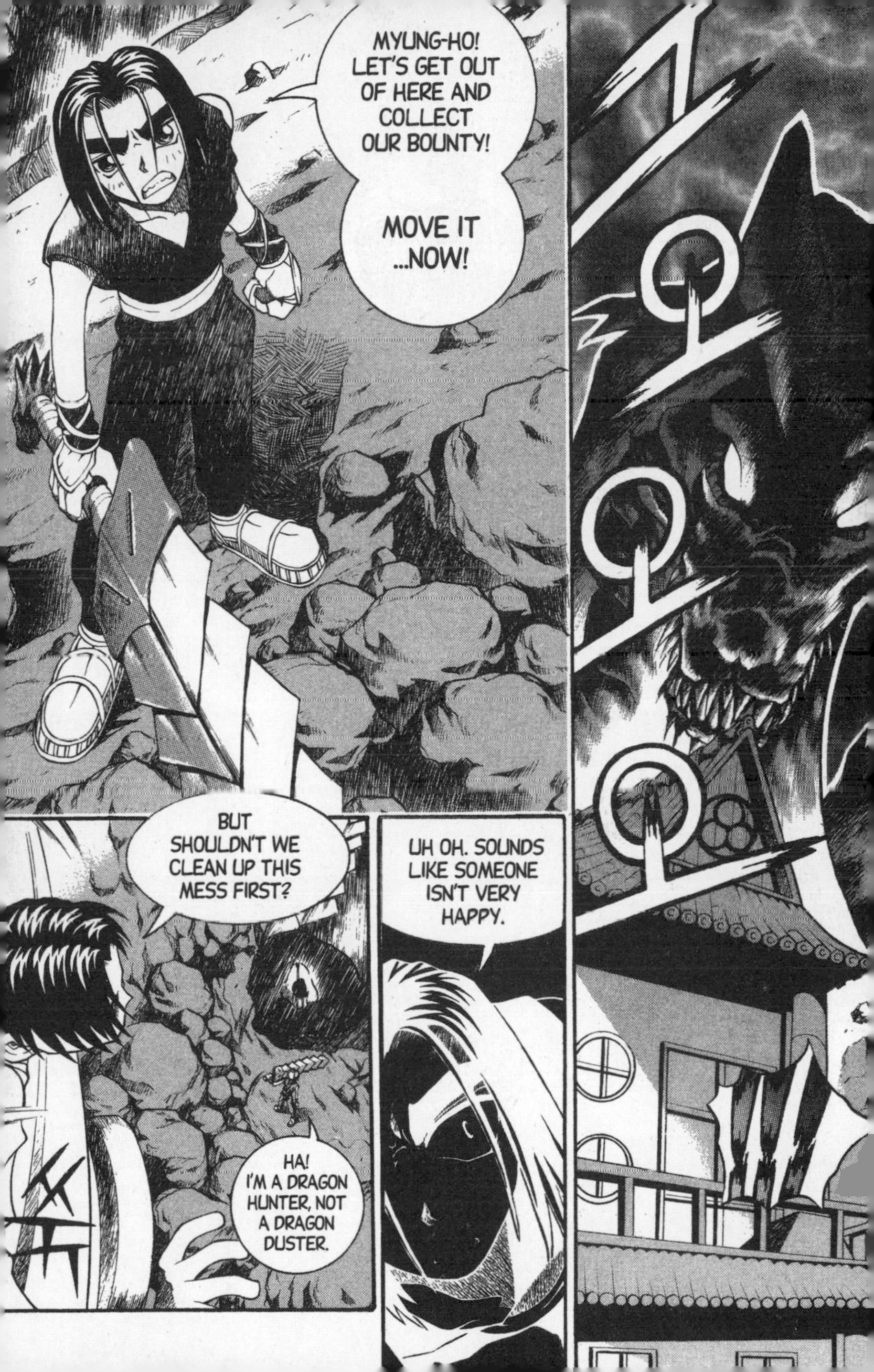
MYUNG-HO! LET'S GET OUT OF HERE AND COLLECT OUR BOUNTY!
MOVE IT ...NOW!
BUT SHOULDN'T WE CLEAN UP THIS MESS FIRST?
HA! I'M A DRAGON HUNTER, NOT A DRAGON DUSTER.
UH OH. SOUNDS LIKE SOMEONE ISN'T VERY HAPPY.

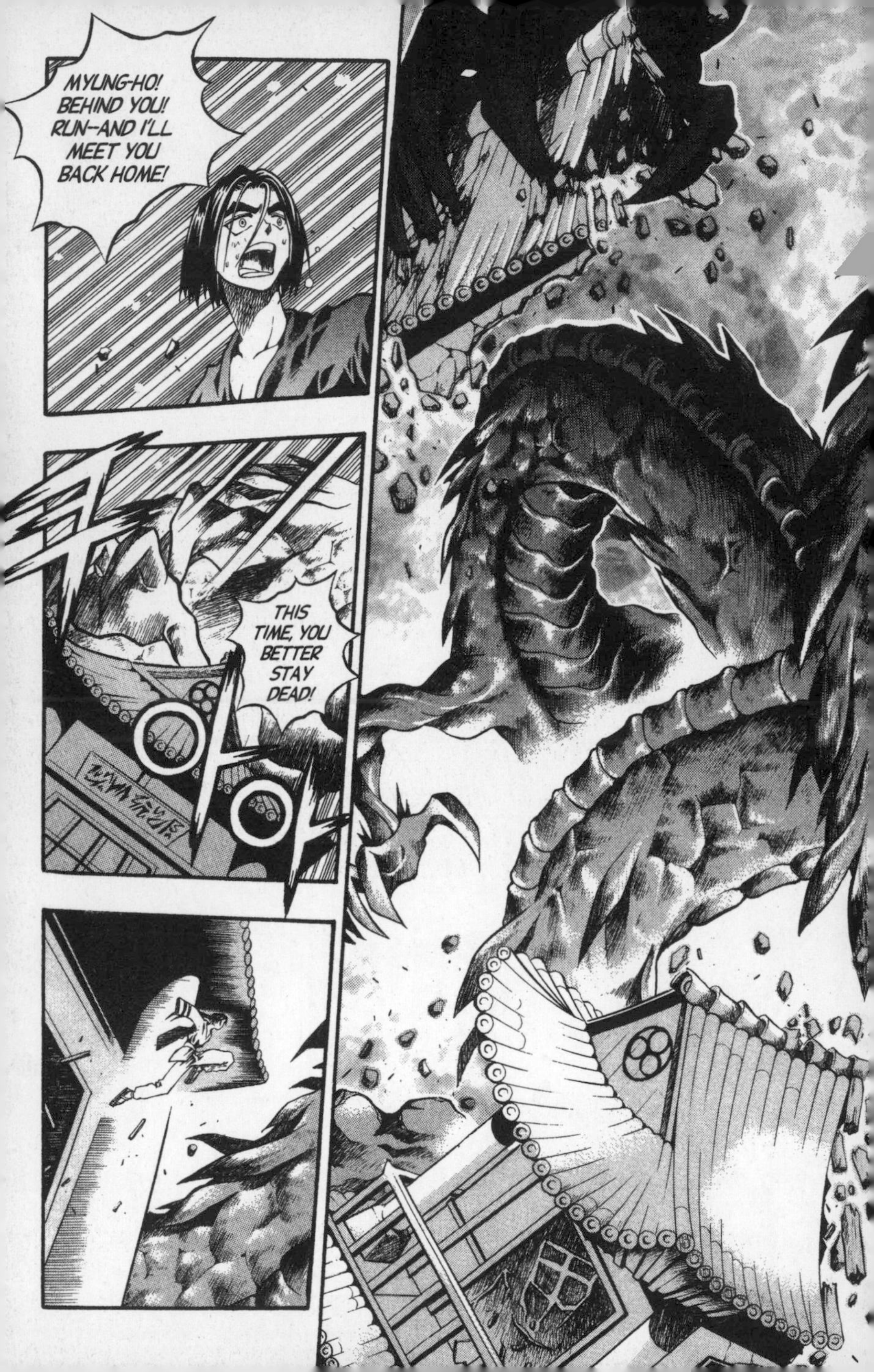
MYUNG-HO! BEHIND YOU! RUN--AND I'LL MEET YOU BACK HOME!
THIS TIME, YOU BETTER STAY DEAD!

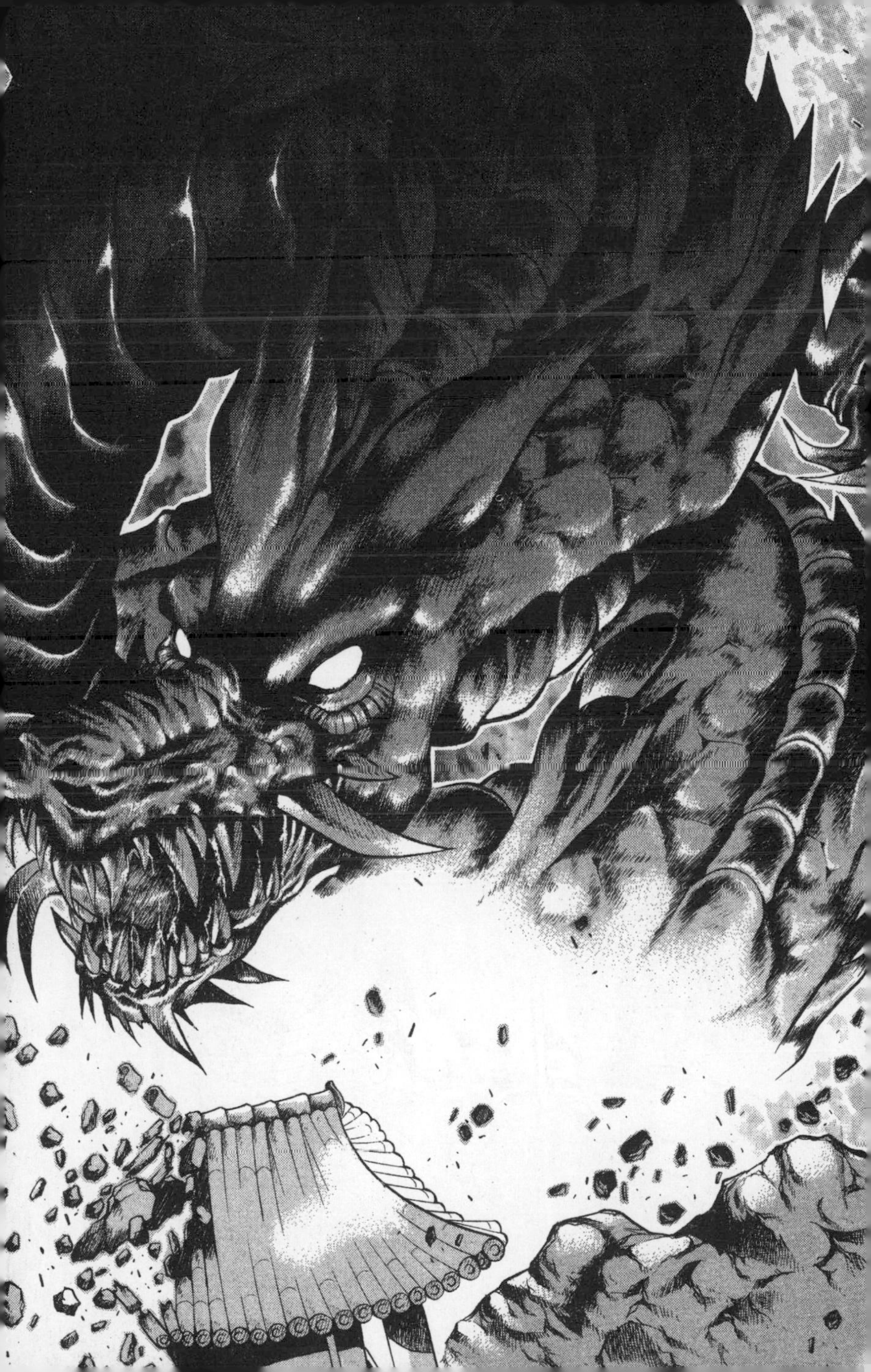

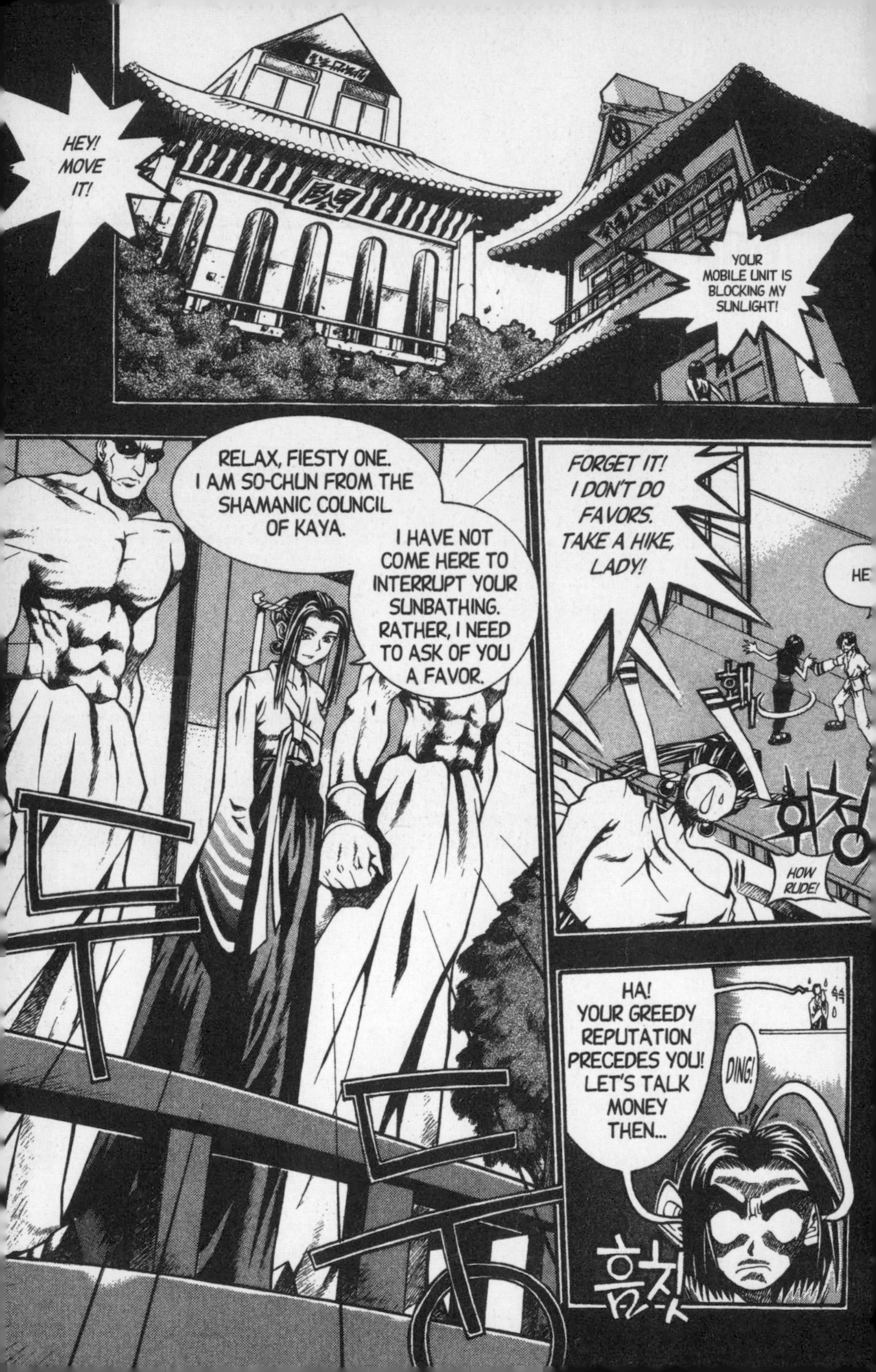
HEY! MOVE IT!
YOUR MOBILE UNIT IS BLOCKING MY SUNLIGHT!
RELAX, FIESTY ONE. I AM SO-CHUN FROM THE SHAMANIC COUNCIL OF KAYA.
I HAVE NOT COME HERE TO INTERRUPT YOUR SUNBATHING. RATHER, I NEED TO ASK OF YOU A FAVOR.
FORGET IT! I DON'T DO FAVORS. TAKE A HIKE, LADY!
HOW RUDE!
HA! YOUR GREEDY REPUTATION PRECEDES YOU! LET'S TALK MONEY THEN...
DING!

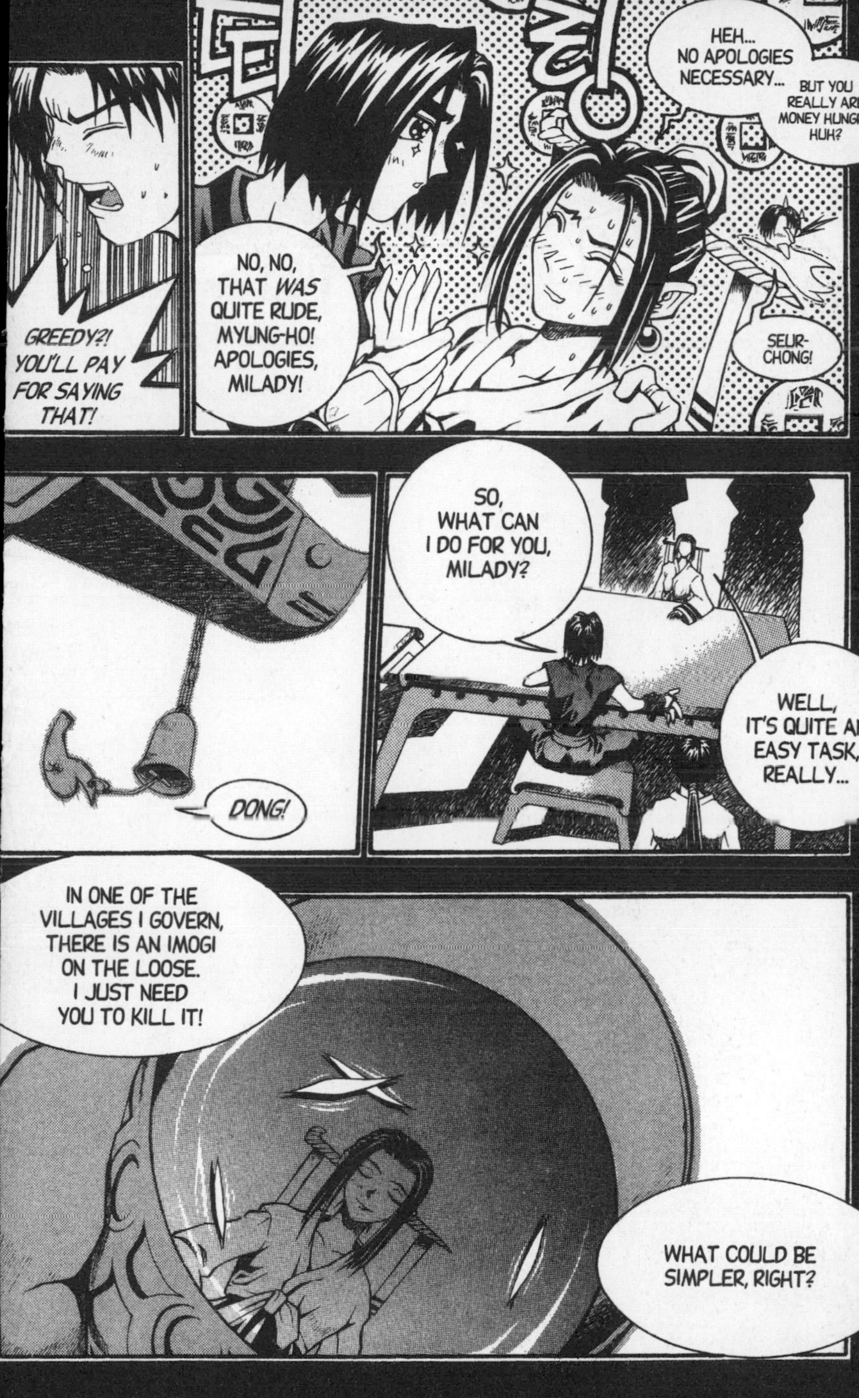
GREEDY?! YOU'LL PAY FOR SAYING THAT!
NO, NO, THAT *WAS* QUITE RUDE, MYUNG-HO! APOLOGIES, MILADY!
HEH... NO APOLOGIES NECESSARY...
BUT YOU REALLY ARE MONEY HUNGRY, HUH?
SEUR-CHONG!
DONG!
SO, WHAT CAN I DO FOR YOU, MILADY?
WELL, IT'S QUITE AN EASY TASK, REALLY...
IN ONE OF THE VILLAGES I GOVERN, THERE IS AN IMOGI ON THE LOOSE. I JUST NEED YOU TO KILL IT!
WHAT COULD BE SIMPLER, RIGHT?

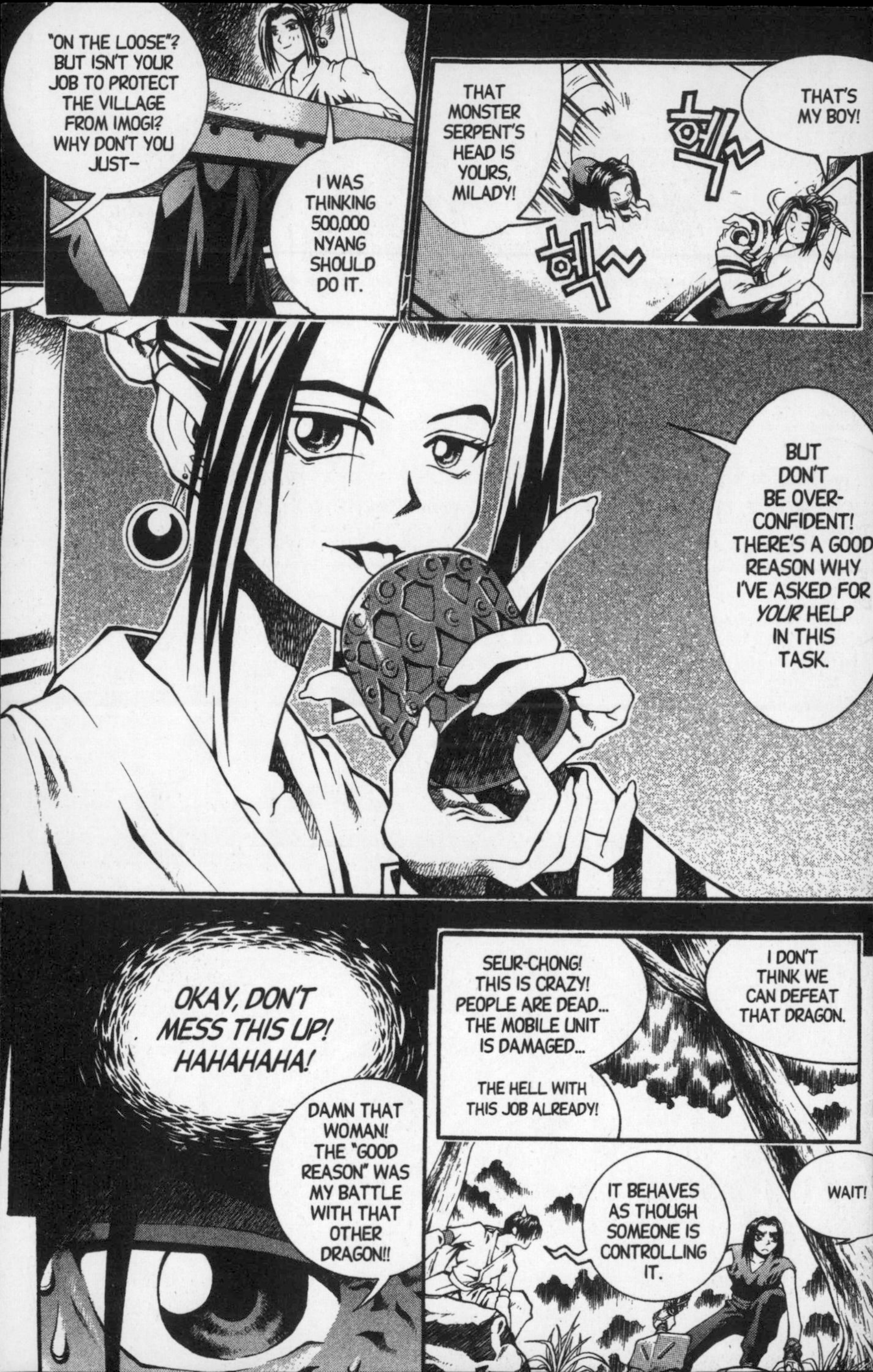
"ON THE LOOSE"? BUT ISN'T YOUR JOB TO PROTECT THE VILLAGE FROM IMOGI? WHY DON'T YOU JUST-
I WAS THINKING 500,000 NYANG SHOULD DO IT.
THAT MONSTER SERPENT'S HEAD IS YOURS, MILADY!
헤~
THAT'S MY BOY!
헤~
BUT DON'T BE OVER-CONFIDENT! THERE'S A GOOD REASON WHY I'VE ASKED FOR *YOUR* HELP IN THIS TASK.
OKAY, DON'T MESS THIS UP! HAHAHAHA!
DAMN THAT WOMAN! THE "GOOD REASON" WAS MY BATTLE WITH THAT OTHER DRAGON!!
SEUR-CHONG! THIS IS CRAZY! PEOPLE ARE DEAD... THE MOBILE UNIT IS DAMAGED...
THE HELL WITH THIS JOB ALREADY!
I DON'T THINK WE CAN DEFEAT THAT DRAGON.
IT BEHAVES AS THOUGH SOMEONE IS CONTROLLING IT.
WAIT!

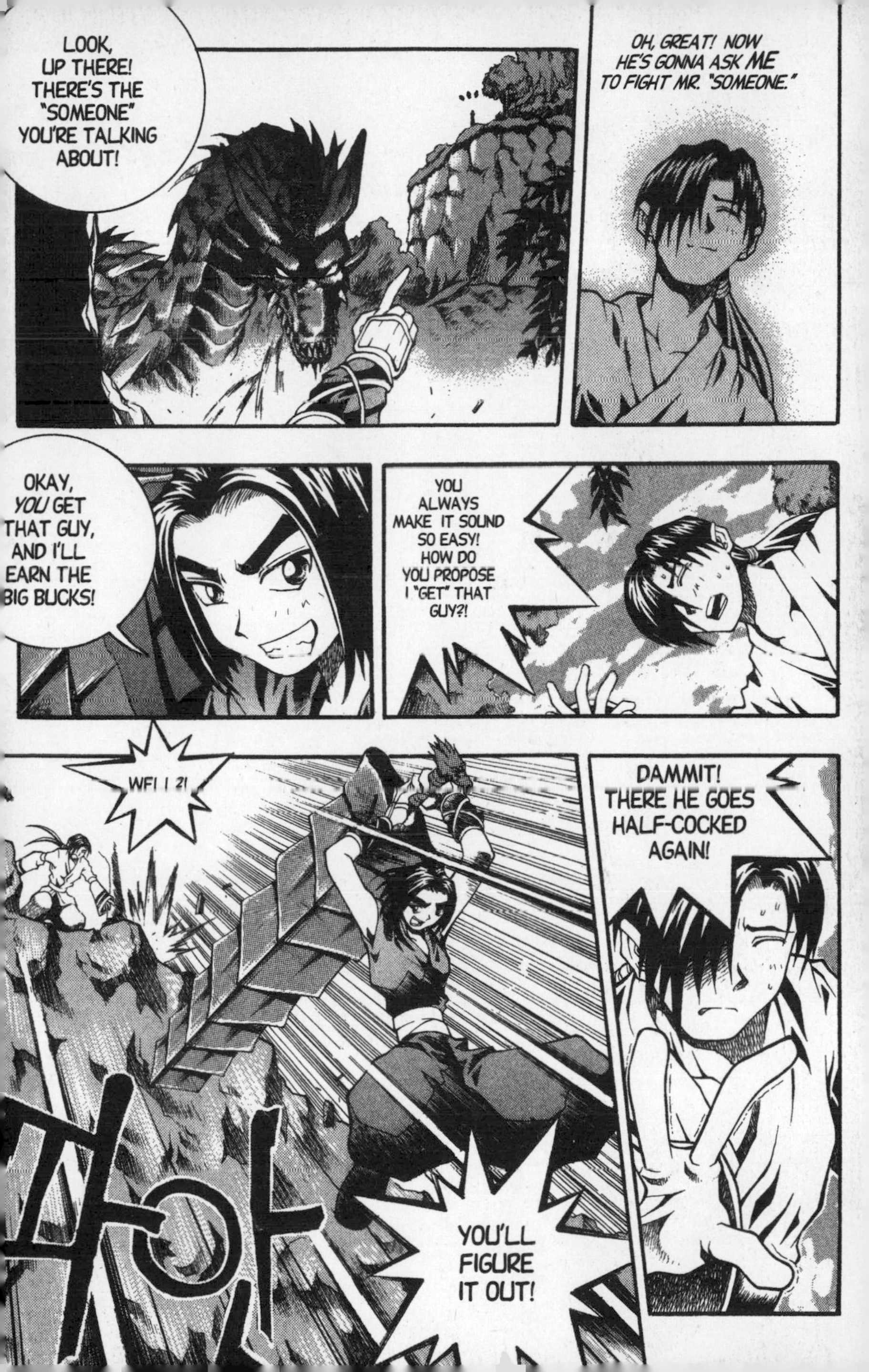
LOOK, UP THERE! THERE'S THE "SOMEONE" YOU'RE TALKING ABOUT!
...
OH, GREAT! NOW HE'S GONNA ASK ME TO FIGHT MR. "SOMEONE."
OKAY, YOU GET THAT GUY, AND I'LL EARN THE BIG BUCKS!
YOU ALWAYS MAKE IT SOUND SO EASY! HOW DO YOU PROPOSE I "GET" THAT GUY?!
WELL?!
YOU'LL FIGURE IT OUT!
DAMMIT! THERE HE GOES HALF-COCKED AGAIN!

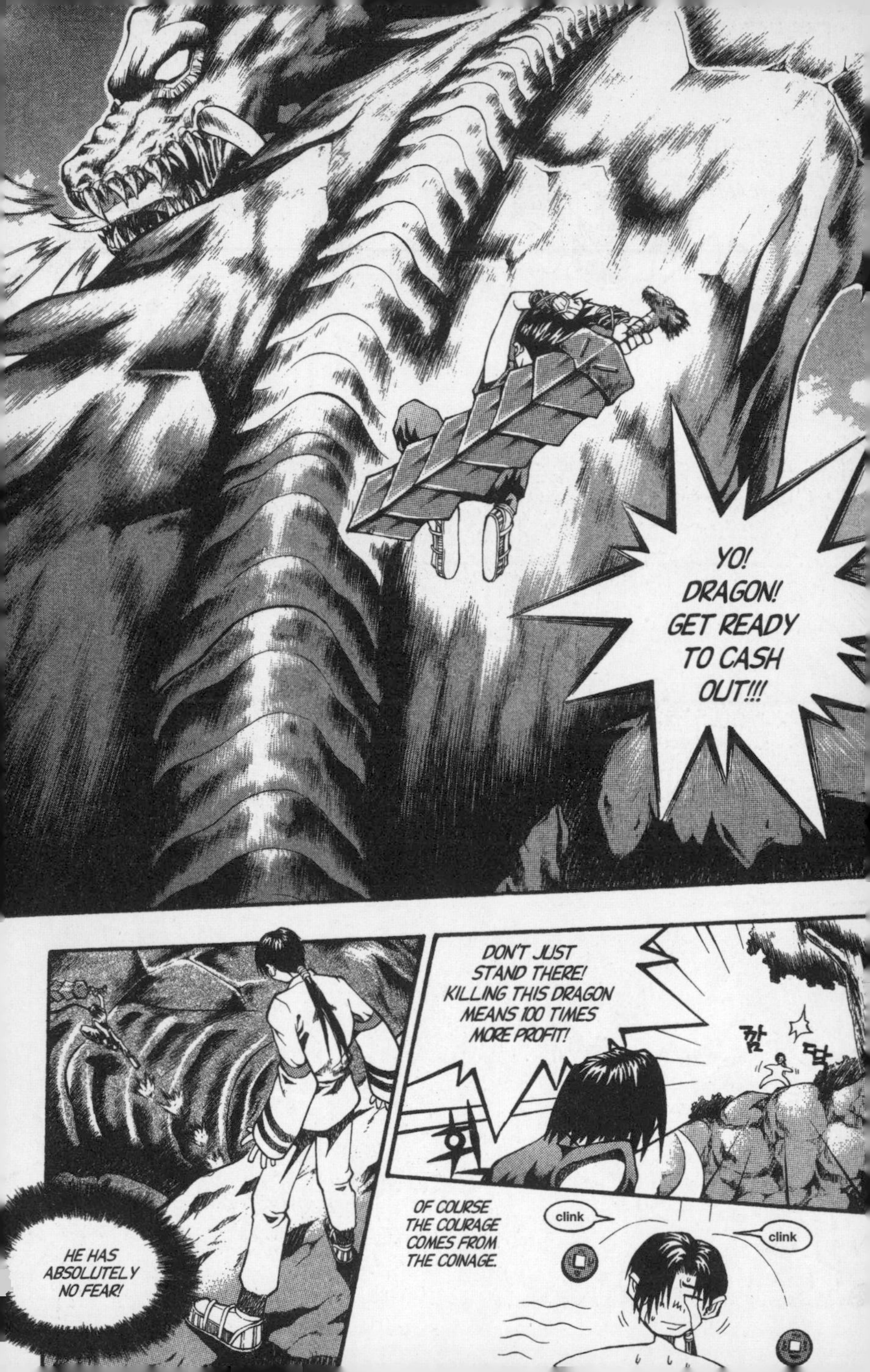
YO! DRAGON! GET READY TO CASH OUT!!!
HE HAS ABSOLUTELY NO FEAR!
DON'T JUST STAND THERE! KILLING THIS DRAGON MEANS 100 TIMES MORE PROFIT!
OF COURSE THE COURAGE COMES FROM THE COINAGE.
clink
clink

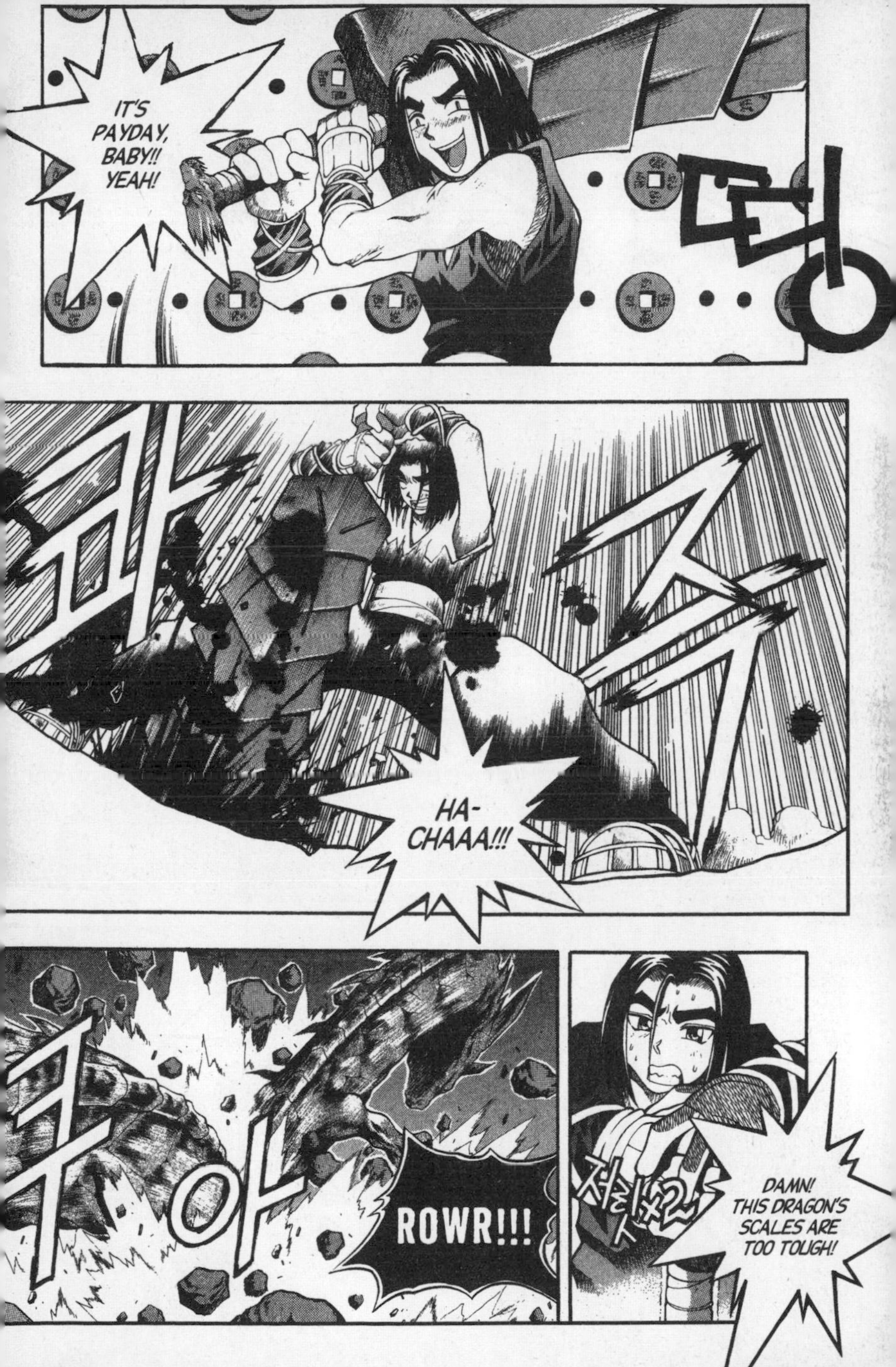
IT'S PAYDAY, BABY!! YEAH!
HA-CHAAA!!!
ROWR!!!
DAMN! THIS DRAGON'S SCALES ARE TOO TOUGH!

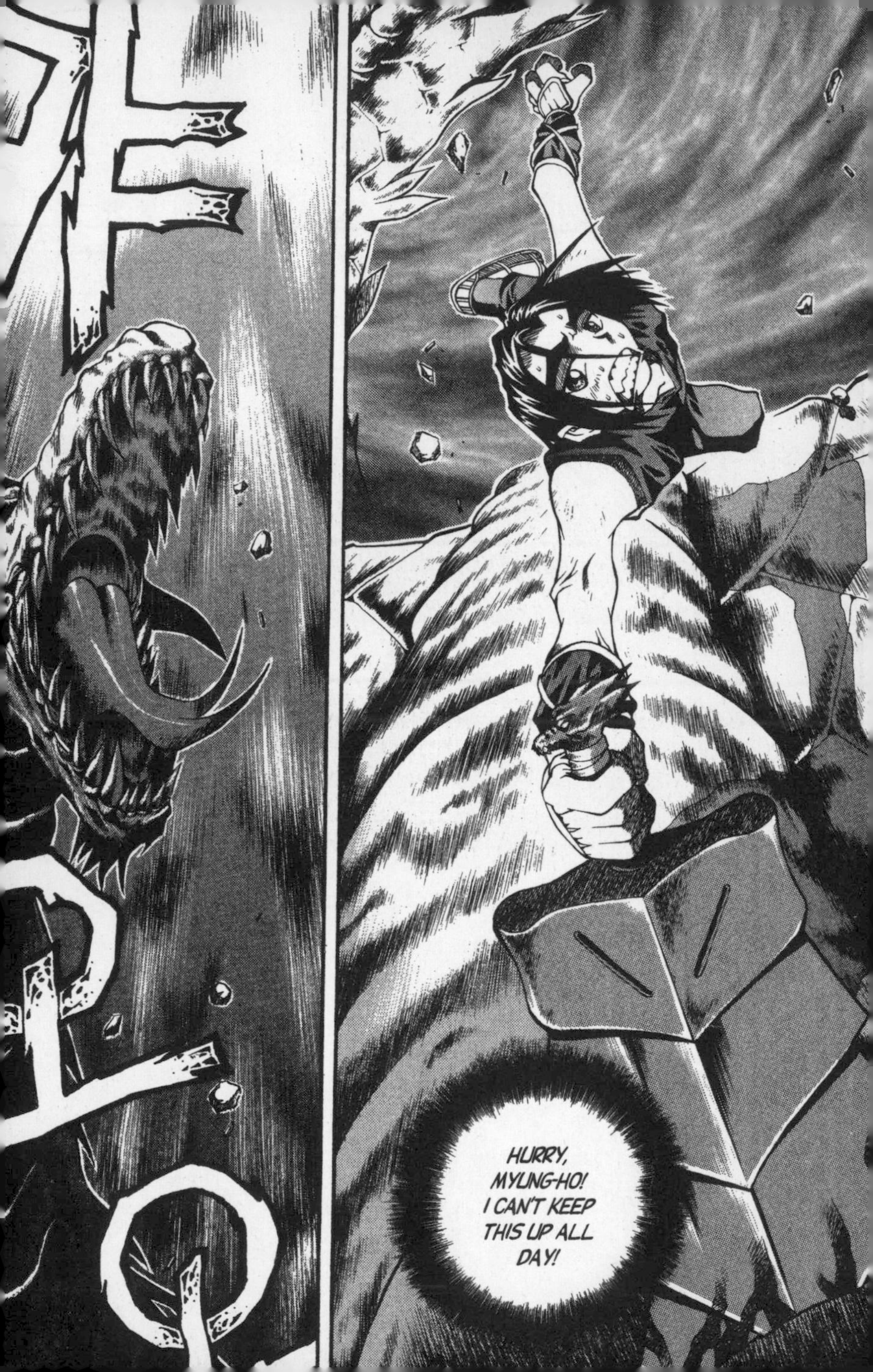
HURRY, MYUNG-HO! I CAN'T KEEP THIS UP ALL DAY!

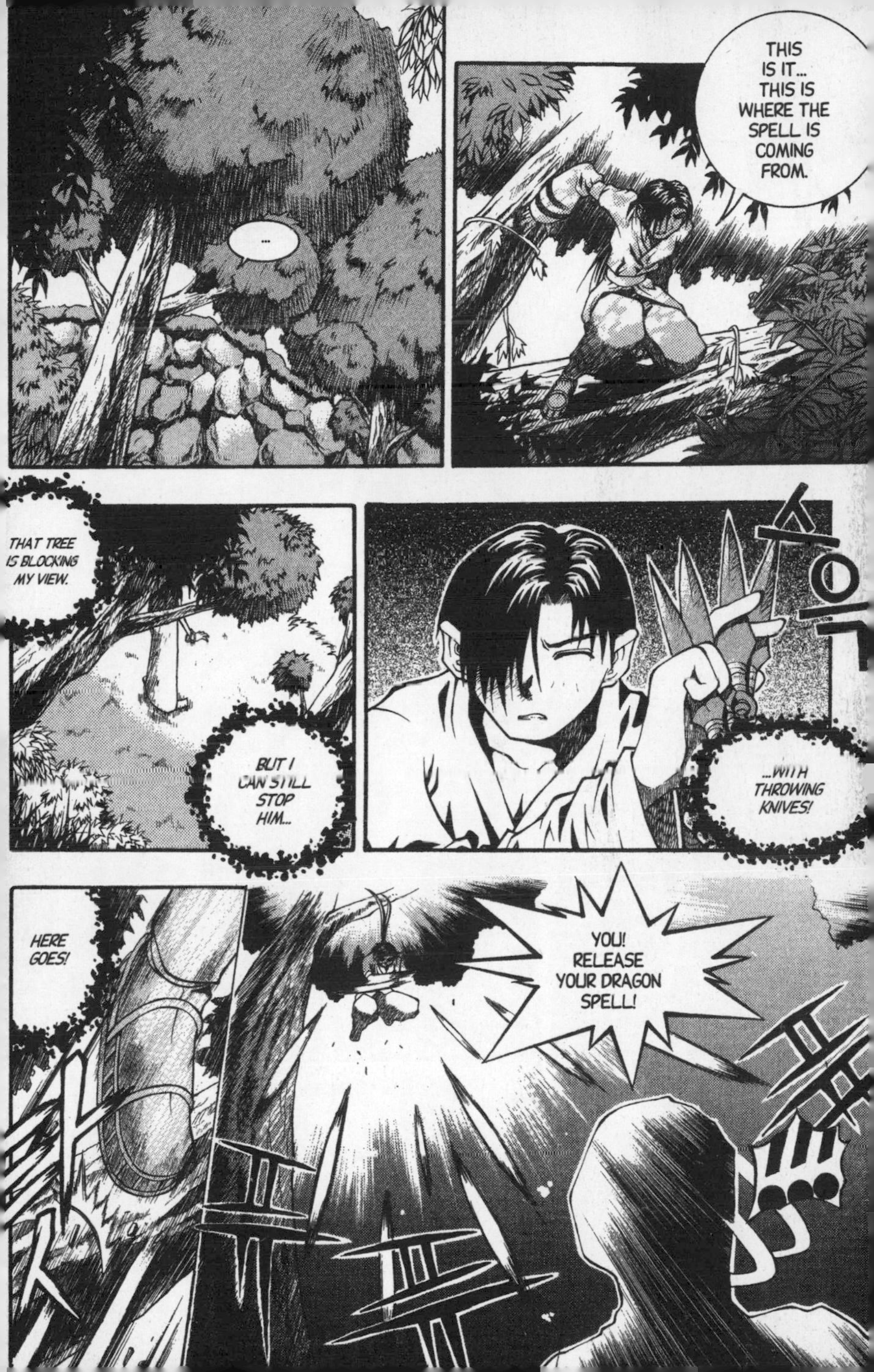
...
THIS IS IT... THIS IS WHERE THE SPELL IS COMING FROM.
THAT TREE IS BLOCKING MY VIEW.
BUT I CAN STILL STOP HIM...
...WITH THROWING KNIVES!
HERE GOES!
YOU! RELEASE YOUR DRAGON SPELL!

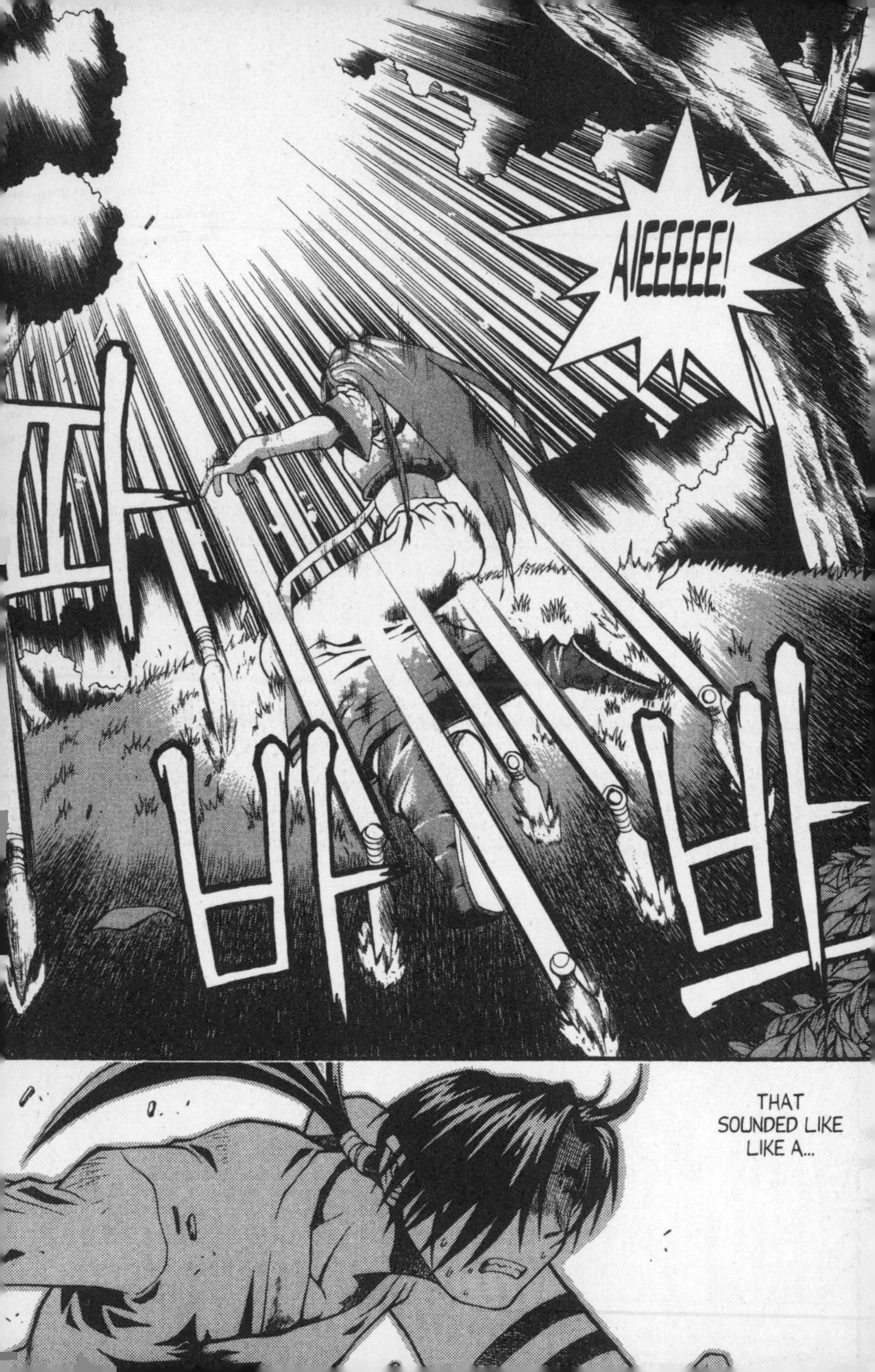
AIEEEEEE!
THAT SOUNDED LIKE LIKE A...

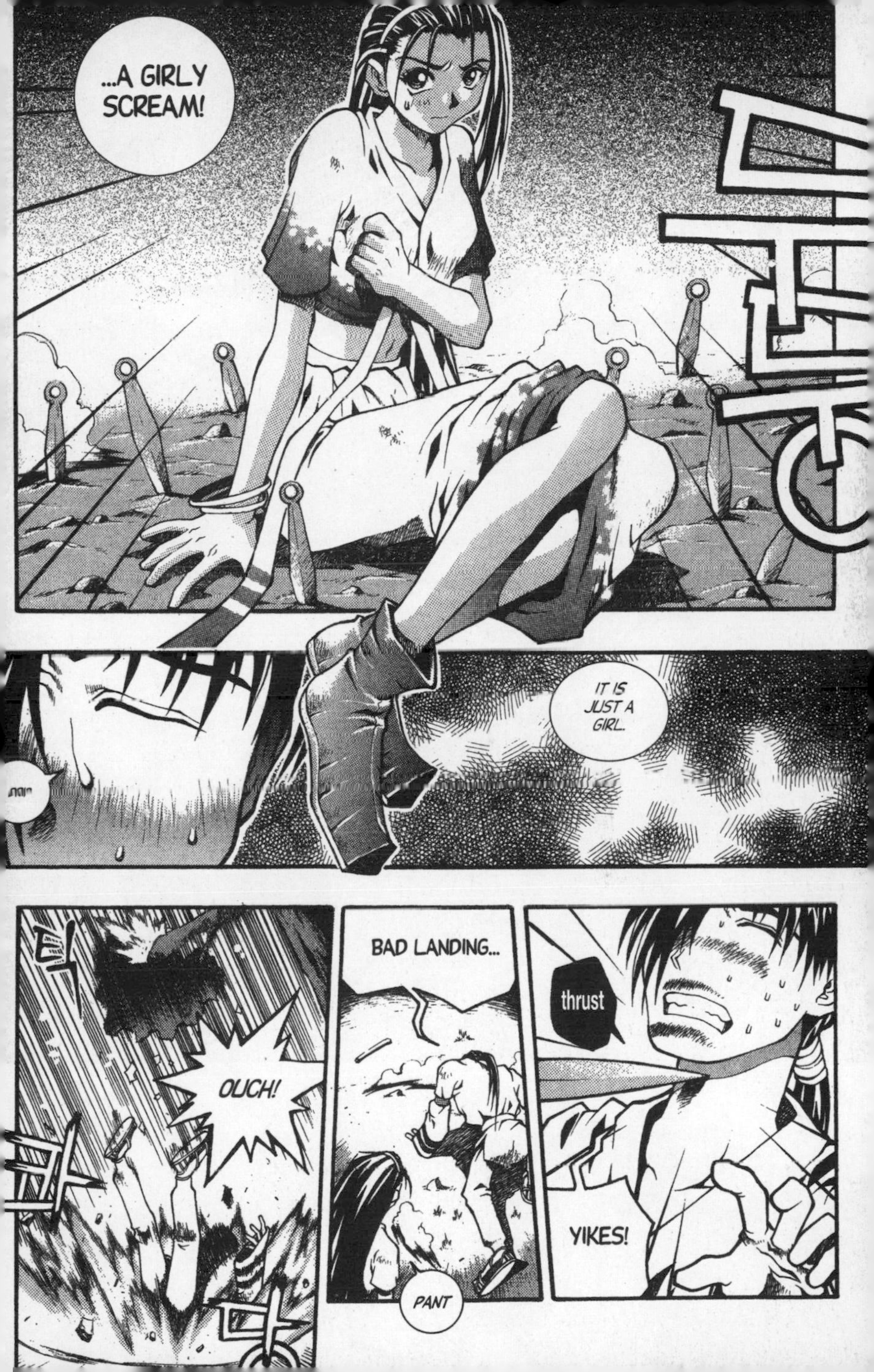
...A GIRLY SCREAM!
IT IS JUST A GIRL.
OUCH!
BAD LANDING...
PANT
thrust
YIKES!

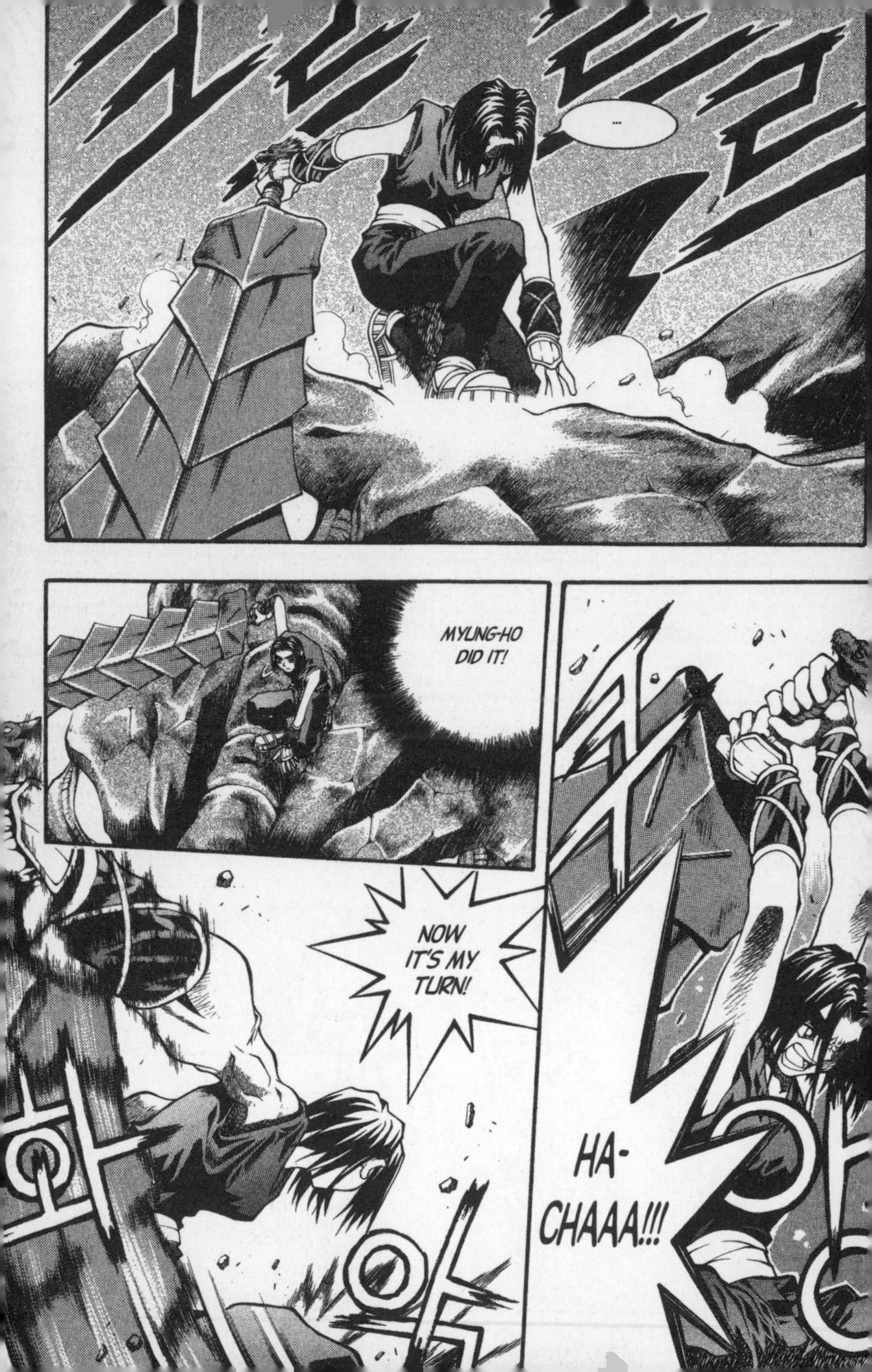
...
MYUNG-HO DID IT!
NOW IT'S MY TURN!
HA-CHAAA!!!

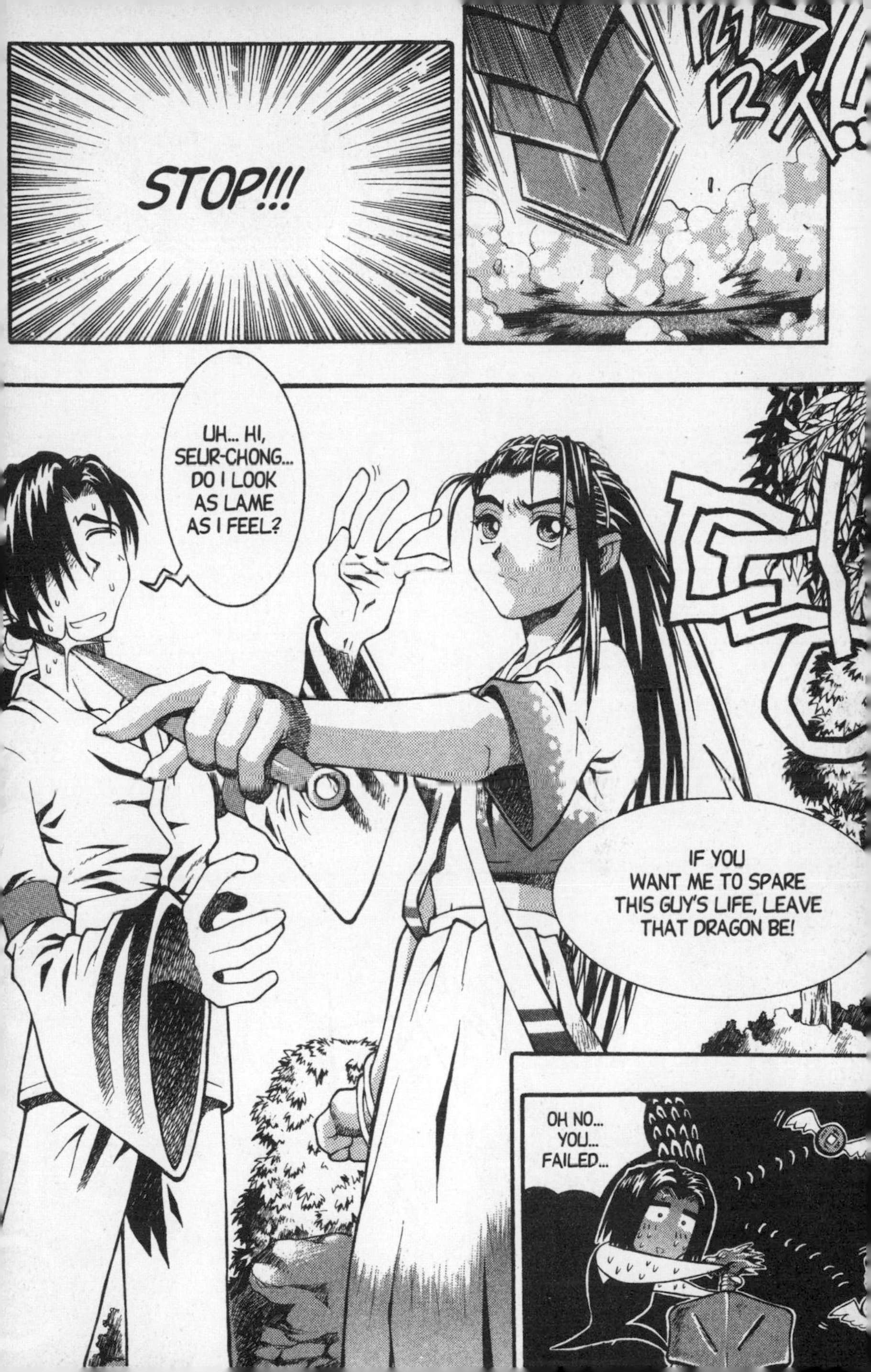
STOP!!!
UH... HI, SEUR-CHONG... DO I LOOK AS LAME AS I FEEL?
IF YOU WANT ME TO SPARE THIS GUY'S LIFE, LEAVE THAT DRAGON BE!
OH NO... YOU... FAILED...

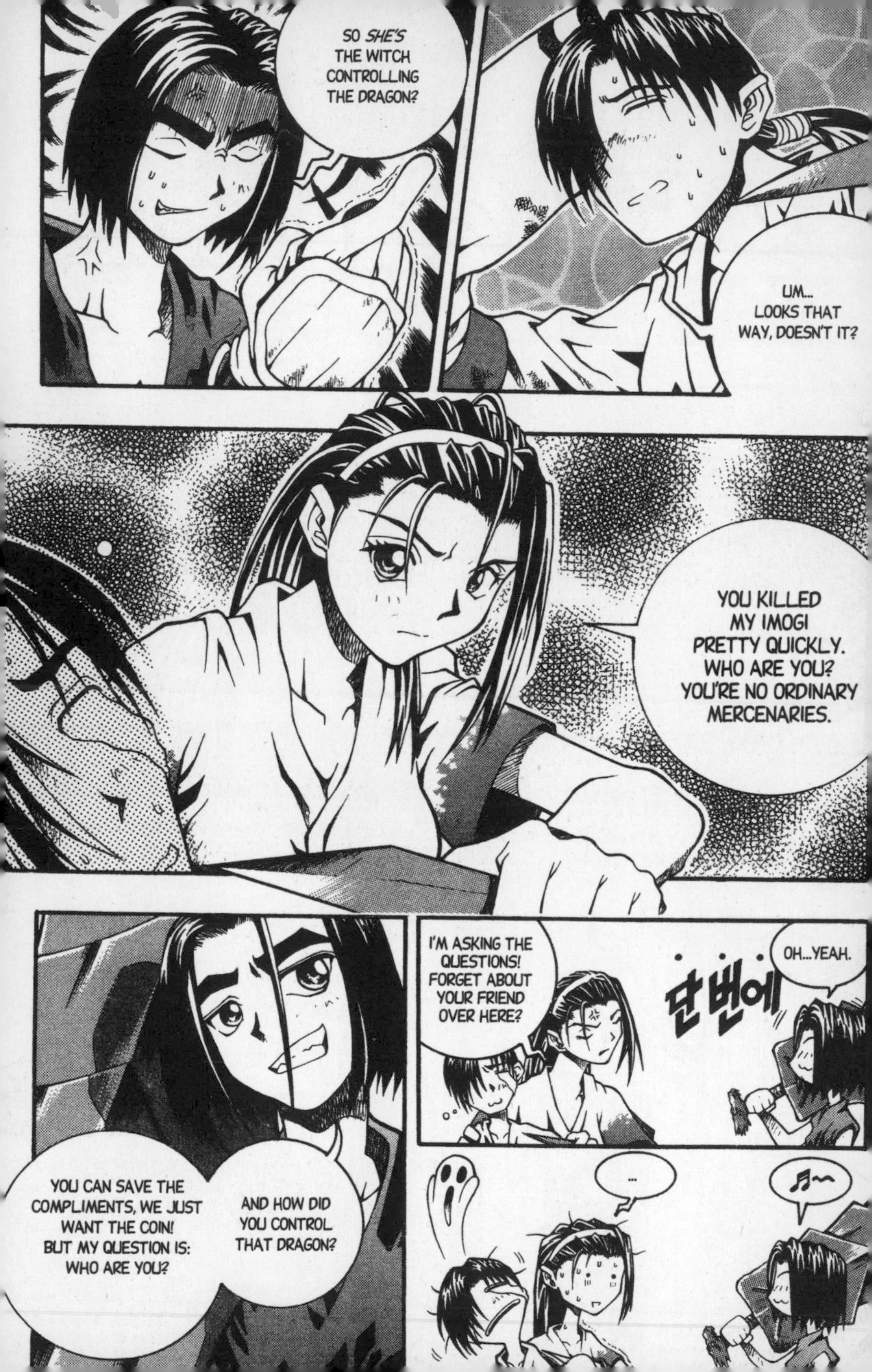
SO SHE'S THE WITCH CONTROLLING THE DRAGON?
UM... LOOKS THAT WAY, DOESN'T IT?
YOU KILLED MY IMOGI PRETTY QUICKLY. WHO ARE YOU? YOU'RE NO ORDINARY MERCENARIES.
YOU CAN SAVE THE COMPLIMENTS, WE JUST WANT THE COIN! BUT MY QUESTION IS: WHO ARE YOU?
AND HOW DID YOU CONTROL THAT DRAGON?
I'M ASKING THE QUESTIONS! FORGET ABOUT YOUR FRIEND OVER HERE?
단 번에
OH...YEAH.
...

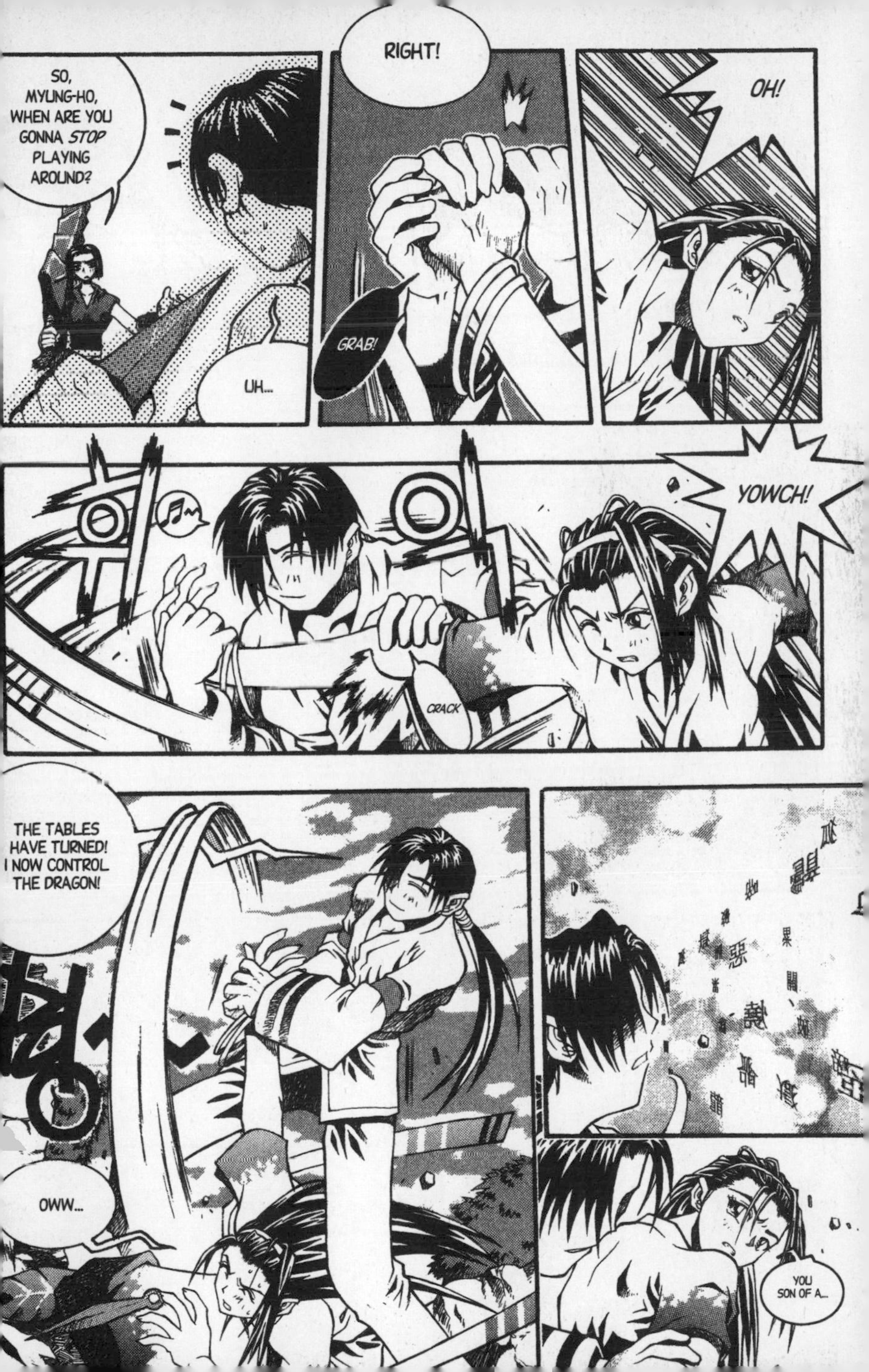
SO, MYUNG-HO, WHEN ARE YOU GONNA *STOP* PLAYING AROUND?
UH...
RIGHT!
GRAB!
OH!
YOWCH!
CRACK
THE TABLES HAVE TURNED! I NOW CONTROL THE DRAGON!
OWW...
YOU SON OF A...

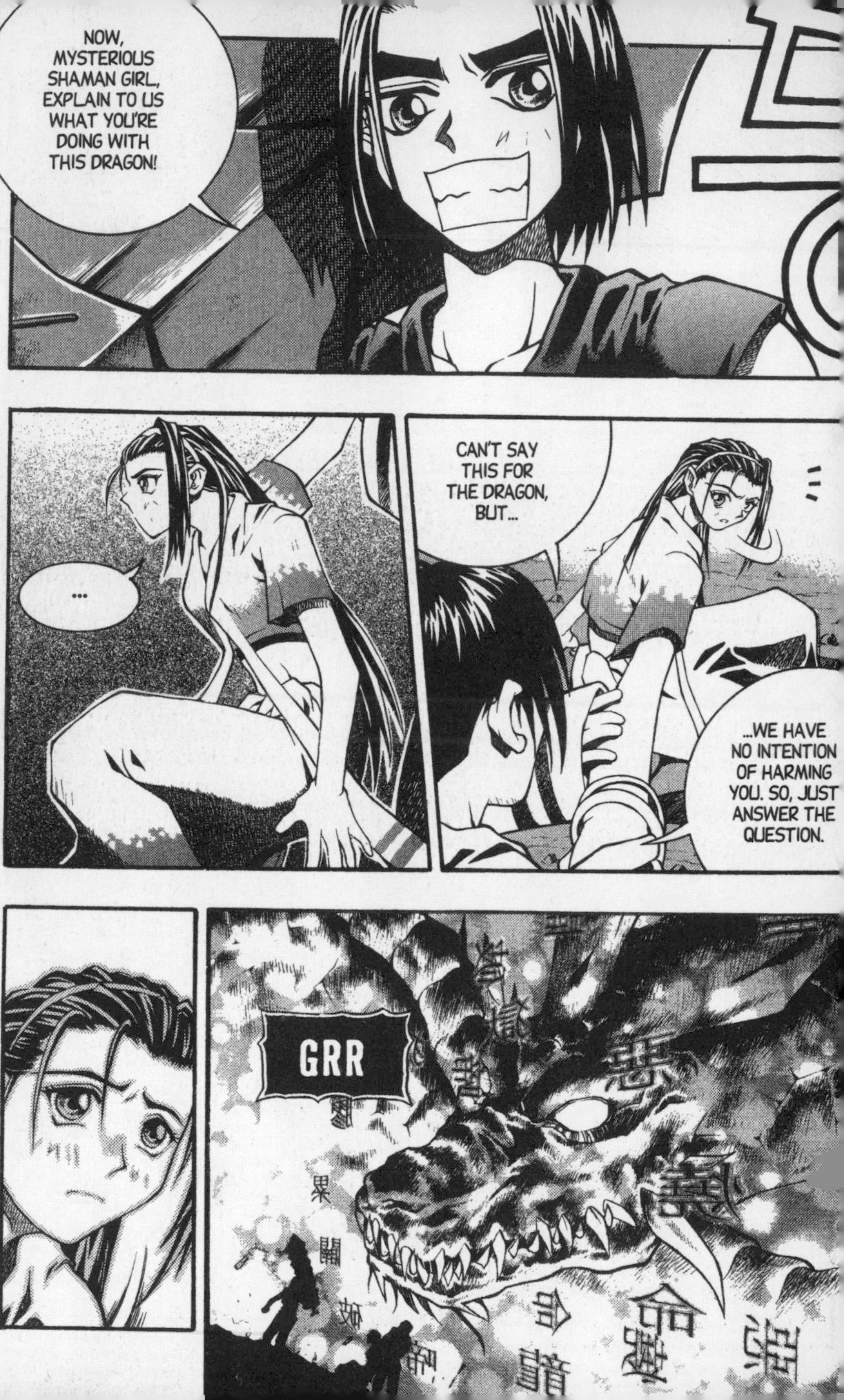
NOW, MYSTERIOUS SHAMAN GIRL, EXPLAIN TO US WHAT YOU'RE DOING WITH THIS DRAGON!
...
CAN'T SAY THIS FOR THE DRAGON, BUT...
...WE HAVE NO INTENTION OF HARMING YOU. SO, JUST ANSWER THE QUESTION.
GRR

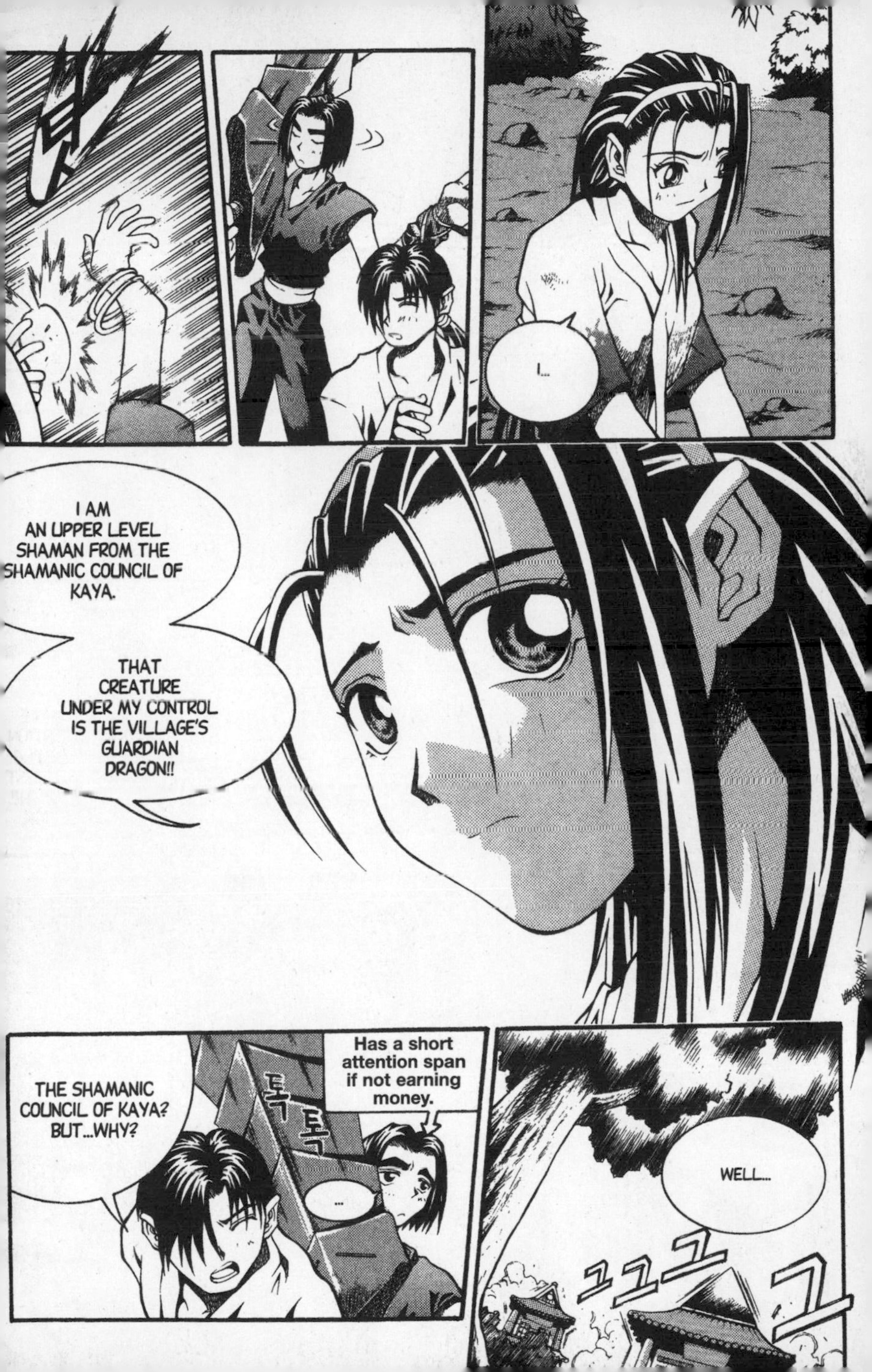
...
I AM AN UPPER LEVEL SHAMAN FROM THE SHAMANIC COUNCIL OF KAYA.
THAT CREATURE UNDER MY CONTROL IS THE VILLAGE'S GUARDIAN DRAGON!!
THE SHAMANIC COUNCIL OF KAYA? BUT...WHY?
톡
톡
Has a short attention span if not earning money.
...
WELL...

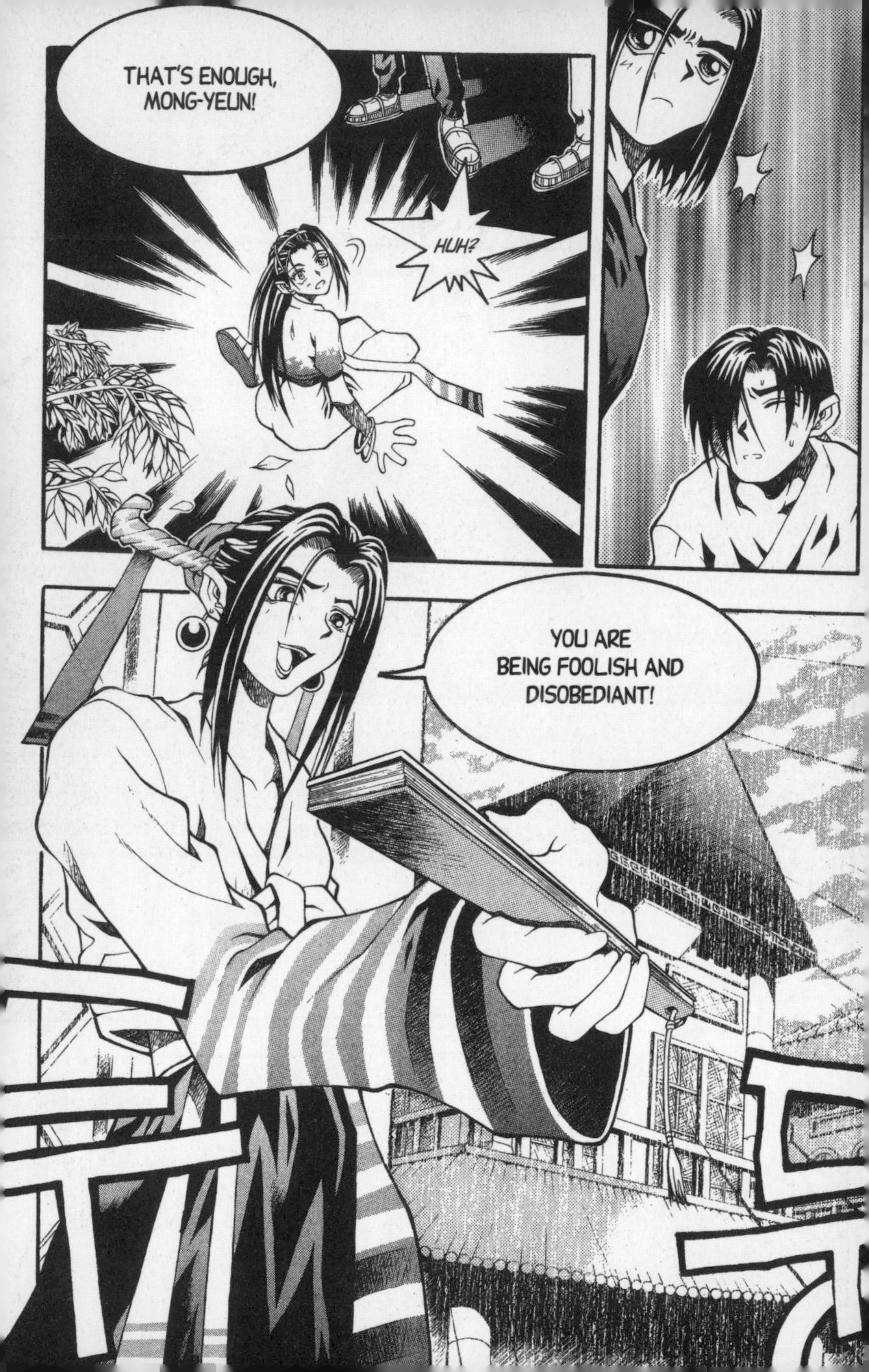
THAT'S ENOUGH, MONG-YEUN!
HUH?
YOU ARE BEING FOOLISH AND DISOBEDIANT!

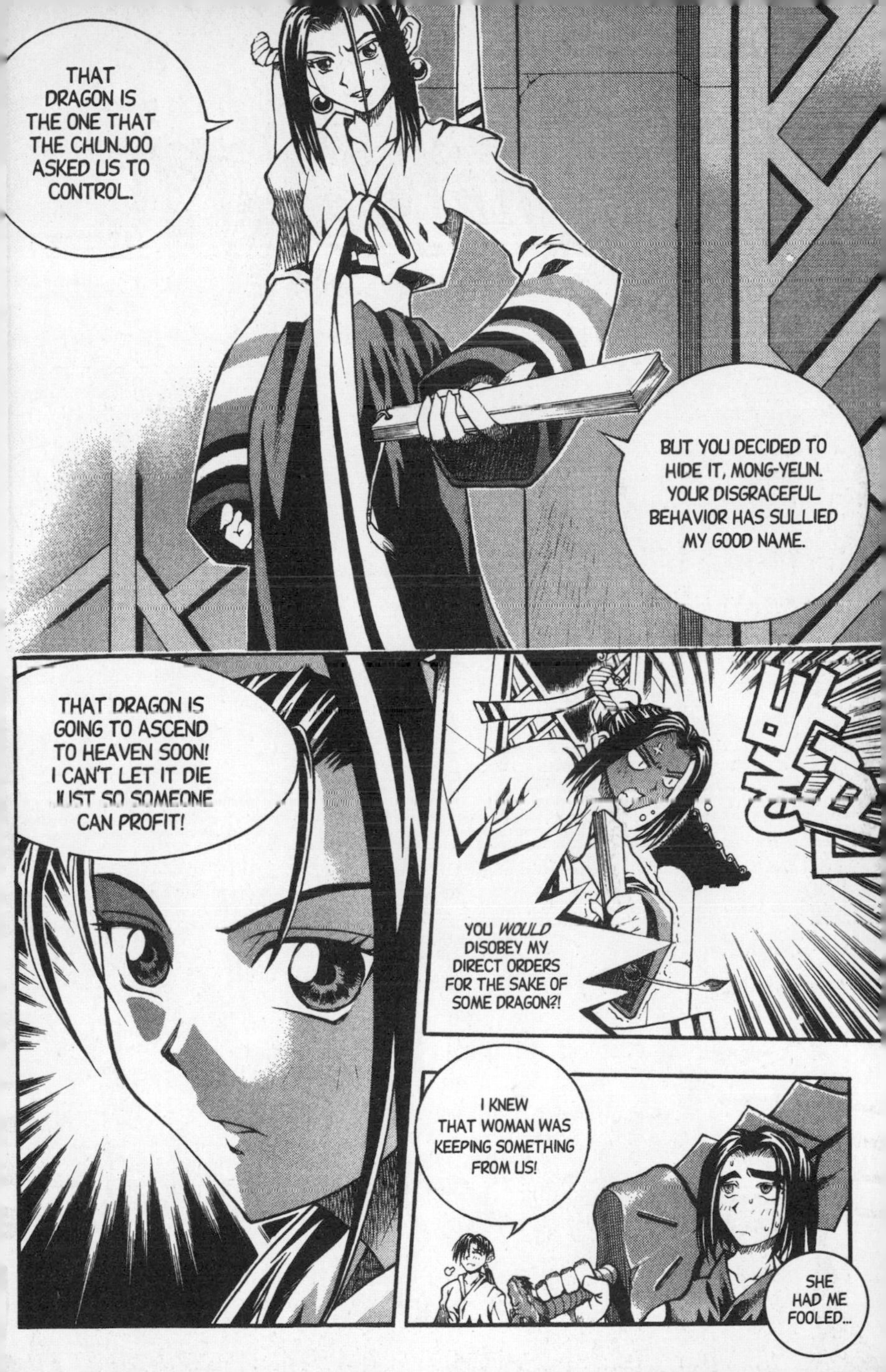
THAT DRAGON IS THE ONE THAT THE CHUNJOO ASKED US TO CONTROL.
BUT YOU DECIDED TO HIDE IT, MONG-YEUN. YOUR DISGRACEFUL BEHAVIOR HAS SULLIED MY GOOD NAME.
THAT DRAGON IS GOING TO ASCEND TO HEAVEN SOON! I CAN'T LET IT DIE JUST SO SOMEONE CAN PROFIT!
YOU *WOULD* DISOBEY MY DIRECT ORDERS FOR THE SAKE OF SOME DRAGON?!
I KNEW THAT WOMAN WAS KEEPING SOMETHING FROM US!
SHE HAD ME FOOLED...

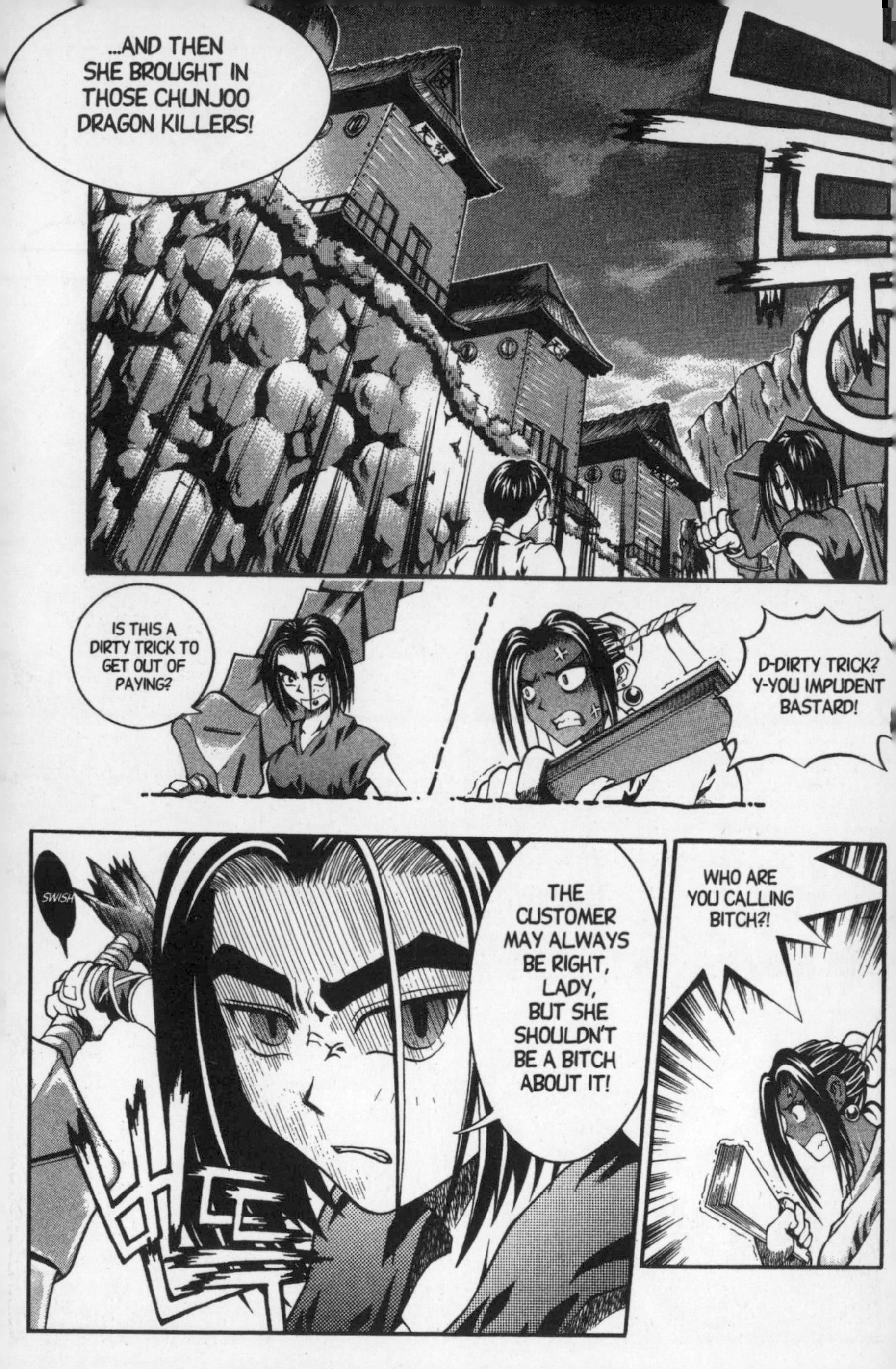
...AND THEN SHE BROUGHT IN THOSE CHUNJOO DRAGON KILLERS!
IS THIS A DIRTY TRICK TO GET OUT OF PAYING?
D-DIRTY TRICK? Y-YOU IMPUDENT BASTARD!
SWISH
THE CUSTOMER MAY ALWAYS BE RIGHT, LADY, BUT SHE SHOULDN'T BE A BITCH ABOUT IT!
WHO ARE YOU CALLING BITCH?!

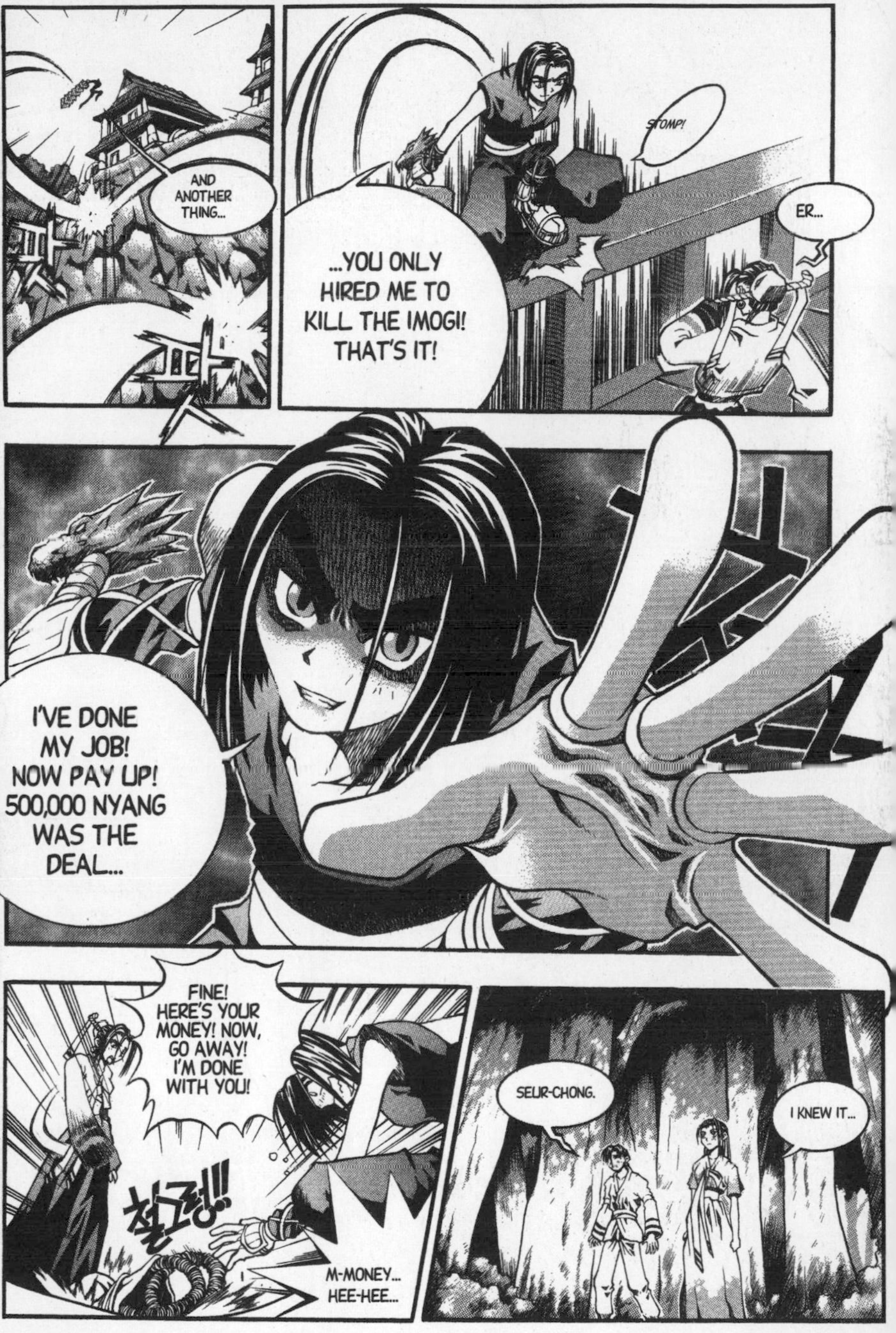
AND ANOTHER THING...
STOMP!
...YOU ONLY HIRED ME TO KILL THE IMOGI! THAT'S IT!
ER...
I'VE DONE MY JOB! NOW PAY UP! 500,000 NYANG WAS THE DEAL...
FINE! HERE'S YOUR MONEY! NOW, GO AWAY! I'M DONE WITH YOU!
철그렁!!
M-MONEY... HEE-HEE...
SEUR-CHONG.
I KNEW IT...

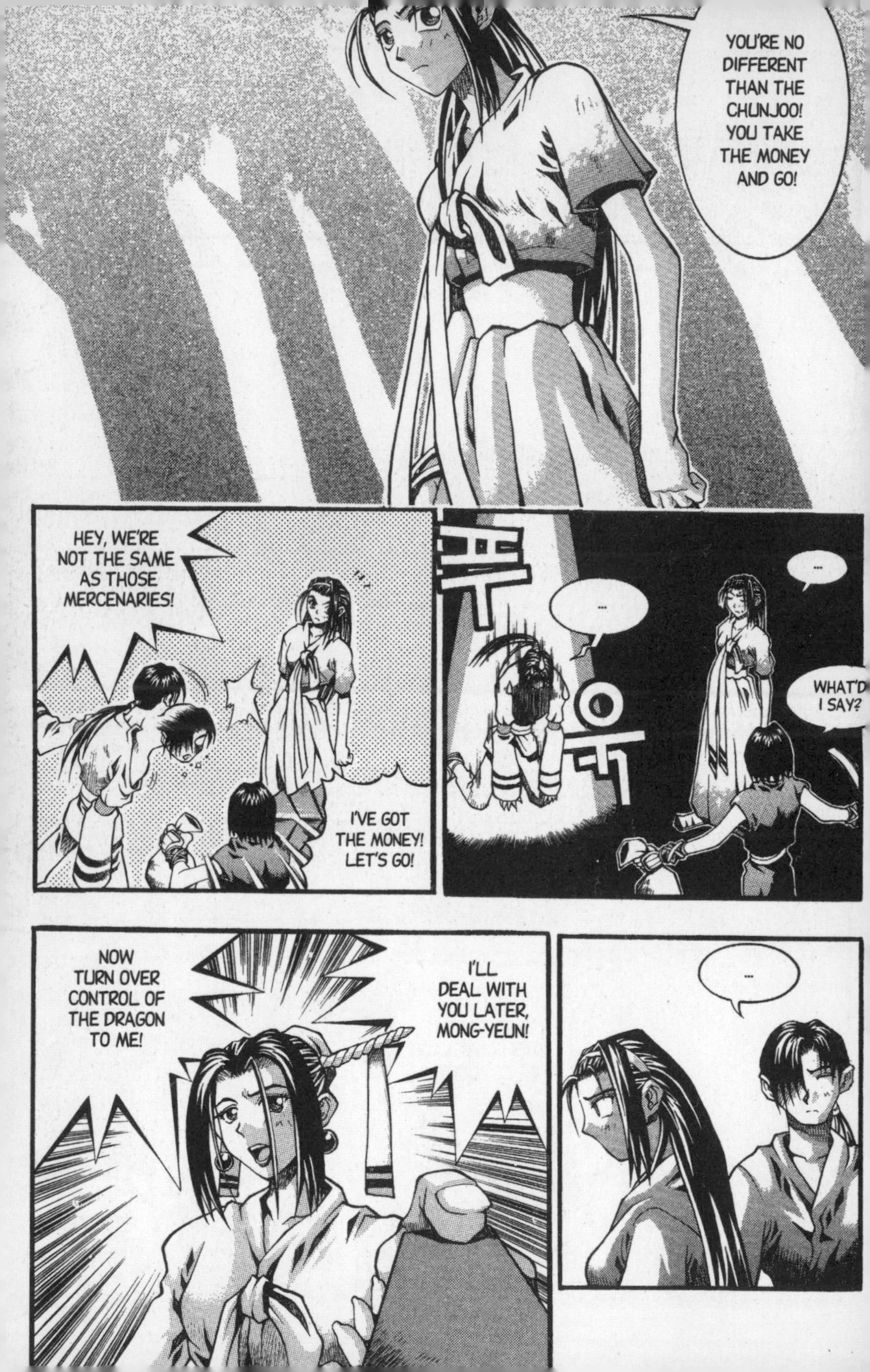
YOU'RE NO DIFFERENT THAN THE CHUNJOO! YOU TAKE THE MONEY AND GO!
HEY, WE'RE NOT THE SAME AS THOSE MERCENARIES!
I'VE GOT THE MONEY! LET'S GO!
...
...
WHAT'D I SAY?
NOW TURN OVER CONTROL OF THE DRAGON TO ME!
I'LL DEAL WITH YOU LATER, MONG-YEUN!
...

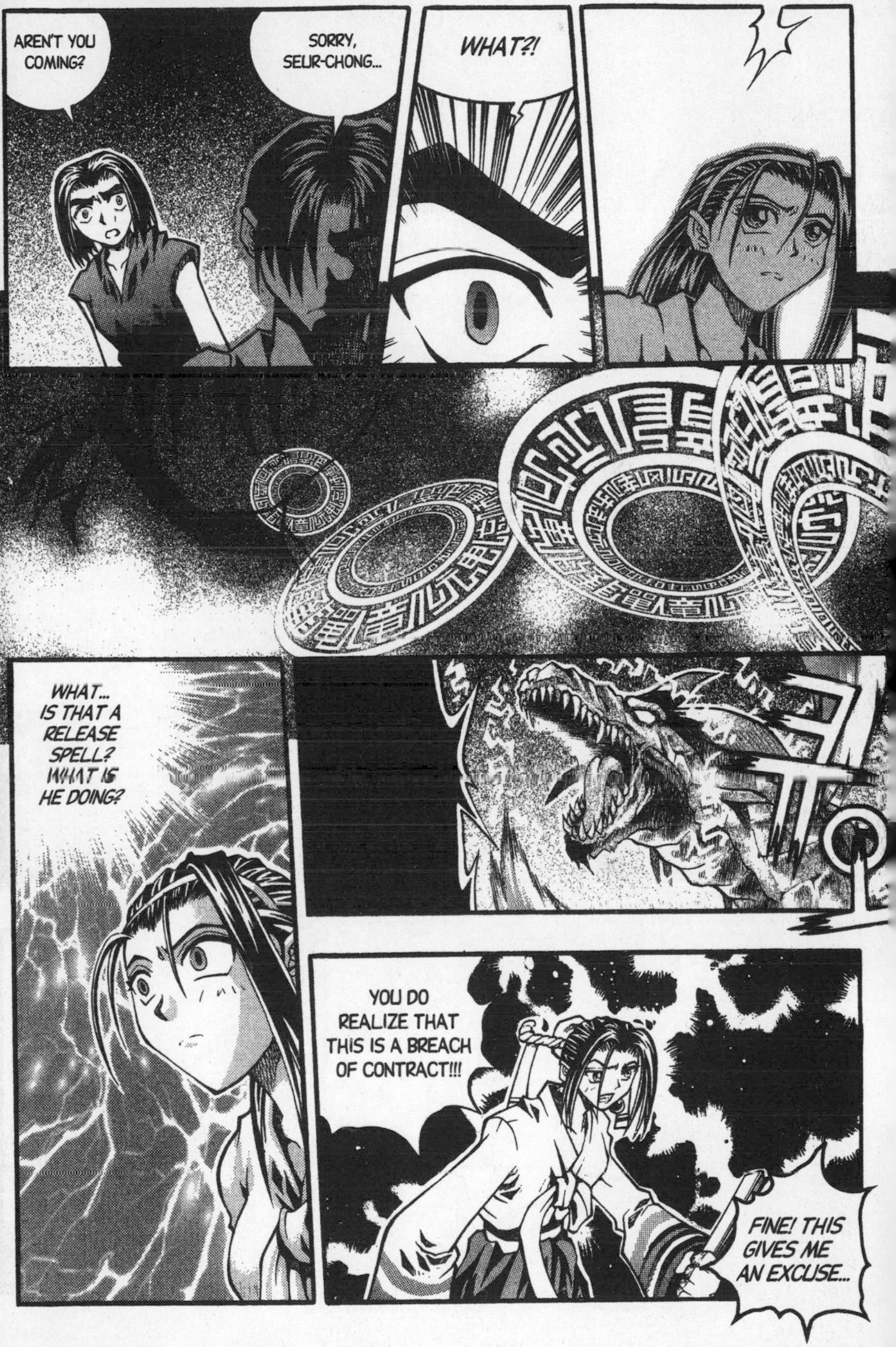
AREN'T YOU COMING?
SORRY, SEUR-CHONG...
WHAT?!
WHAT... IS THAT A RELEASE SPELL? WHAT IS HE DOING?
YOU DO REALIZE THAT THIS IS A BREACH OF CONTRACT!!!
FINE! THIS GIVES ME AN EXCUSE...

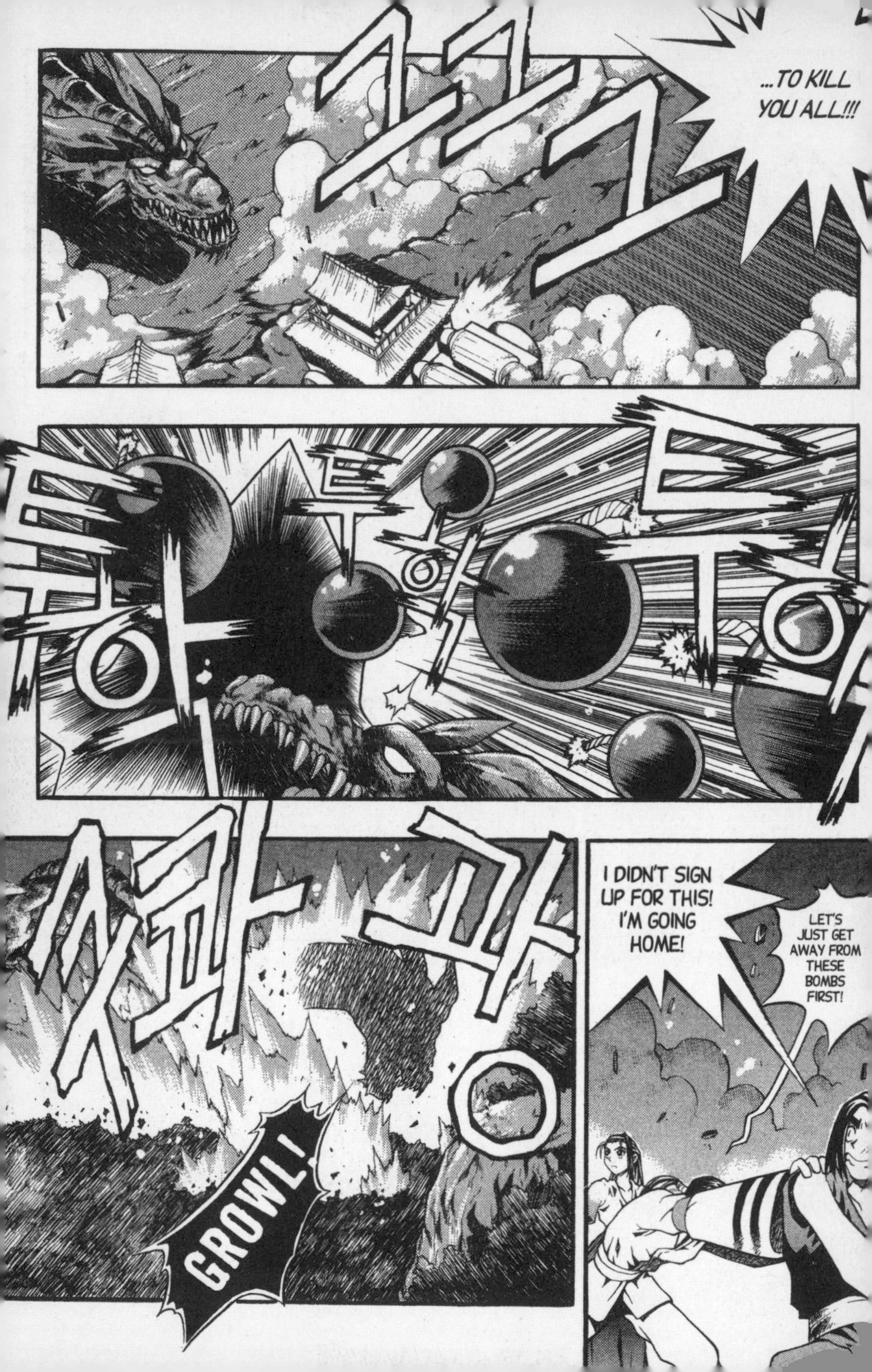
...TO KILL YOU ALL!!!
GROWL!
I DIDN'T SIGN UP FOR THIS! I'M GOING HOME!
LET'S JUST GET AWAY FROM THESE BOMBS FIRST!

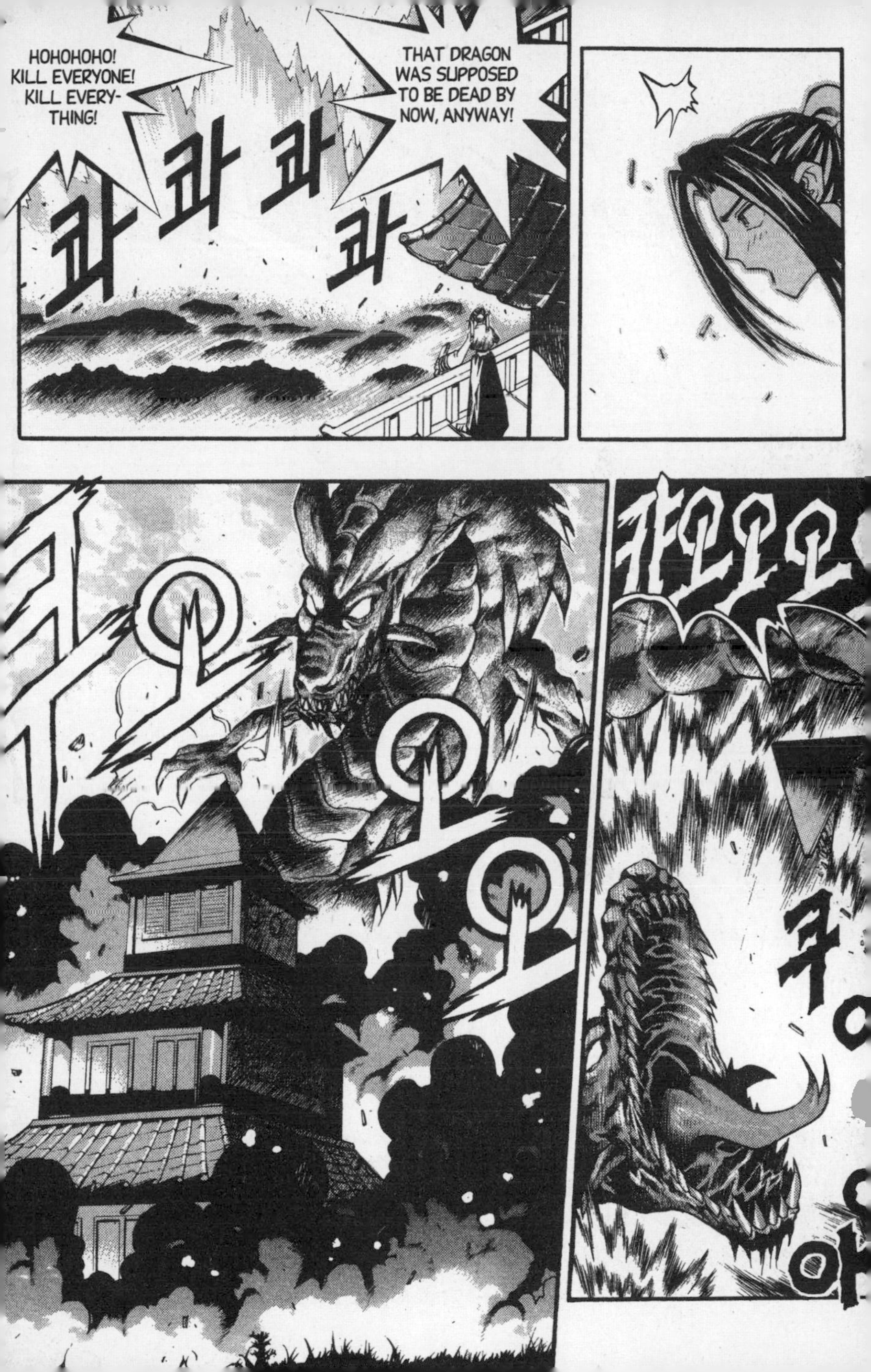
HOHOHOHO! KILL EVERYONE! KILL EVERY-THING!
THAT DRAGON WAS SUPPOSED TO BE DEAD BY NOW, ANYWAY!
콰콰콰콰

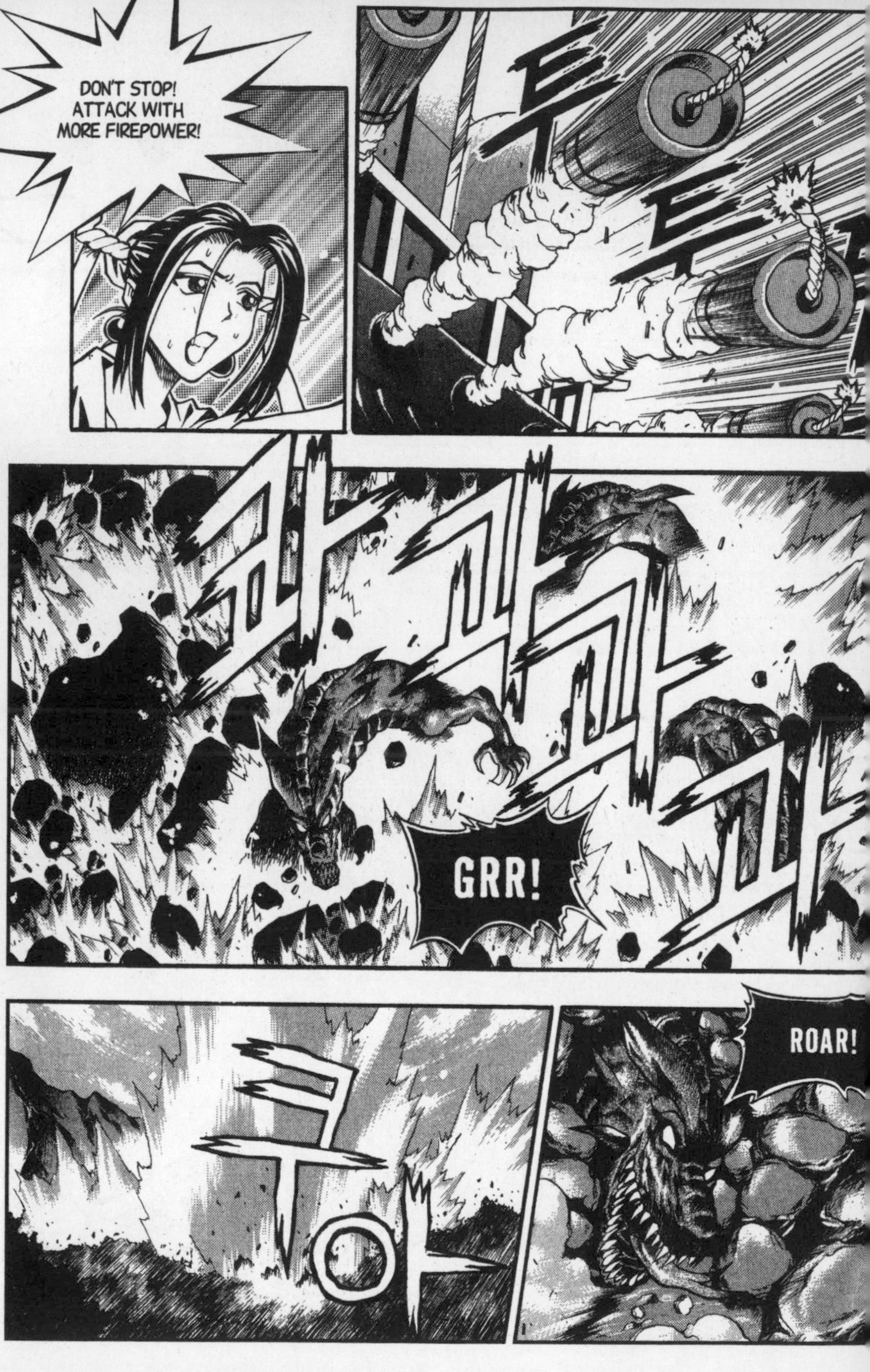
DON'T STOP! ATTACK WITH MORE FIREPOWER!
GRR!
ROAR!

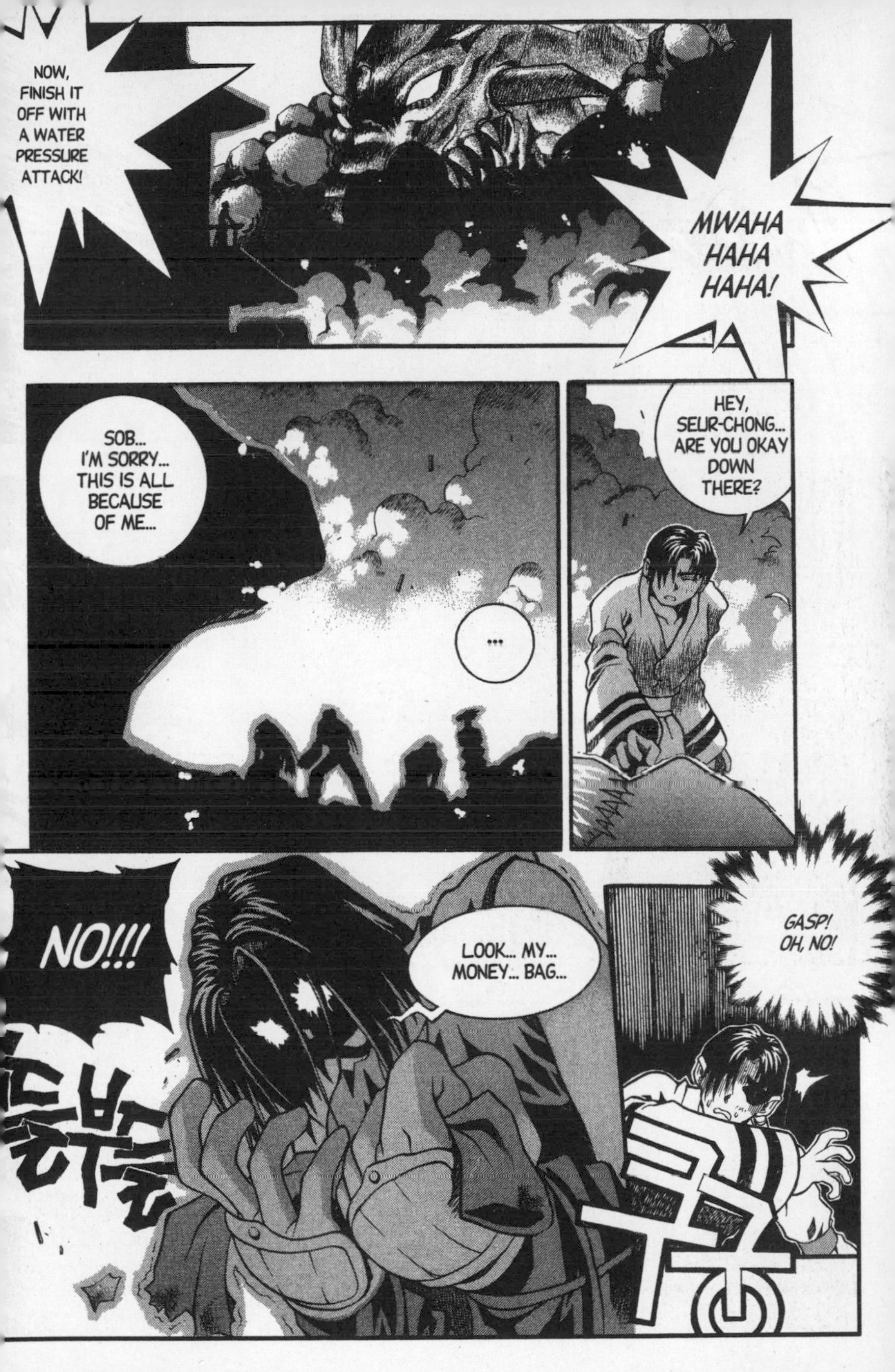
NOW, FINISH IT OFF WITH A WATER PRESSURE ATTACK!
MWAHA HAHA HAHA!
SOB... I'M SORRY... THIS IS ALL BECAUSE OF ME...
...
HEY, SEUR-CHONG... ARE YOU OKAY DOWN THERE?
NO!!!
LOOK... MY... MONEY... BAG...
GASP! OH, NO!

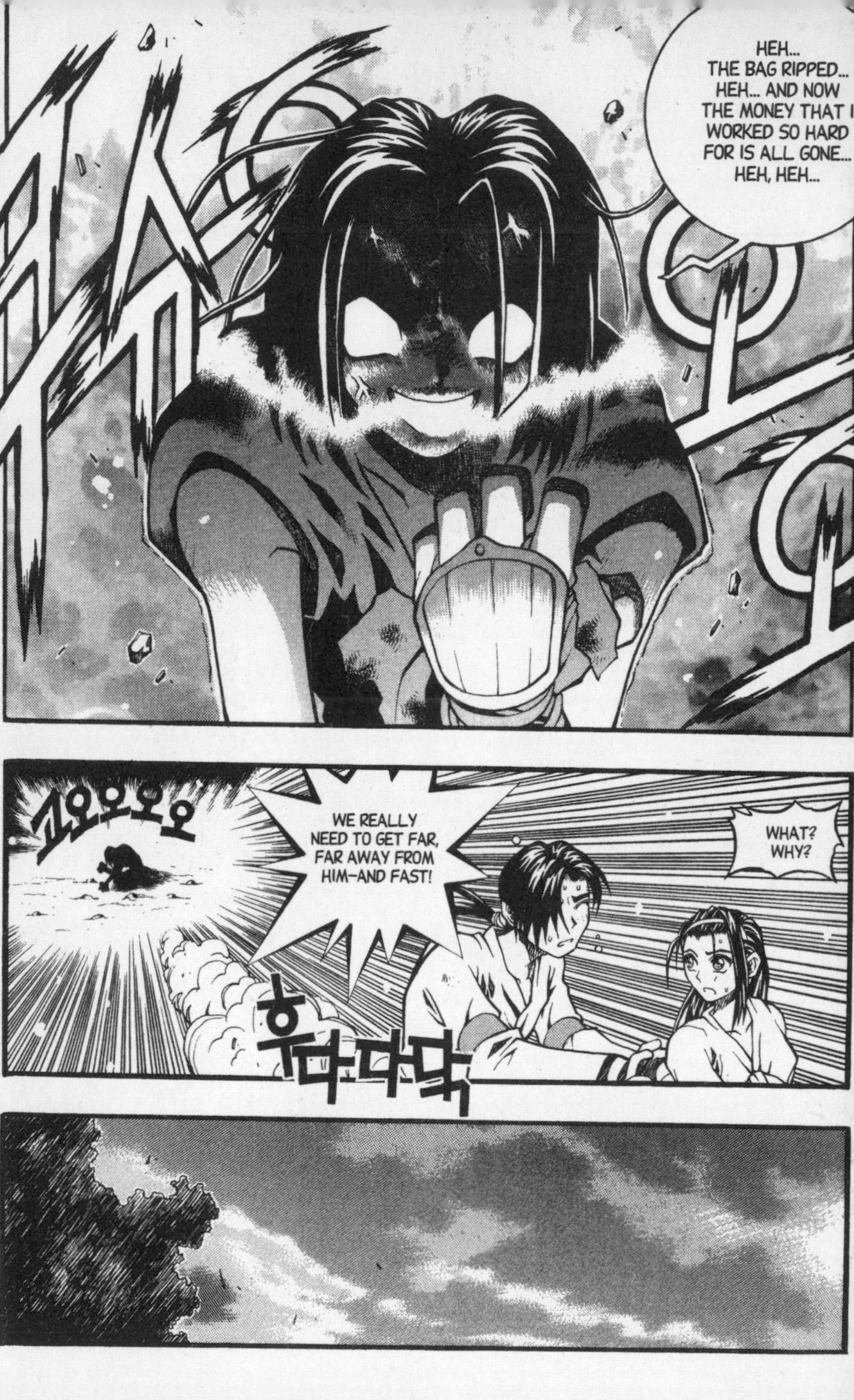
HEH... THE BAG RIPPED... HEH... AND NOW THE MONEY THAT I WORKED SO HARD FOR IS ALL GONE... HEH, HEH...
고오오오오
WE REALLY NEED TO GET FAR, FAR AWAY FROM HIM–AND FAST!
WHAT? WHY?
후다다닥

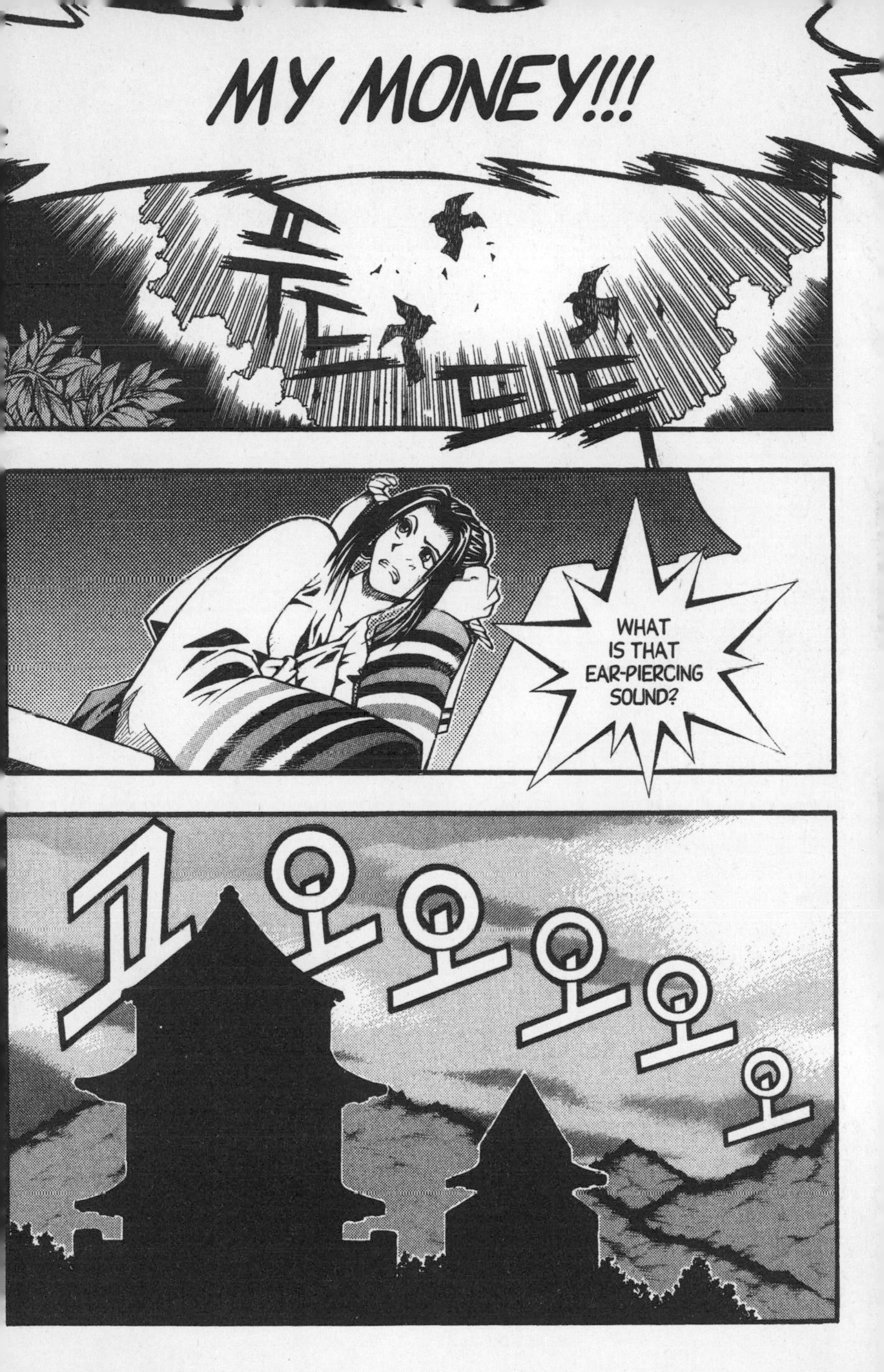
MY MONEY!!!
WHAT IS THAT EAR-PIERCING SOUND?

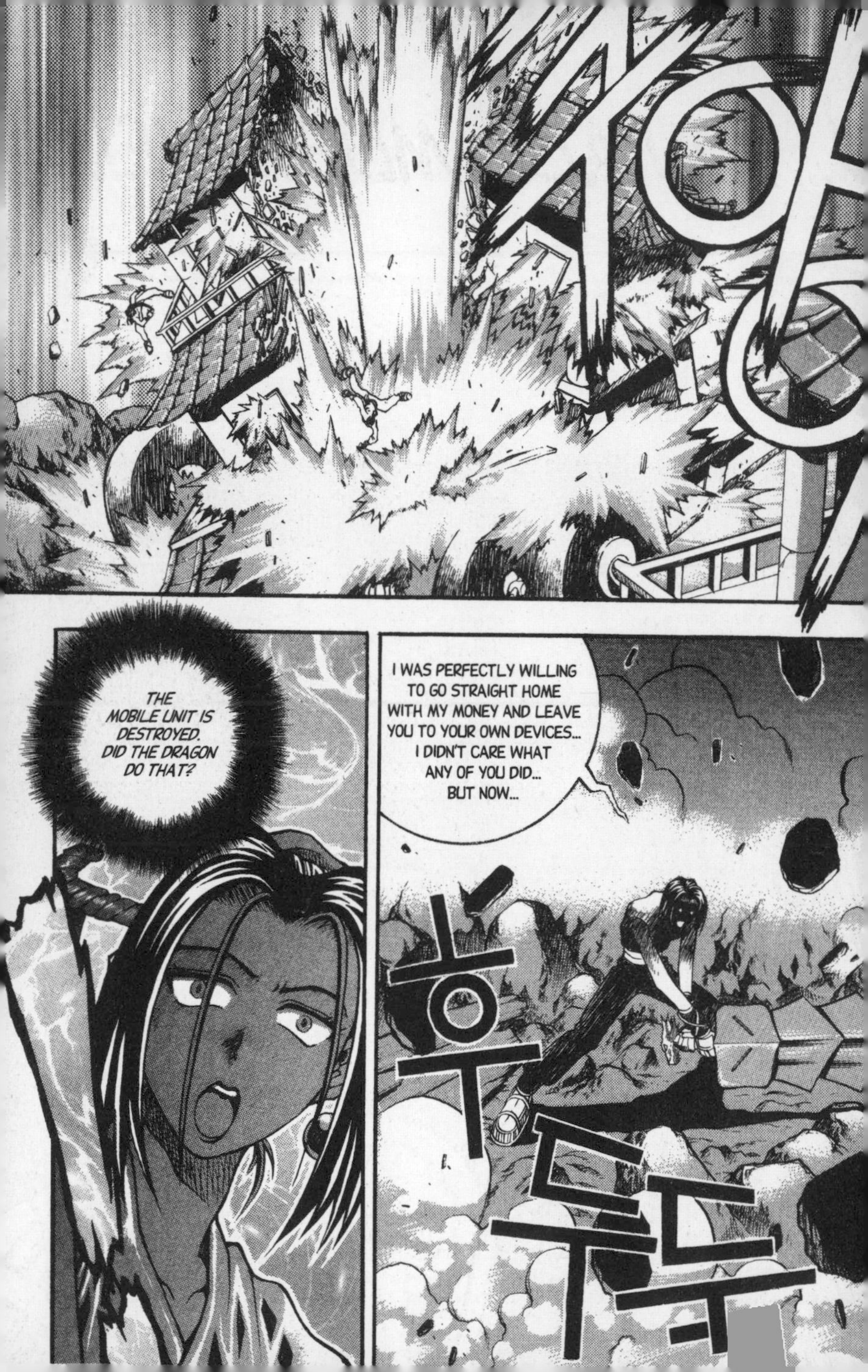
THE MOBILE UNIT IS DESTROYED. DID THE DRAGON DO THAT?
I WAS PERFECTLY WILLING TO GO STRAIGHT HOME WITH MY MONEY AND LEAVE YOU TO YOUR OWN DEVICES... I DIDN'T CARE WHAT ANY OF YOU DID... BUT NOW...

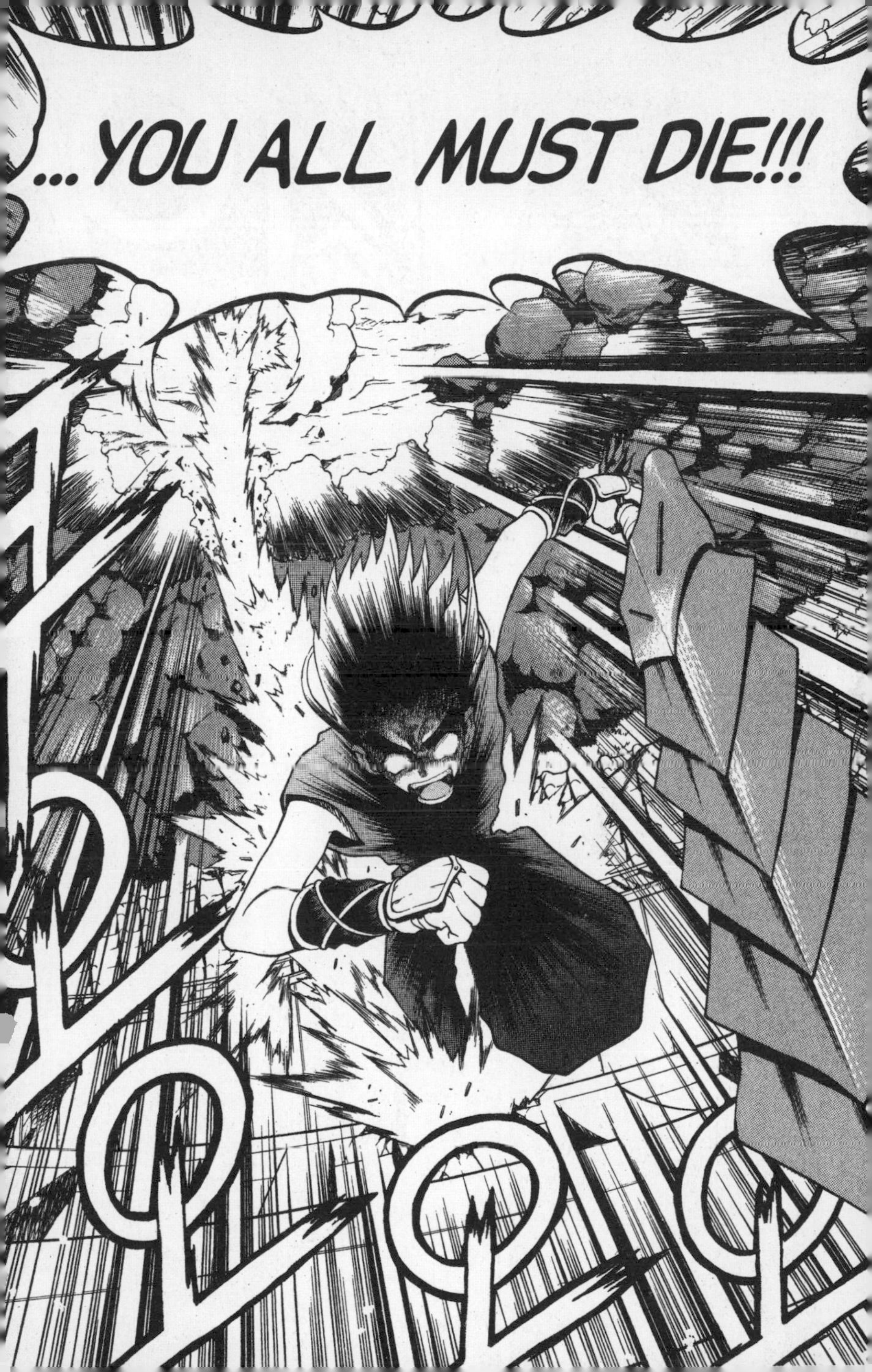
...YOU ALL MUST DIE!!!

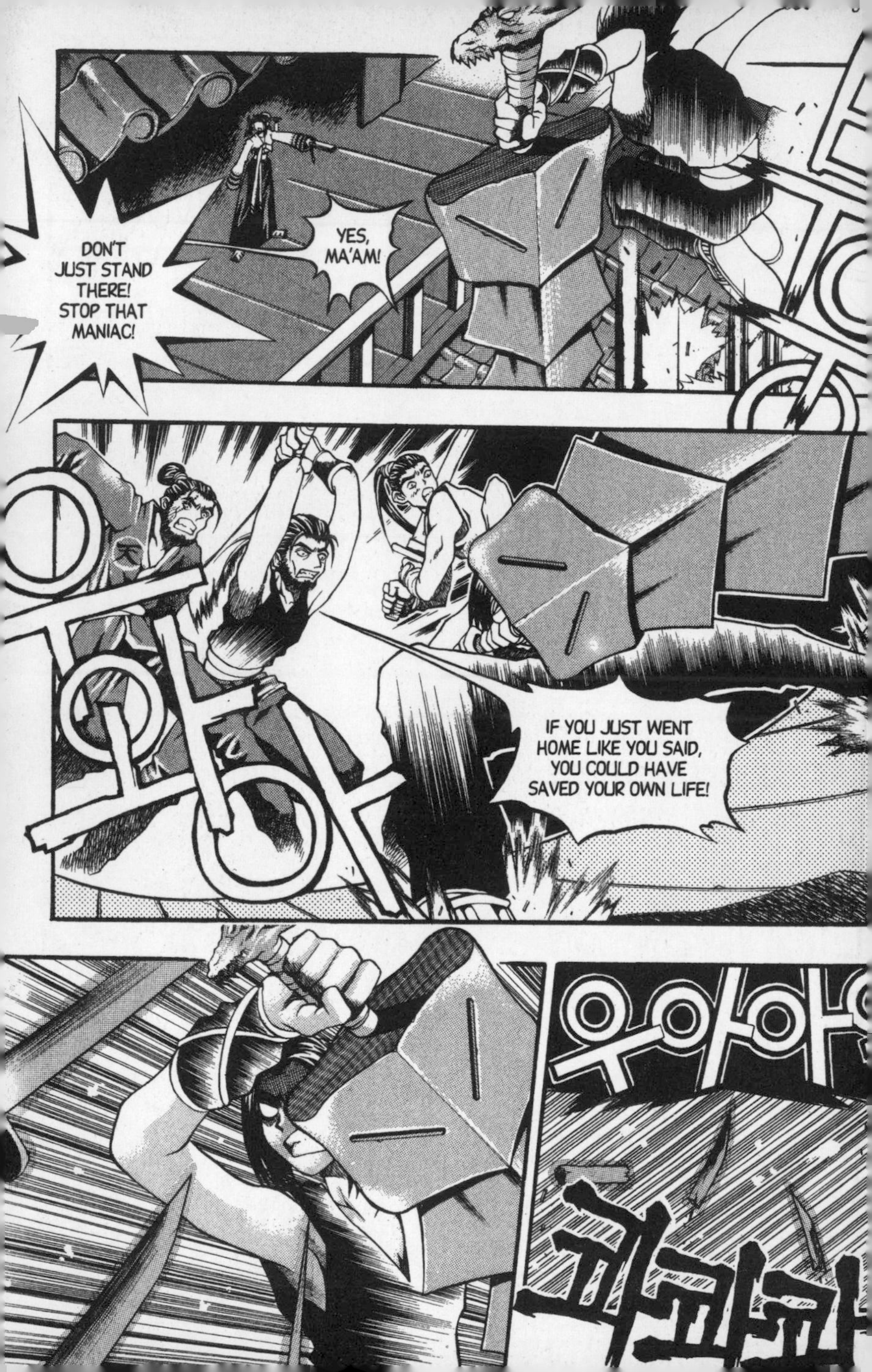
DON'T JUST STAND THERE! STOP THAT MANIAC!
YES, MA'AM!
IF YOU JUST WENT HOME LIKE YOU SAID, YOU COULD HAVE SAVED YOUR OWN LIFE!

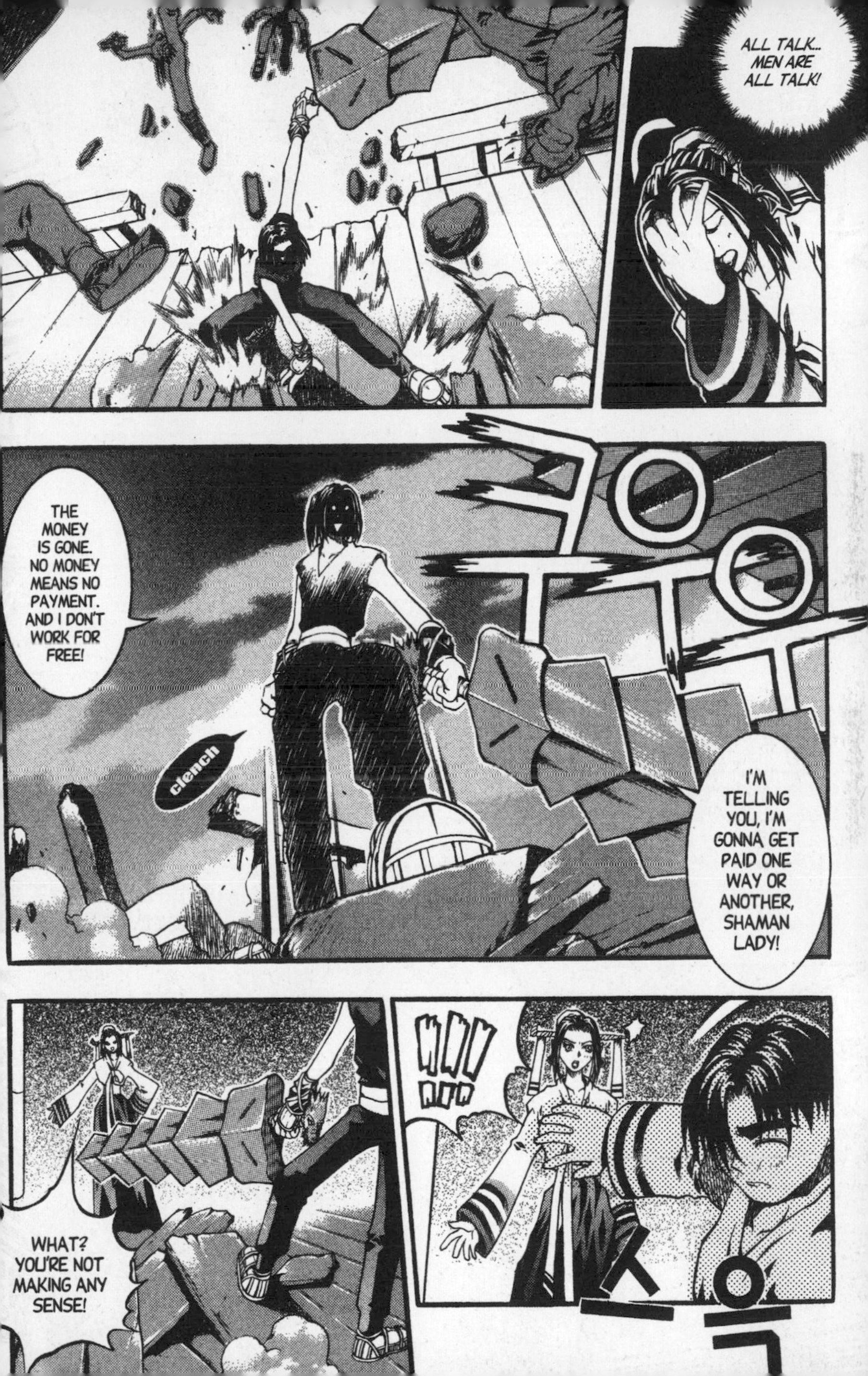
ALL TALK... MEN ARE ALL TALK!
THE MONEY IS GONE. NO MONEY MEANS NO PAYMENT. AND I DON'T WORK FOR FREE!
clench
I'M TELLING YOU, I'M GONNA GET PAID ONE WAY OR ANOTHER, SHAMAN LADY!
WHAT? YOU'RE NOT MAKING ANY SENSE!

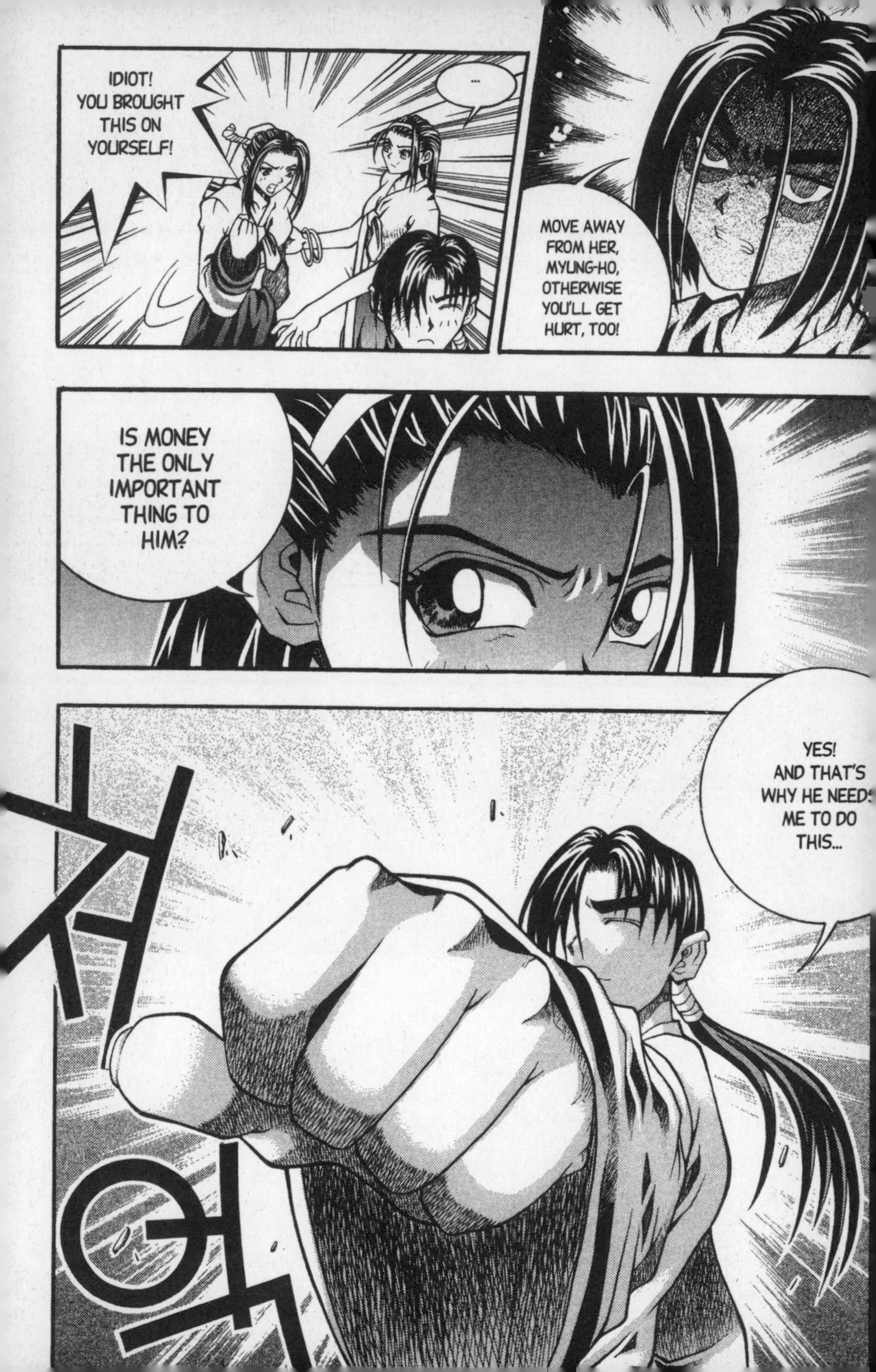
IDIOT! YOU BROUGHT THIS ON YOURSELF!
...
MOVE AWAY FROM HER, MYUNG-HO, OTHERWISE YOU'LL GET HURT, TOO!
IS MONEY THE ONLY IMPORTANT THING TO HIM?
YES! AND THAT'S WHY HE NEEDS ME TO DO THIS...

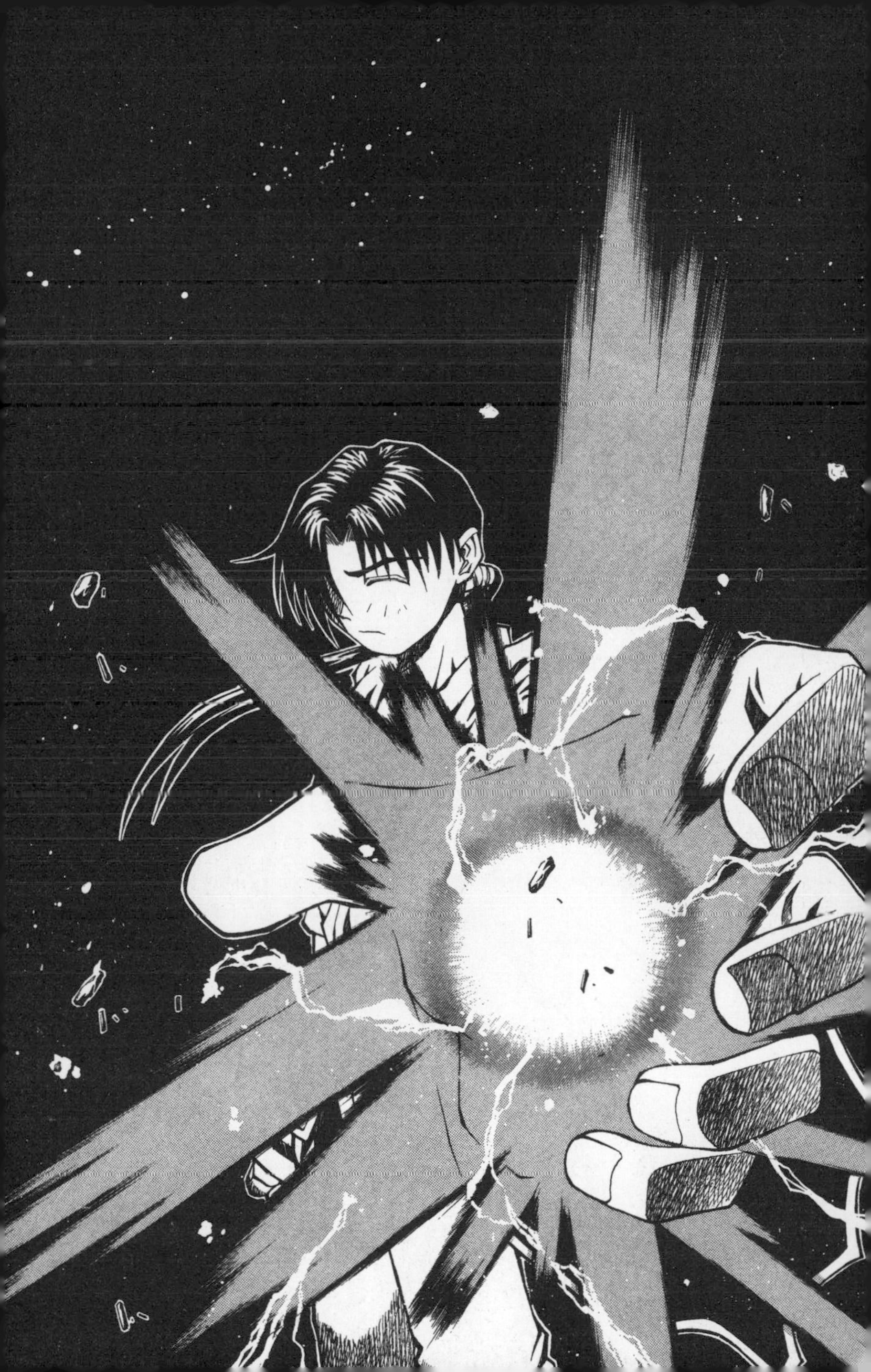

I'M WARNING YOU. MOVE AWAY FROM HER, MYUNG-HO!

RELAX. YOU WANT MONEY? I'LL GIVE YOU SOME.

NO MORE WARNINGS!

THE ONE THING I CAN'T FORGIVE IS BEING RIPPED OFF!!

GRAB

IS HE SERIOUS? HE'D EVEN KILL HIS OWN PARTNER OVER THIS? MAYBE I SHOULD JUST PAY HIM AGAIN?

DISTRACTING SEUR-CHONG WITH SHINY, VALUABLE OBJECTS.

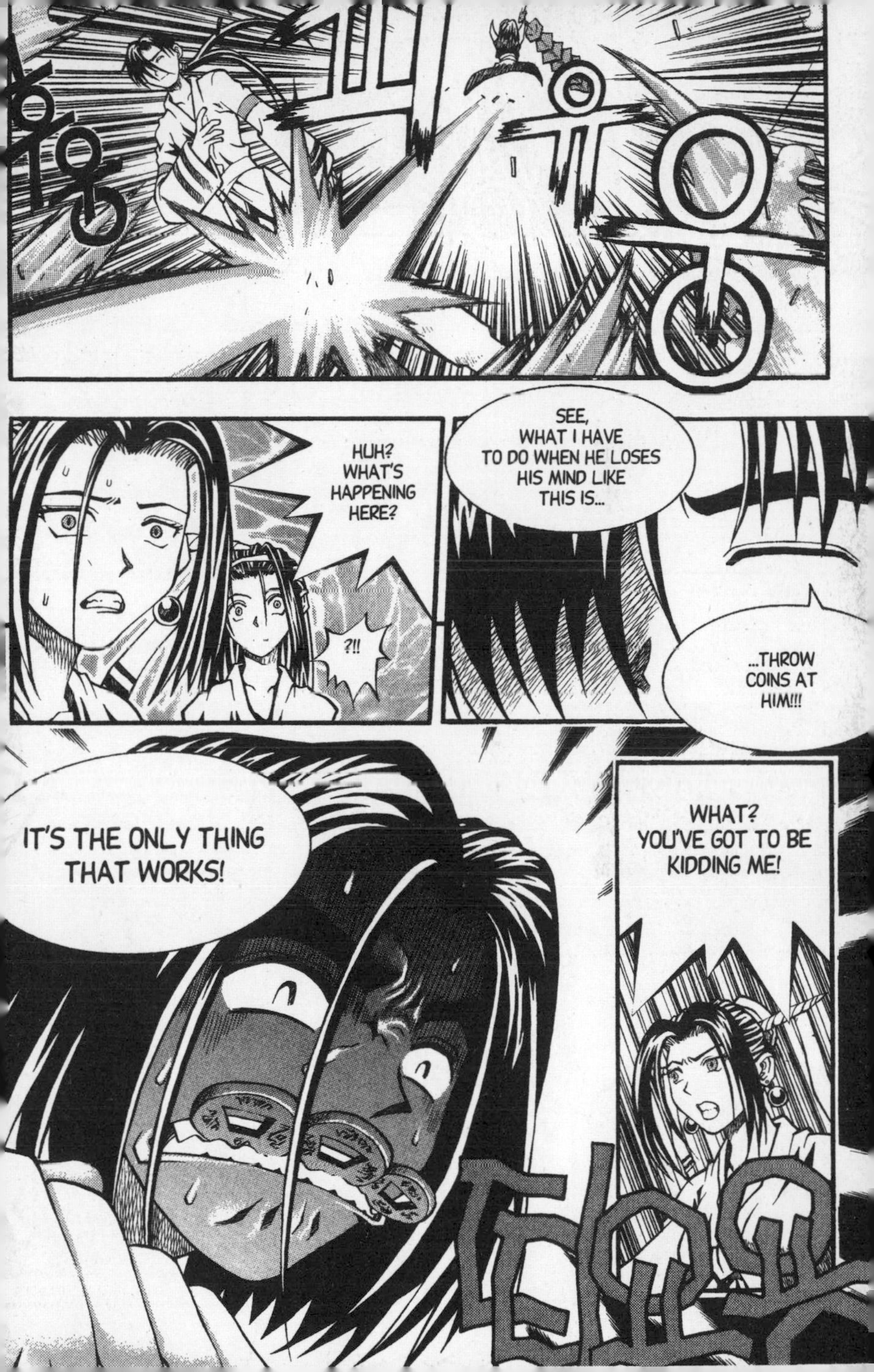
HUH? WHAT'S HAPPENING HERE?
?!!
SEE, WHAT I HAVE TO DO WHEN HE LOSES HIS MIND LIKE THIS IS...
...THROW COINS AT HIM!!!
IT'S THE ONLY THING THAT WORKS!
WHAT? YOU'VE GOT TO BE KIDDING ME!

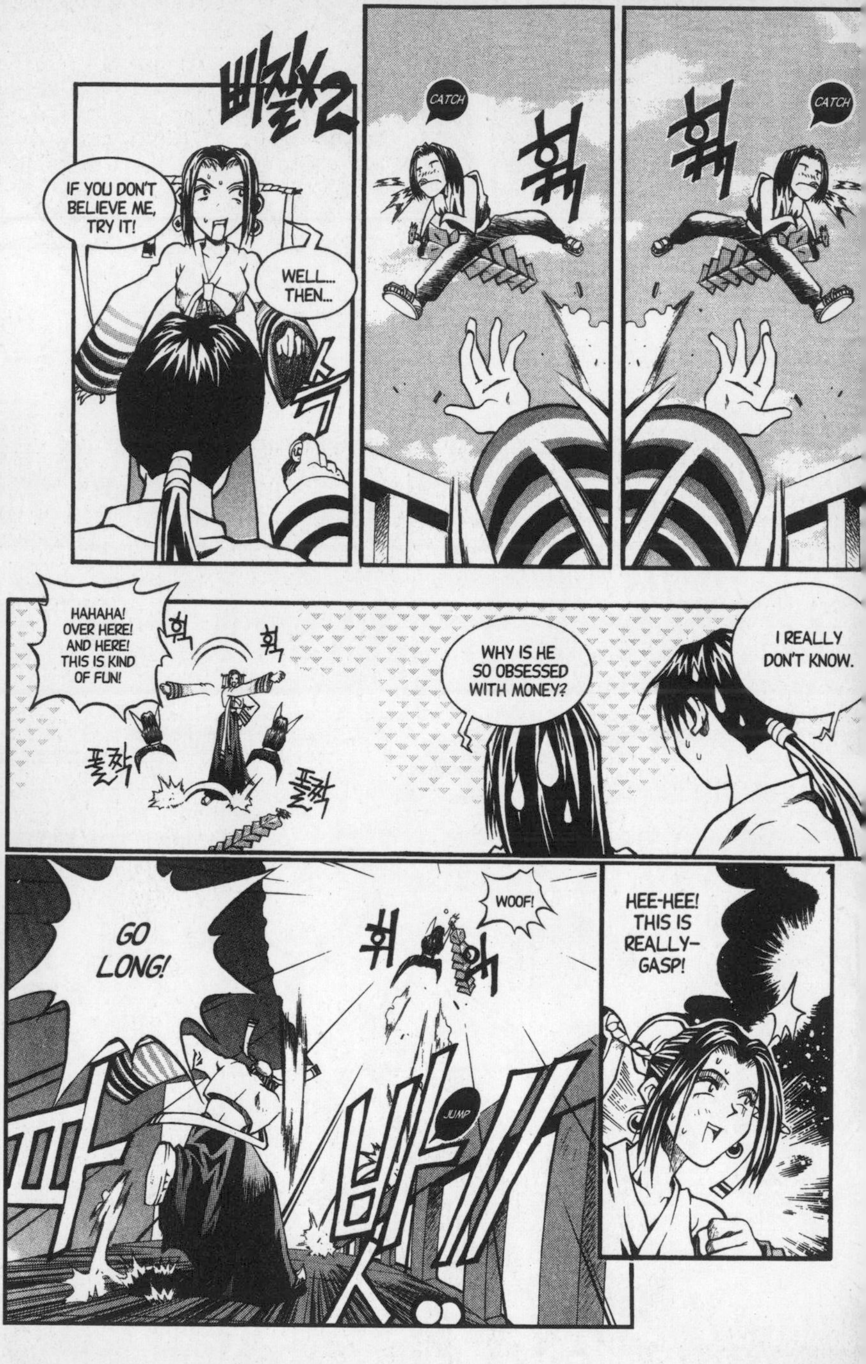
IF YOU DON'T BELIEVE ME, TRY IT!
WELL... THEN...
CATCH
CATCH
HAHAHA! OVER HERE! AND HERE! THIS IS KIND OF FUN!
WHY IS HE SO OBSESSED WITH MONEY?
I REALLY DON'T KNOW.
GO LONG!
WOOF!
JUMP
HEE-HEE! THIS IS REALLY— GASP!

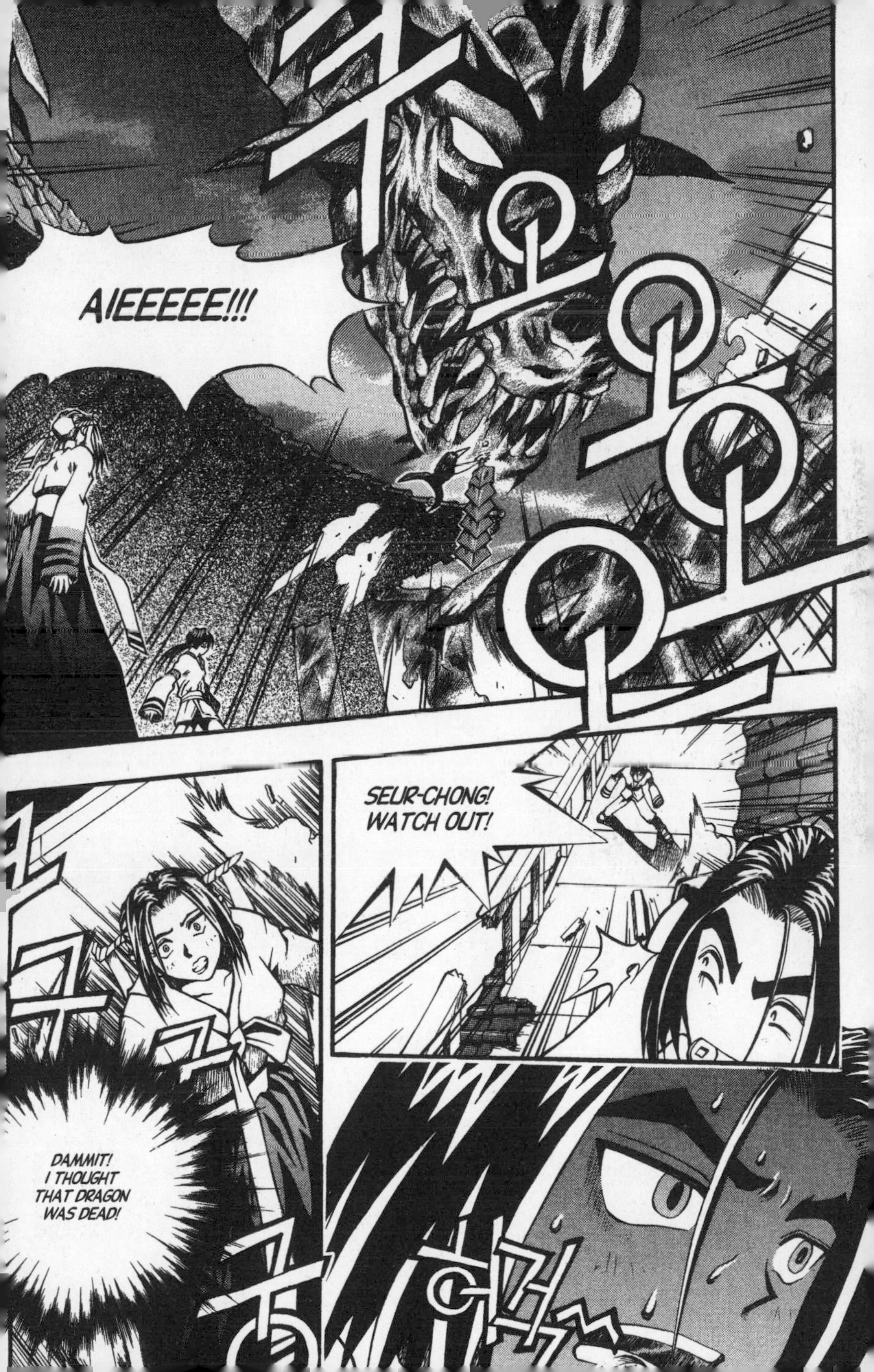
AIEEEEE!!!
SEUR-CHONG! WATCH OUT!
DAMMIT! I THOUGHT THAT DRAGON WAS DEAD!

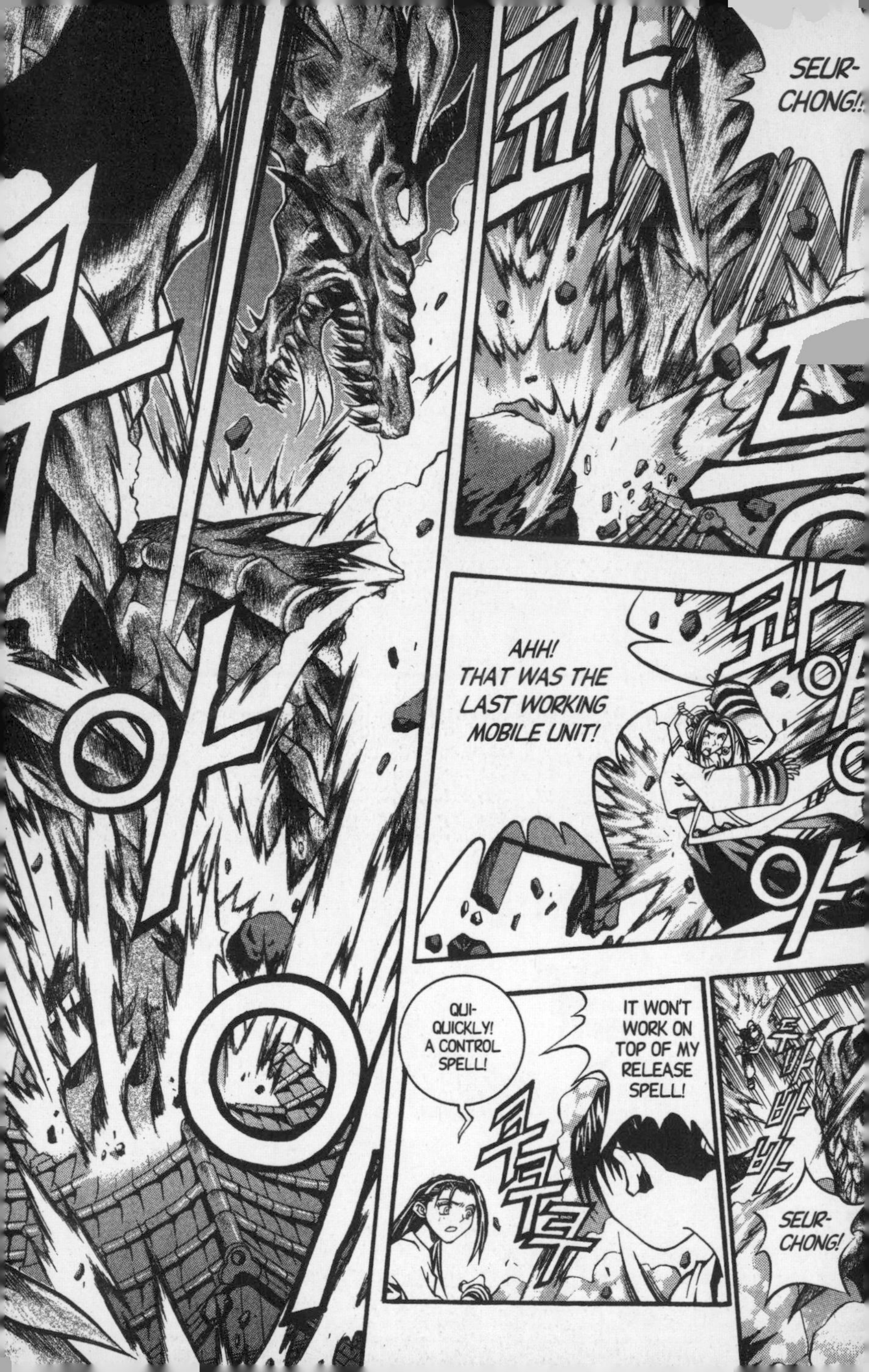
SEUR-CHONG!!
AHH! THAT WAS THE LAST WORKING MOBILE UNIT!
QUI-QUICKLY! A CONTROL SPELL!
IT WON'T WORK ON TOP OF MY RELEASE SPELL!
SEUR-CHONG!

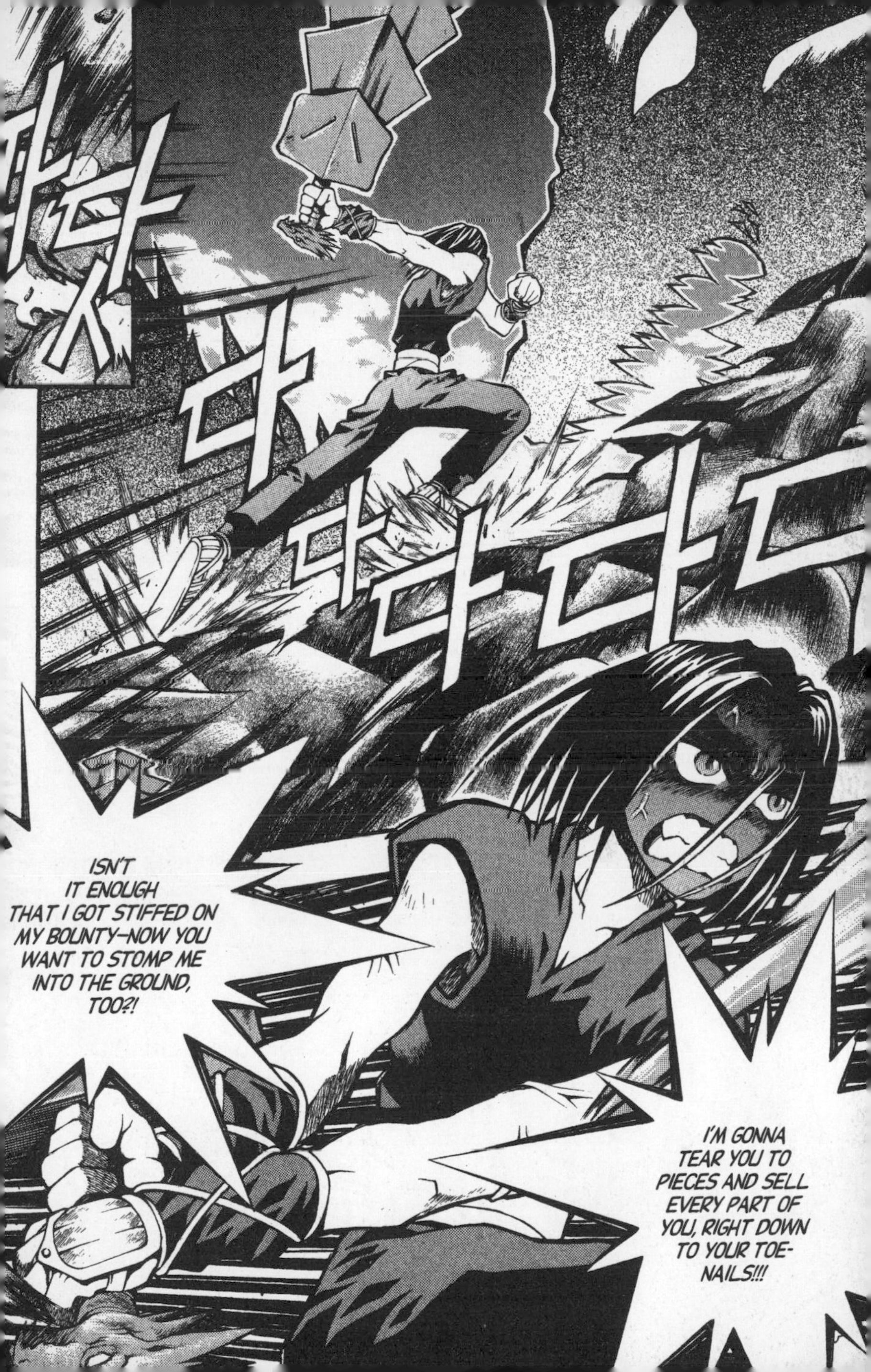
ISN'T IT ENOUGH THAT I GOT STIFFED ON MY BOUNTY–NOW YOU WANT TO STOMP ME INTO THE GROUND, TOO?!
I'M GONNA TEAR YOU TO PIECES AND SELL EVERY PART OF YOU, RIGHT DOWN TO YOUR TOE-NAILS!!!

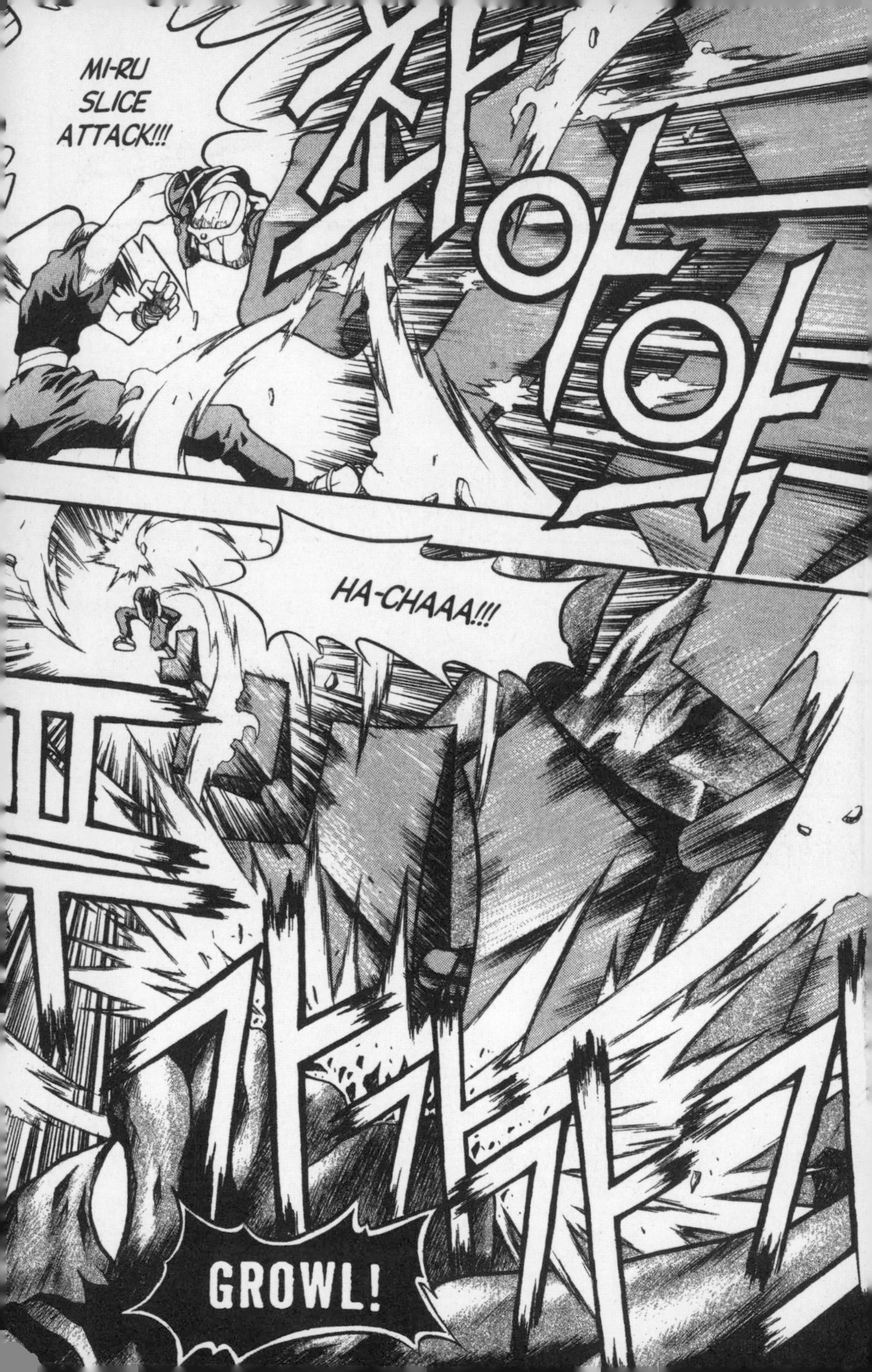
MI-RU SLICE ATTACK!!!
HA-CHAAA!!!
GROWL!

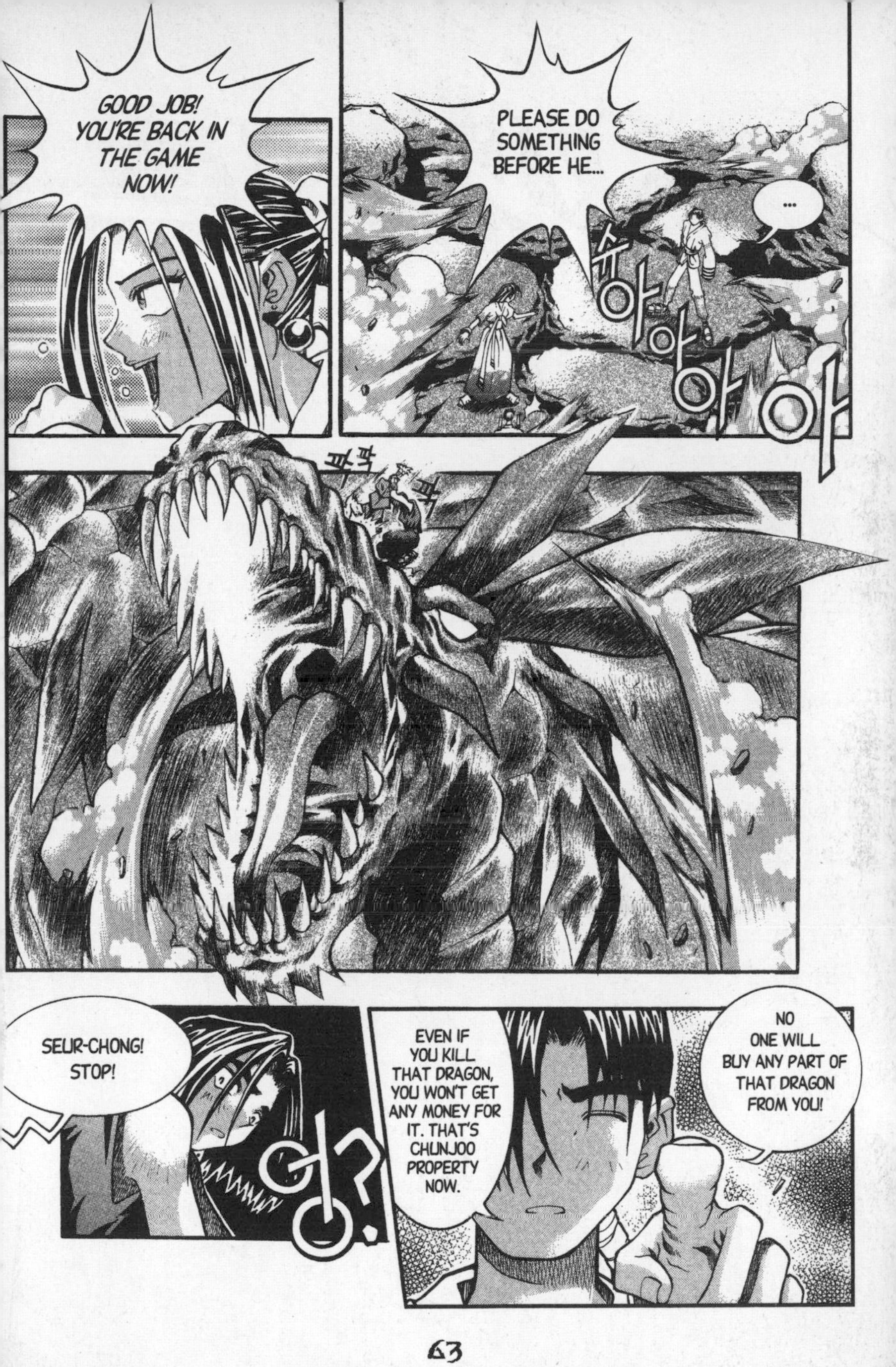
GOOD JOB! YOU'RE BACK IN THE GAME NOW!
PLEASE DO SOMETHING BEFORE HE...
...
슈아아아아
퍽퍽
퍽
SEUR-CHONG! STOP!
엉?
EVEN IF YOU KILL THAT DRAGON, YOU WON'T GET ANY MONEY FOR IT. THAT'S CHUNJOO PROPERTY NOW.
NO ONE WILL BUY ANY PART OF THAT DRAGON FROM YOU!

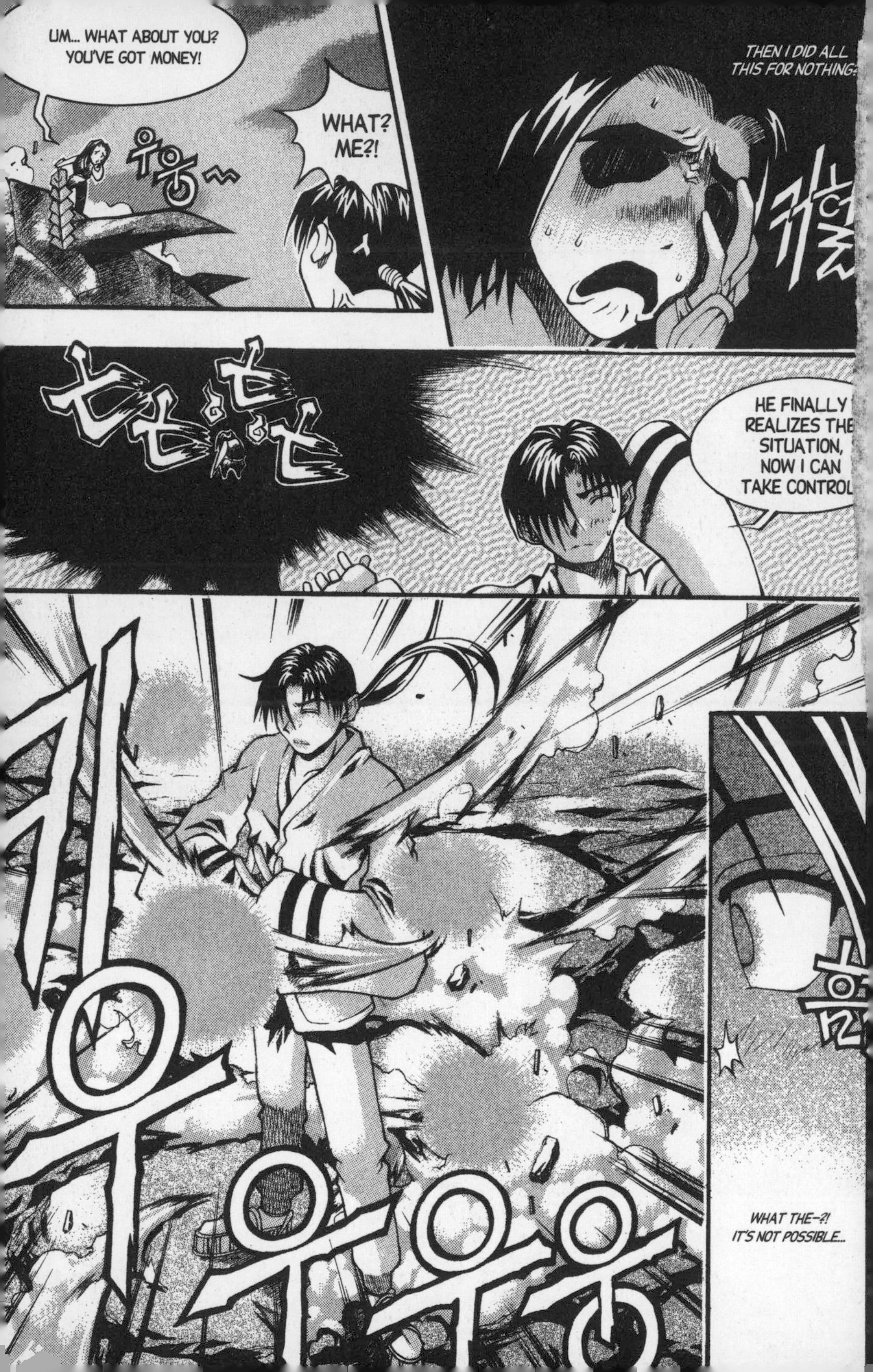
UM... WHAT ABOUT YOU? YOU'VE GOT MONEY!
WHAT? ME?!
THEN I DID ALL THIS FOR NOTHING?
HE FINALLY REALIZES THE SITUATION, NOW I CAN TAKE CONTROL
WHAT THE—?! IT'S NOT POSSIBLE...

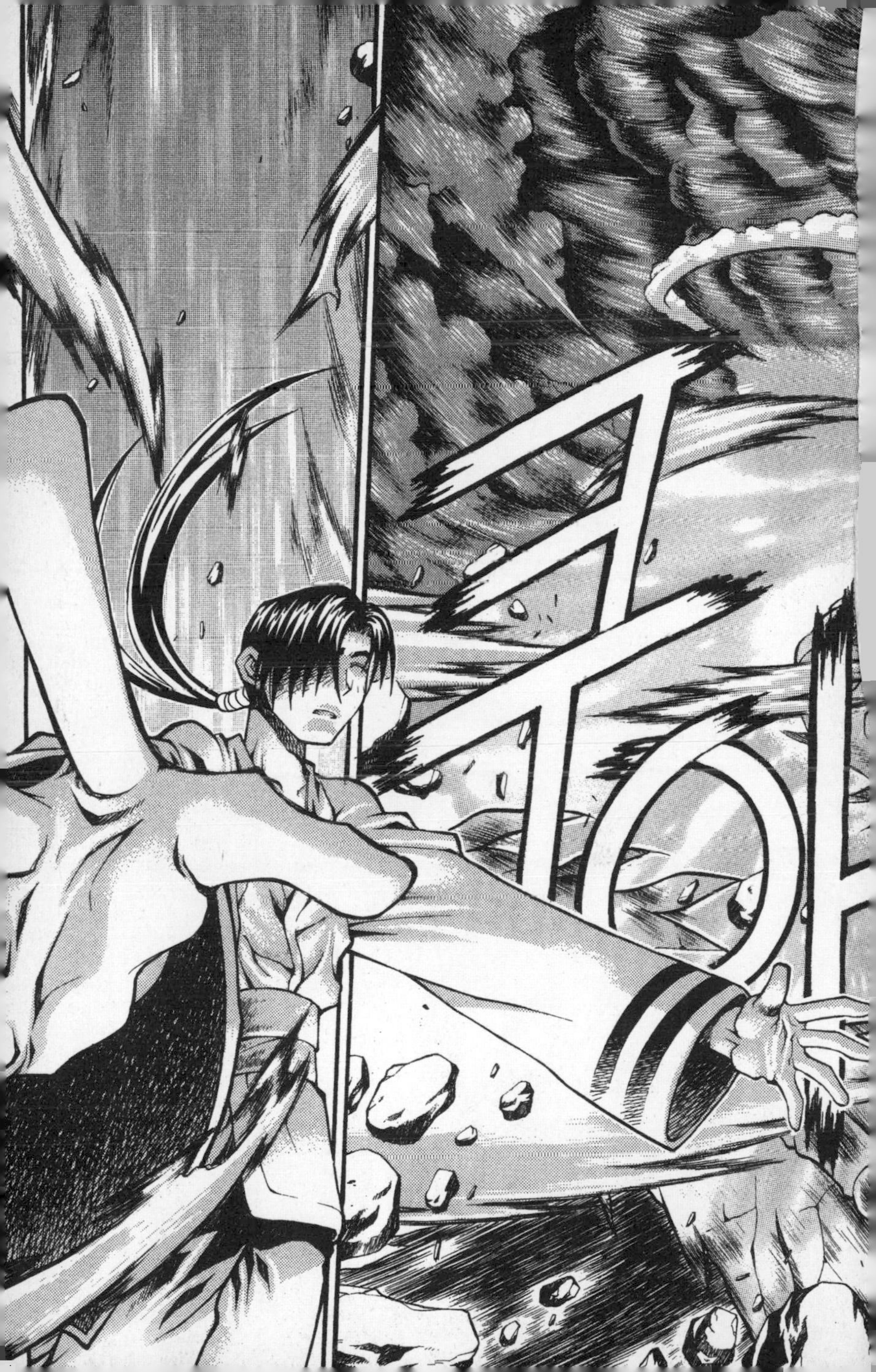

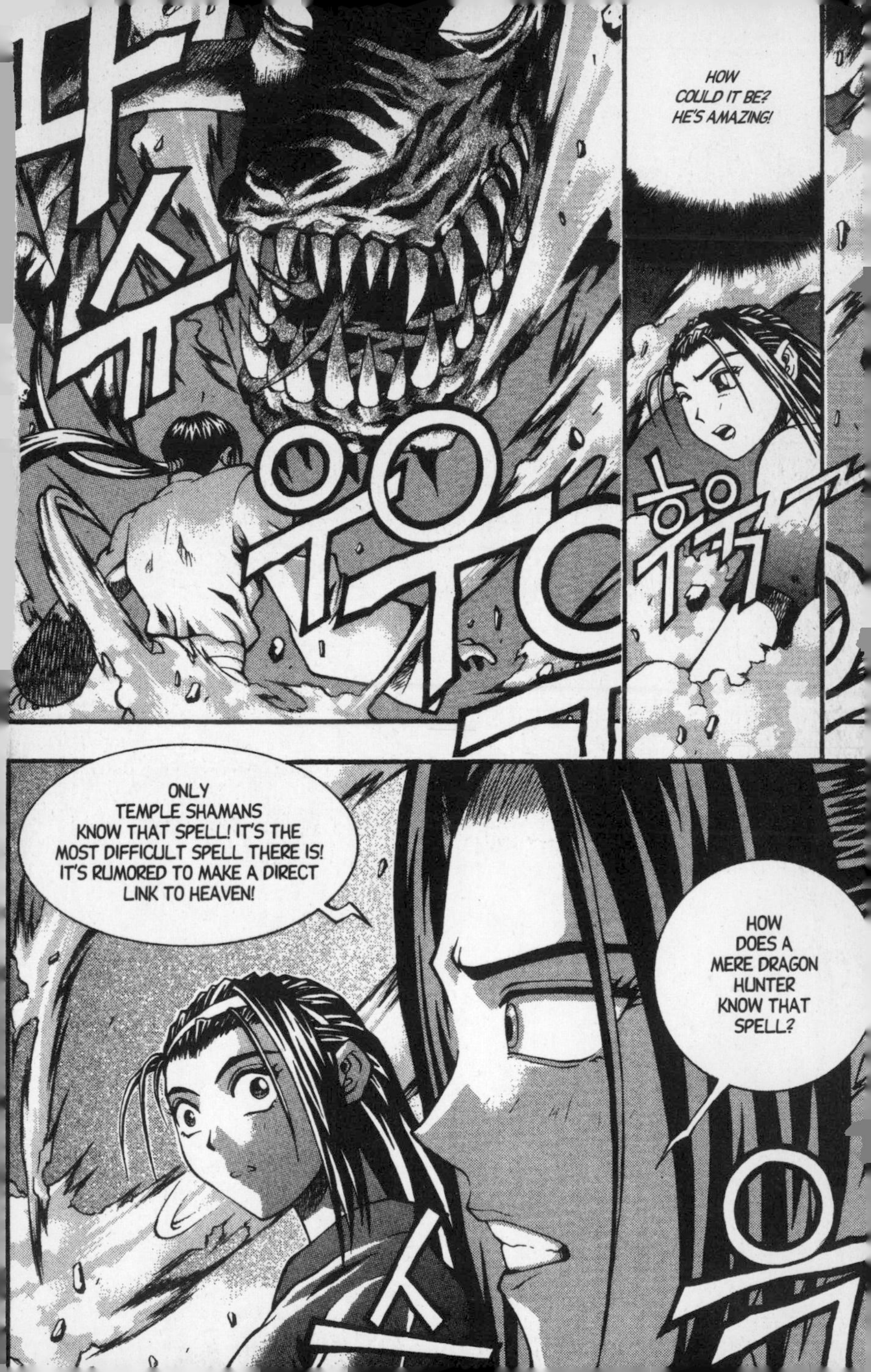
HOW COULD IT BE? HE'S AMAZING!
ONLY TEMPLE SHAMANS KNOW THAT SPELL! IT'S THE MOST DIFFICULT SPELL THERE IS! IT'S RUMORED TO MAKE A DIRECT LINK TO HEAVEN!
HOW DOES A MERE DRAGON HUNTER KNOW THAT SPELL?

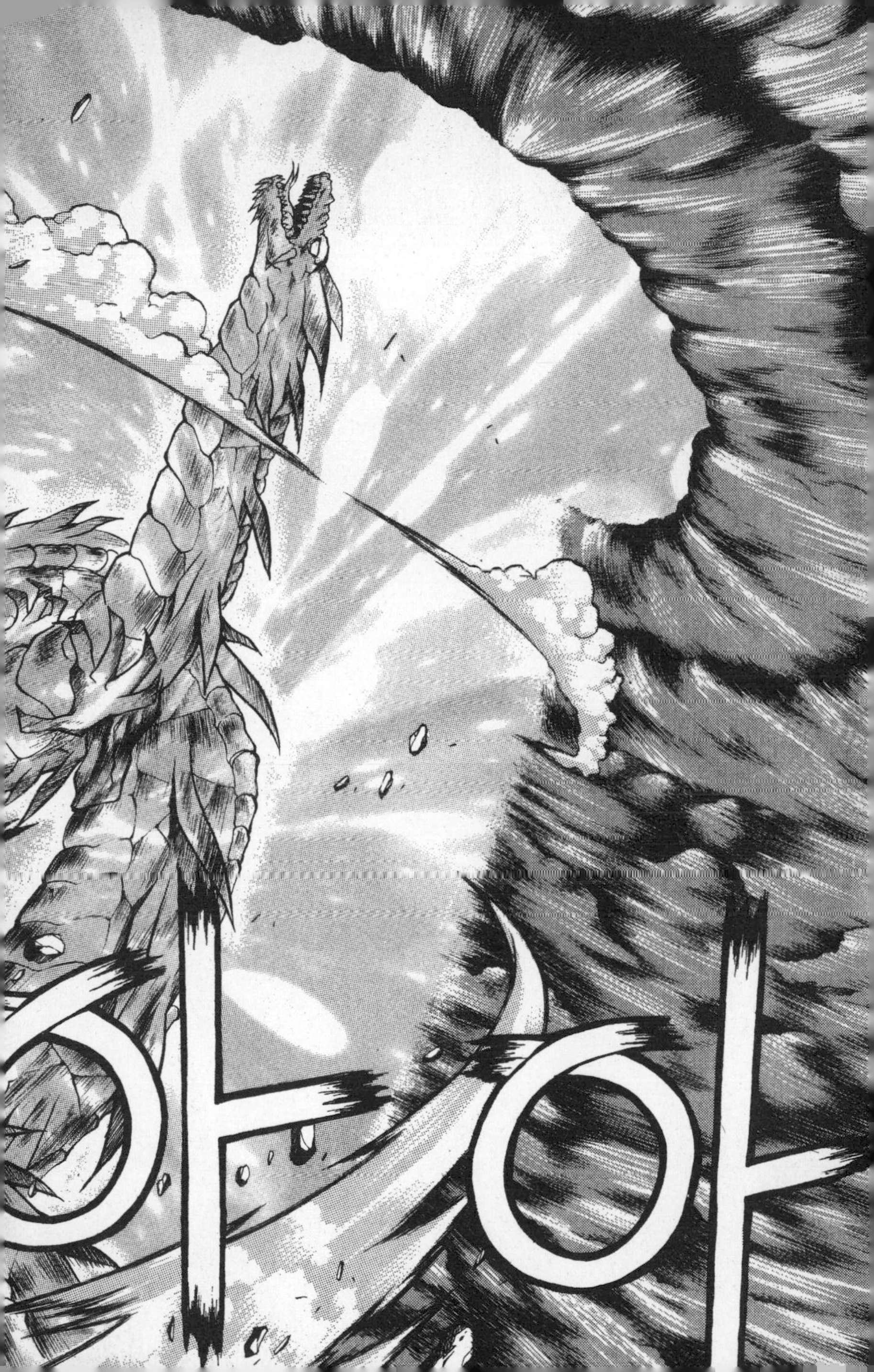
아아

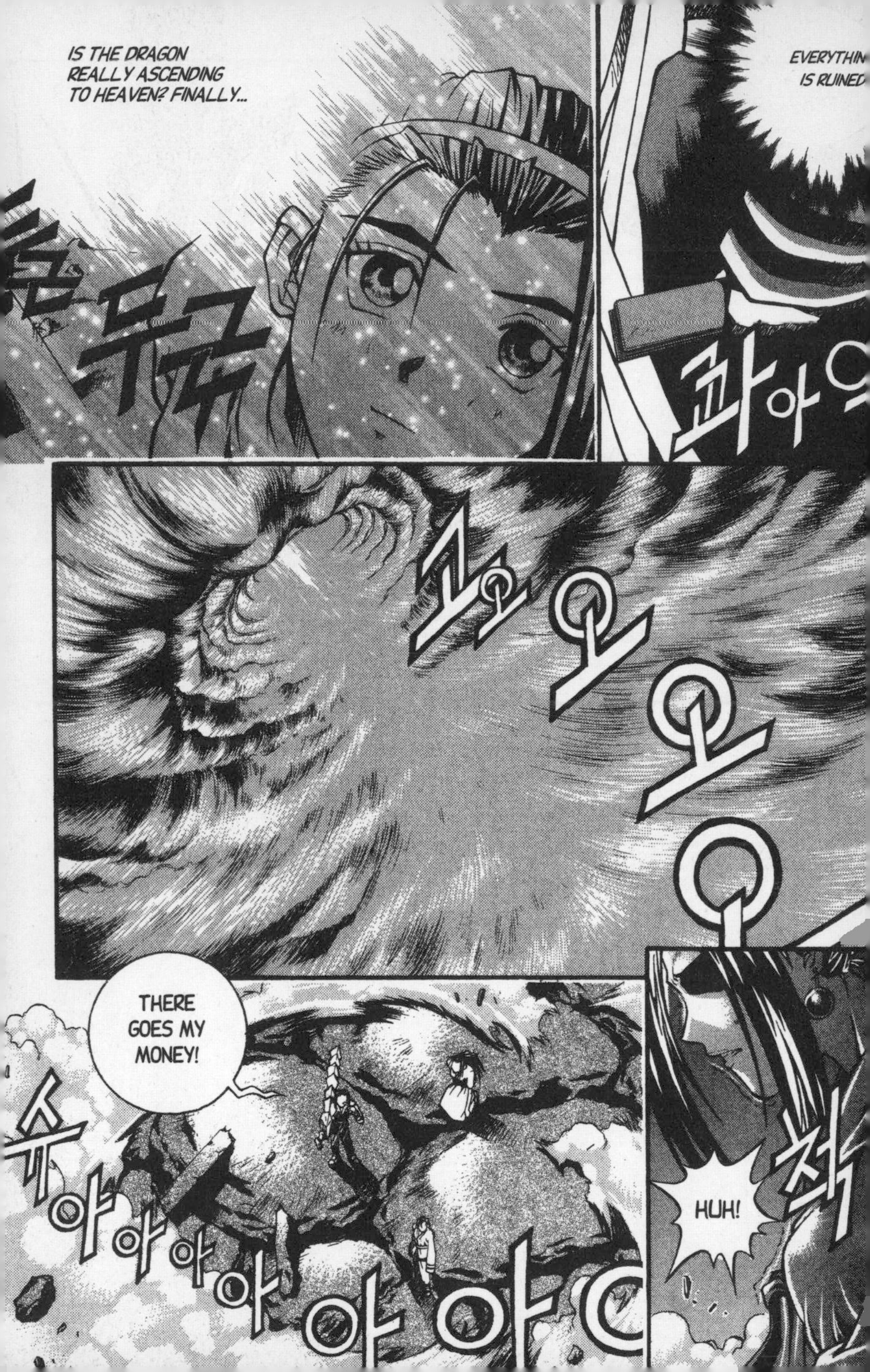
IS THE DRAGON REALLY ASCENDING TO HEAVEN? FINALLY...
EVERYTHIN IS RUINED
THERE GOES MY MONEY!
HUH!
척

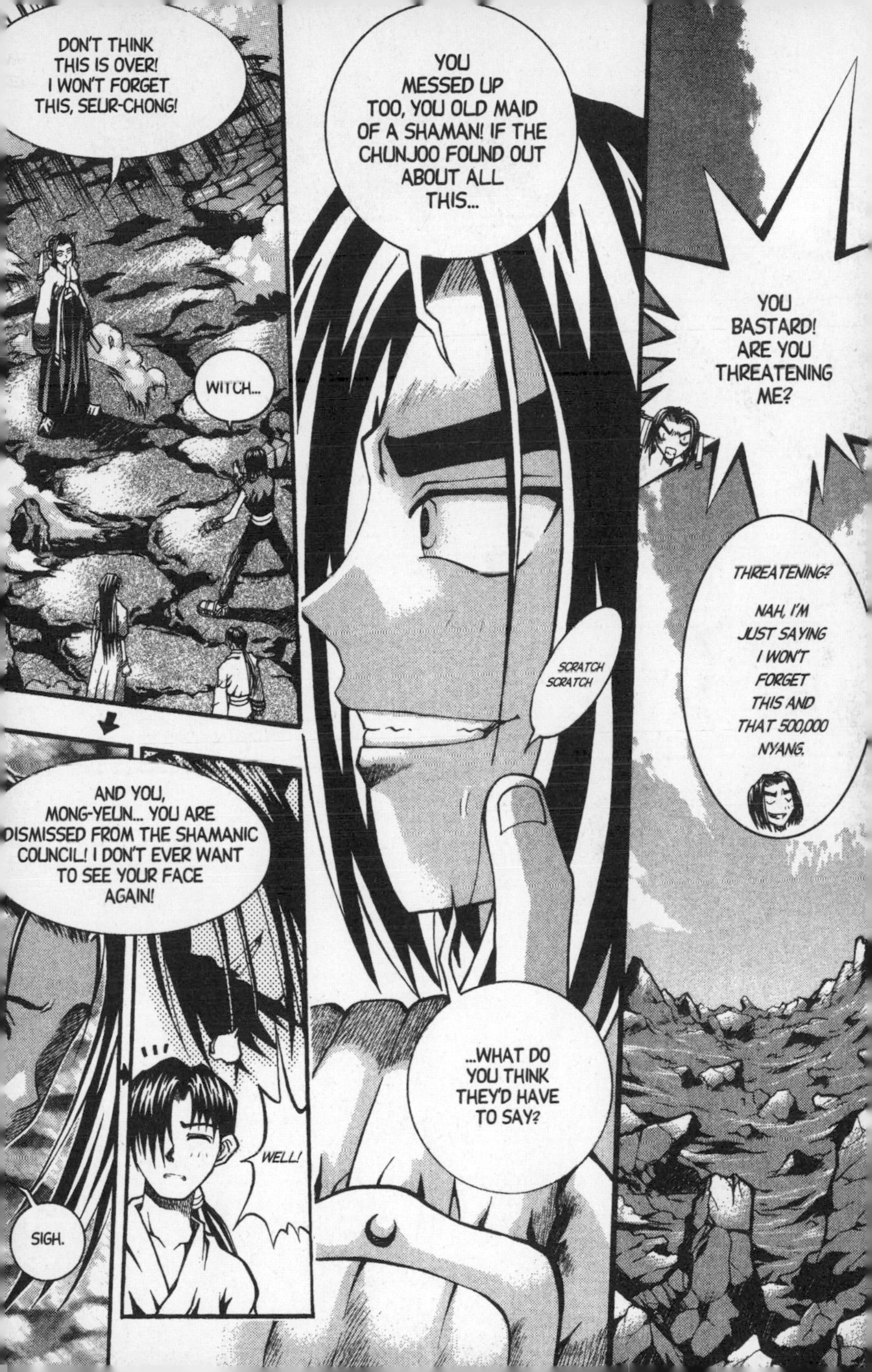
DON'T THINK THIS IS OVER! I WON'T FORGET THIS, SEUR-CHONG!
WITCH...
AND YOU, MONG-YEUN... YOU ARE DISMISSED FROM THE SHAMANIC COUNCIL! I DON'T EVER WANT TO SEE YOUR FACE AGAIN!
WELL!
SIGH.
YOU MESSED UP TOO, YOU OLD MAID OF A SHAMAN! IF THE CHUNJOO FOUND OUT ABOUT ALL THIS...
SCRATCH SCRATCH
...WHAT DO YOU THINK THEY'D HAVE TO SAY?
YOU BASTARD! ARE YOU THREATENING ME?
THREATENING?
NAH, I'M JUST SAYING I WON'T FORGET THIS AND THAT 500,000 NYANG.

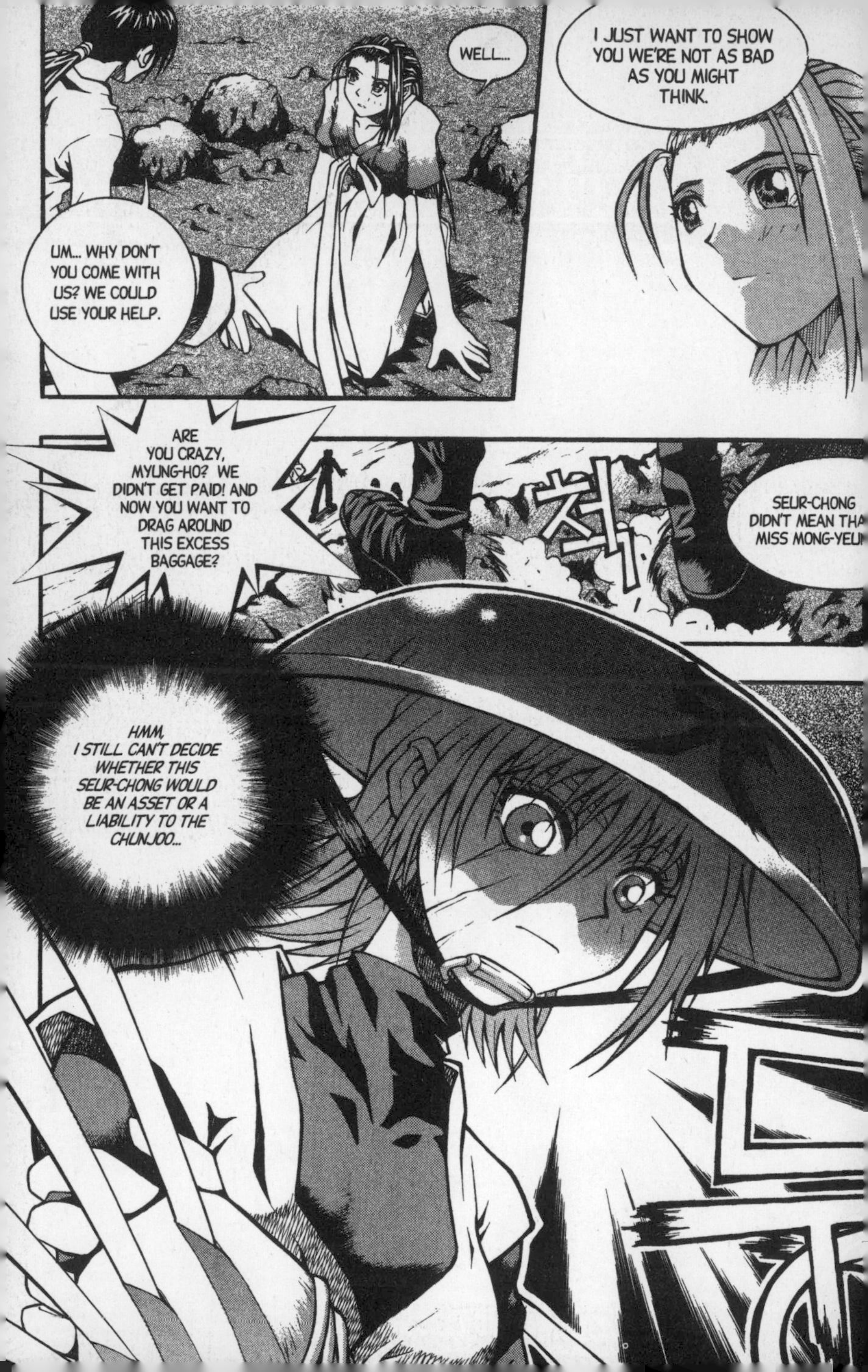
WELL...
UM... WHY DON'T YOU COME WITH US? WE COULD USE YOUR HELP.
I JUST WANT TO SHOW YOU WE'RE NOT AS BAD AS YOU MIGHT THINK.
ARE YOU CRAZY, MYUNG-HO? WE DIDN'T GET PAID! AND NOW YOU WANT TO DRAG AROUND THIS EXCESS BAGGAGE?
SEUR-CHONG DIDN'T MEAN THA MISS MONG-YEU
HMM, I STILL CAN'T DECIDE WHETHER THIS SEUR-CHONG WOULD BE AN ASSET OR A LIABILITY TO THE CHUNJOO...

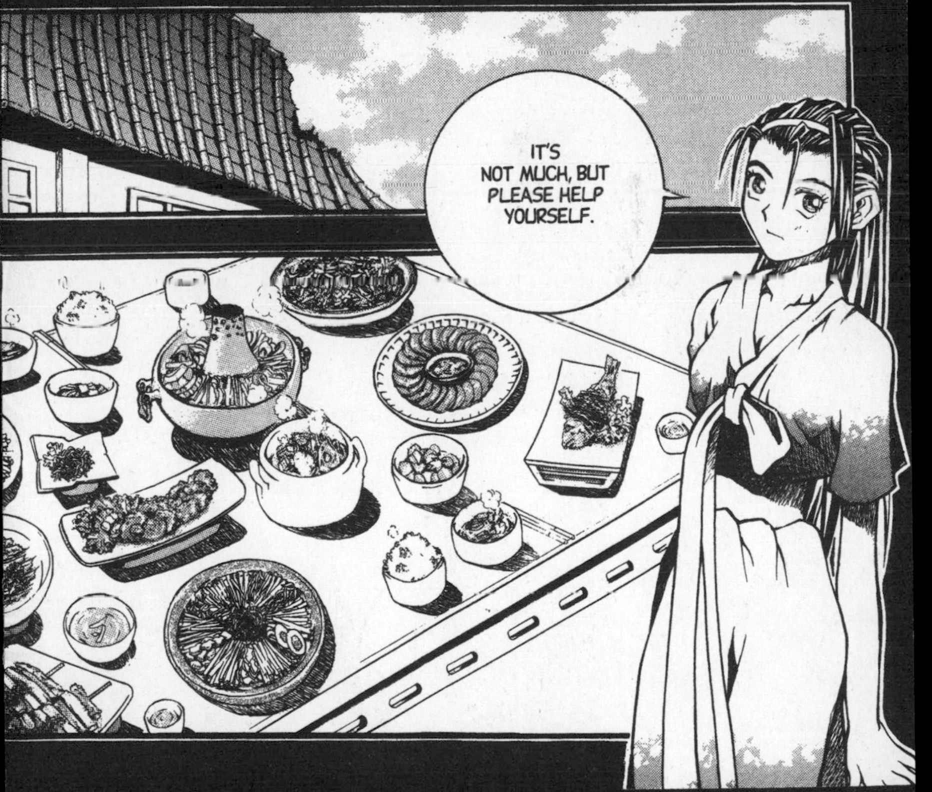
IT'S NOT MUCH, BUT PLEASE HELP YOURSELF.

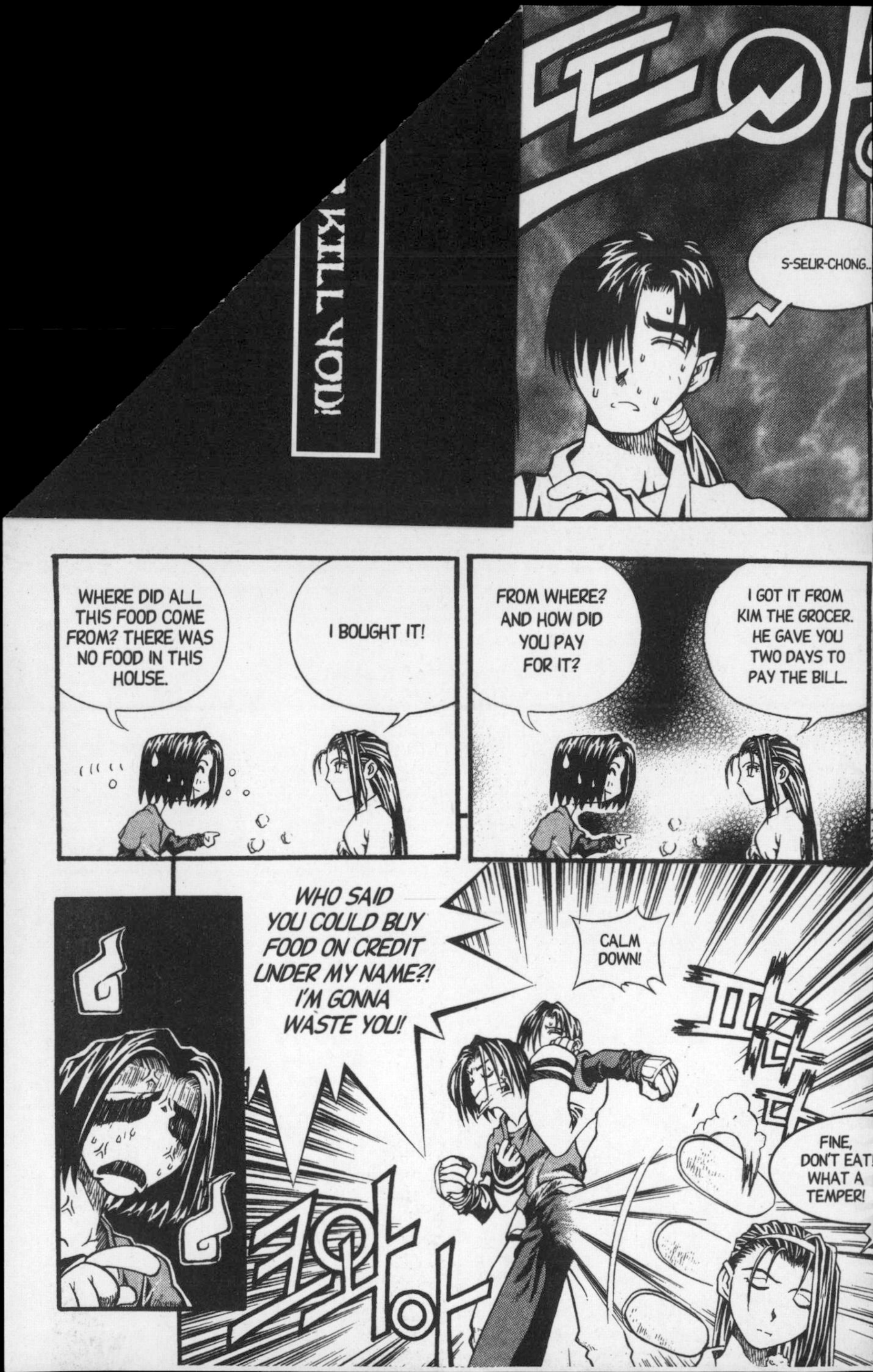
KILL YOU!
S-SEUR-CHONG...
WHERE DID ALL THIS FOOD COME FROM? THERE WAS NO FOOD IN THIS HOUSE.
I BOUGHT IT!
FROM WHERE? AND HOW DID YOU PAY FOR IT?
I GOT IT FROM KIM THE GROCER. HE GAVE YOU TWO DAYS TO PAY THE BILL.
WHO SAID YOU COULD BUY FOOD ON CREDIT UNDER MY NAME?! I'M GONNA WASTE YOU!
CALM DOWN!
FINE, DON'T EAT! WHAT A TEMPER!

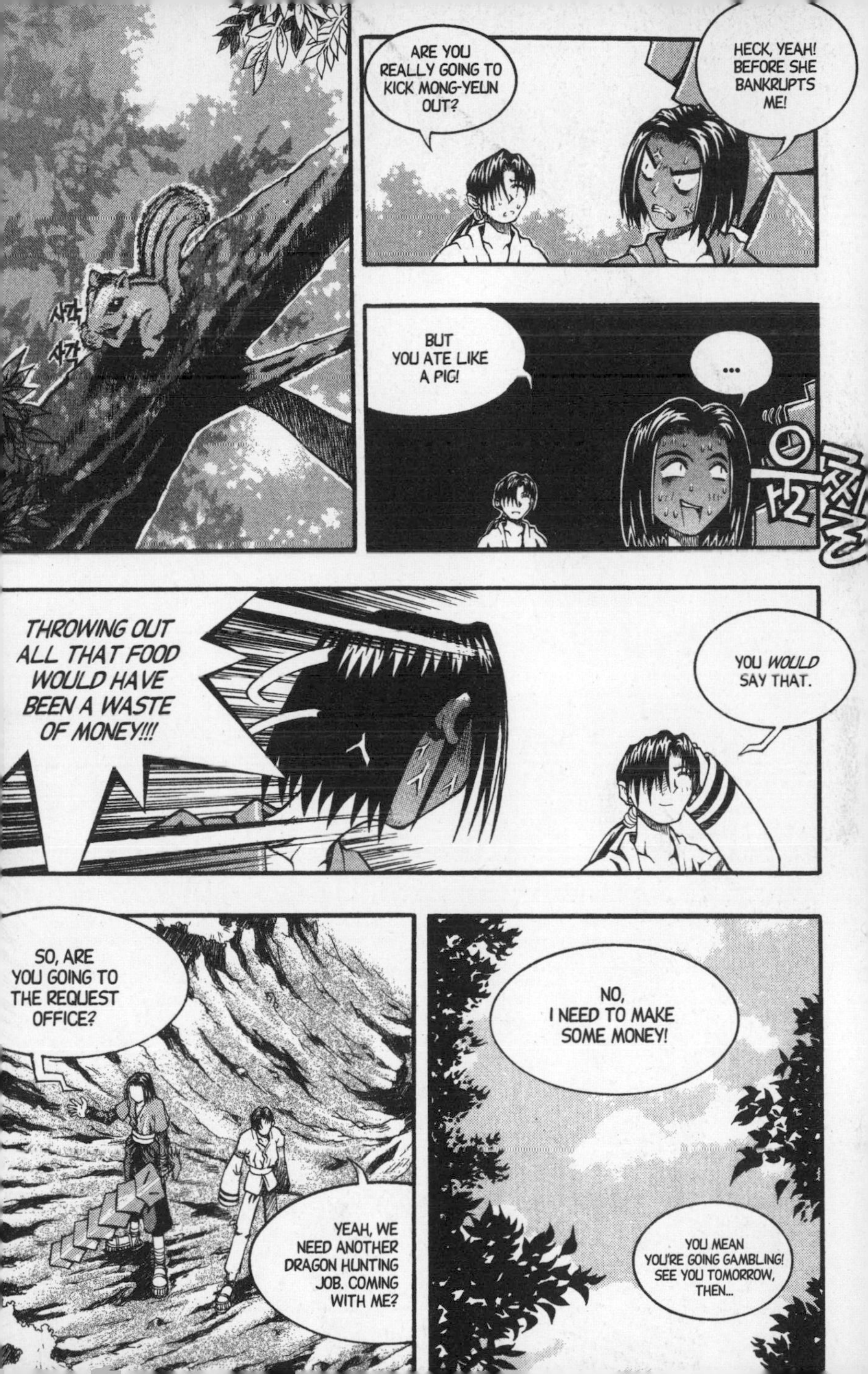
사각
사각
ARE YOU REALLY GOING TO KICK MONG-YEUN OUT?
HECK, YEAH! BEFORE SHE BANKRUPTS ME!
BUT YOU ATE LIKE A PIG!
...
THROWING OUT ALL THAT FOOD WOULD HAVE BEEN A WASTE OF MONEY!!!
YOU *WOULD* SAY THAT.
SO, ARE YOU GOING TO THE REQUEST OFFICE?
YEAH, WE NEED ANOTHER DRAGON HUNTING JOB. COMING WITH ME?
NO, I NEED TO MAKE SOME MONEY!
YOU MEAN YOU'RE GOING GAMBLING! SEE YOU TOMORROW, THEN...

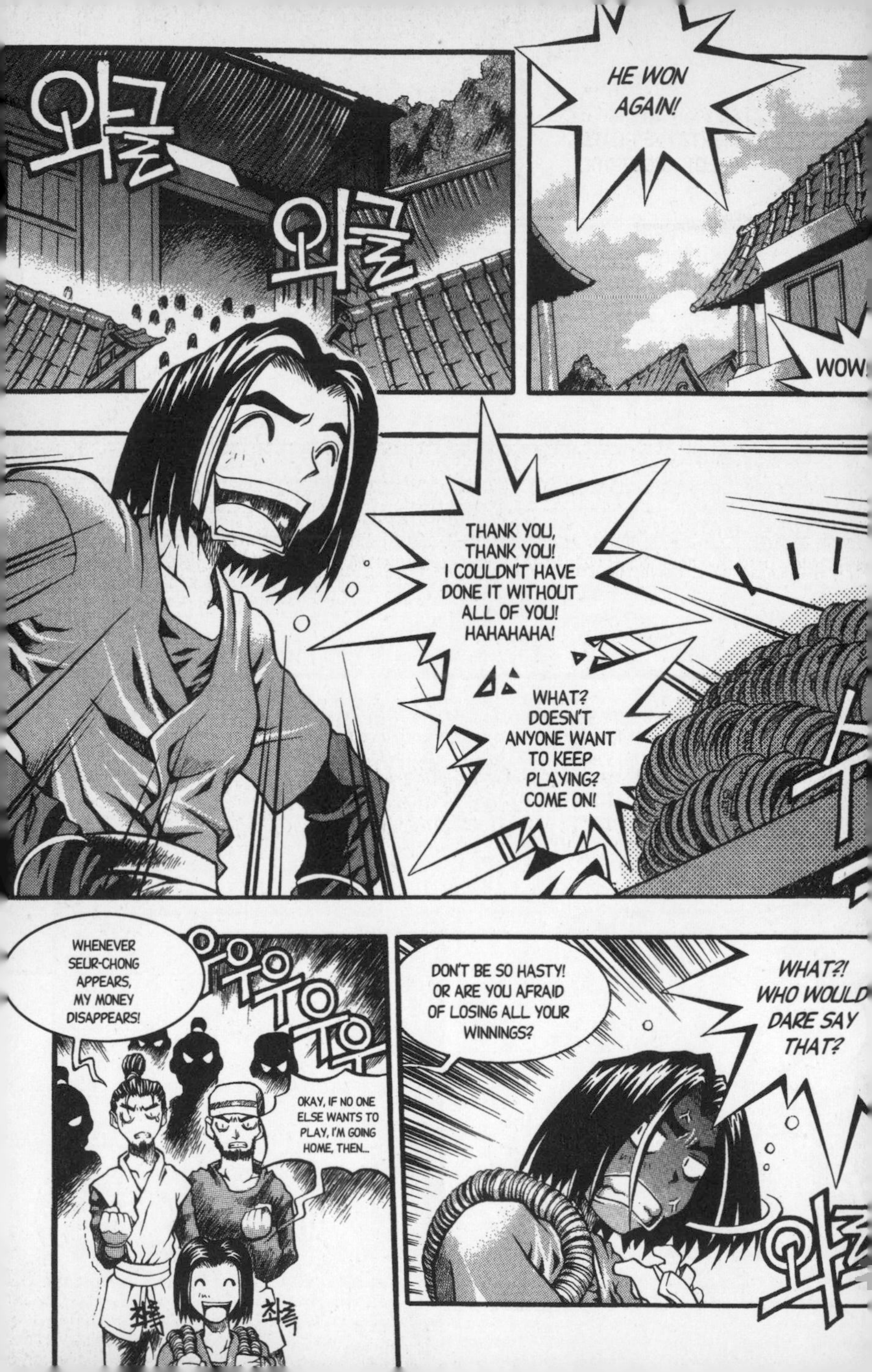
와글
와글
HE WON AGAIN!
WOW!
THANK YOU, THANK YOU! I COULDN'T HAVE DONE IT WITHOUT ALL OF YOU! HAHAHAHA!
WHAT? DOESN'T ANYONE WANT TO KEEP PLAYING? COME ON!
WHENEVER SEUR-CHONG APPEARS, MY MONEY DISAPPEARS!
OKAY, IF NO ONE ELSE WANTS TO PLAY, I'M GOING HOME, THEN...
DON'T BE SO HASTY! OR ARE YOU AFRAID OF LOSING ALL YOUR WINNINGS?
WHAT?! WHO WOULD DARE SAY THAT?

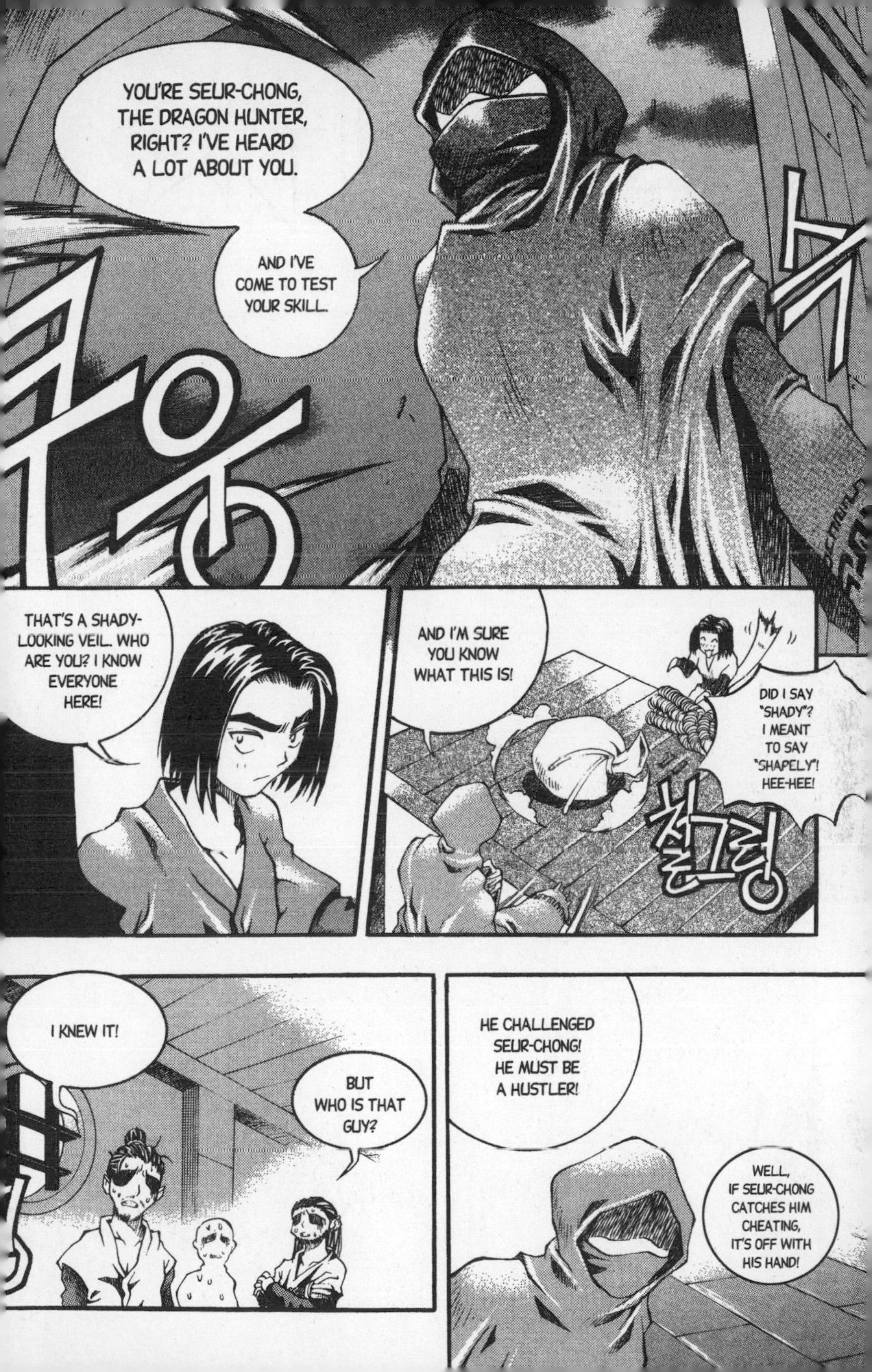
YOU'RE SEUR-CHONG, THE DRAGON HUNTER, RIGHT? I'VE HEARD A LOT ABOUT YOU.
AND I'VE COME TO TEST YOUR SKILL.
THAT'S A SHADY-LOOKING VEIL. WHO ARE YOU? I KNOW EVERYONE HERE!
AND I'M SURE YOU KNOW WHAT THIS IS!
DID I SAY "SHADY"? I MEANT TO SAY "SHAPELY"! HEE-HEE!
철그렁
I KNEW IT!
BUT WHO IS THAT GUY?
HE CHALLENGED SEUR-CHONG! HE MUST BE A HUSTLER!
WELL, IF SEUR-CHONG CATCHES HIM CHEATING, IT'S OFF WITH HIS HAND!

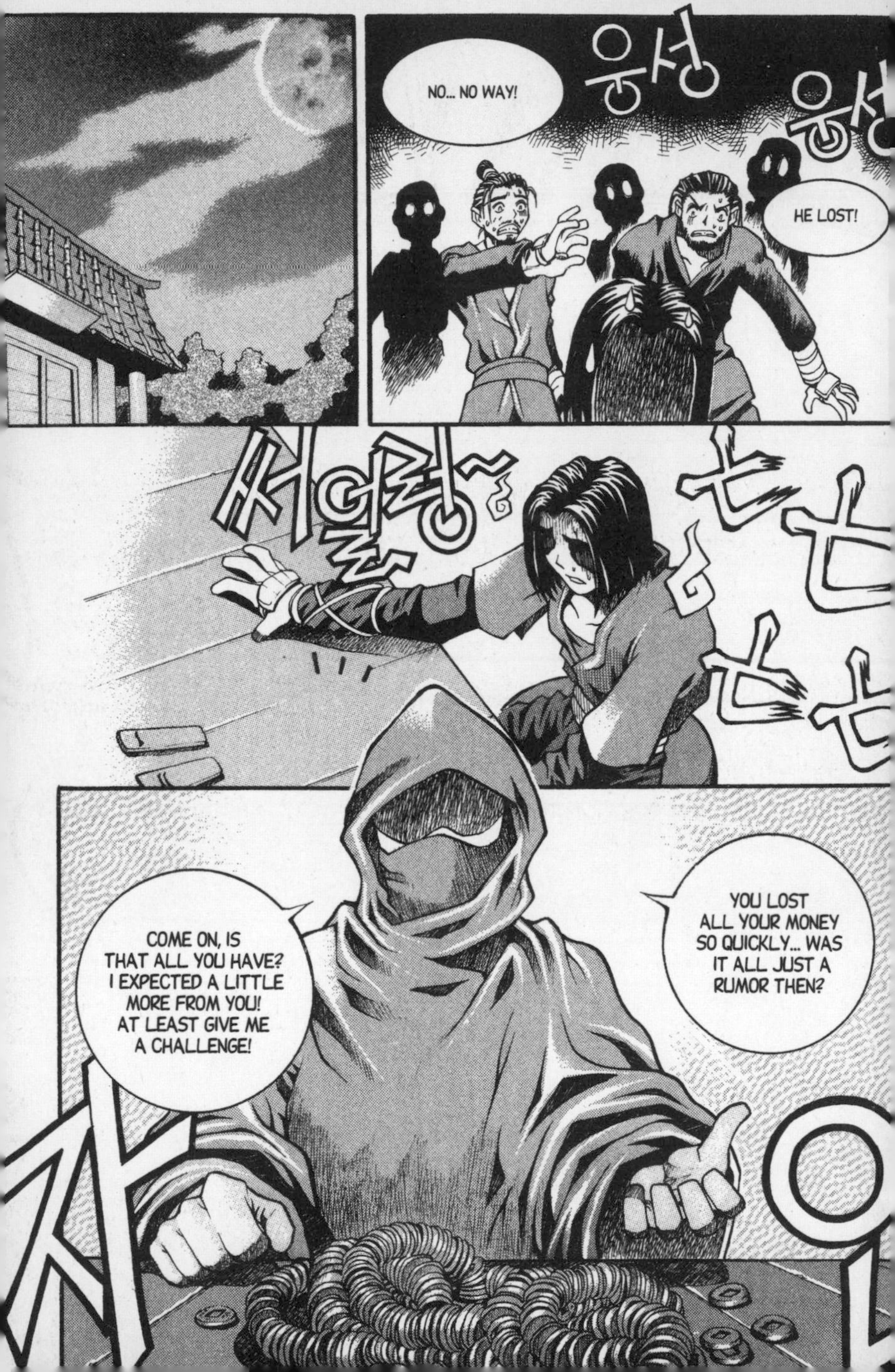
NO... NO WAY!
웅성
웅성
HE LOST!
COME ON, IS THAT ALL YOU HAVE? I EXPECTED A LITTLE MORE FROM YOU! AT LEAST GIVE ME A CHALLENGE!
YOU LOST ALL YOUR MONEY SO QUICKLY... WAS IT ALL JUST A RUMOR THEN?

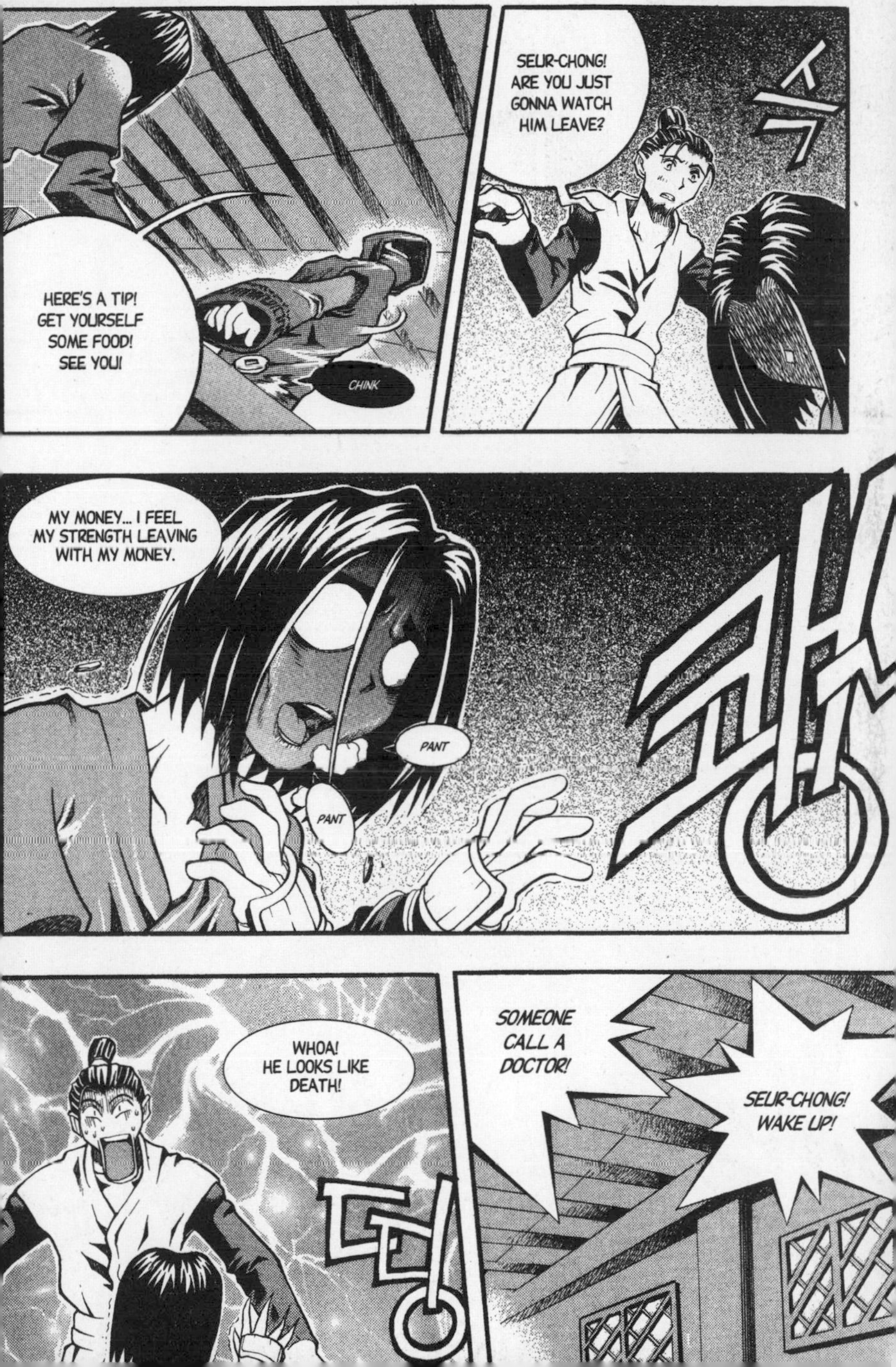
HERE'S A TIP! GET YOURSELF SOME FOOD! SEE YOU!
CHINK
SEUR-CHONG! ARE YOU JUST GONNA WATCH HIM LEAVE?
MY MONEY... I FEEL MY STRENGTH LEAVING WITH MY MONEY.
PANT
PANT
WHOA! HE LOOKS LIKE DEATH!
SOMEONE CALL A DOCTOR!
SEUR-CHONG! WAKE UP!

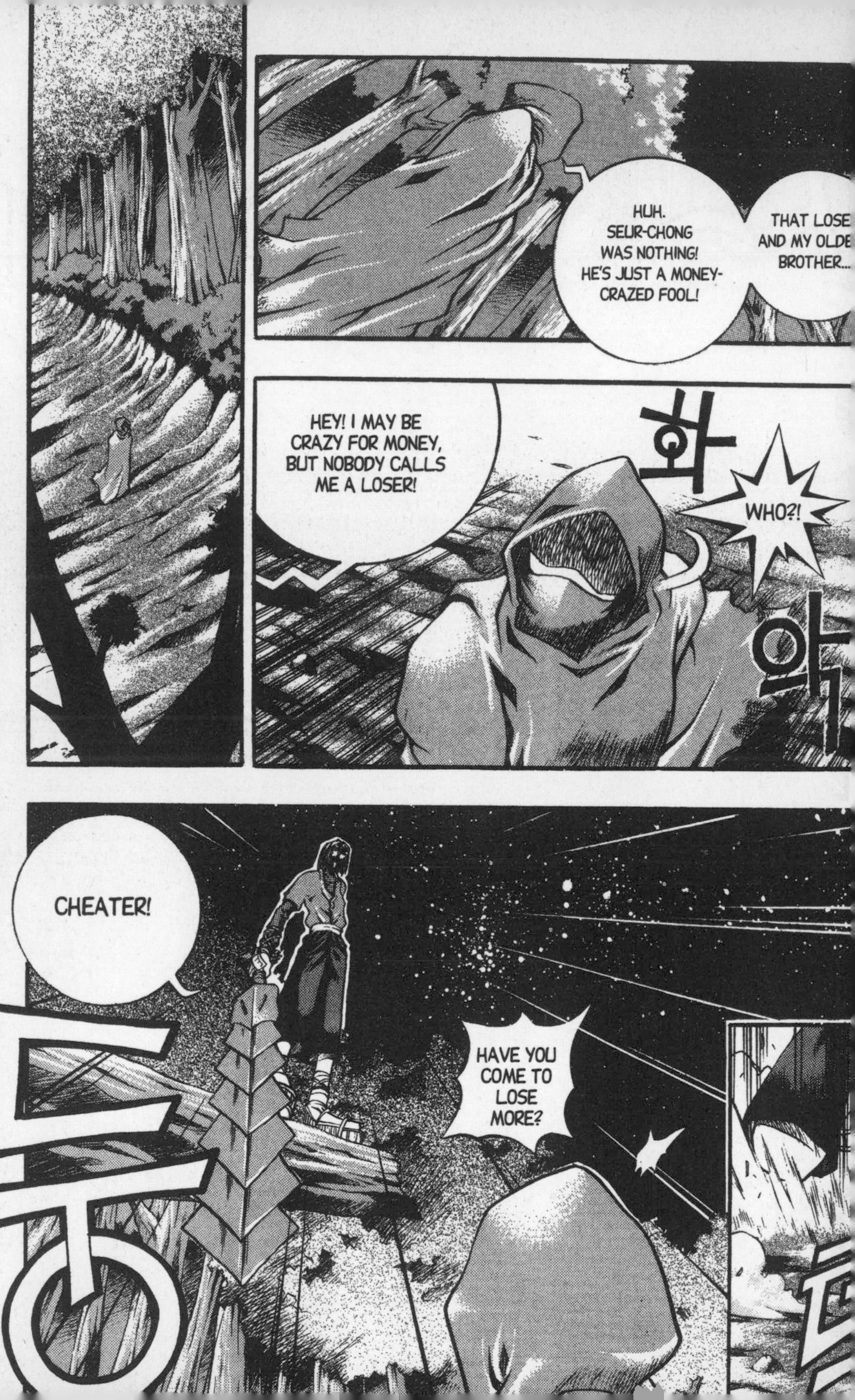
HUH. SEUR-CHONG WAS NOTHING! HE'S JUST A MONEY-CRAZED FOOL!
THAT LOSE AND MY OLDE BROTHER...
HEY! I MAY BE CRAZY FOR MONEY, BUT NOBODY CALLS ME A LOSER!
WHO?!
CHEATER!
HAVE YOU COME TO LOSE MORE?

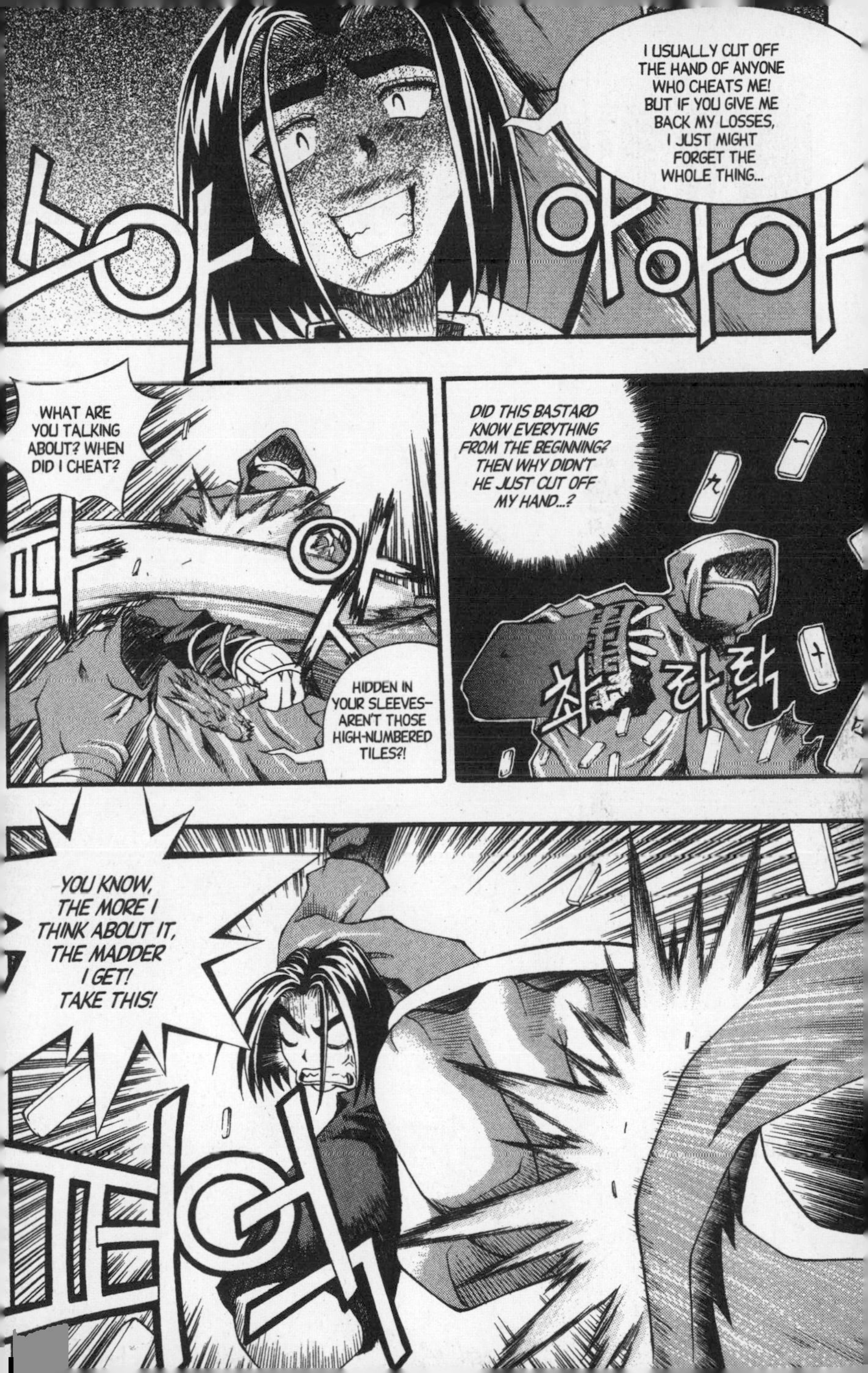
I USUALLY CUT OFF THE HAND OF ANYONE WHO CHEATS ME! BUT IF YOU GIVE ME BACK MY LOSSES, I JUST MIGHT FORGET THE WHOLE THING...
WHAT ARE YOU TALKING ABOUT? WHEN DID I CHEAT?
HIDDEN IN YOUR SLEEVES-- AREN'T THOSE HIGH-NUMBERED TILES?!
DID THIS BASTARD KNOW EVERYTHING FROM THE BEGINNING? THEN WHY DIDN'T HE JUST CUT OFF MY HAND...?
YOU KNOW, THE MORE I THINK ABOUT IT, THE MADDER I GET! TAKE THIS!

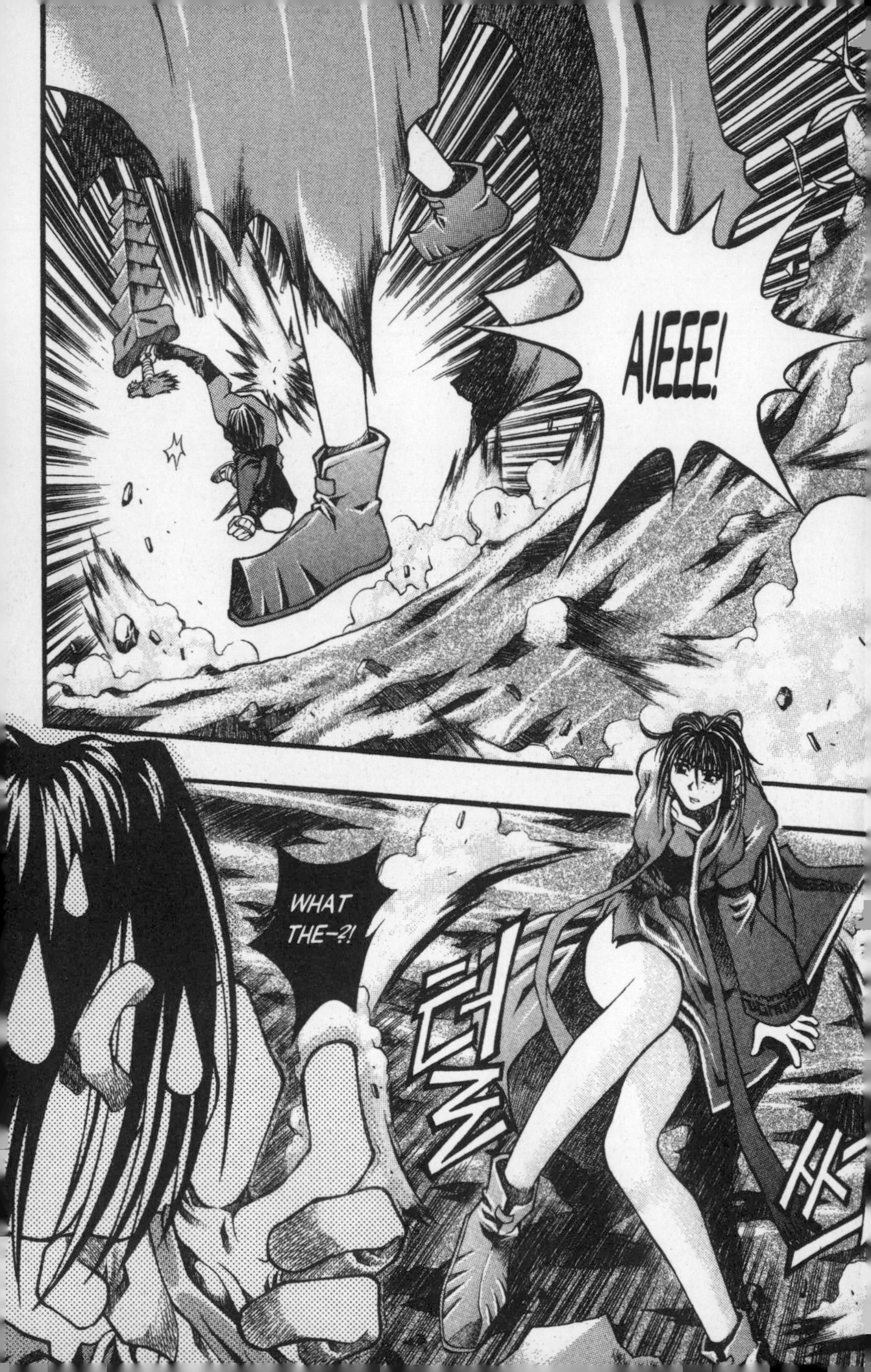
AIEEE!
WHAT THE–?!

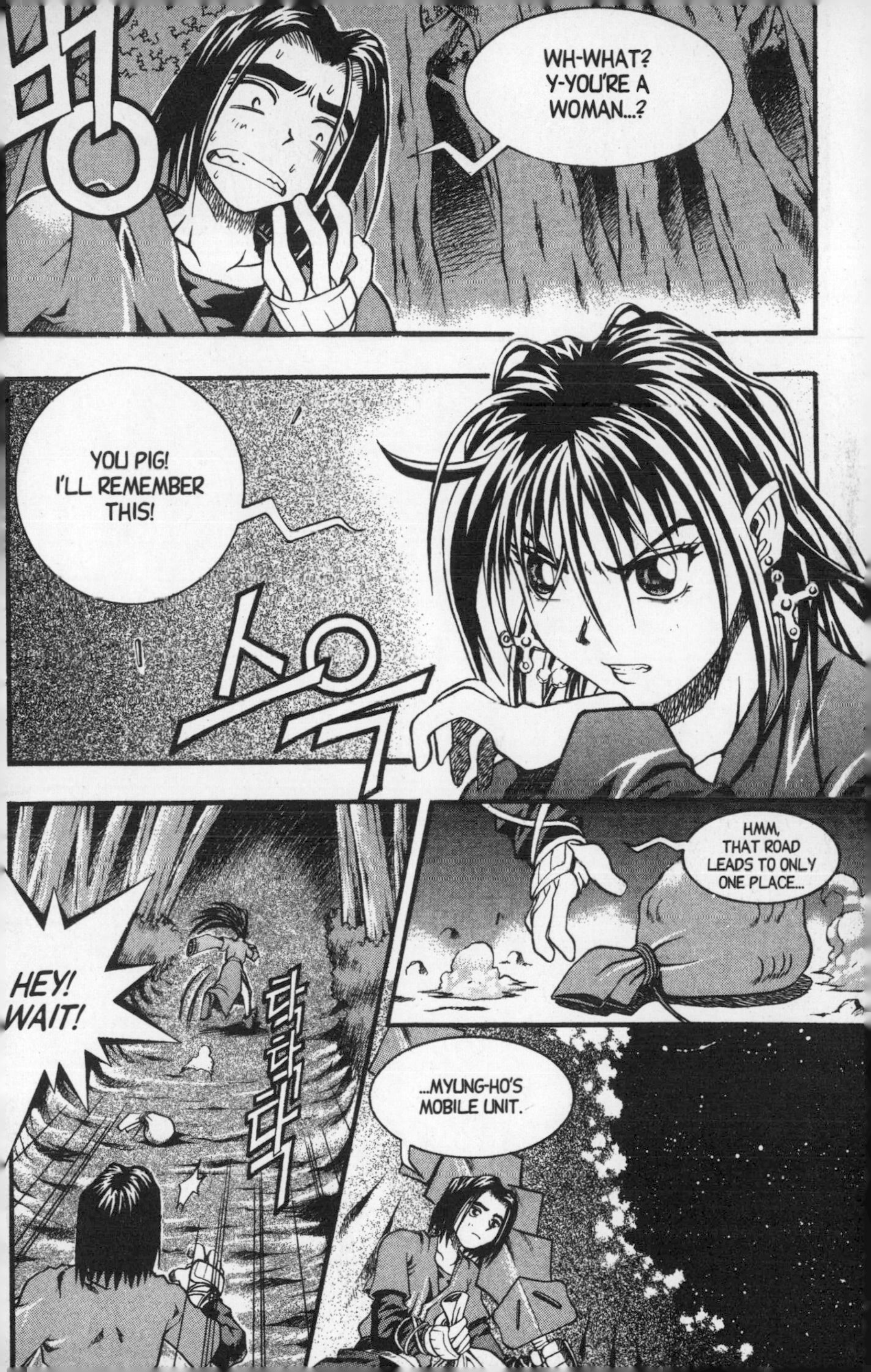
WH-WHAT? Y-YOU'RE A WOMAN...?
YOU PIG! I'LL REMEMBER THIS!
HEY! WAIT!
HMM, THAT ROAD LEADS TO ONLY ONE PLACE...
...MYUNG-HO'S MOBILE UNIT.

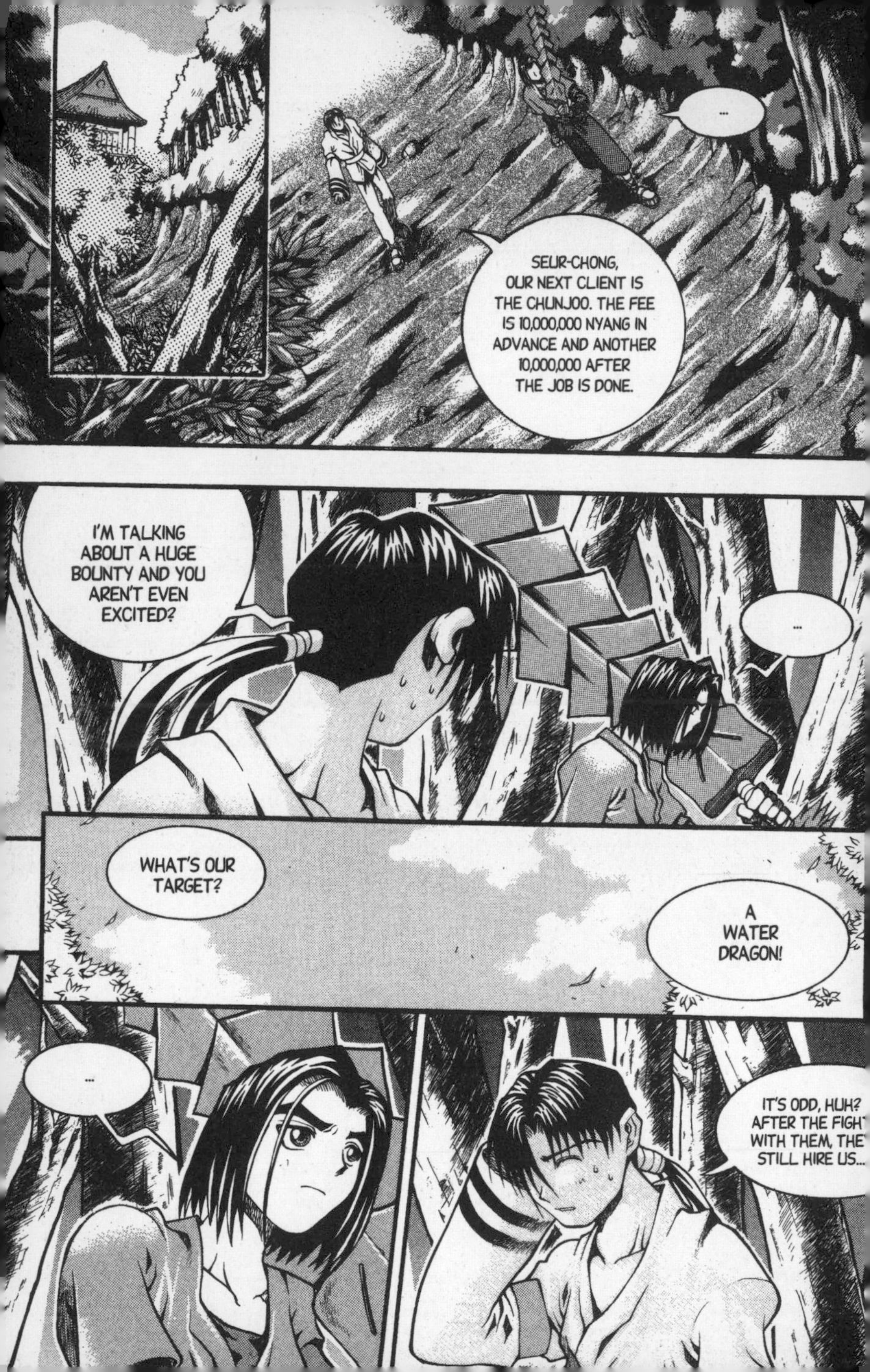
...
SEUR-CHONG, OUR NEXT CLIENT IS THE CHUNJOO. THE FEE IS 10,000,000 NYANG IN ADVANCE AND ANOTHER 10,000,000 AFTER THE JOB IS DONE.
I'M TALKING ABOUT A HUGE BOUNTY AND YOU AREN'T EVEN EXCITED?
...
WHAT'S OUR TARGET?
A WATER DRAGON!
...
IT'S ODD, HUH? AFTER THE FIGHT WITH THEM, THE STILL HIRE US...

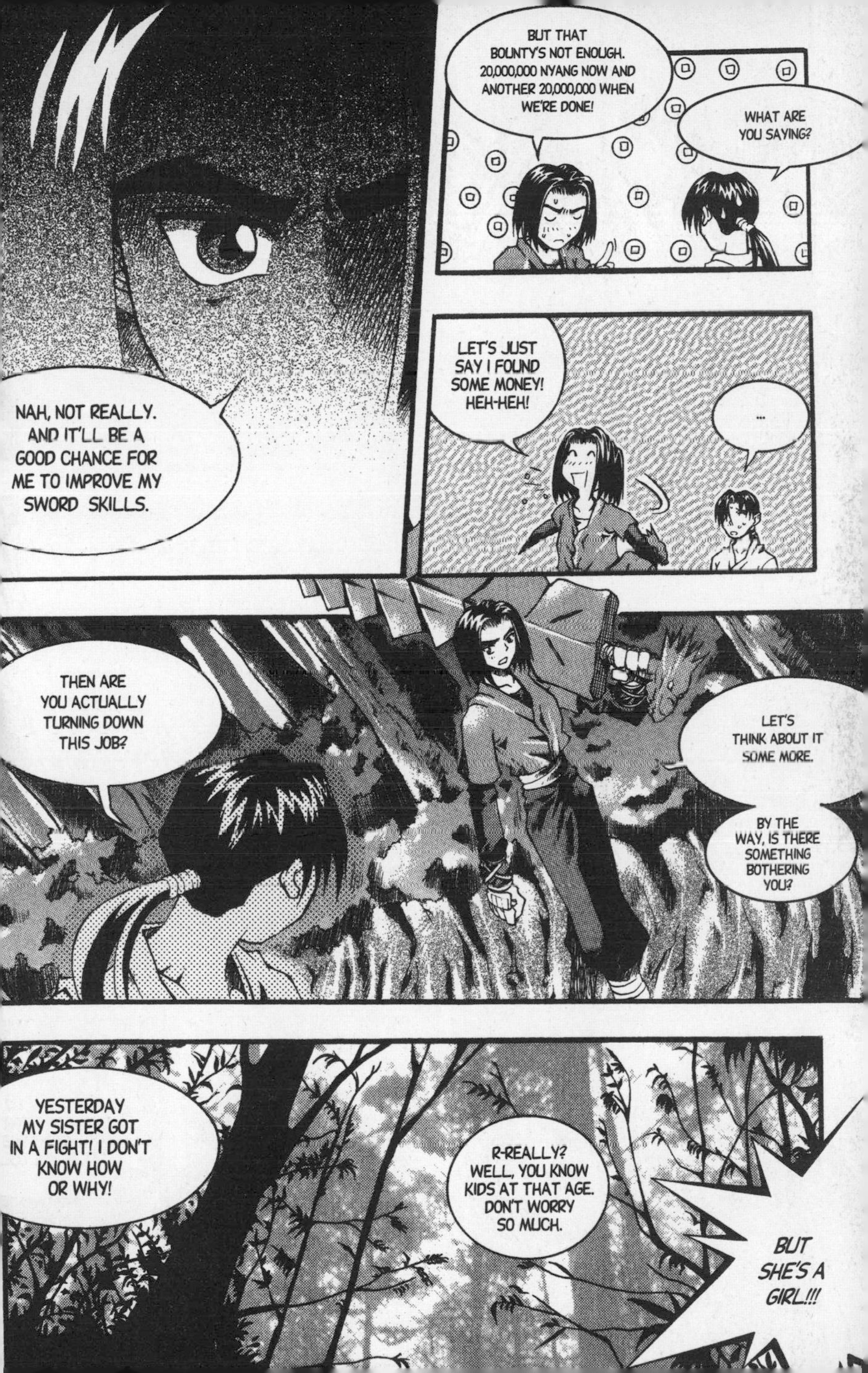
NAH, NOT REALLY. AND IT'LL BE A GOOD CHANCE FOR ME TO IMPROVE MY SWORD SKILLS.
BUT THAT BOUNTY'S NOT ENOUGH. 20,000,000 NYANG NOW AND ANOTHER 20,000,000 WHEN WE'RE DONE!
WHAT ARE YOU SAYING?
LET'S JUST SAY I FOUND SOME MONEY! HEH-HEH!
...
THEN ARE YOU ACTUALLY TURNING DOWN THIS JOB?
LET'S THINK ABOUT IT SOME MORE.
BY THE WAY, IS THERE SOMETHING BOTHERING YOU?
YESTERDAY MY SISTER GOT IN A FIGHT! I DON'T KNOW HOW OR WHY!
R-REALLY? WELL, YOU KNOW KIDS AT THAT AGE. DON'T WORRY SO MUCH.
BUT SHE'S A GIRL!!!

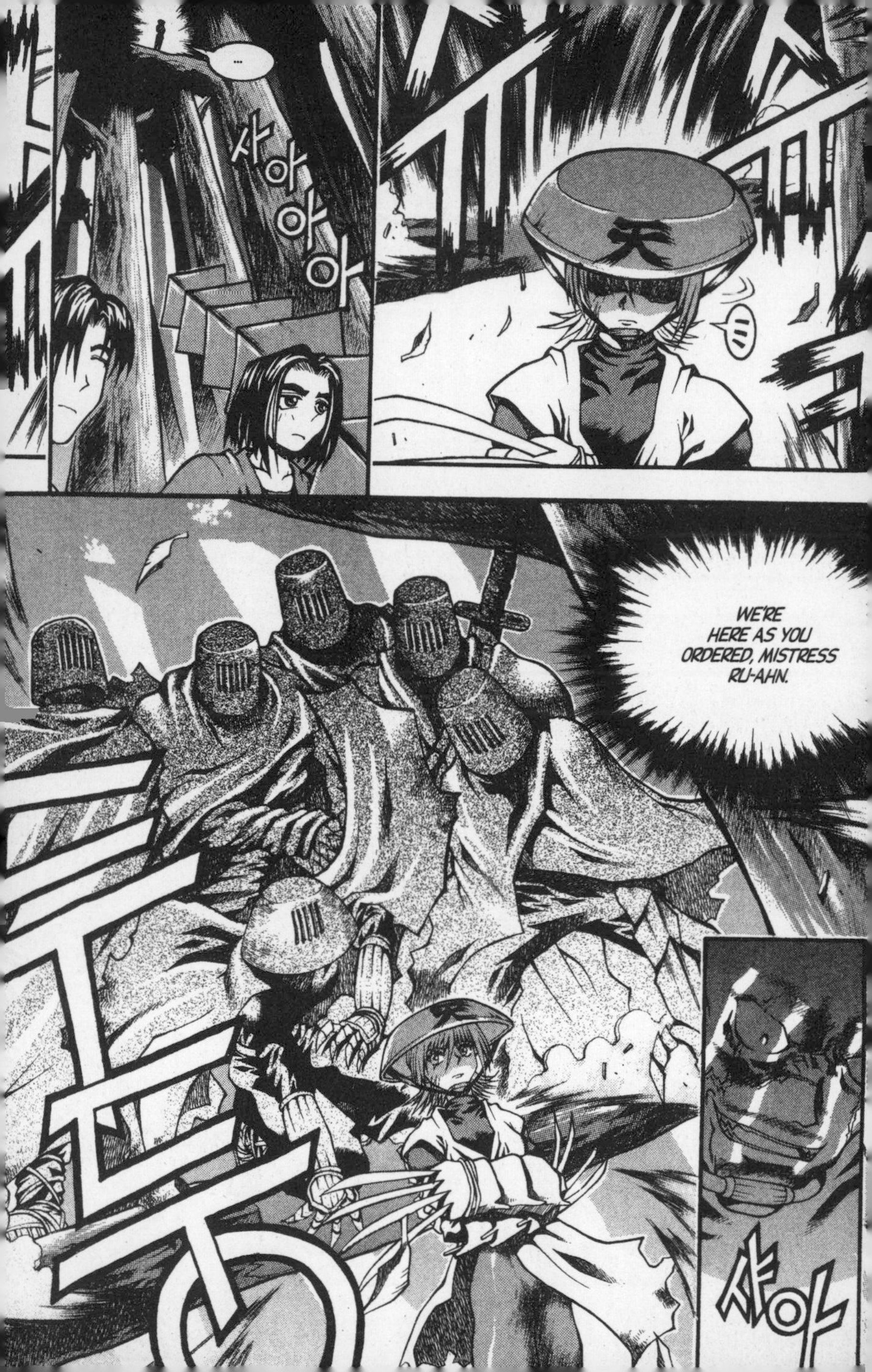
...
사아아아
WE'RE HERE AS YOU ORDERED, MISTRESS RU-AHN.
샤아

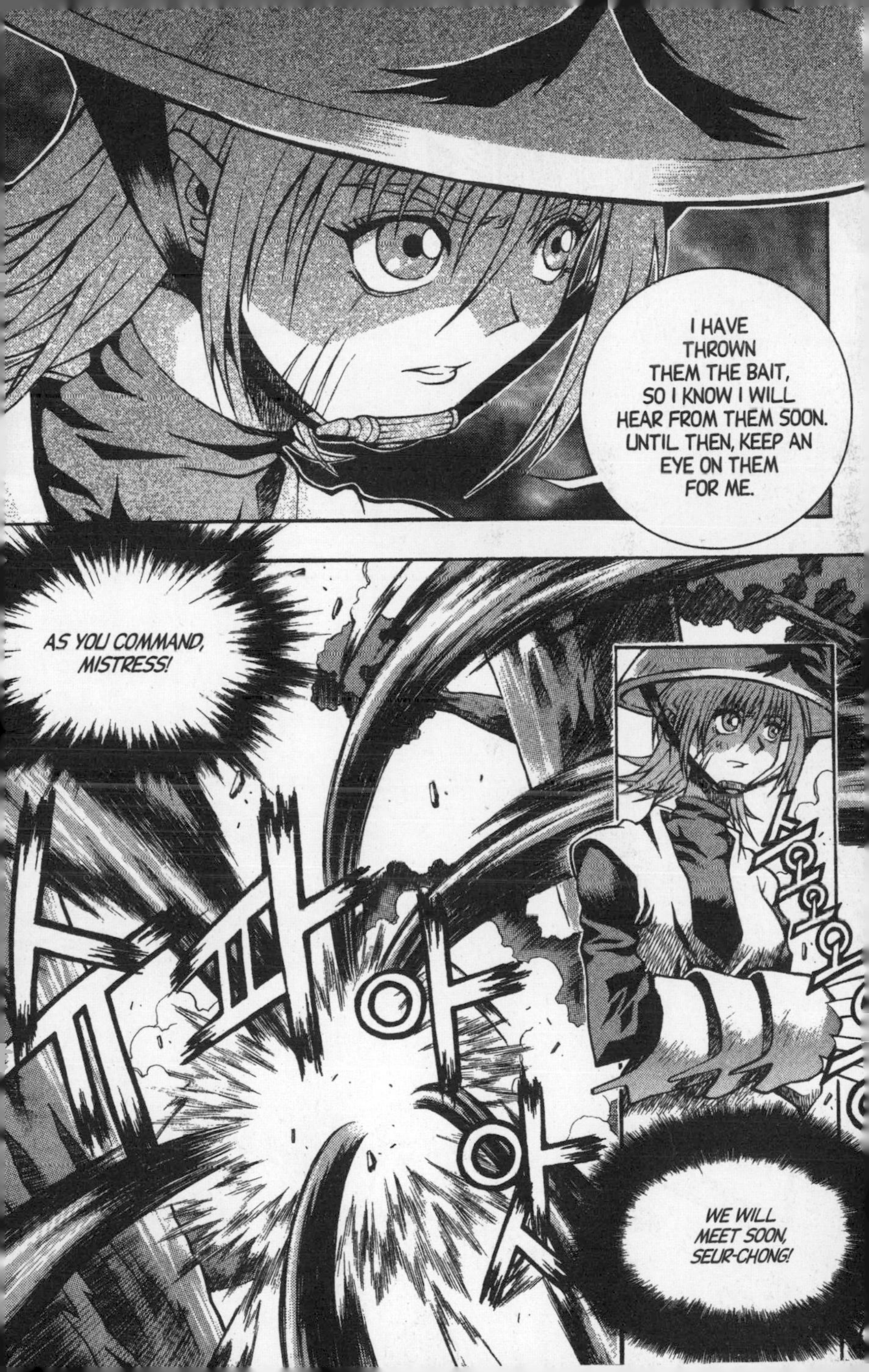
I HAVE THROWN THEM THE BAIT, SO I KNOW I WILL HEAR FROM THEM SOON. UNTIL THEN, KEEP AN EYE ON THEM FOR ME.
AS YOU COMMAND, MISTRESS!
WE WILL MEET SOON, SEUR-CHONG!

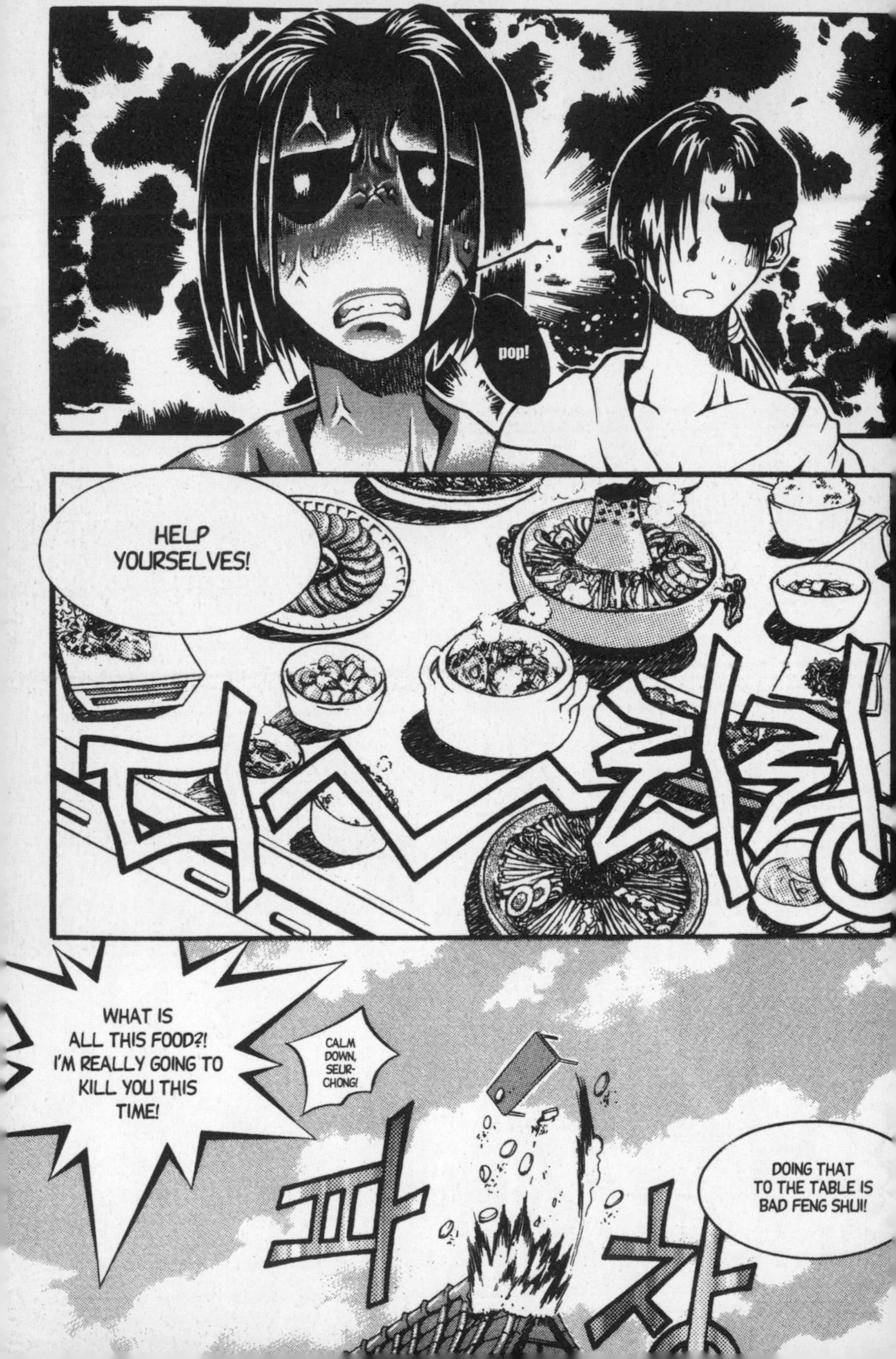

pop!
HELP YOURSELVES!
WHAT IS ALL THIS FOOD?! I'M REALLY GOING TO KILL YOU THIS TIME!
CALM DOWN, SEUR-CHONG!
DOING THAT TO THE TABLE IS BAD FENG SHUI!

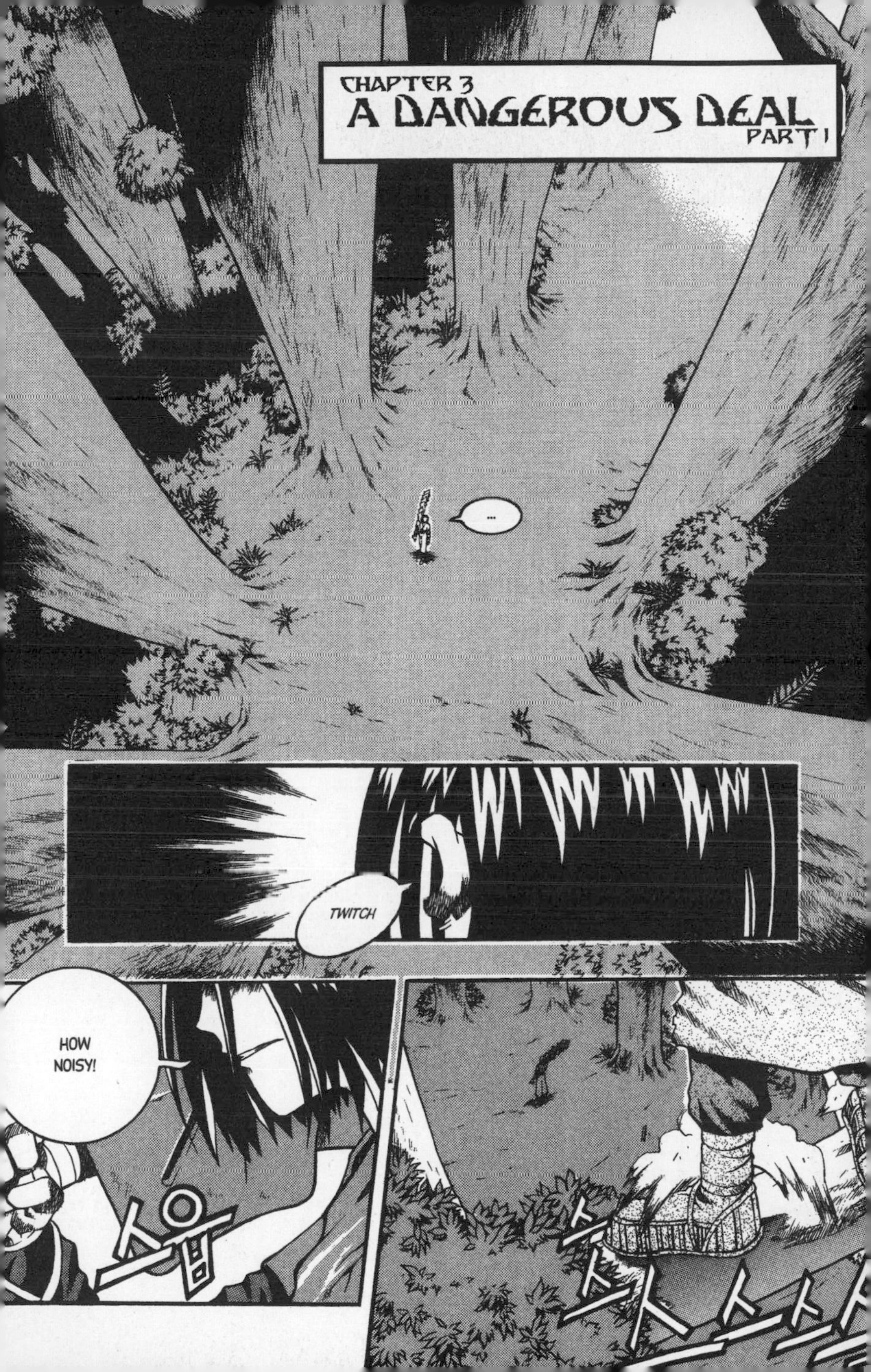
CHAPTER 3
A DANGEROUS DEAL
PART 1
...
TWITCH
HOW NOISY!
스읍

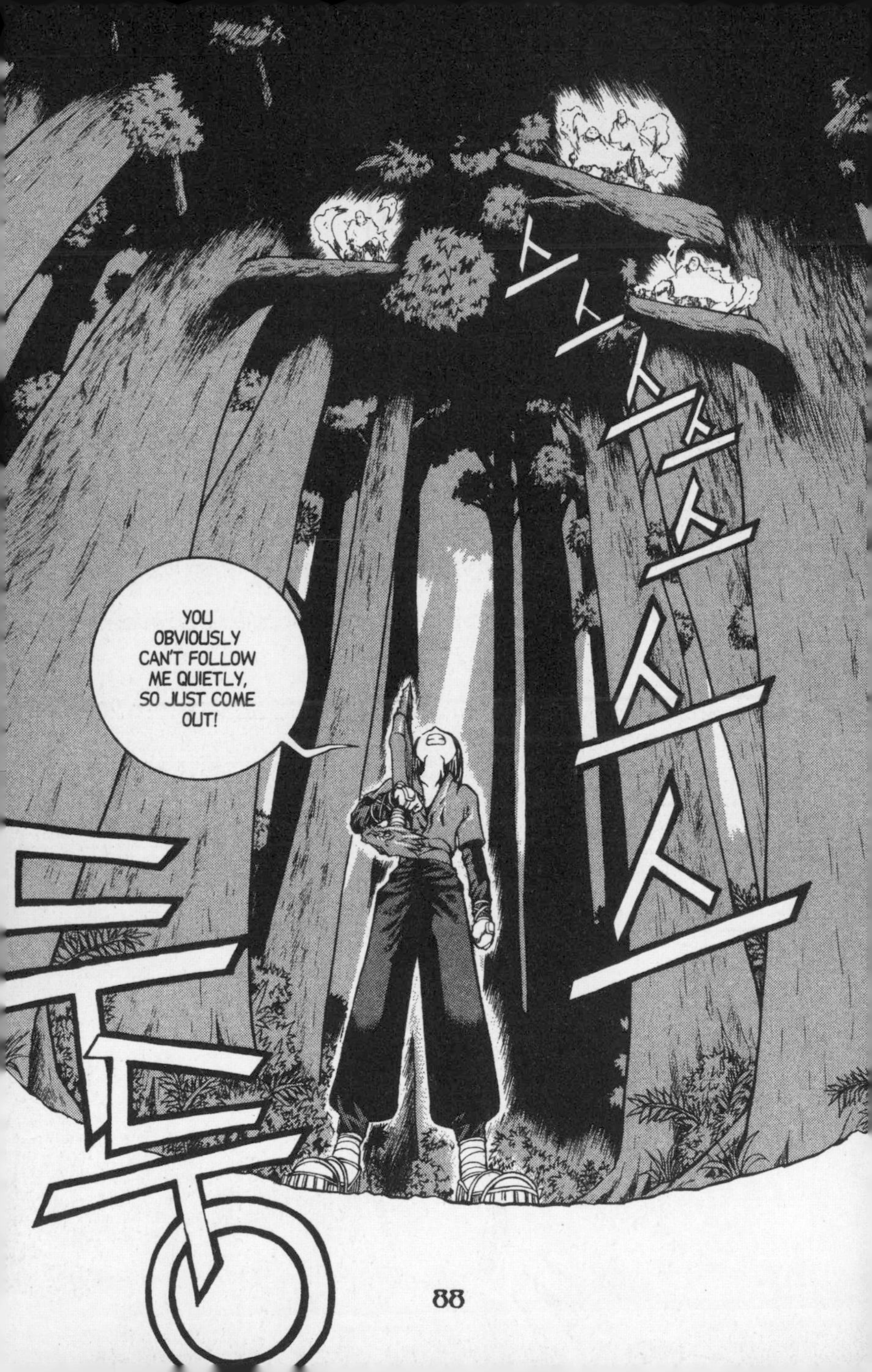
YOU OBVIOUSLY CAN'T FOLLOW ME QUIETLY, SO JUST COME OUT!

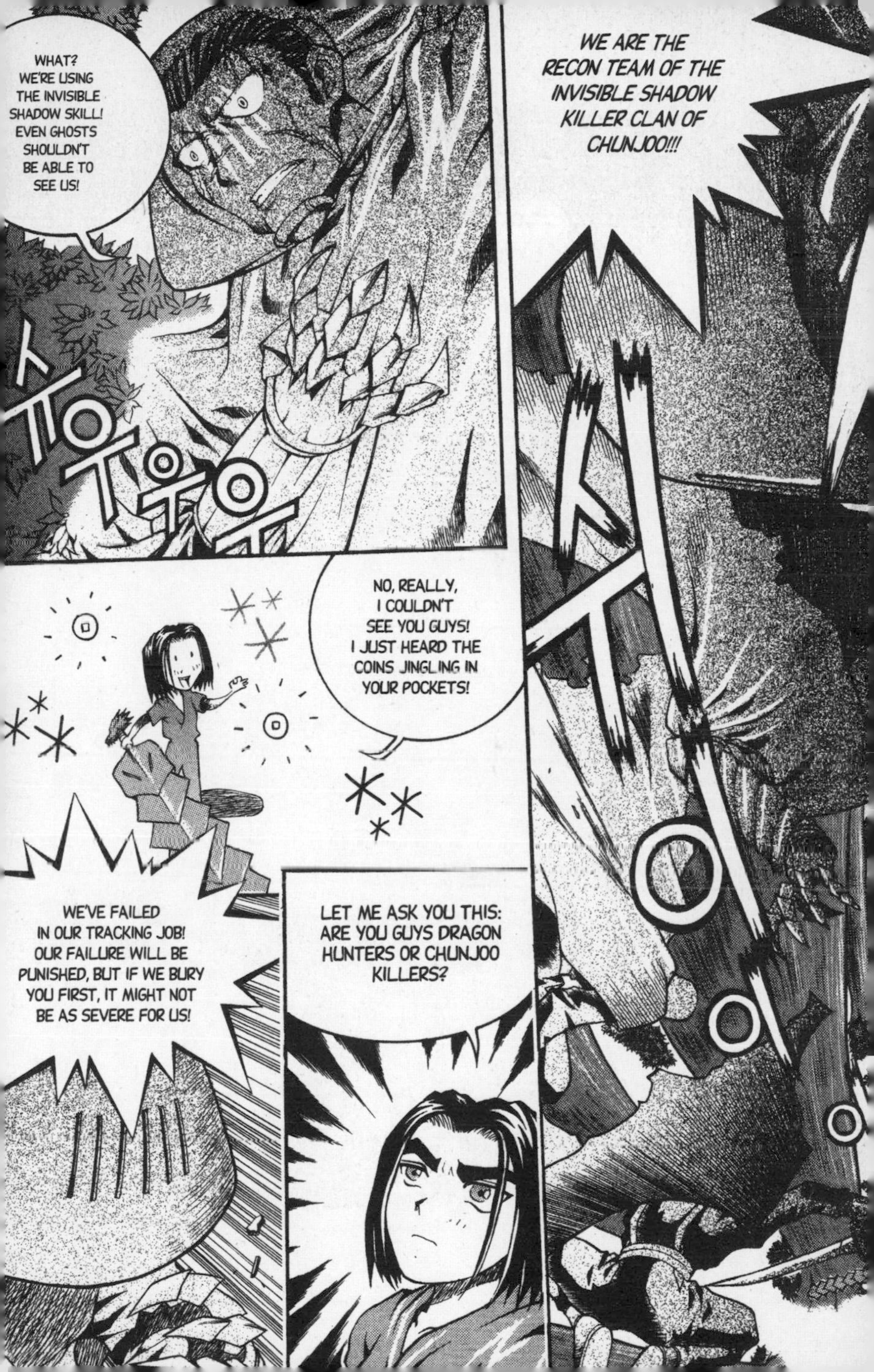
WHAT? WE'RE USING THE INVISIBLE SHADOW SKILL! EVEN GHOSTS SHOULDN'T BE ABLE TO SEE US!
NO, REALLY, I COULDN'T SEE YOU GUYS! I JUST HEARD THE COINS JINGLING IN YOUR POCKETS!
WE'VE FAILED IN OUR TRACKING JOB! OUR FAILURE WILL BE PUNISHED, BUT IF WE BURY YOU FIRST, IT MIGHT NOT BE AS SEVERE FOR US!
LET ME ASK YOU THIS: ARE YOU GUYS DRAGON HUNTERS OR CHUNJOO KILLERS?
WE ARE THE RECON TEAM OF THE INVISIBLE SHADOW KILLER CLAN OF CHUNJOO!!!

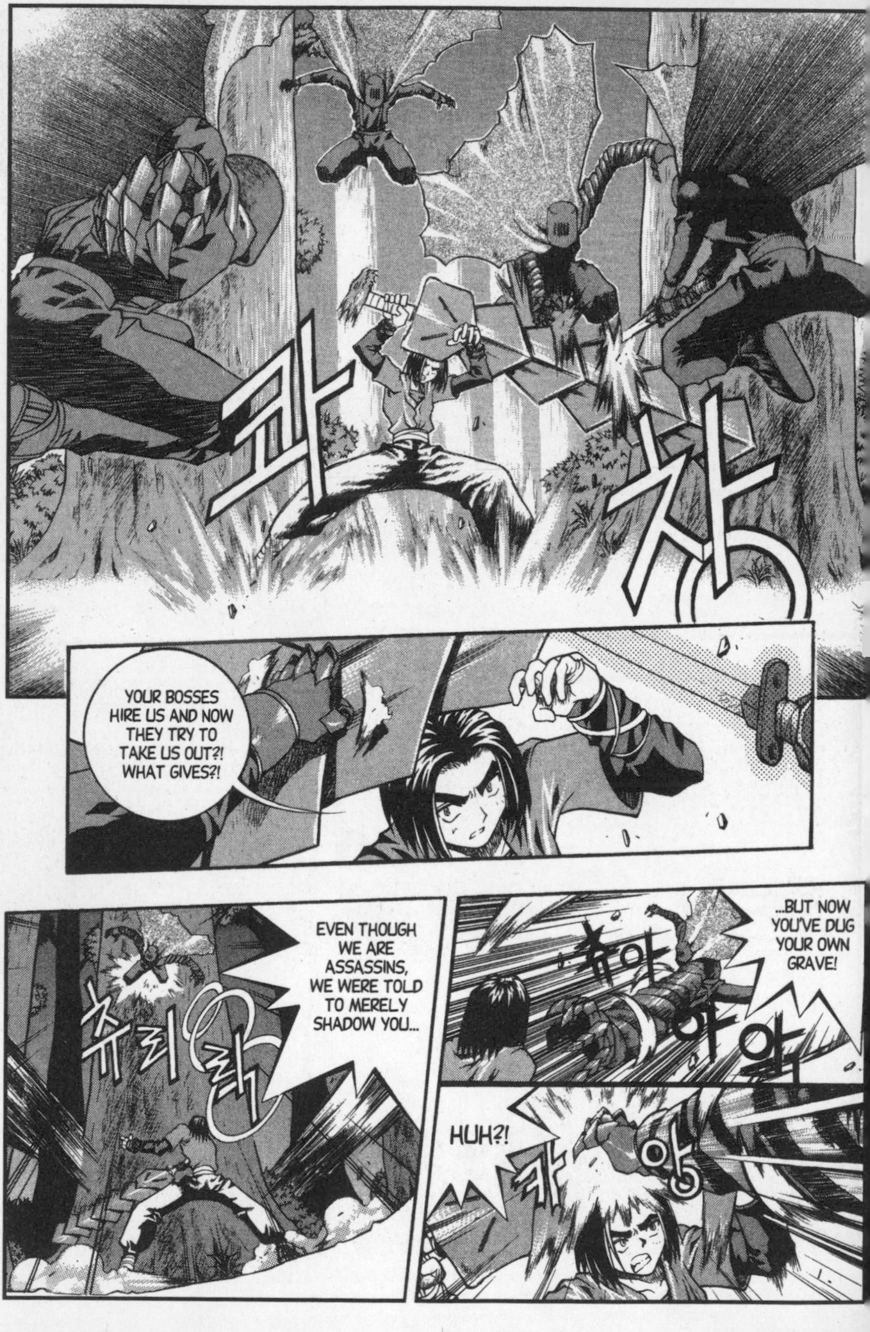
YOUR BOSSES HIRE US AND NOW THEY TRY TO TAKE US OUT?! WHAT GIVES?!
EVEN THOUGH WE ARE ASSASSINS, WE WERE TOLD TO MERELY SHADOW YOU...
...BUT NOW YOU'VE DUG YOUR OWN GRAVE!
HUH?!

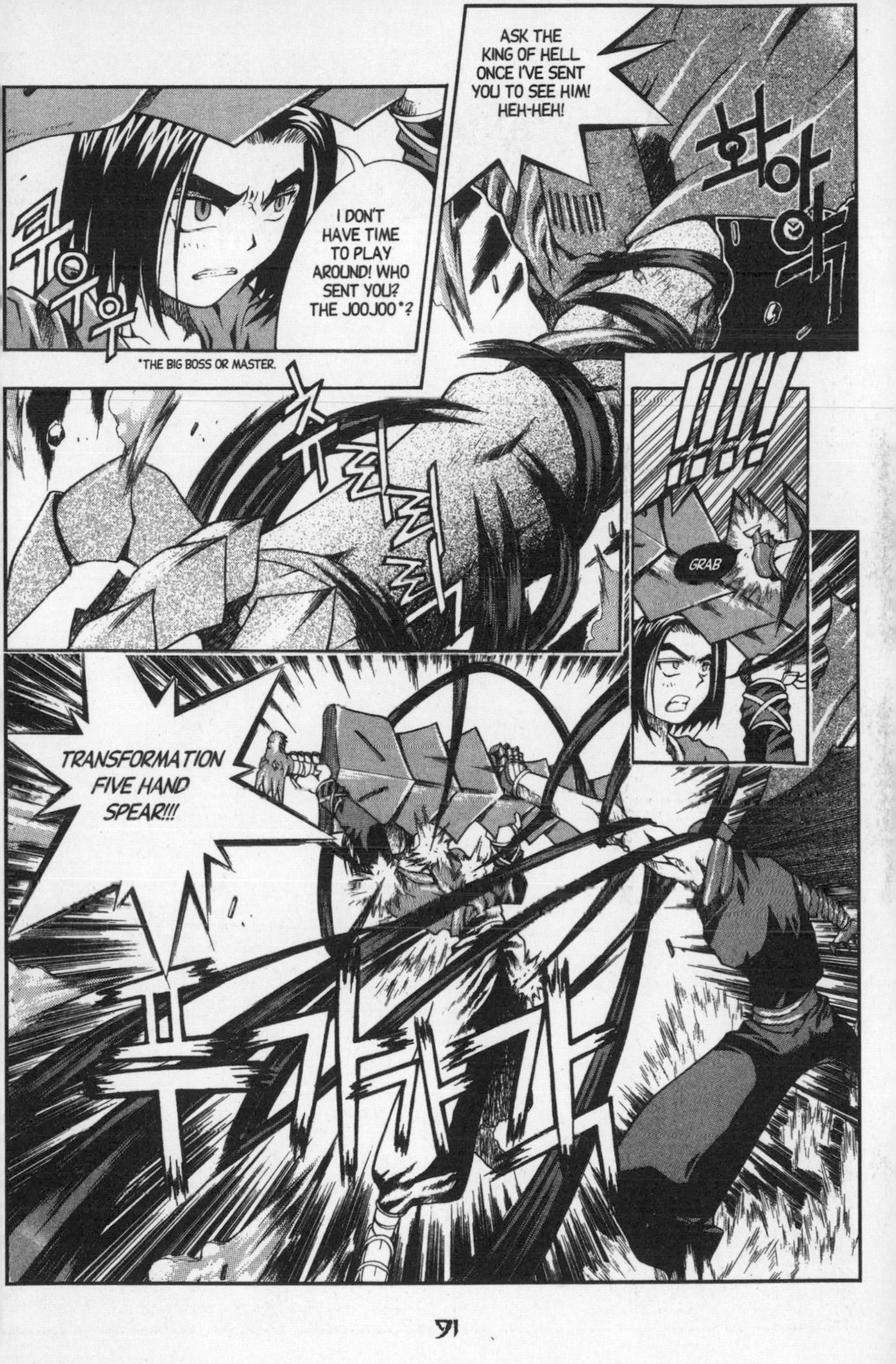

I DON'T HAVE TIME TO PLAY AROUND! WHO SENT YOU? THE JOOJOO*?
*THE BIG BOSS OR MASTER.
ASK THE KING OF HELL ONCE I'VE SENT YOU TO SEE HIM! HEH-HEH!
!!!!
GRAB
TRANSFORMATION FIVE HAND SPEAR!!!

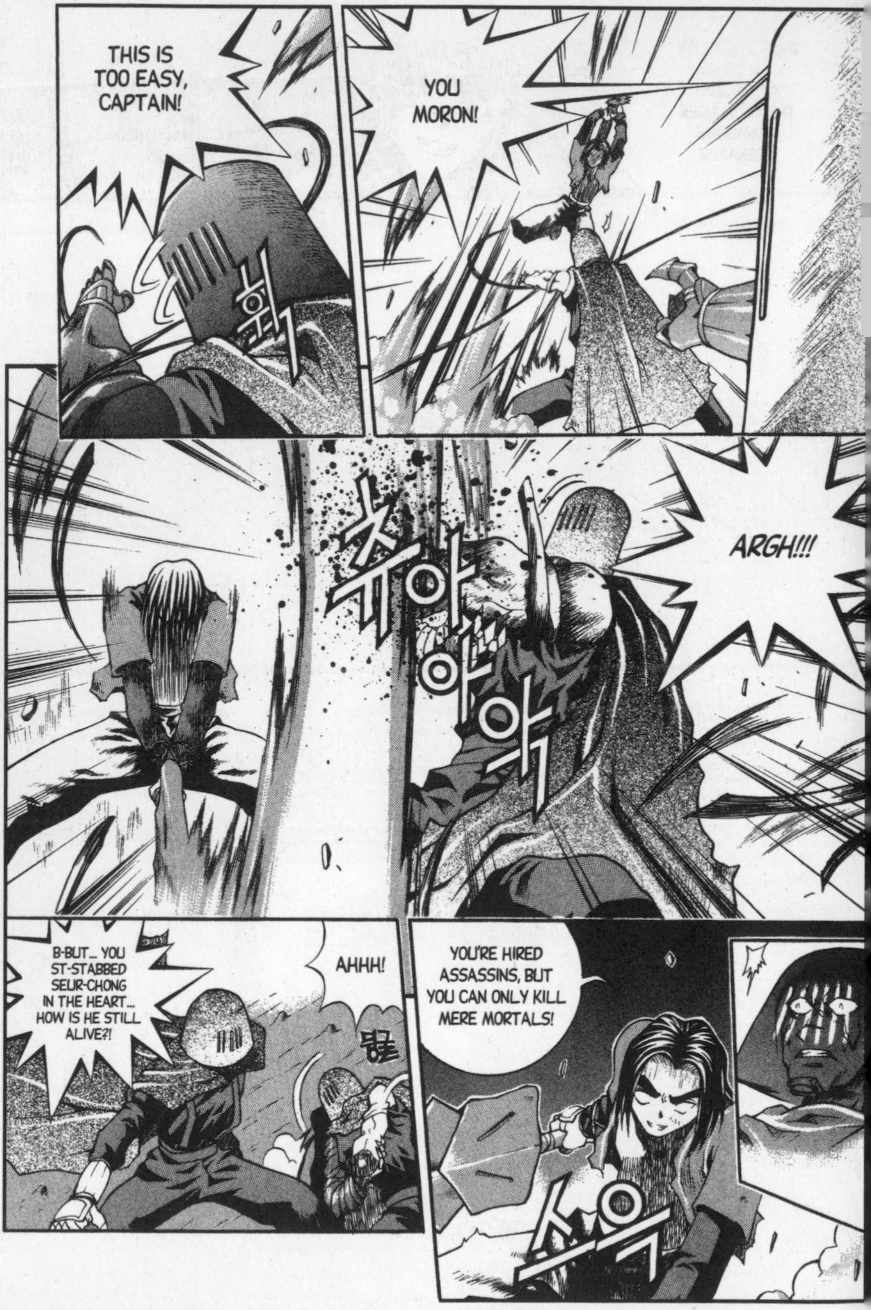

THIS IS TOO EASY, CAPTAIN!
YOU MORON!
ARGH!!!
B-BUT... YOU ST-STABBED SEUR-CHONG IN THE HEART... HOW IS HE STILL ALIVE?!
AHHH!
YOU'RE HIRED ASSASSINS, BUT YOU CAN ONLY KILL MERE MORTALS!

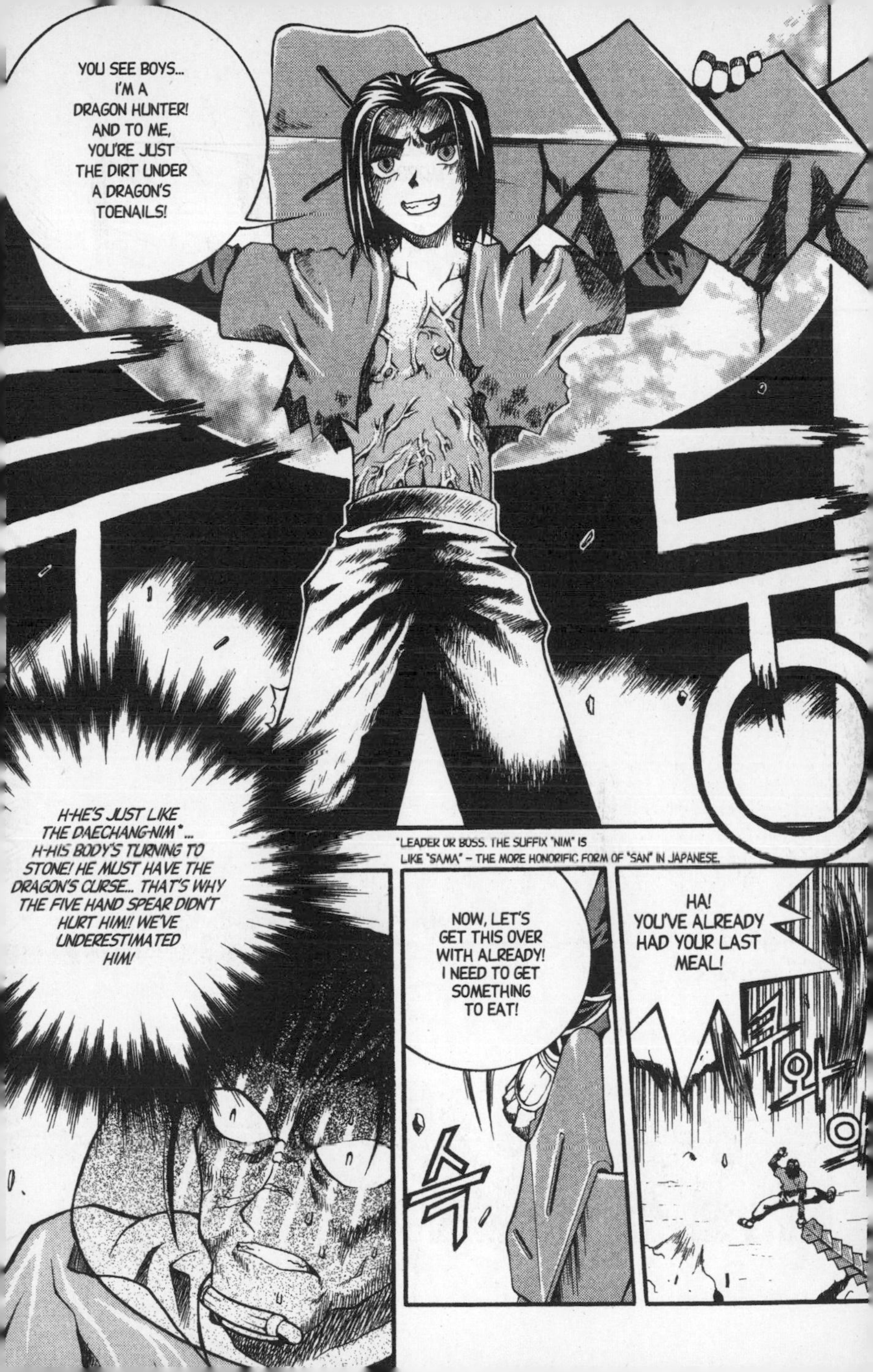
YOU SEE BOYS... I'M A DRAGON HUNTER! AND TO ME, YOU'RE JUST THE DIRT UNDER A DRAGON'S TOENAILS!
H-HE'S JUST LIKE THE DAECHANG-NIM*... H-HIS BODY'S TURNING TO STONE! HE MUST HAVE THE DRAGON'S CURSE... THAT'S WHY THE FIVE HAND SPEAR DIDN'T HURT HIM!! WE'VE UNDERESTIMATED HIM!
NOW, LET'S GET THIS OVER WITH ALREADY! I NEED TO GET SOMETHING TO EAT!
HA! YOU'VE ALREADY HAD YOUR LAST MEAL!

*LEADER OR BOSS. THE SUFFIX "NIM" IS LIKE "SAMA" – THE MORE HONORIFIC FORM OF "SAN" IN JAPANESE.

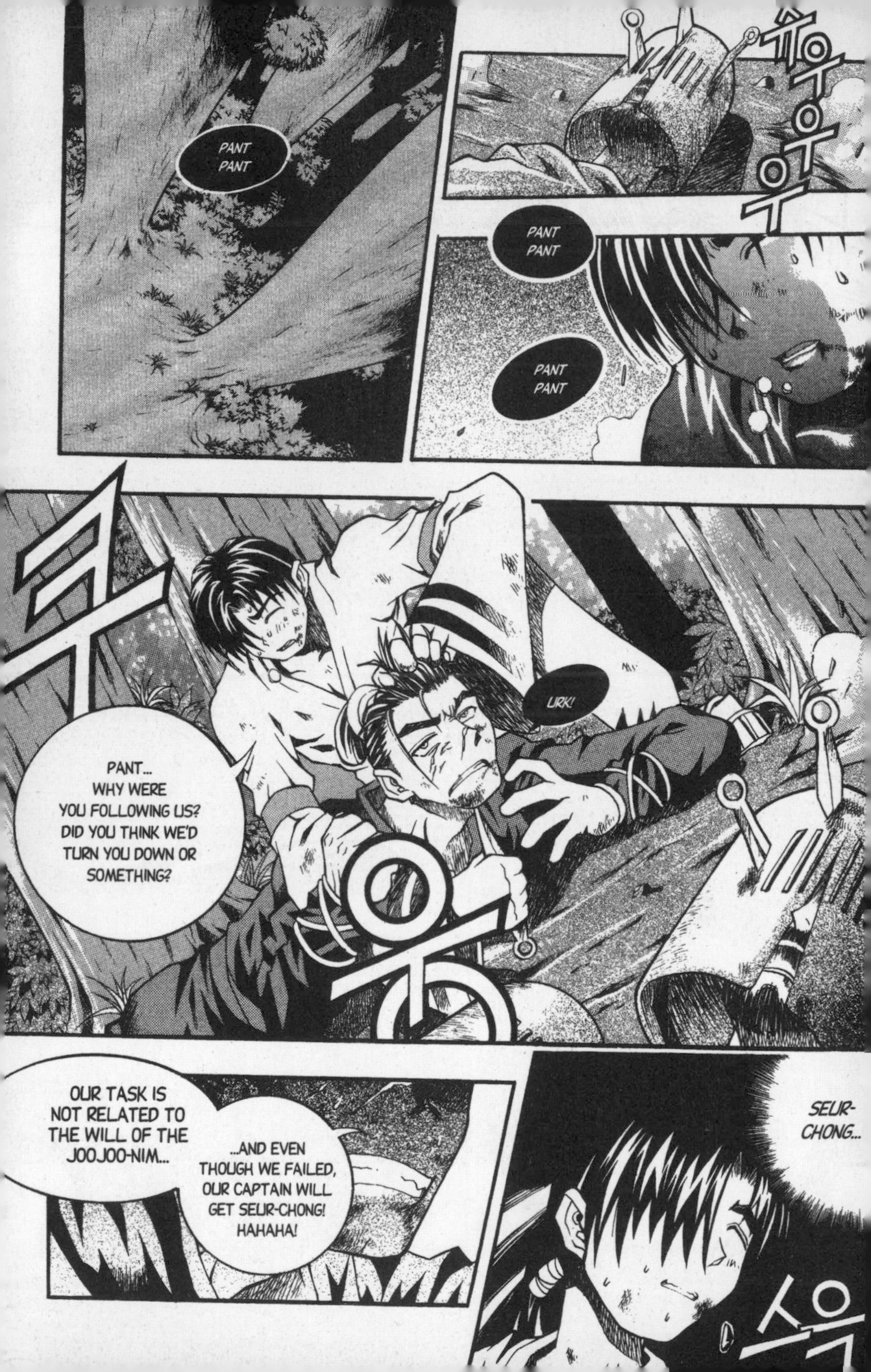
PANT PANT
PANT PANT
PANT PANT
URK!
PANT... WHY WERE YOU FOLLOWING US? DID YOU THINK WE'D TURN YOU DOWN OR SOMETHING?
OUR TASK IS NOT RELATED TO THE WILL OF THE JOOJOO-NIM...
...AND EVEN THOUGH WE FAILED, OUR CAPTAIN WILL GET SEUR-CHONG! HAHAHA!
SEUR-CHONG...

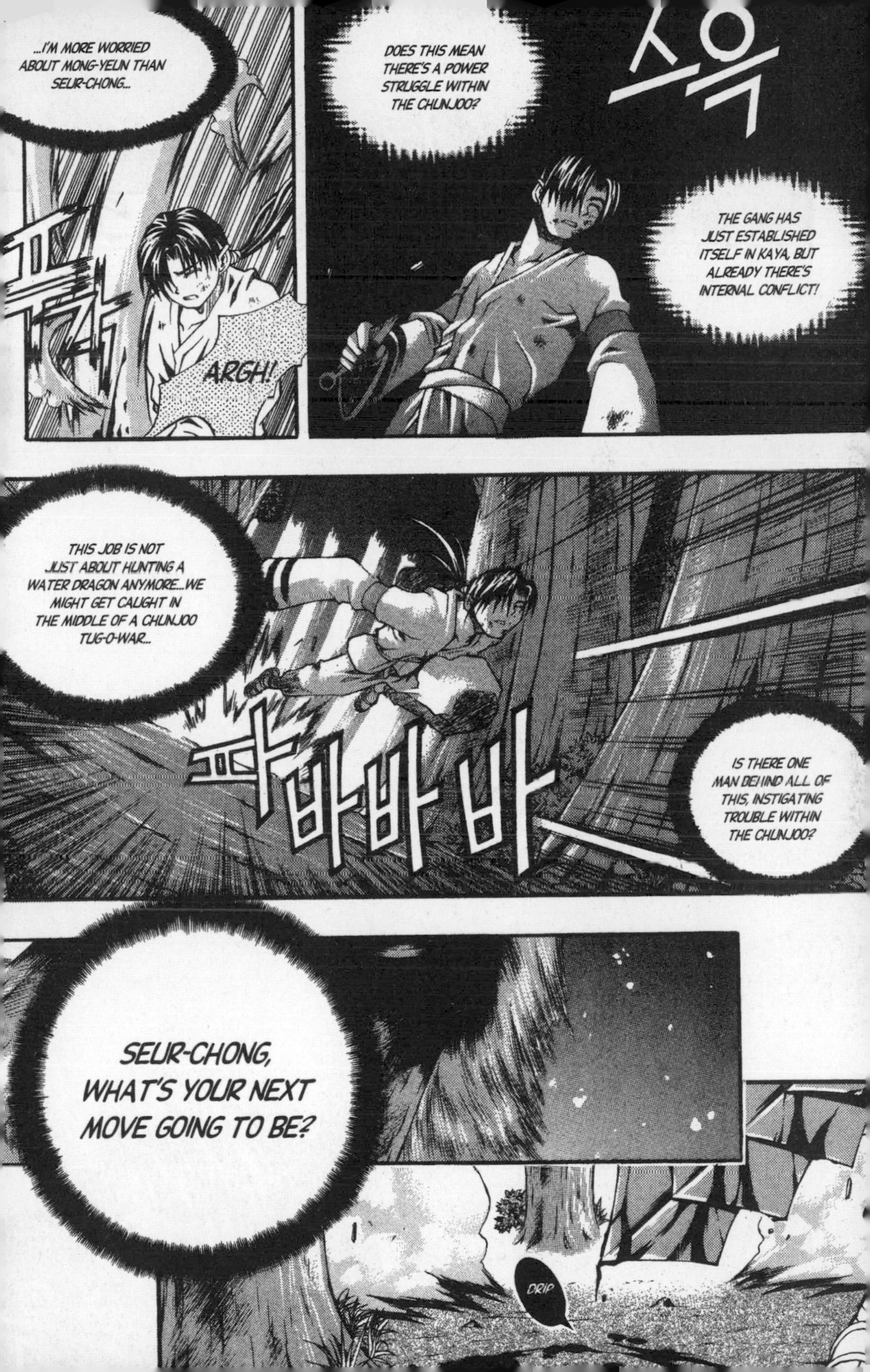
...I'M MORE WORRIED ABOUT MONG-YEUN THAN SEUR-CHONG...
ARGH!
DOES THIS MEAN THERE'S A POWER STRUGGLE WITHIN THE CHUNJOO?
스윽
THE GANG HAS JUST ESTABLISHED ITSELF IN KAYA, BUT ALREADY THERE'S INTERNAL CONFLICT!
THIS JOB IS NOT JUST ABOUT HUNTING A WATER DRAGON ANYMORE...WE MIGHT GET CAUGHT IN THE MIDDLE OF A CHUNJOO TUG-O-WAR...
파바바바
IS THERE ONE MAN BEHIND ALL OF THIS, INSTIGATING TROUBLE WITHIN THE CHUNJOO?
SEUR-CHONG, WHAT'S YOUR NEXT MOVE GOING TO BE?
DRIP

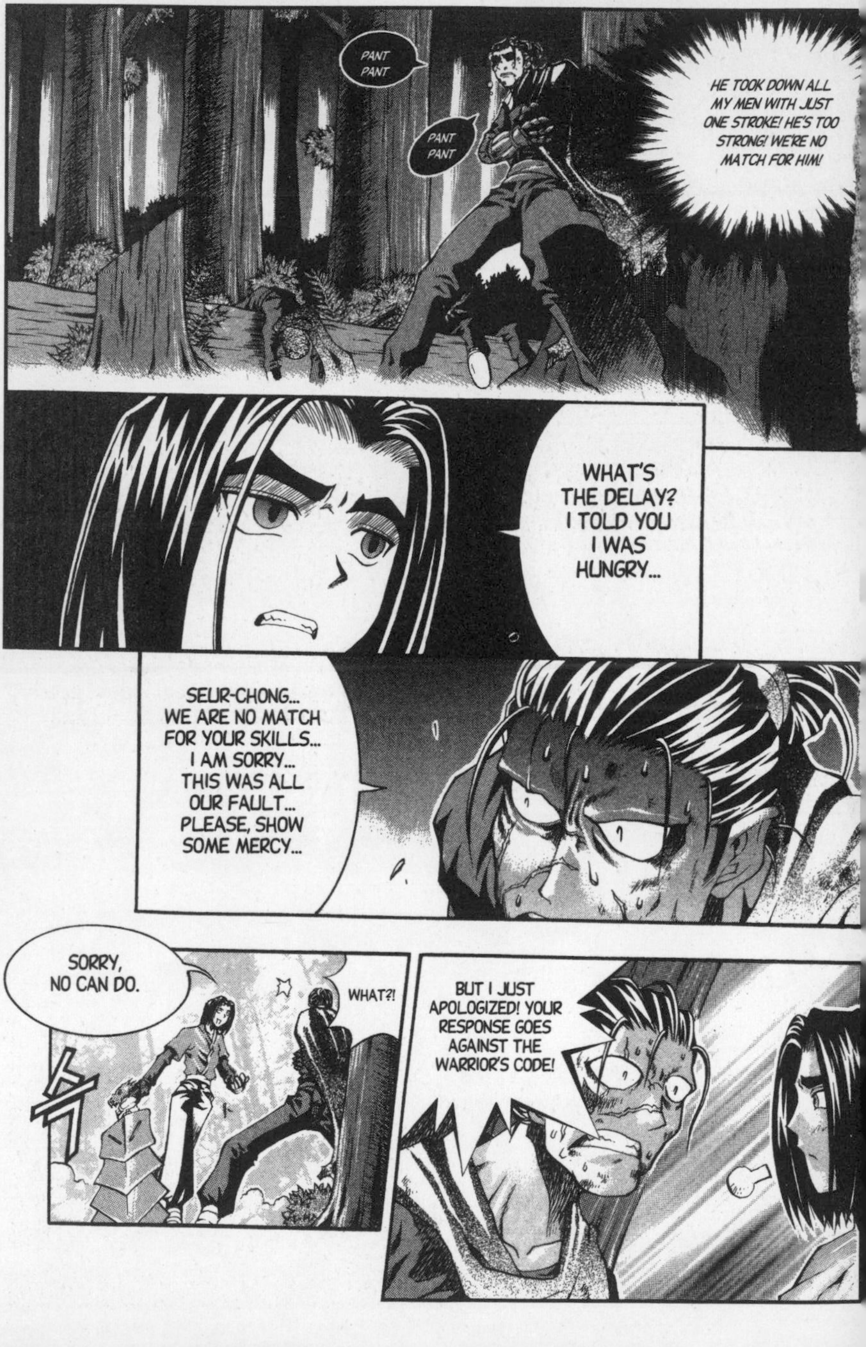
PANT PANT
PANT PANT
HE TOOK DOWN ALL MY MEN WITH JUST ONE STROKE! HE'S TOO STRONG! WE'RE NO MATCH FOR HIM!
WHAT'S THE DELAY? I TOLD YOU I WAS HUNGRY...
SEUR-CHONG... WE ARE NO MATCH FOR YOUR SKILLS... I AM SORRY... THIS WAS ALL OUR FAULT... PLEASE, SHOW SOME MERCY...
SORRY, NO CAN DO.
WHAT?!
BUT I JUST APOLOGIZED! YOUR RESPONSE GOES AGAINST THE WARRIOR'S CODE!

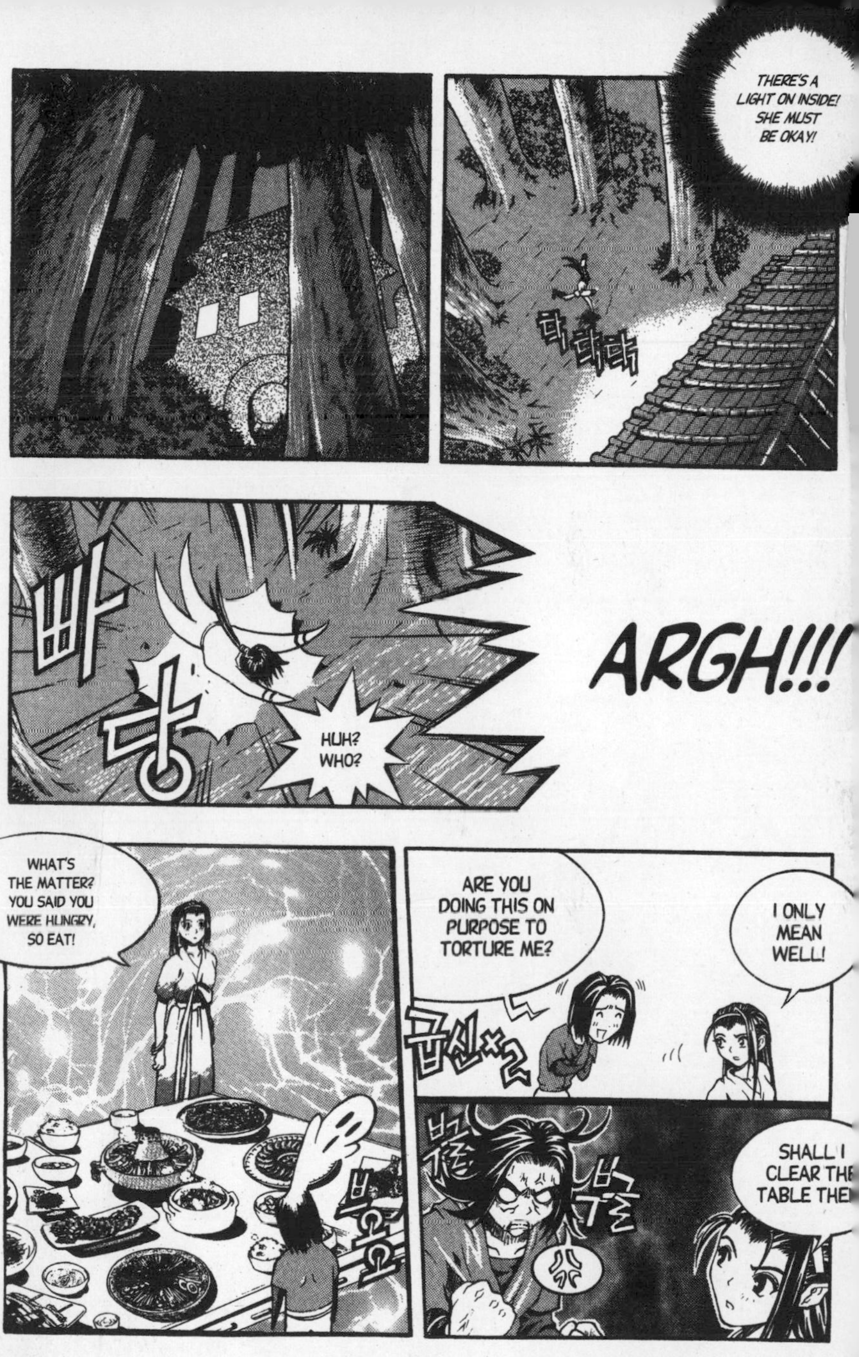

THERE'S A LIGHT ON INSIDE! SHE MUST BE OKAY!
ARGH!!!
HUH? WHO?
WHAT'S THE MATTER? YOU SAID YOU WERE HUNGRY, SO EAT!
ARE YOU DOING THIS ON PURPOSE TO TORTURE ME?
굽신×2
I ONLY MEAN WELL!
SHALL I CLEAR THE TABLE THE

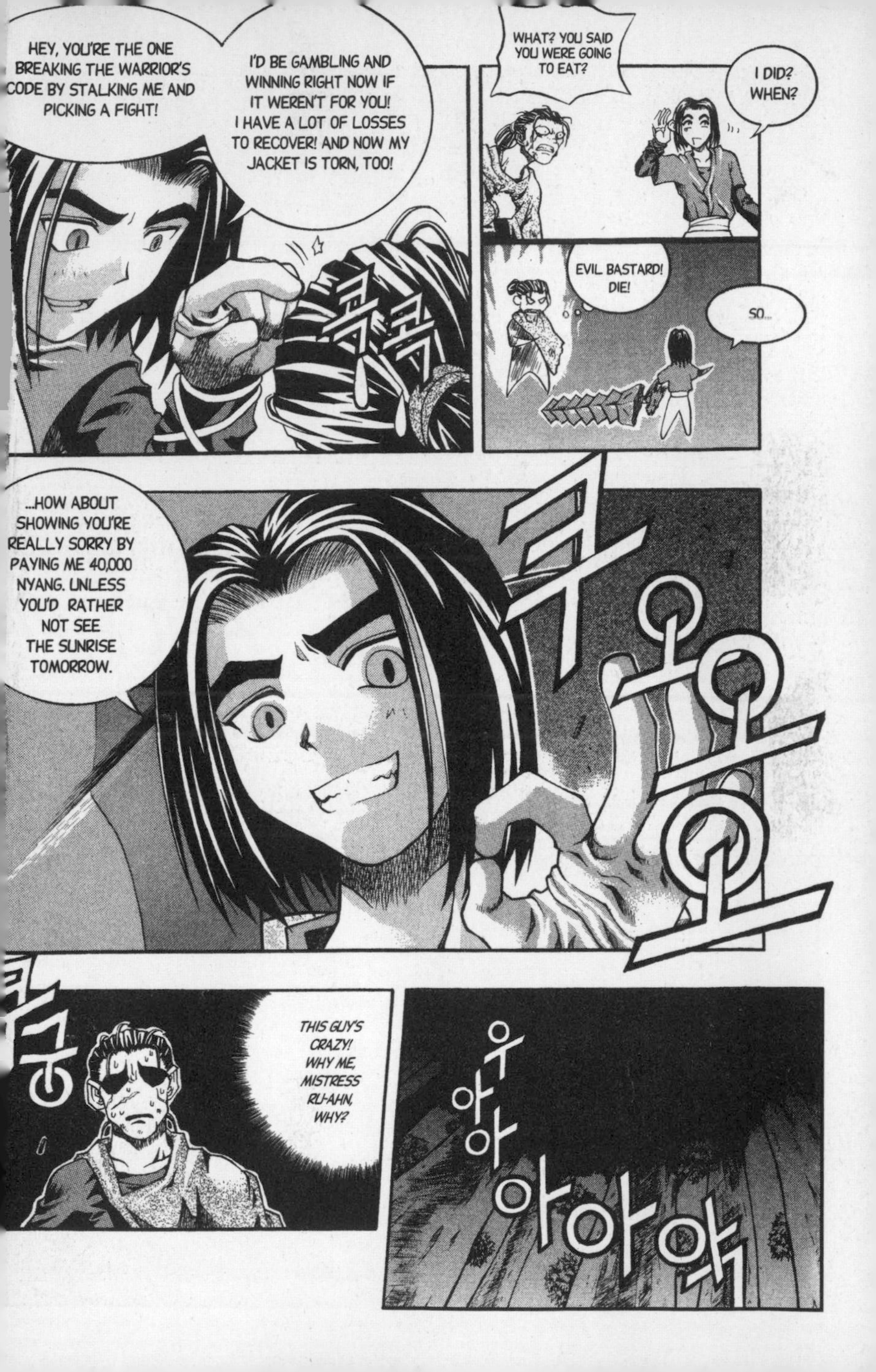

HEY, YOU'RE THE ONE BREAKING THE WARRIOR'S CODE BY STALKING ME AND PICKING A FIGHT!
I'D BE GAMBLING AND WINNING RIGHT NOW IF IT WEREN'T FOR YOU! I HAVE A LOT OF LOSSES TO RECOVER! AND NOW MY JACKET IS TORN, TOO!
콕콕
WHAT? YOU SAID YOU WERE GOING TO EAT?
I DID? WHEN?
EVIL BASTARD! DIE!
SO...
...HOW ABOUT SHOWING YOU'RE REALLY SORRY BY PAYING ME 40,000 NYANG. UNLESS YOU'D RATHER NOT SEE THE SUNRISE TOMORROW.
THIS GUY'S CRAZY! WHY ME, MISTRESS RU-AHN, WHY?

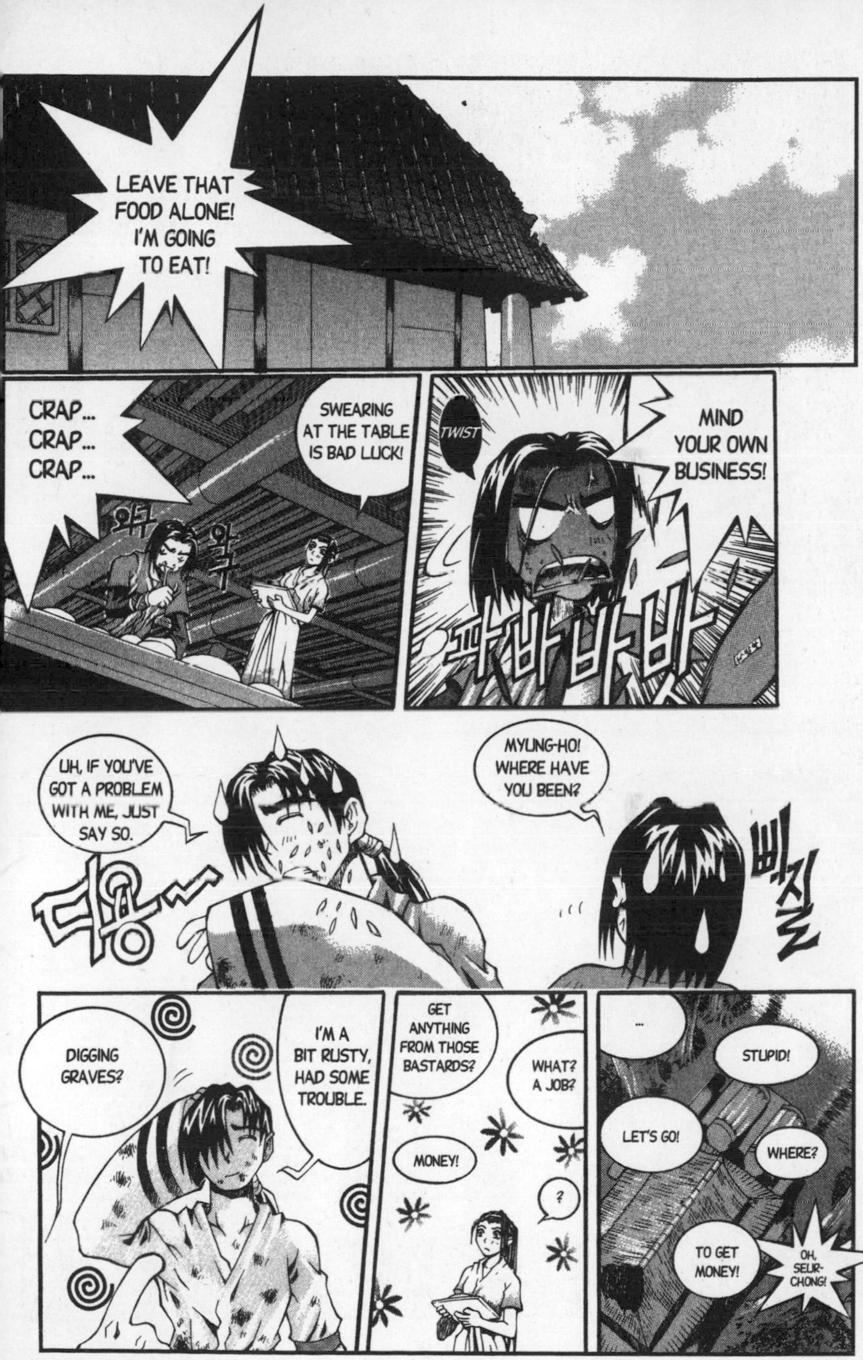
LEAVE THAT FOOD ALONE! I'M GOING TO EAT!
CRAP... CRAP... CRAP...
SWEARING AT THE TABLE IS BAD LUCK!
TWIST
MIND YOUR OWN BUSINESS!
UH, IF YOU'VE GOT A PROBLEM WITH ME, JUST SAY SO.
MYUNG-HO! WHERE HAVE YOU BEEN?
DIGGING GRAVES?
I'M A BIT RUSTY, HAD SOME TROUBLE.
GET ANYTHING FROM THOSE BASTARDS?
WHAT? A JOB?
MONEY!
?
...
STUPID!
LET'S GO!
WHERE?
TO GET MONEY!
OH, SEUR-CHONG!

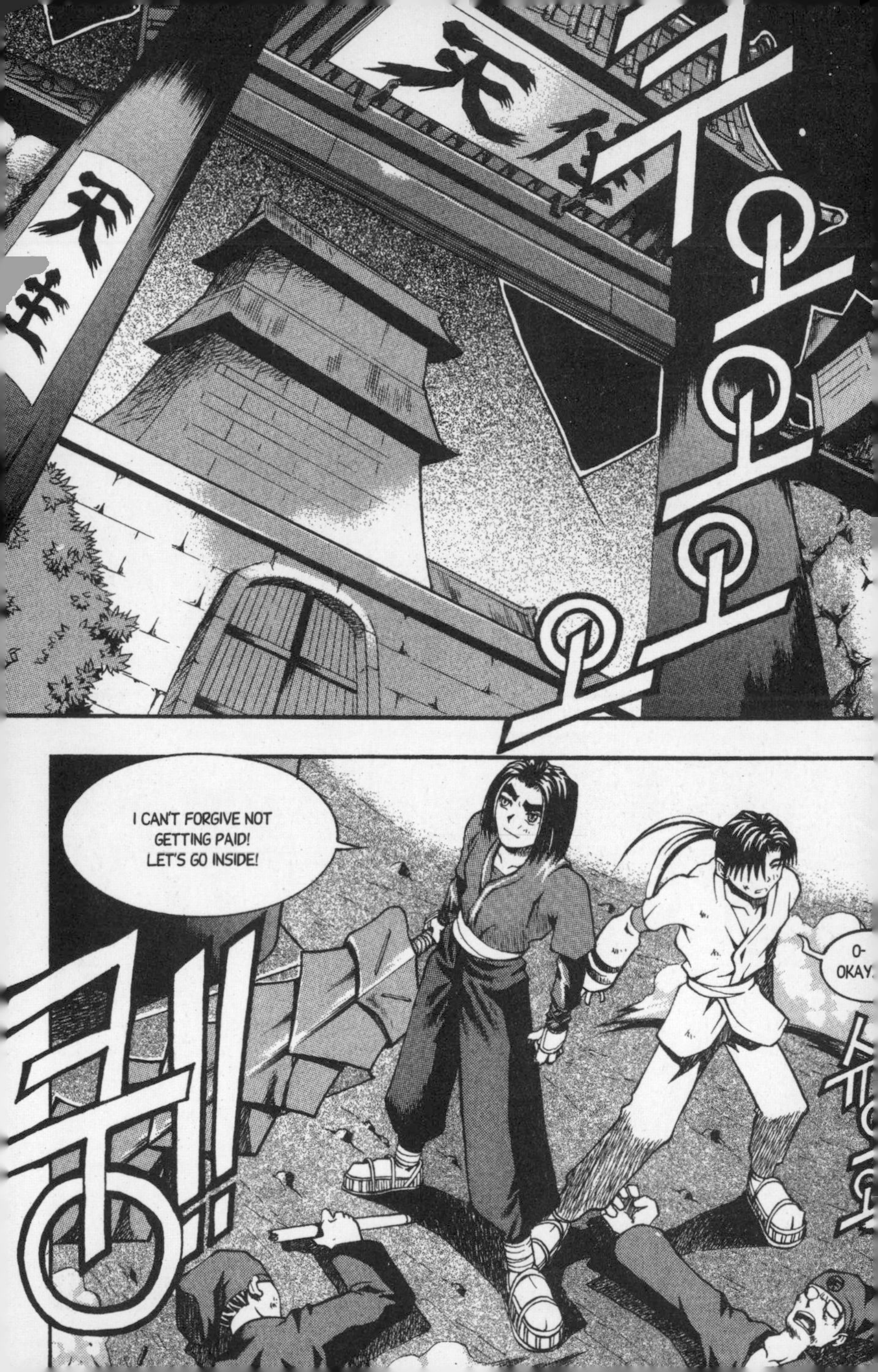
I CAN'T FORGIVE NOT GETTING PAID! LET'S GO INSIDE!
O-OKAY.

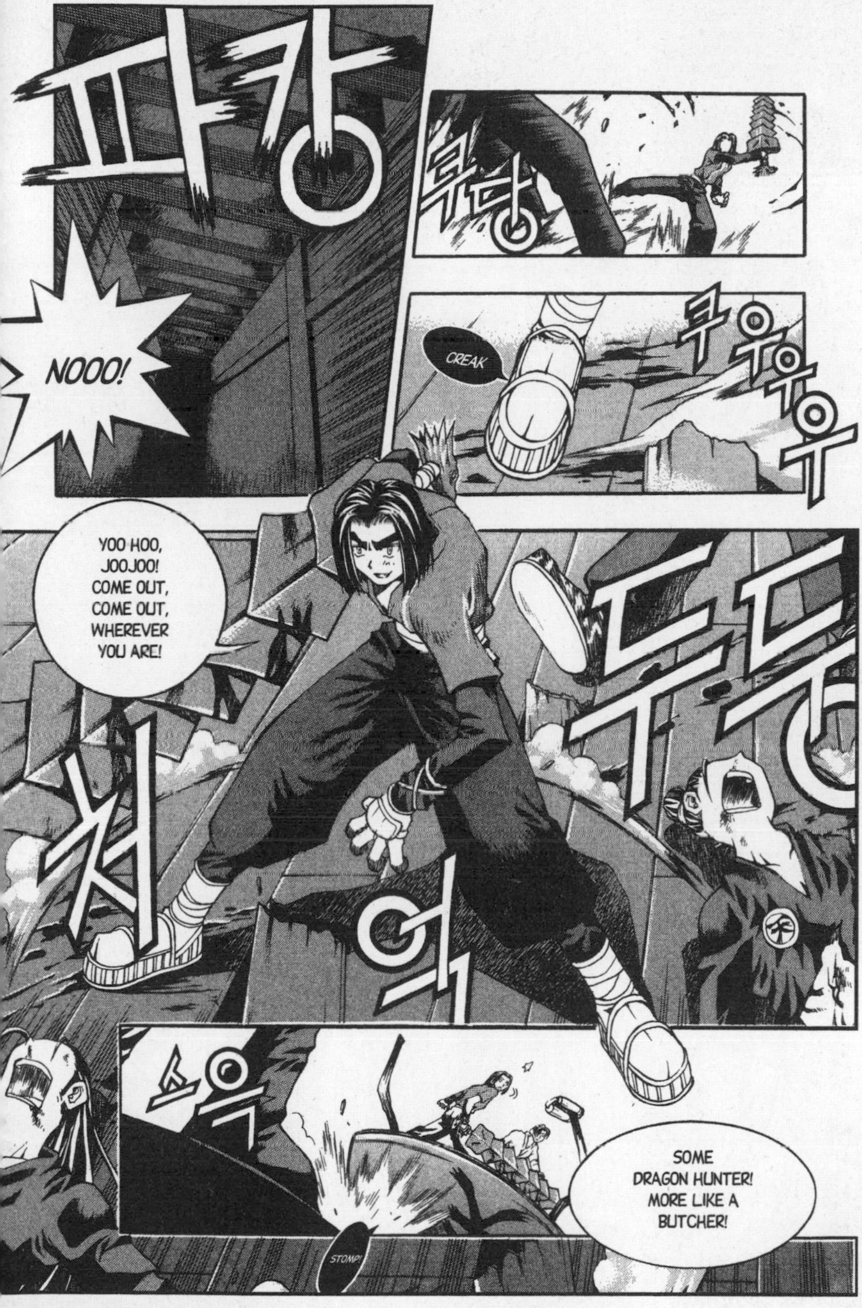
NOOO!
CREAK
YOO HOO, JOOJOO! COME OUT, COME OUT, WHEREVER YOU ARE!
STOMP!
SOME DRAGON HUNTER! MORE LIKE A BUTCHER!

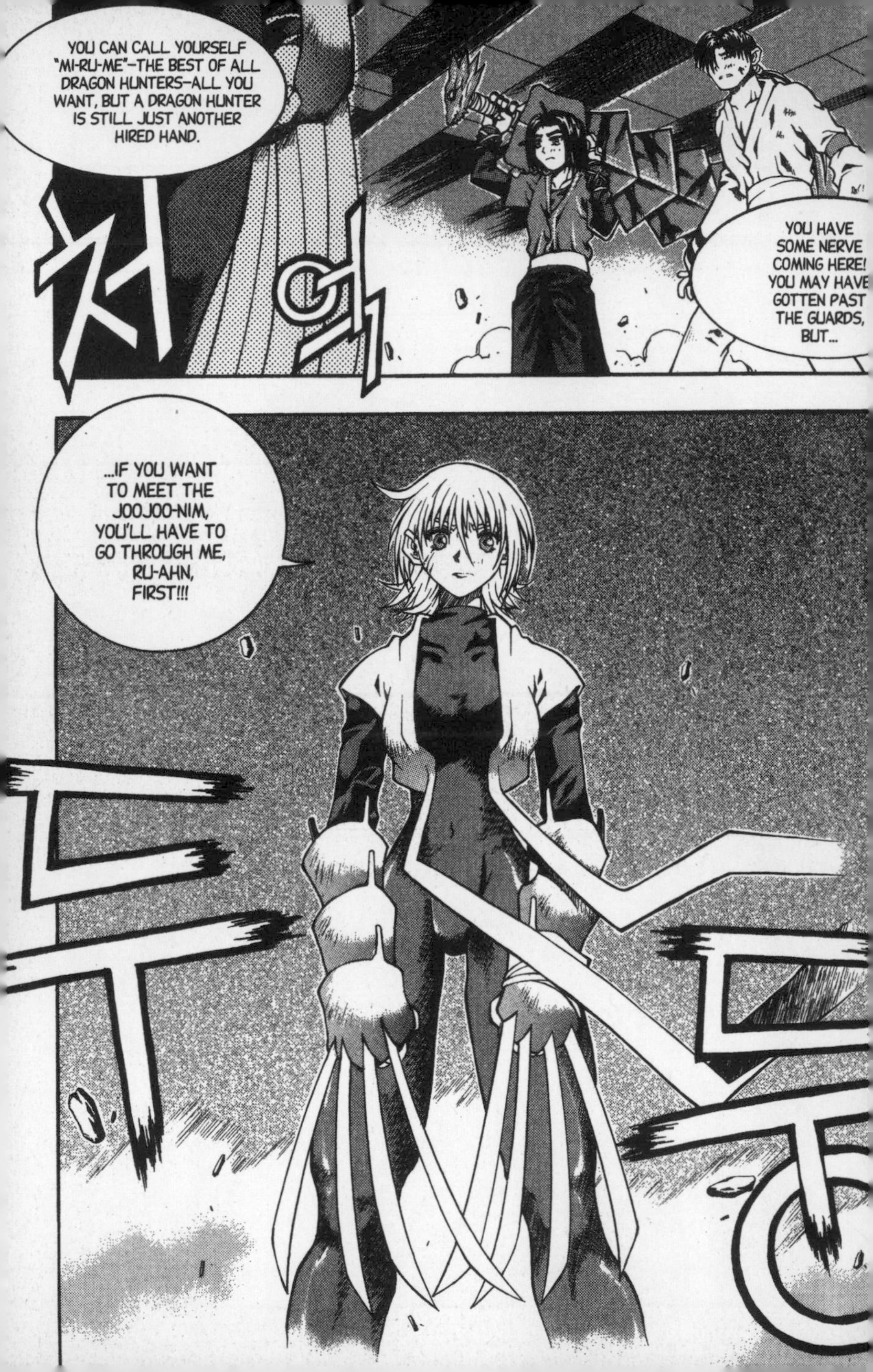
YOU CAN CALL YOURSELF "MI-RU-ME"—THE BEST OF ALL DRAGON HUNTERS—ALL YOU WANT, BUT A DRAGON HUNTER IS STILL JUST ANOTHER HIRED HAND.
YOU HAVE SOME NERVE COMING HERE! YOU MAY HAVE GOTTEN PAST THE GUARDS, BUT...
...IF YOU WANT TO MEET THE JOOJOO-NIM, YOU'LL HAVE TO GO THROUGH ME, RU-AHN, FIRST!!!

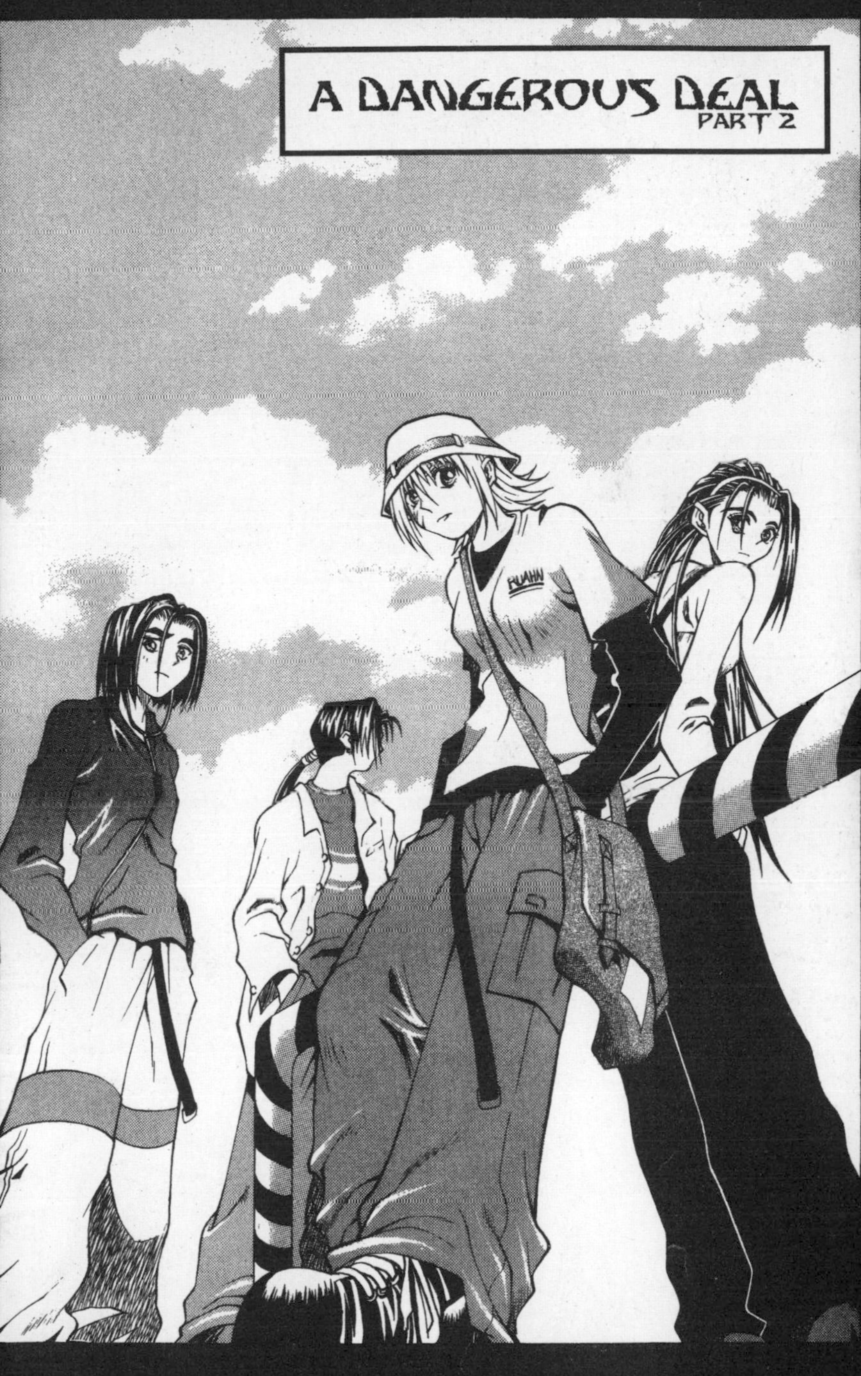
A DANGEROUS DEAL
PART 2
RUAHN

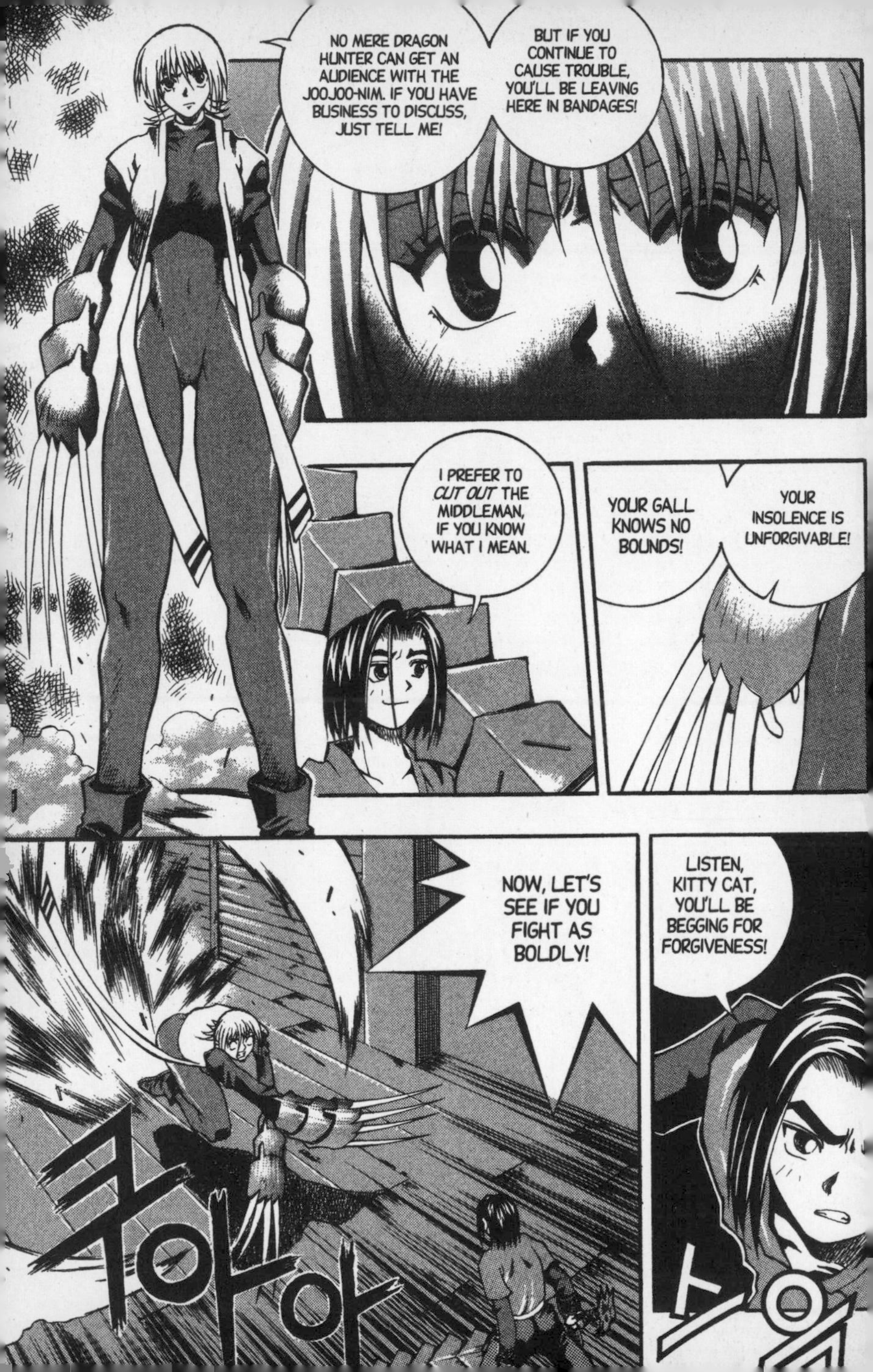
NO MERE DRAGON HUNTER CAN GET AN AUDIENCE WITH THE JOOJOO-NIM. IF YOU HAVE BUSINESS TO DISCUSS, JUST TELL ME!
BUT IF YOU CONTINUE TO CAUSE TROUBLE, YOU'LL BE LEAVING HERE IN BANDAGES!
I PREFER TO *CUT OUT* THE MIDDLEMAN, IF YOU KNOW WHAT I MEAN.
YOUR GALL KNOWS NO BOUNDS!
YOUR INSOLENCE IS UNFORGIVABLE!
NOW, LET'S SEE IF YOU FIGHT AS BOLDLY!
LISTEN, KITTY CAT, YOU'LL BE BEGGING FOR FORGIVENESS!

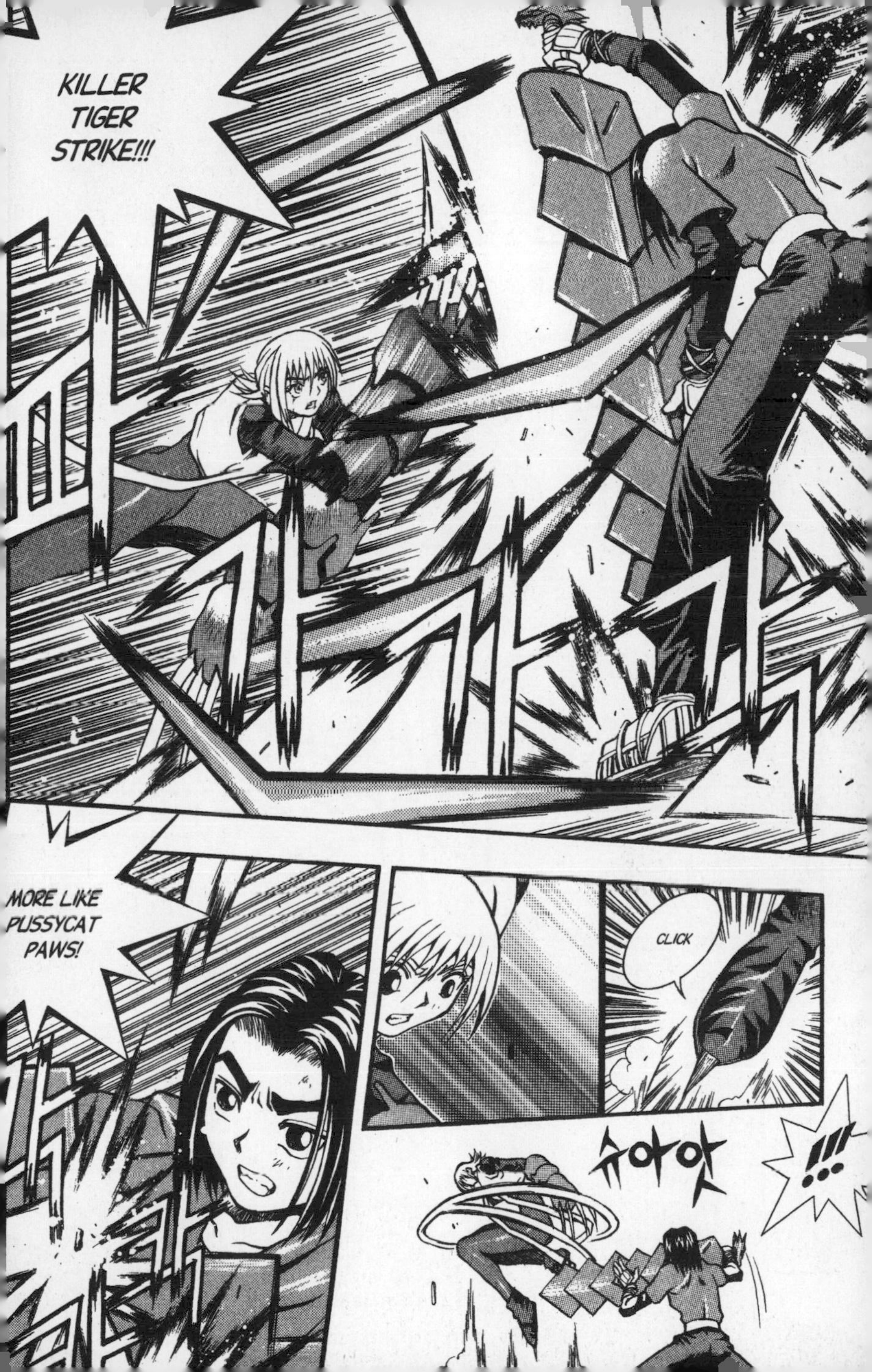
KILLER TIGER STRIKE!!!
MORE LIKE PUSSYCAT PAWS!
CLICK
!!!

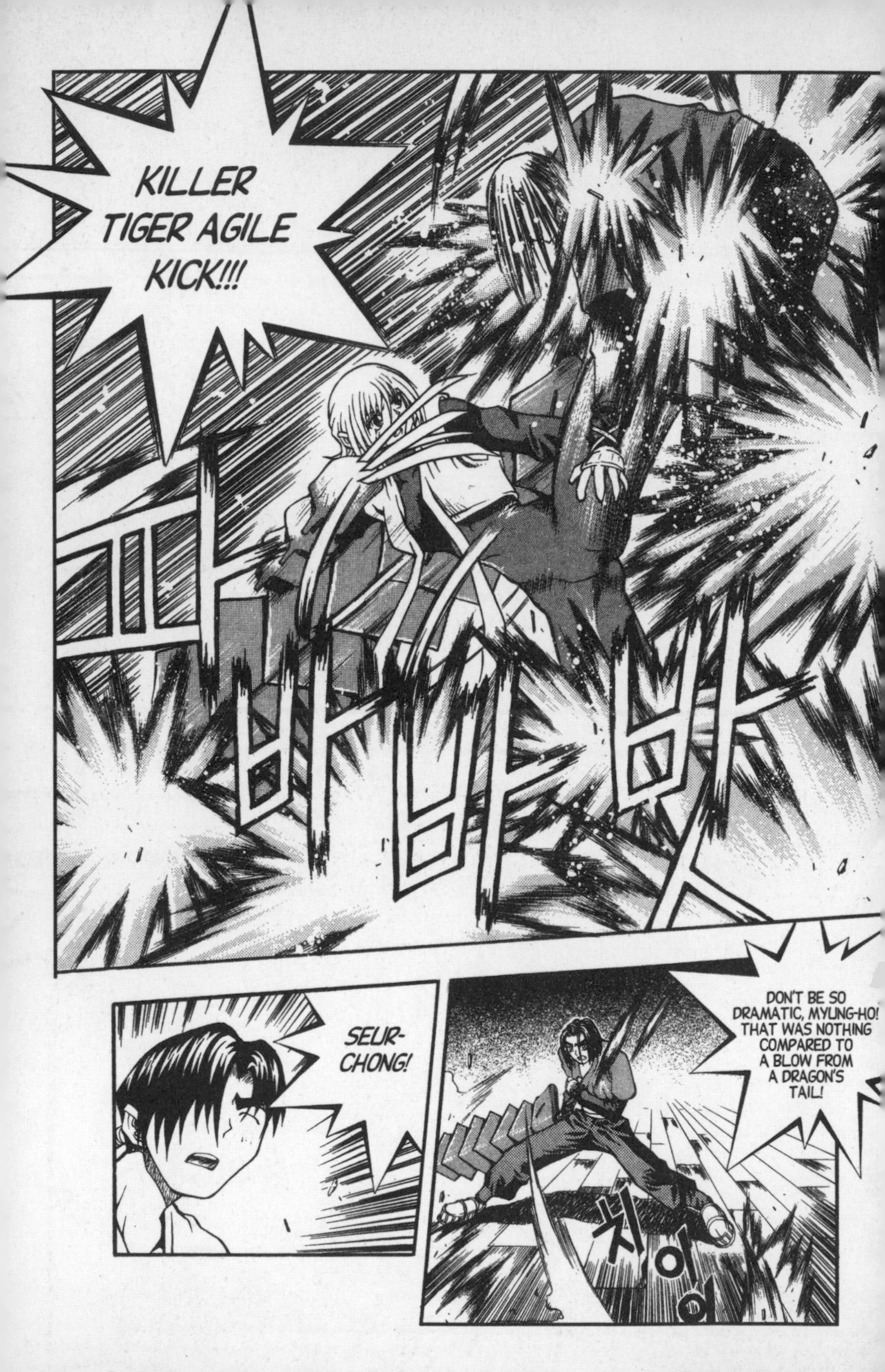
KILLER TIGER AGILE KICK!!!
SEUR-CHONG!
DON'T BE SO DRAMATIC, MYUNG-HO! THAT WAS NOTHING COMPARED TO A BLOW FROM A DRAGON'S TAIL!

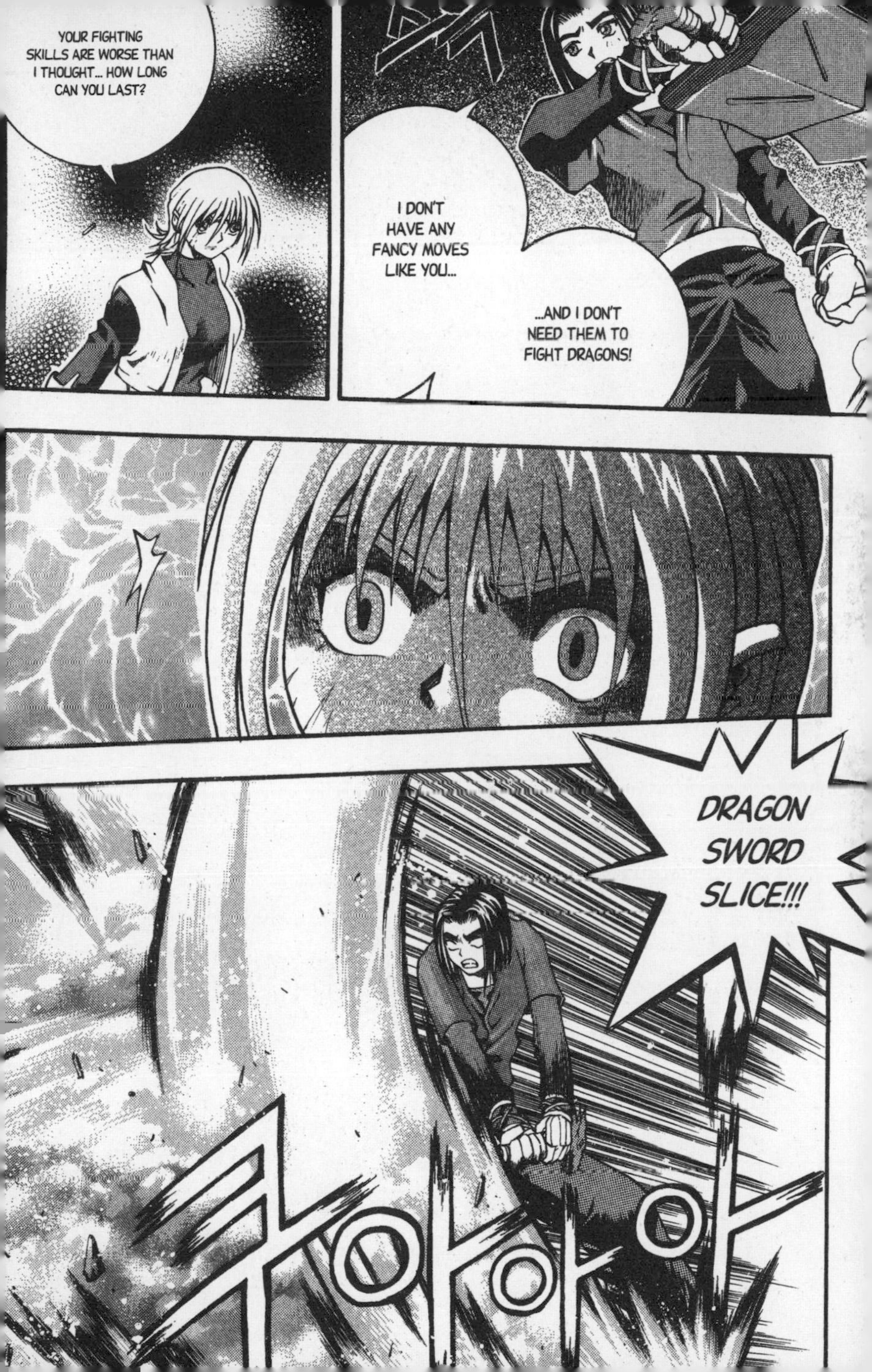
YOUR FIGHTING SKILLS ARE WORSE THAN I THOUGHT... HOW LONG CAN YOU LAST?
I DON'T HAVE ANY FANCY MOVES LIKE YOU...
...AND I DON'T NEED THEM TO FIGHT DRAGONS!
DRAGON SWORD SLICE!!!

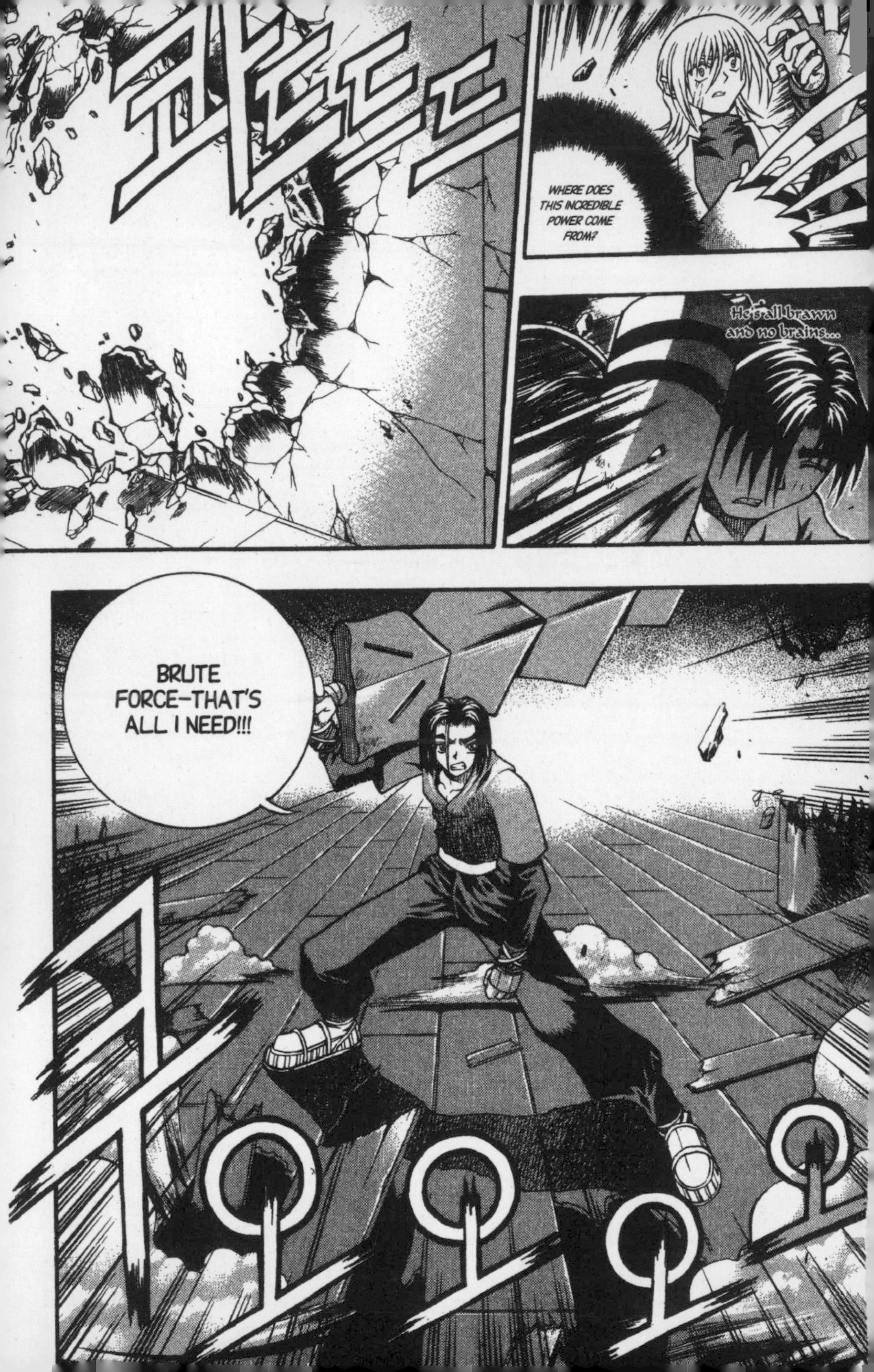
WHERE DOES THIS INCREDIBLE POWER COME FROM?
He's all brawn and no brains...
BRUTE FORCE—THAT'S ALL I NEED!!!

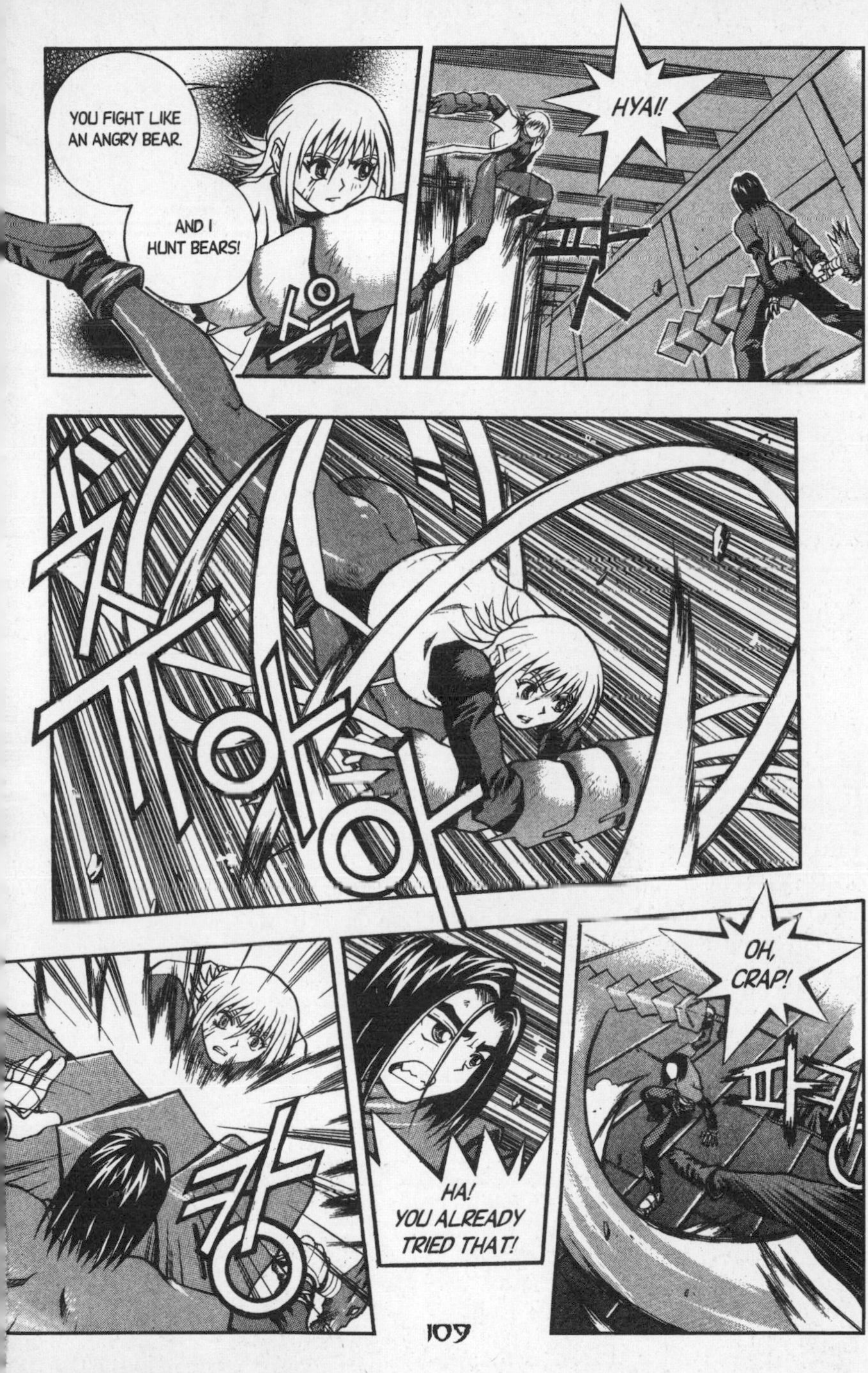

YOU FIGHT LIKE AN ANGRY BEAR.
AND I HUNT BEARS!
HYA!!
HA! YOU ALREADY TRIED THAT!
OH, CRAP!

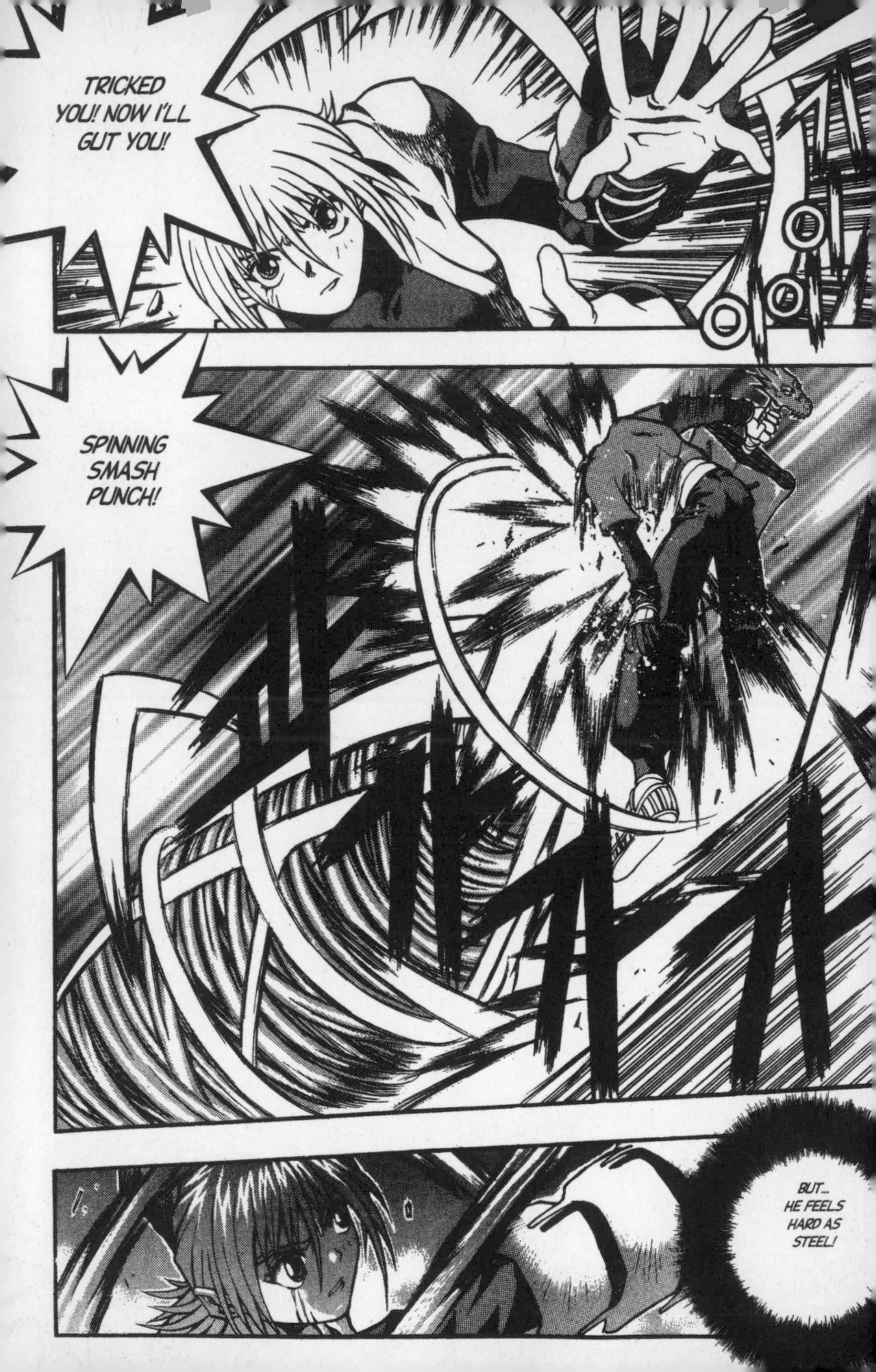
TRICKED YOU! NOW I'LL GUT YOU!
SPINNING SMASH PUNCH!
BUT... HE FEELS HARD AS STEEL!

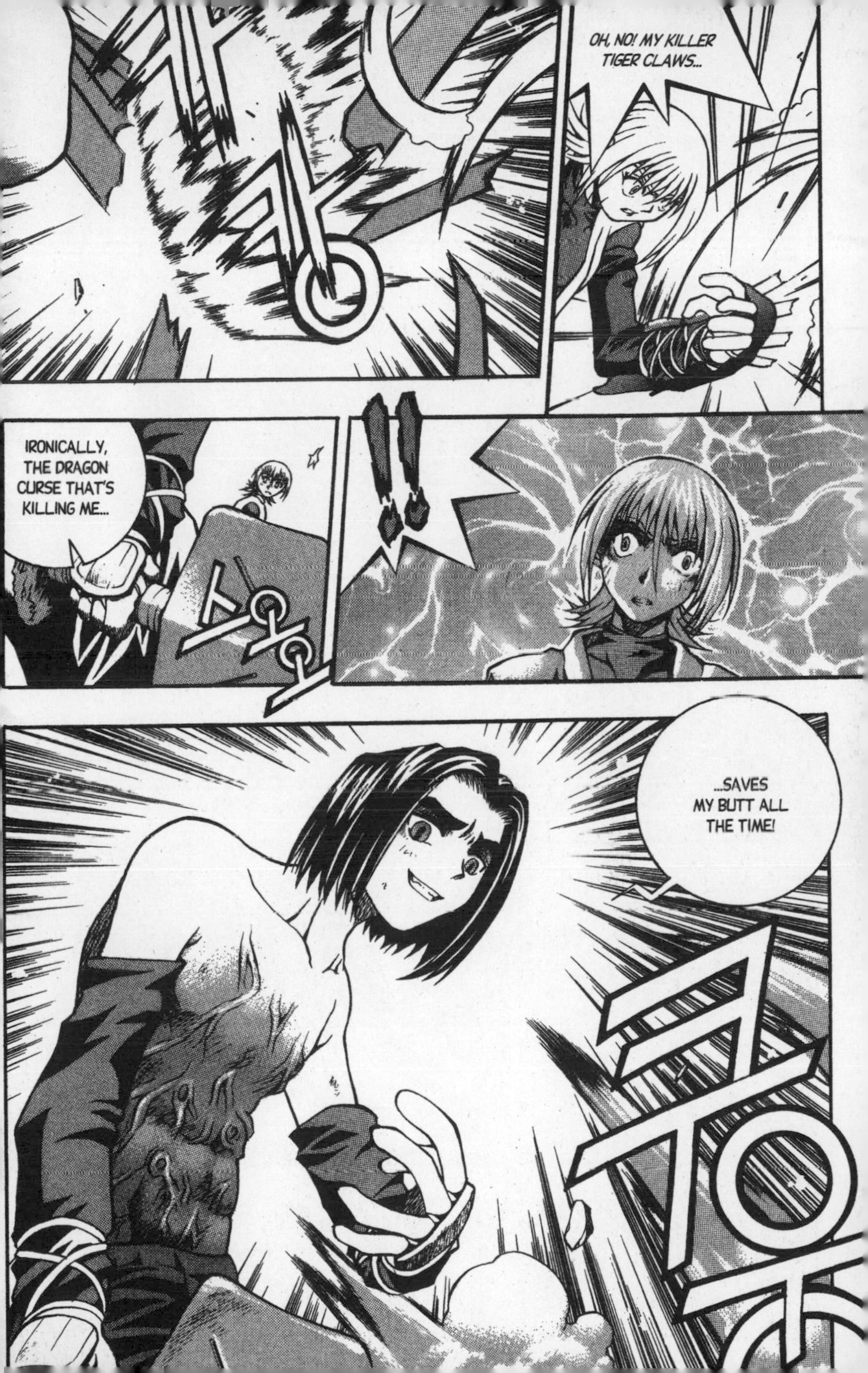
OH, NO! MY KILLER TIGER CLAWS...
IRONICALLY, THE DRAGON CURSE THAT'S KILLING ME...
!!
...SAVES MY BUTT ALL THE TIME!

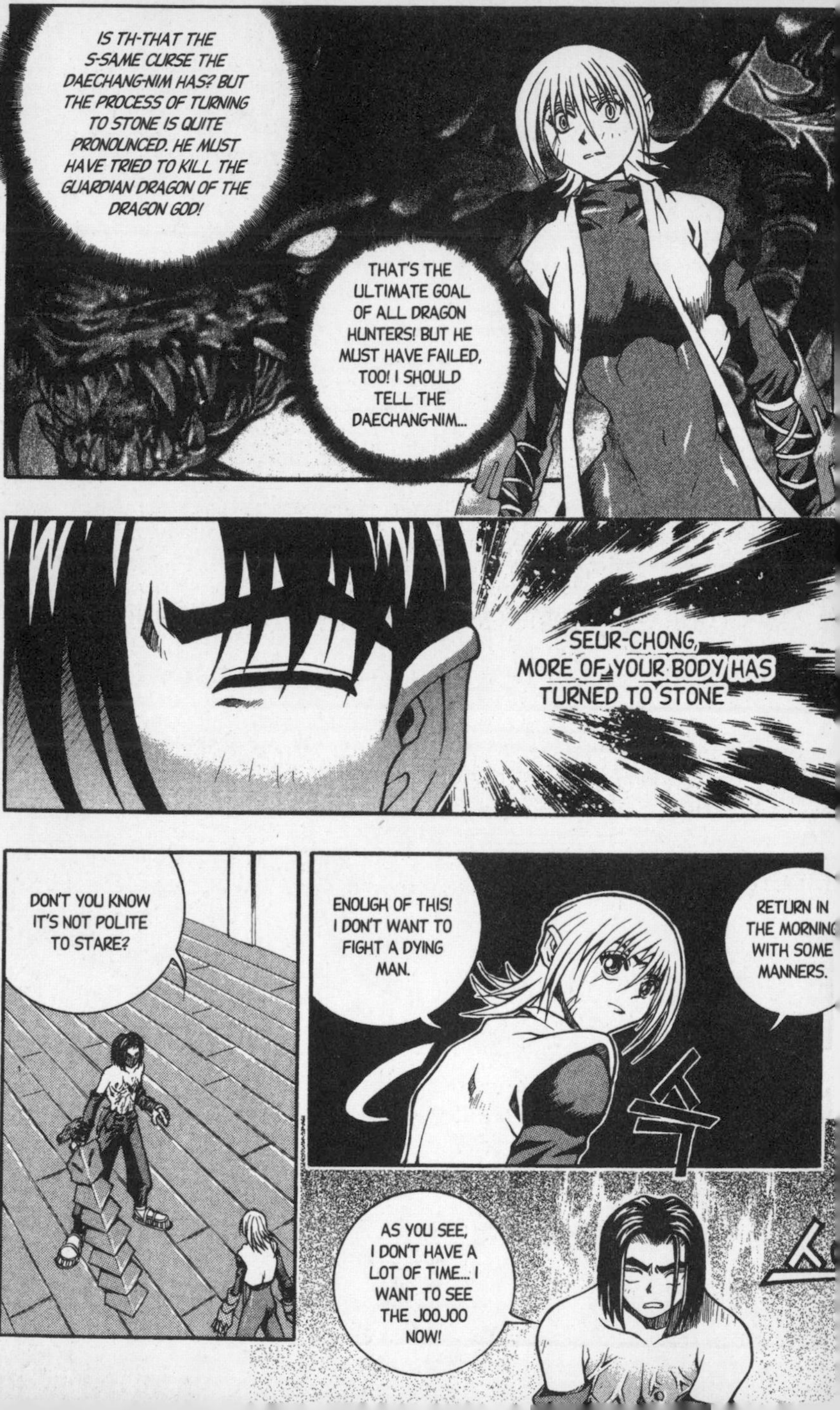
IS TH-THAT THE S-SAME CURSE THE DAECHANG-NIM HAS? BUT THE PROCESS OF TURNING TO STONE IS QUITE PRONOUNCED. HE MUST HAVE TRIED TO KILL THE GUARDIAN DRAGON OF THE DRAGON GOD!
THAT'S THE ULTIMATE GOAL OF ALL DRAGON HUNTERS! BUT HE MUST HAVE FAILED, TOO! I SHOULD TELL THE DAECHANG-NIM...
SEUR-CHONG, MORE OF YOUR BODY HAS TURNED TO STONE
DON'T YOU KNOW IT'S NOT POLITE TO STARE?
ENOUGH OF THIS! I DON'T WANT TO FIGHT A DYING MAN.
RETURN IN THE MORNING WITH SOME MANNERS.
AS YOU SEE, I DON'T HAVE A LOT OF TIME... I WANT TO SEE THE JOOJOO NOW!

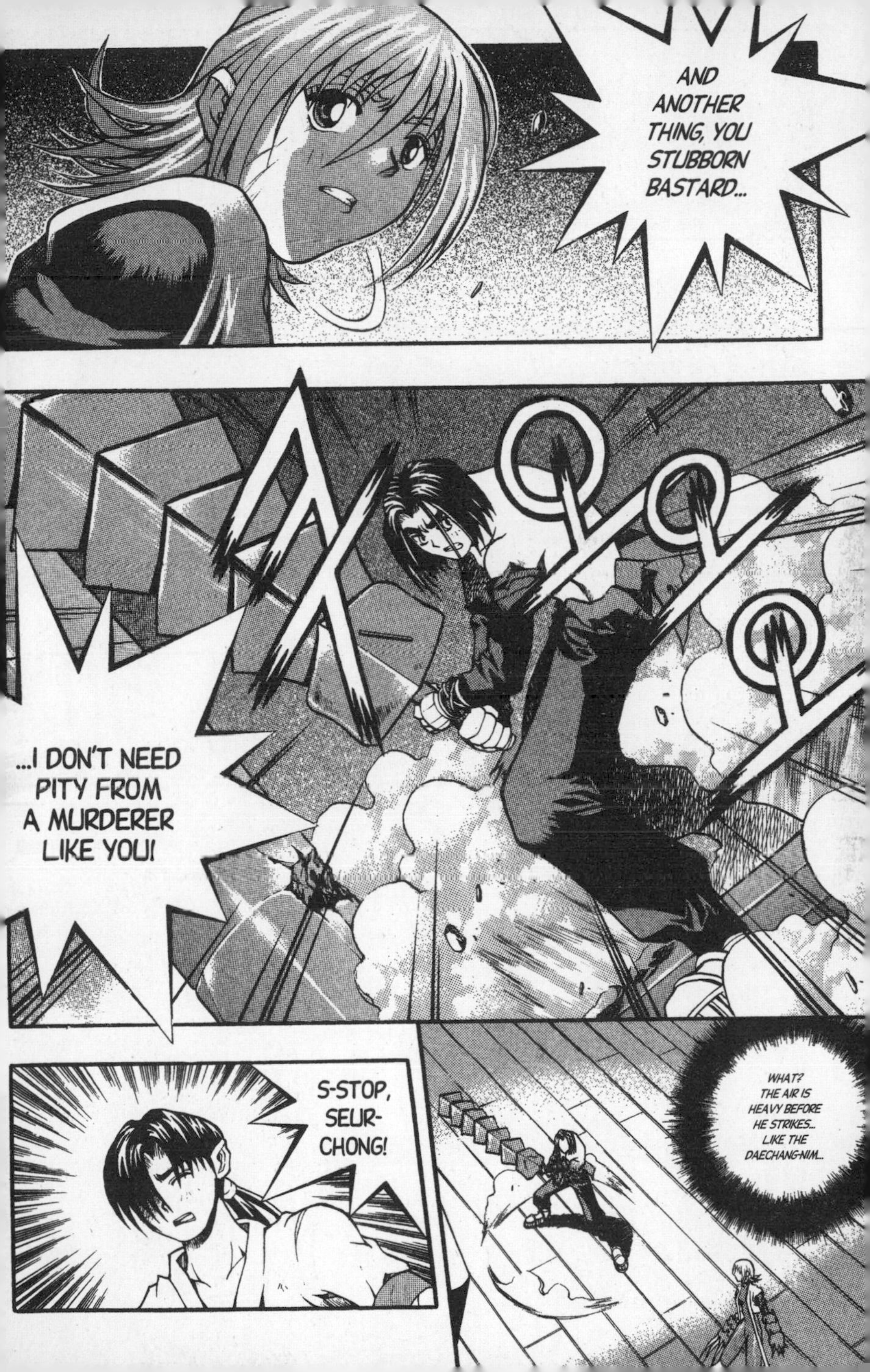
AND ANOTHER THING, YOU STUBBORN BASTARD...
...I DON'T NEED PITY FROM A MURDERER LIKE YOU!
S-STOP, SEUR-CHONG!
WHAT? THE AIR IS HEAVY BEFORE HE STRIKES... LIKE THE DAECHANG-NIM...

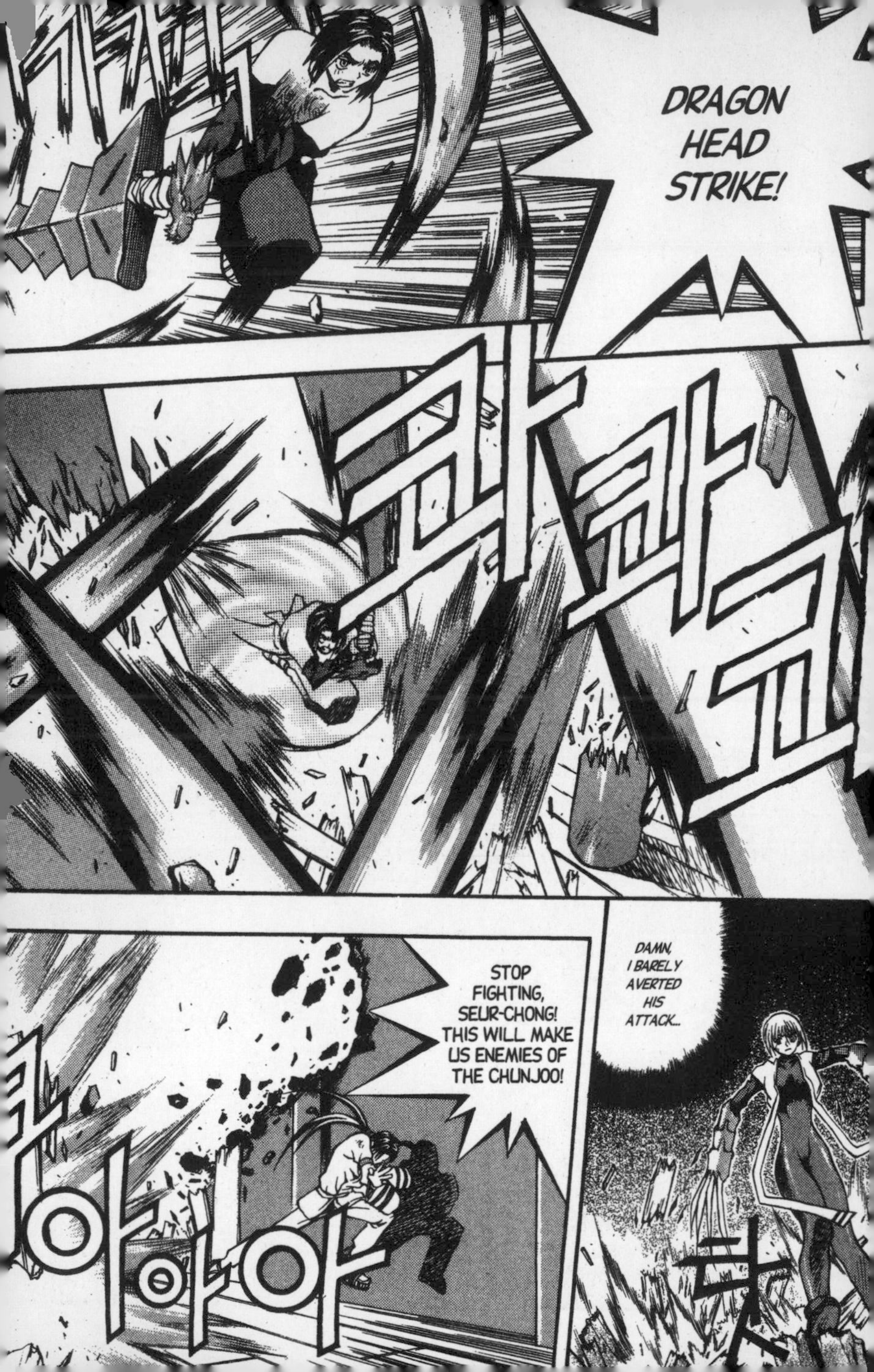
DRAGON HEAD STRIKE!
STOP FIGHTING, SEUR-CHONG! THIS WILL MAKE US ENEMIES OF THE CHUNJOO!
DAMN, I BARELY AVERTED HIS ATTACK...

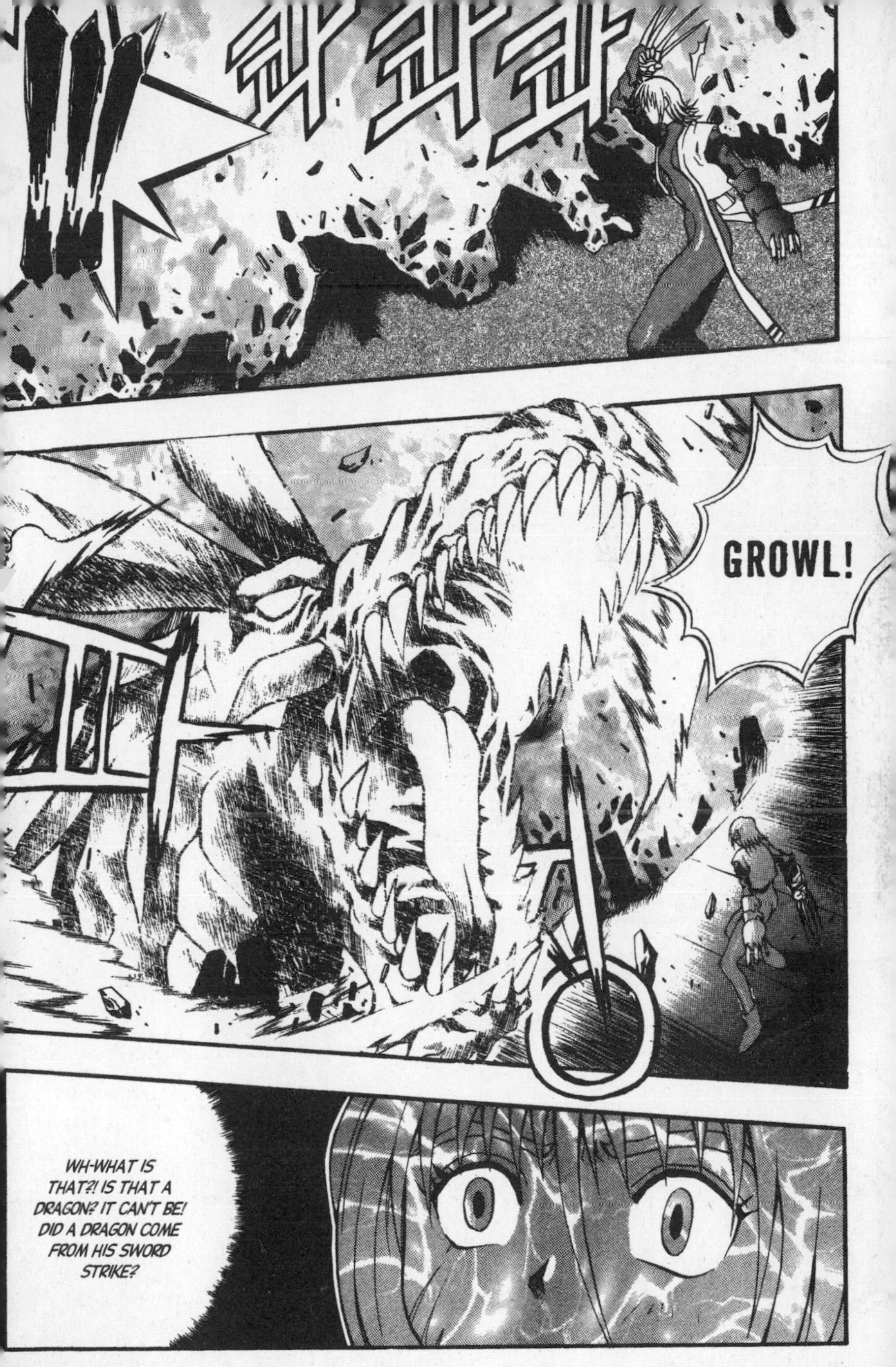
GROWL!
WH-WHAT IS THAT?! IS THAT A DRAGON? IT CAN'T BE! DID A DRAGON COME FROM HIS SWORD STRIKE?

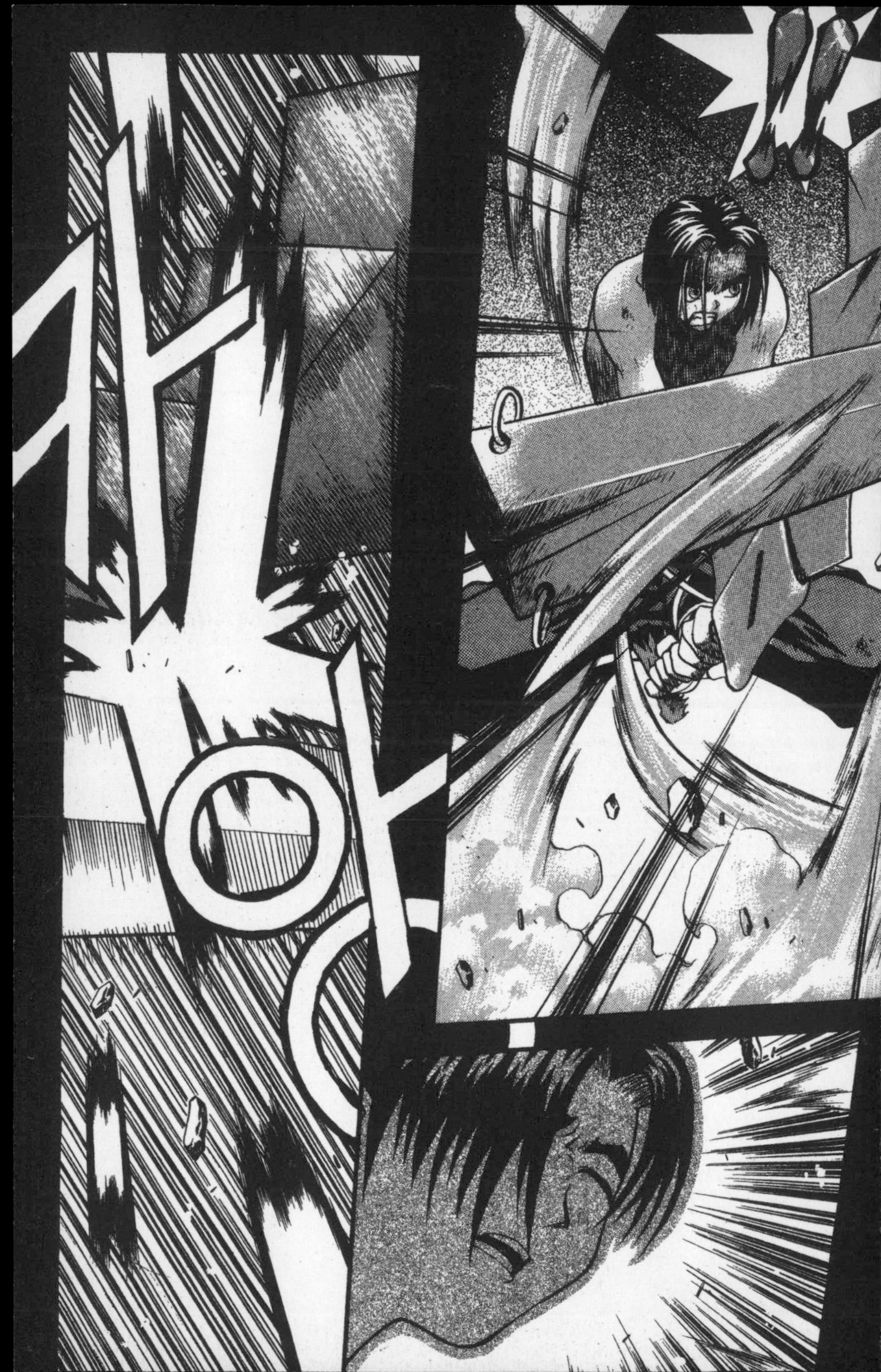

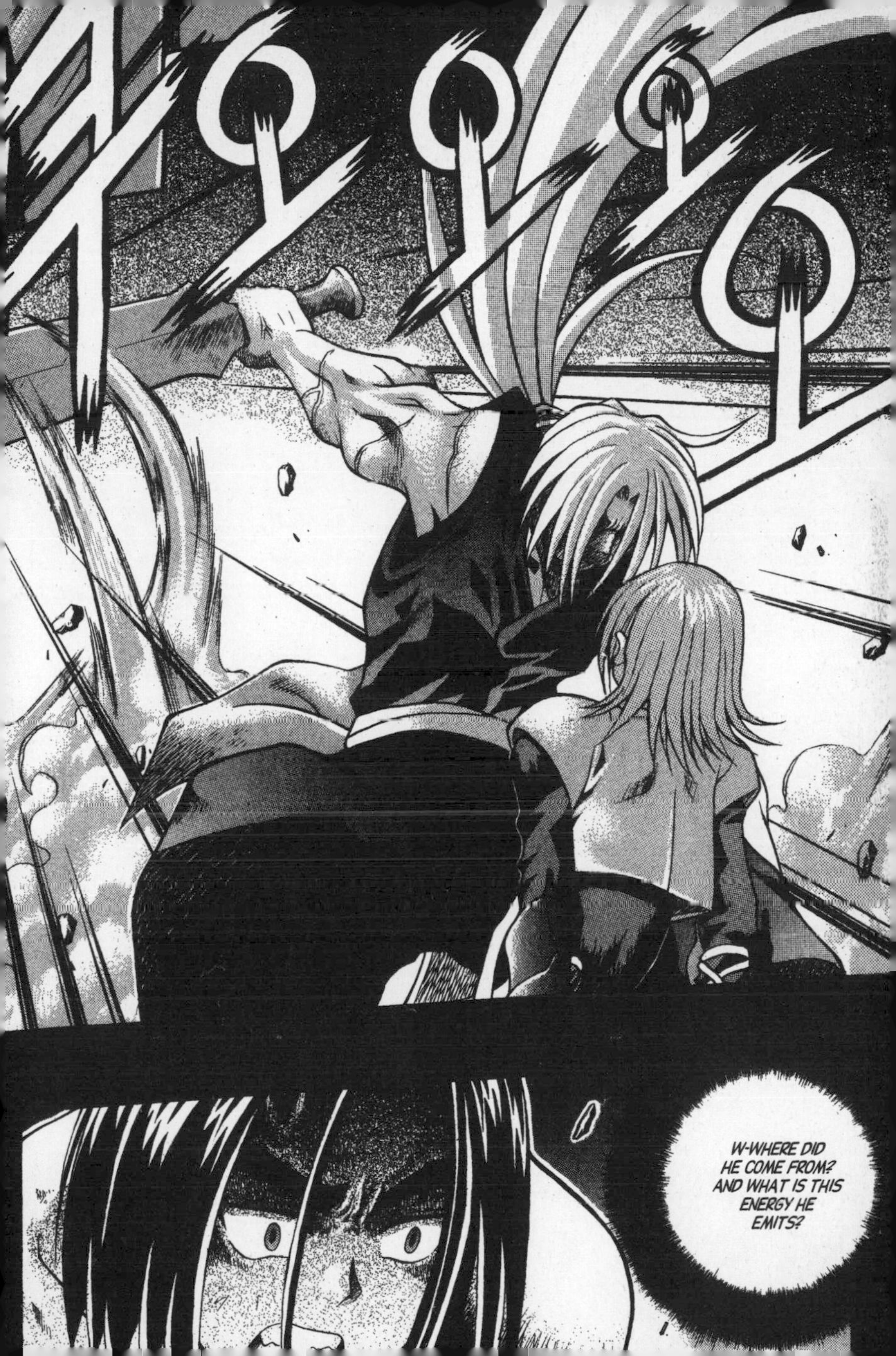
W-WHERE DID HE COME FROM? AND WHAT IS THIS ENERGY HE EMITS?

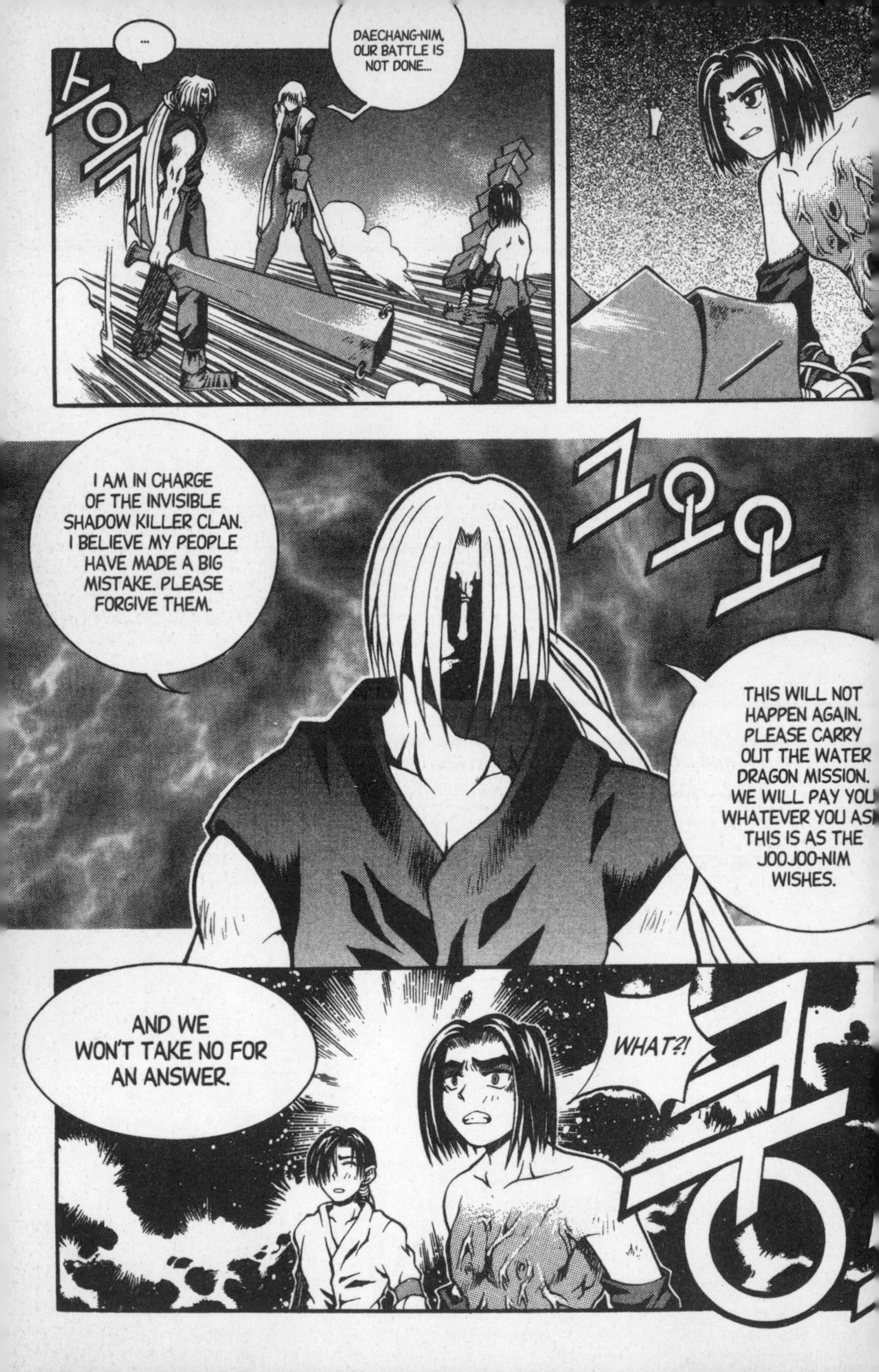
...
DAECHANG-NIM, OUR BATTLE IS NOT DONE...
I AM IN CHARGE OF THE INVISIBLE SHADOW KILLER CLAN. I BELIEVE MY PEOPLE HAVE MADE A BIG MISTAKE. PLEASE FORGIVE THEM.
THIS WILL NOT HAPPEN AGAIN. PLEASE CARRY OUT THE WATER DRAGON MISSION. WE WILL PAY YOU WHATEVER YOU AS[K] THIS IS AS THE JOOJOO-NIM WISHES.
AND WE WON'T TAKE NO FOR AN ANSWER.
WHAT?!

CHAPTER 4

SIGNS OF UNHAPPINESS

PART 1

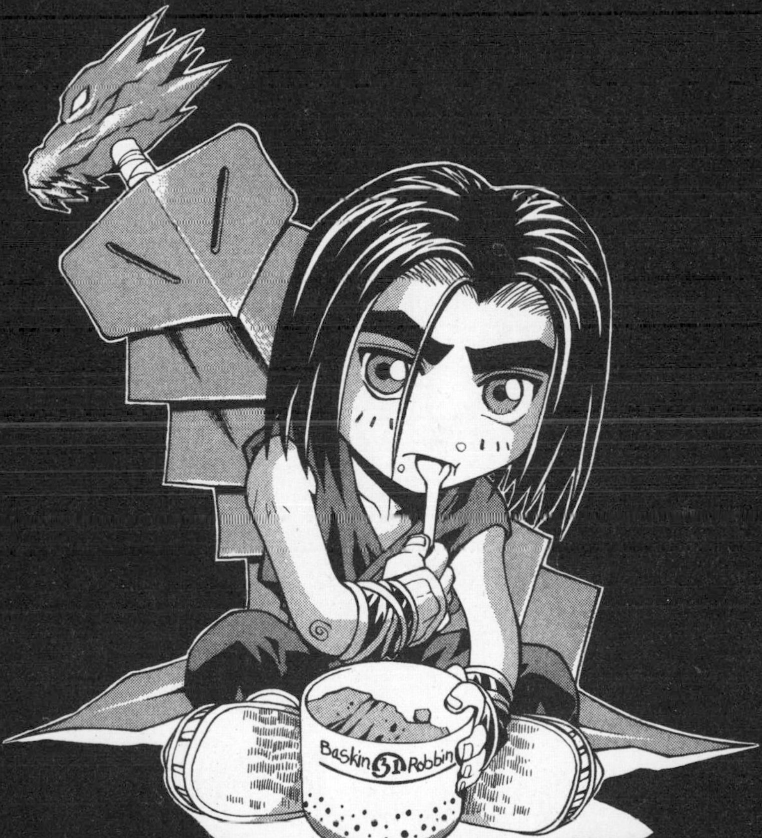
Baskin 31 Robbin

SO, WHY DID YOU GIVE UP SO EASILY? THAT WASN'T LIKE YOU...

OR MAYBE BEING PAID WHATEVER YOU ASKED WAS AN OFFER YOU COULDN'T REFUSE?

...AND YOU DIDN'T EVEN FINISH YOUR FIGHT WITH RU-AHN...

멈칫!!

...

I ONLY USED 80 PERCENT OF MY POWER FOR THAT LAST STRIKE. THAT'S ENOUGH TO SERIOUSLY INJURE A DRAGON, BUT...

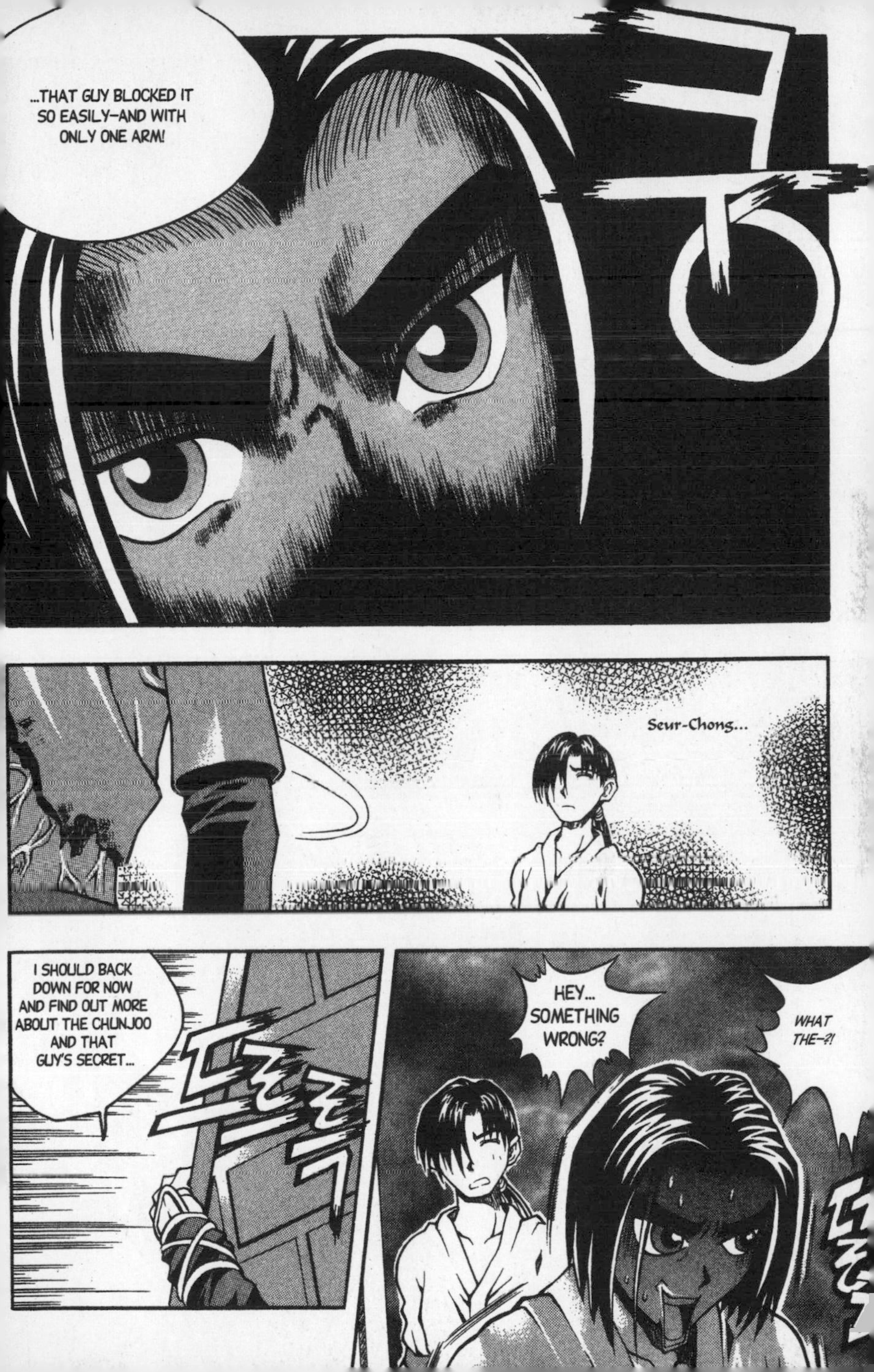
...THAT GUY BLOCKED IT SO EASILY—AND WITH ONLY ONE ARM!
Seur-Chong...
I SHOULD BACK DOWN FOR NOW AND FIND OUT MORE ABOUT THE CHUNJOO AND THAT GUY'S SECRET...
HEY... SOMETHING WRONG?
WHAT THE-?!

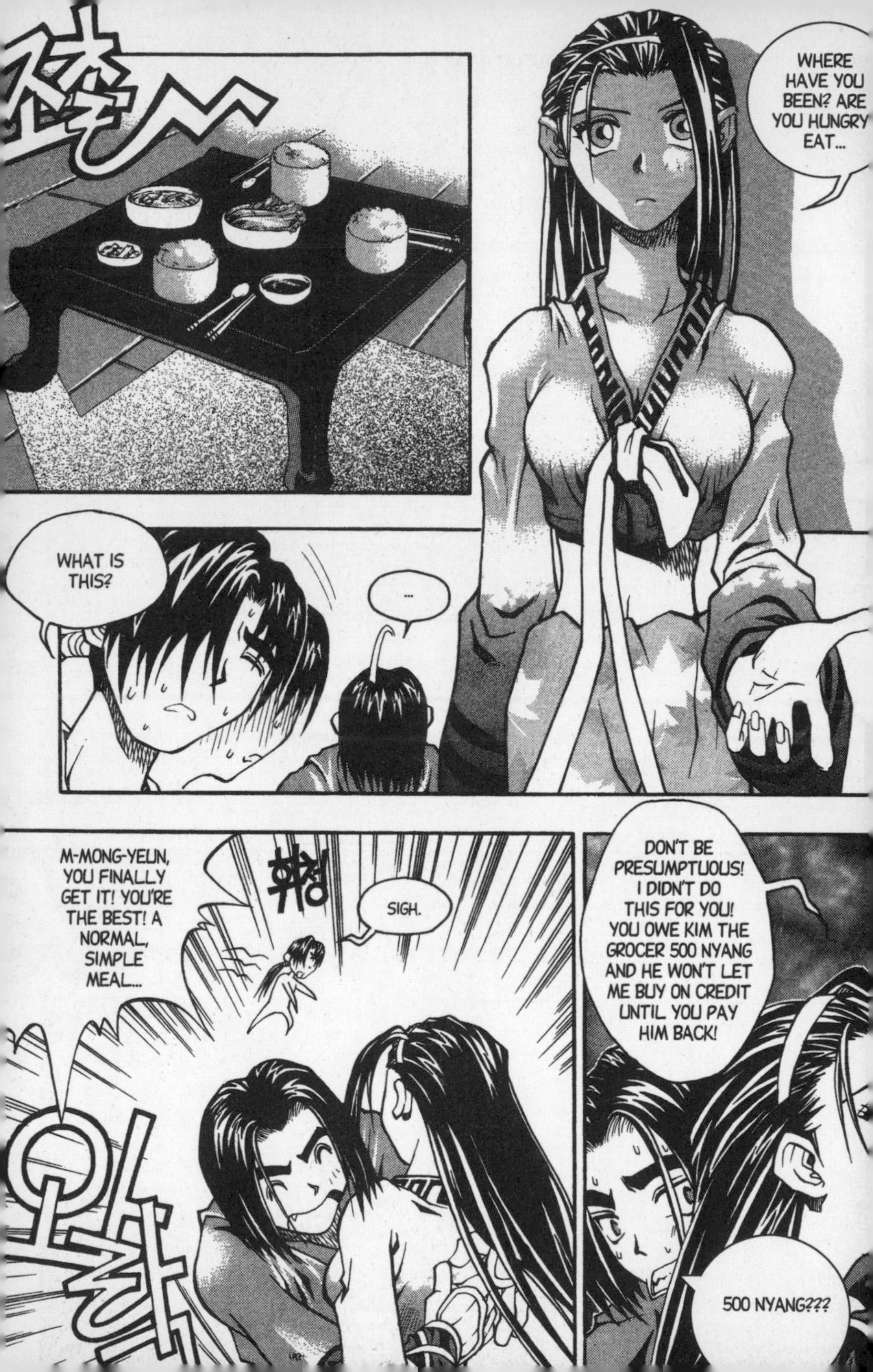
WHAT IS THIS?
...
WHERE HAVE YOU BEEN? ARE YOU HUNGRY EAT...
M-MONG-YEUN, YOU FINALLY GET IT! YOU'RE THE BEST! A NORMAL, SIMPLE MEAL...
SIGH.
DON'T BE PRESUMPTUOUS! I DIDN'T DO THIS FOR YOU! YOU OWE KIM THE GROCER 500 NYANG AND HE WON'T LET ME BUY ON CREDIT UNTIL YOU PAY HIM BACK!
500 NYANG???

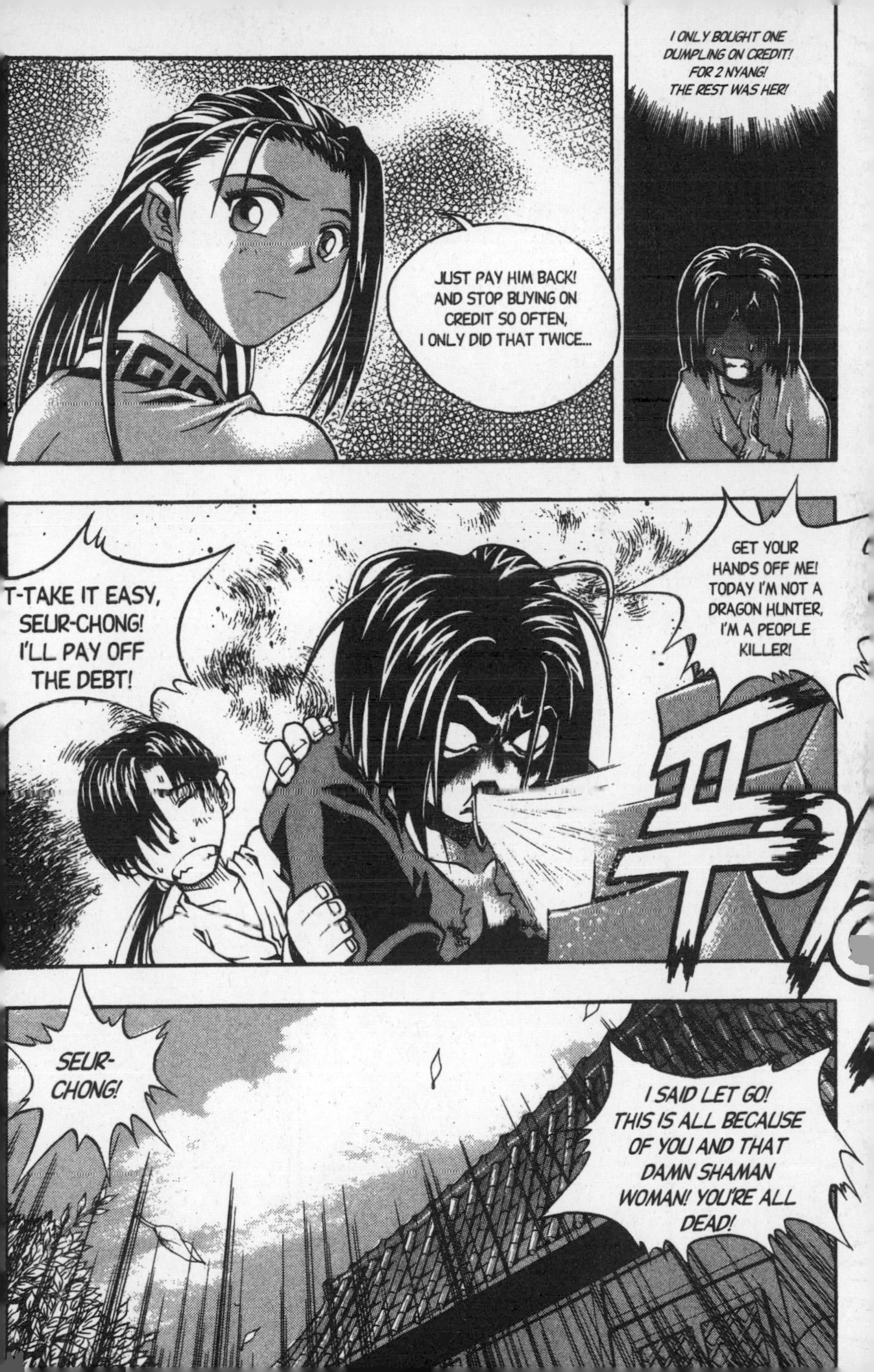
JUST PAY HIM BACK! AND STOP BUYING ON CREDIT SO OFTEN, I ONLY DID THAT TWICE...
I ONLY BOUGHT ONE DUMPLING ON CREDIT! FOR 2 NYANG! THE REST WAS HER!
T-TAKE IT EASY, SEUR-CHONG! I'LL PAY OFF THE DEBT!
GET YOUR HANDS OFF ME! TODAY I'M NOT A DRAGON HUNTER, I'M A PEOPLE KILLER!
SEUR-CHONG!
I SAID LET GO! THIS IS ALL BECAUSE OF YOU AND THAT DAMN SHAMAN WOMAN! YOU'RE ALL DEAD!

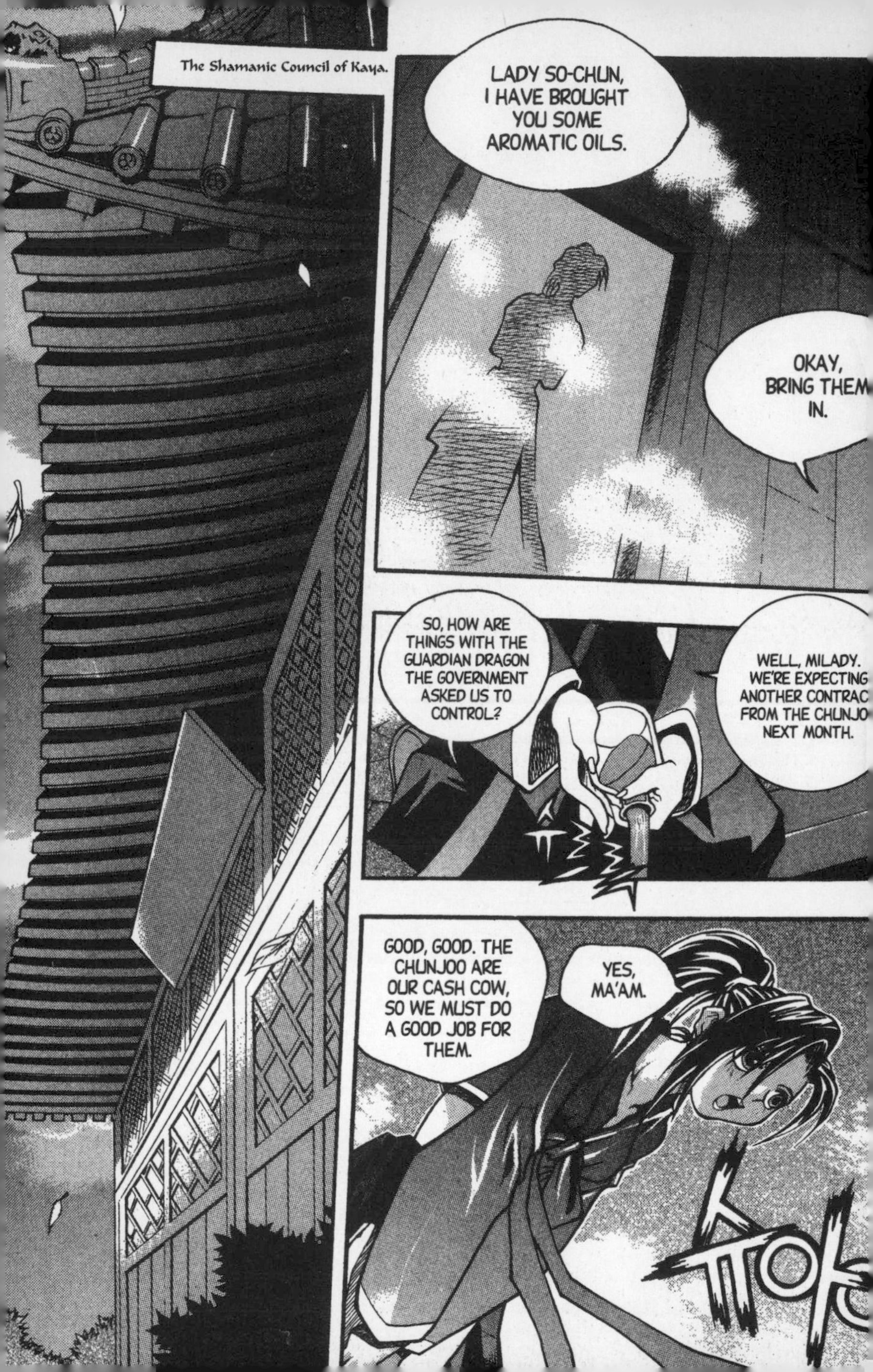

The Shamanic Council of Kaya.
LADY SO-CHUN, I HAVE BROUGHT YOU SOME AROMATIC OILS.
OKAY, BRING THEM IN.
SO, HOW ARE THINGS WITH THE GUARDIAN DRAGON THE GOVERNMENT ASKED US TO CONTROL?
WELL, MILADY. WE'RE EXPECTING ANOTHER CONTRAC FROM THE CHUNJO NEXT MONTH.
GOOD, GOOD. THE CHUNJOO ARE OUR CASH COW, SO WE MUST DO A GOOD JOB FOR THEM.
YES, MA'AM.
TTOK

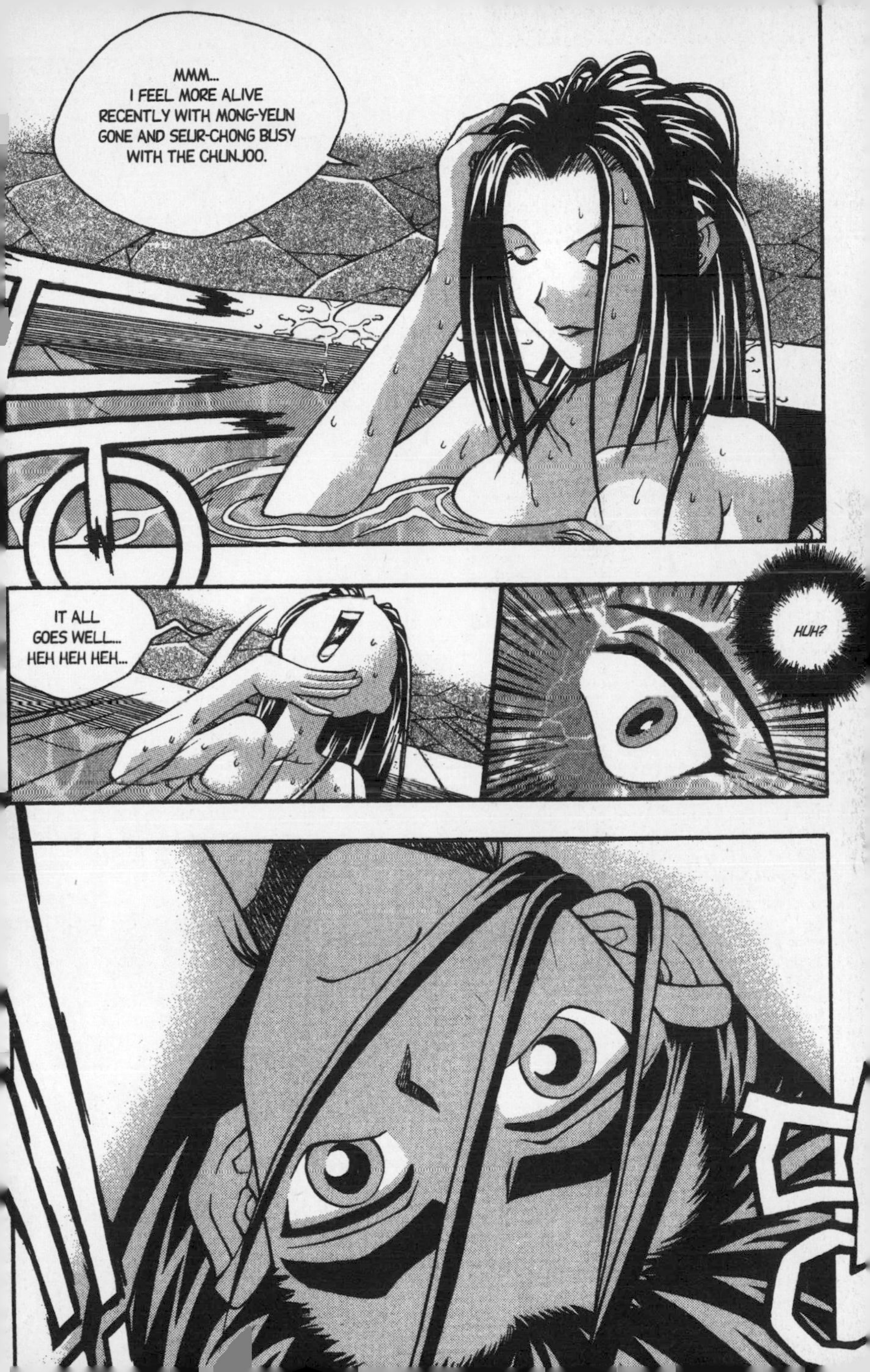
MMM... I FEEL MORE ALIVE RECENTLY WITH MONG-YEUN GONE AND SEUR-CHONG BUSY WITH THE CHUNJOO.
IT ALL GOES WELL... HEH HEH HEH...
HUH?

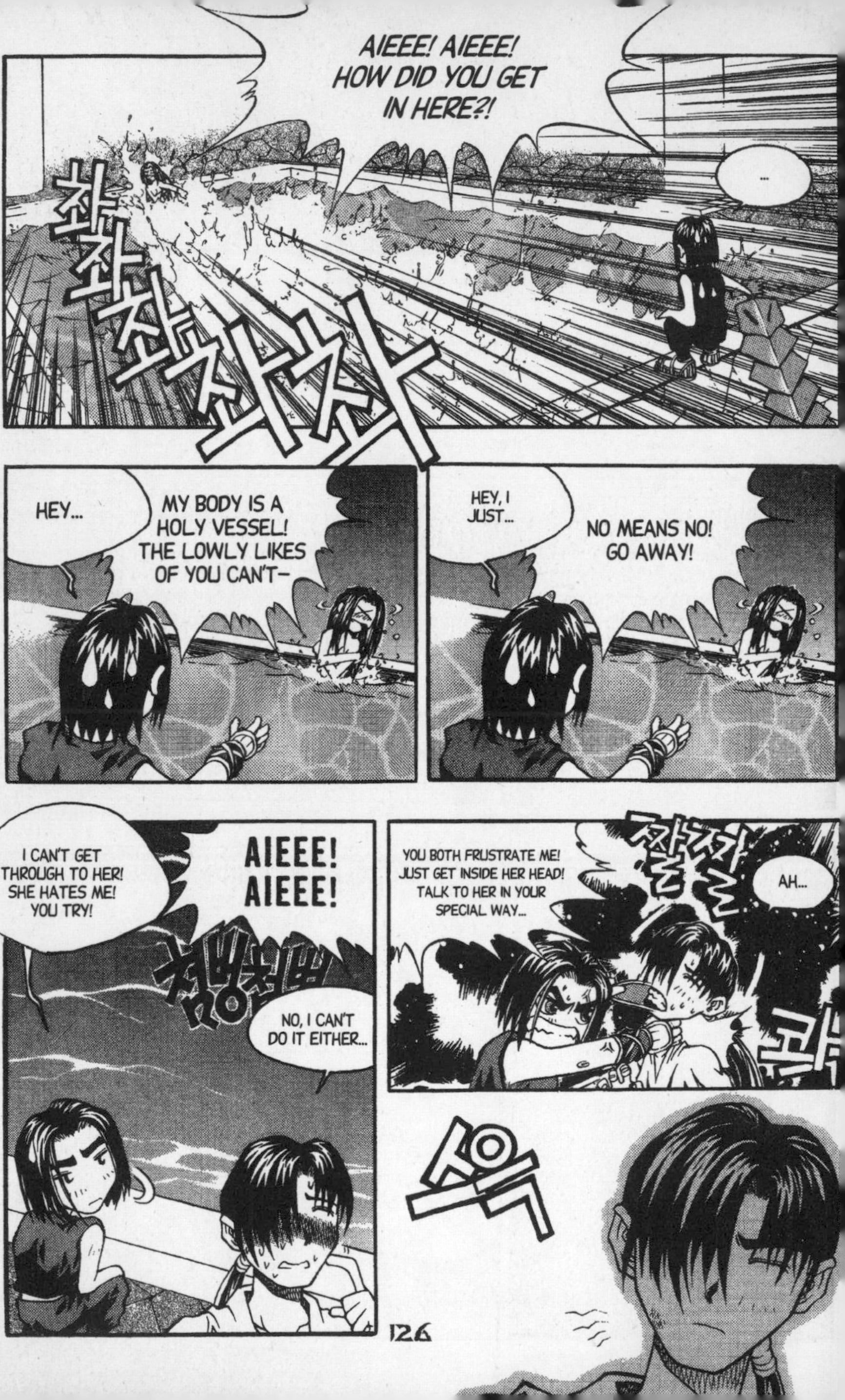
AIEEE! AIEEE! HOW DID YOU GET IN HERE?!
...
HEY...
MY BODY IS A HOLY VESSEL! THE LOWLY LIKES OF YOU CAN'T–
HEY, I JUST...
NO MEANS NO! GO AWAY!
I CAN'T GET THROUGH TO HER! SHE HATES ME! YOU TRY!
AIEEE! AIEEE!
NO, I CAN'T DO IT EITHER...
YOU BOTH FRUSTRATE ME! JUST GET INSIDE HER HEAD! TALK TO HER IN YOUR SPECIAL WAY...
AH...

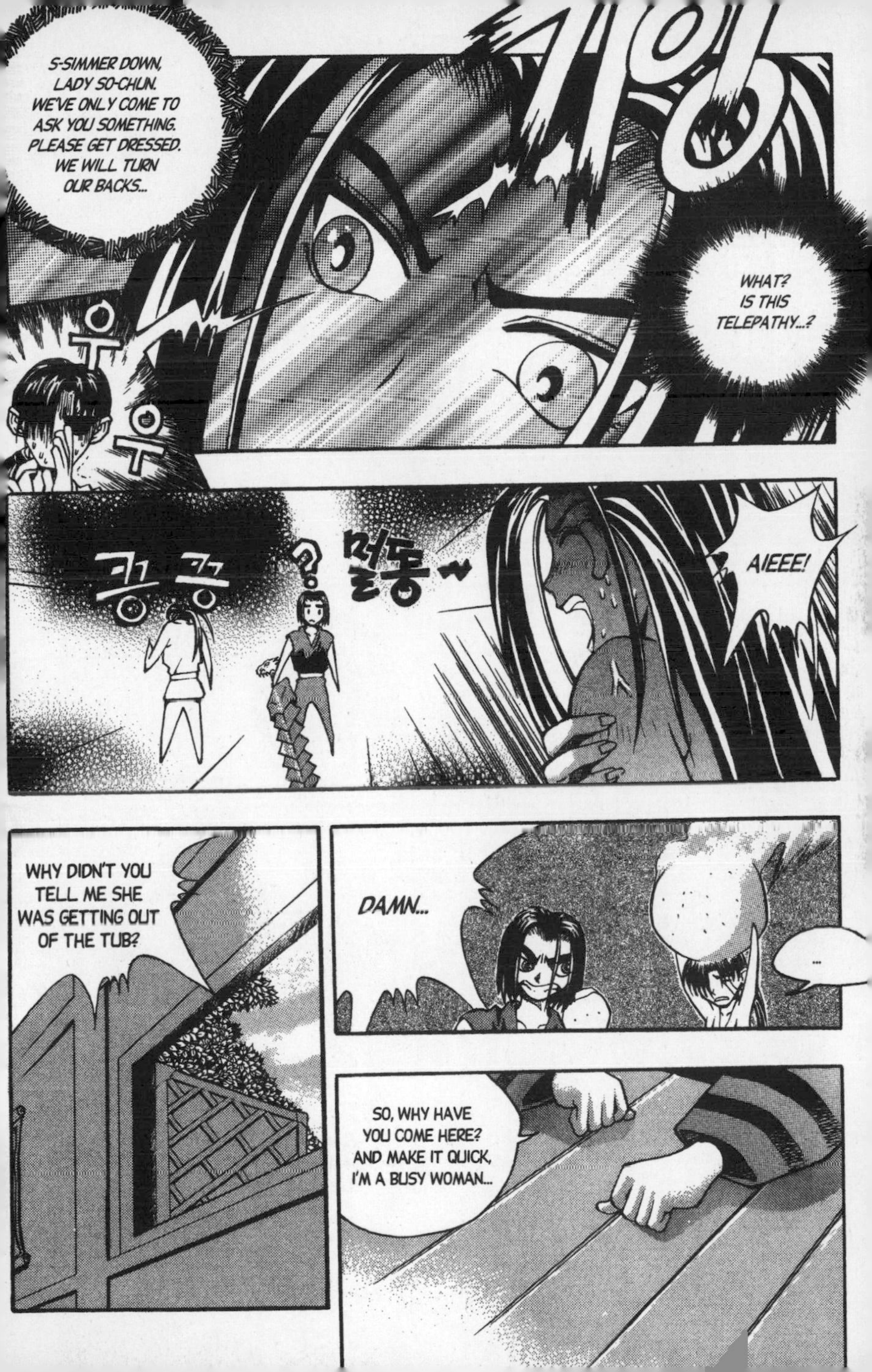
S-SIMMER DOWN, LADY SO-CHUN. WE'VE ONLY COME TO ASK YOU SOMETHING. PLEASE GET DRESSED. WE WILL TURN OUR BACKS...
WHAT? IS THIS TELEPATHY...?
쿵 쿵
?
AIEEE!
WHY DIDN'T YOU TELL ME SHE WAS GETTING OUT OF THE TUB?
DAMN...
...
SO, WHY HAVE YOU COME HERE? AND MAKE IT QUICK, I'M A BUSY WOMAN...

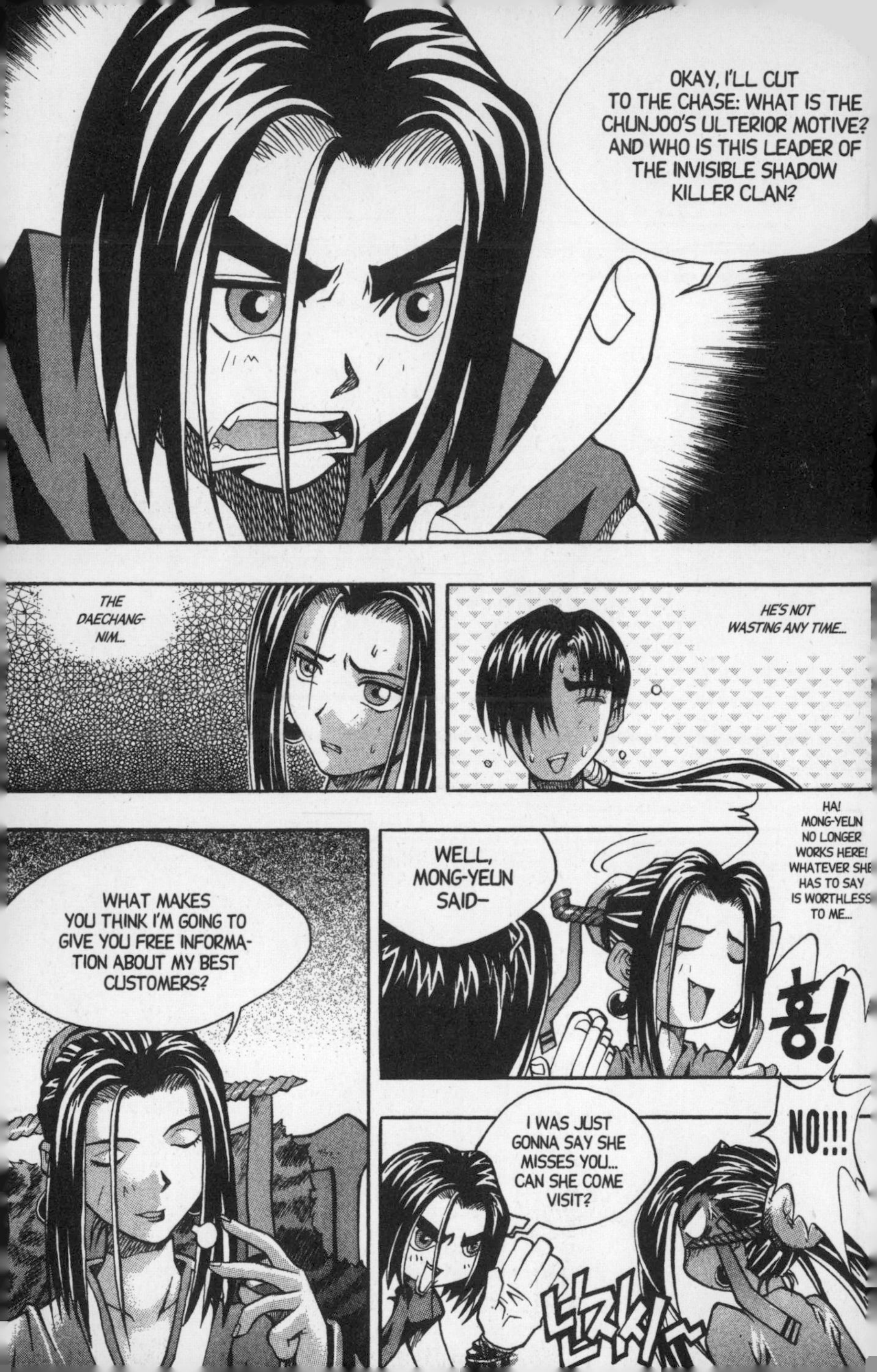
OKAY, I'LL CUT TO THE CHASE: WHAT IS THE CHUNJOO'S ULTERIOR MOTIVE? AND WHO IS THIS LEADER OF THE INVISIBLE SHADOW KILLER CLAN?
THE DAECHANG-NIM...
HE'S NOT WASTING ANY TIME...
WHAT MAKES YOU THINK I'M GOING TO GIVE YOU FREE INFORMATION ABOUT MY BEST CUSTOMERS?
WELL, MONG-YEUN SAID-
HA! MONG-YEUN NO LONGER WORKS HERE! WHATEVER SHE HAS TO SAY IS WORTHLESS TO ME...
흥!
I WAS JUST GONNA SAY SHE MISSES YOU... CAN SHE COME VISIT?
NO!!!

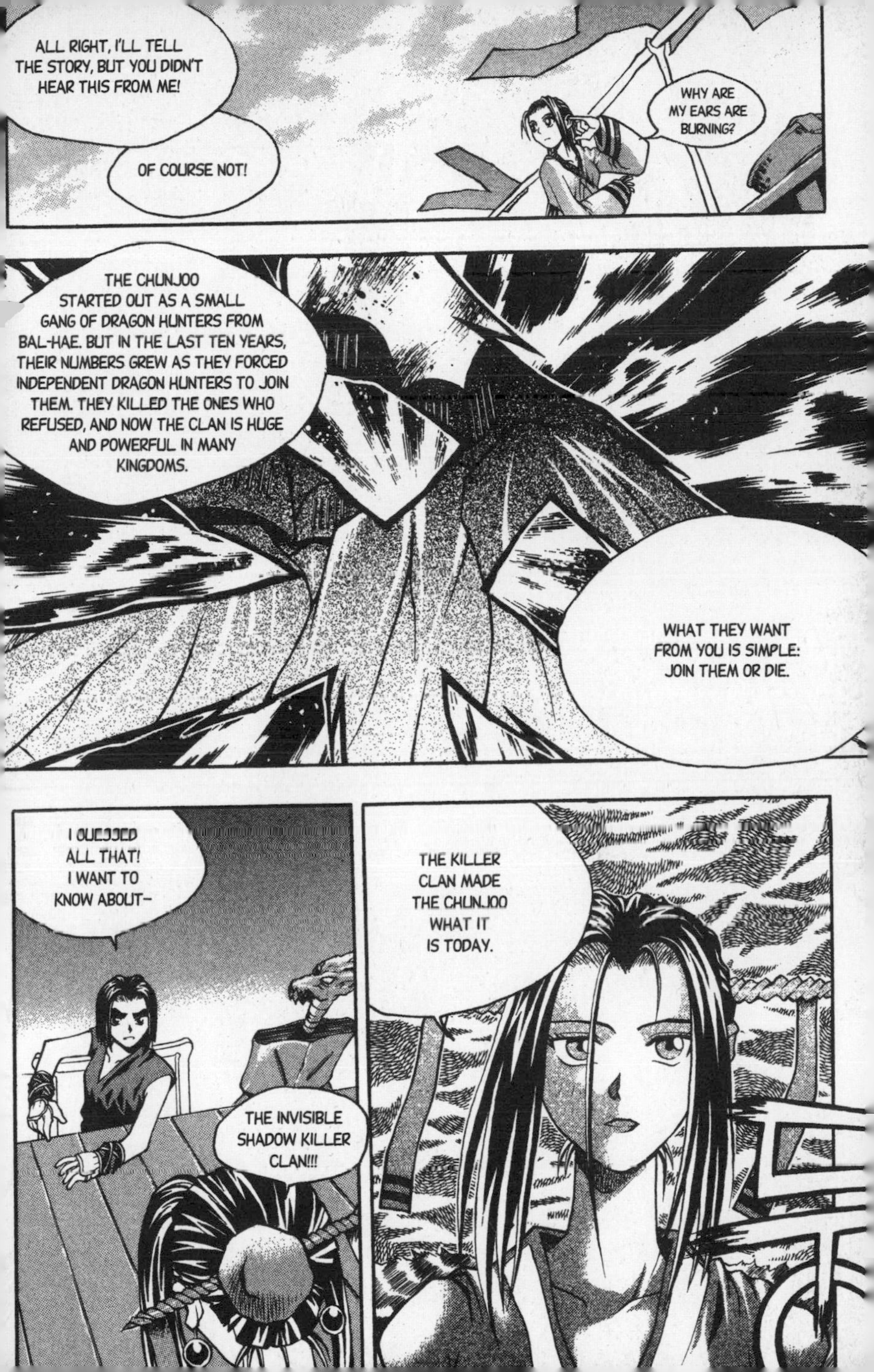
ALL RIGHT, I'LL TELL THE STORY, BUT YOU DIDN'T HEAR THIS FROM ME!
OF COURSE NOT!
WHY ARE MY EARS ARE BURNING?
THE CHUNJOO STARTED OUT AS A SMALL GANG OF DRAGON HUNTERS FROM BAL-HAE. BUT IN THE LAST TEN YEARS, THEIR NUMBERS GREW AS THEY FORCED INDEPENDENT DRAGON HUNTERS TO JOIN THEM. THEY KILLED THE ONES WHO REFUSED, AND NOW THE CLAN IS HUGE AND POWERFUL IN MANY KINGDOMS.
WHAT THEY WANT FROM YOU IS SIMPLE: JOIN THEM OR DIE.
I GUESSED ALL THAT! I WANT TO KNOW ABOUT-
THE INVISIBLE SHADOW KILLER CLAN!!!
THE KILLER CLAN MADE THE CHUNJOO WHAT IT IS TODAY.

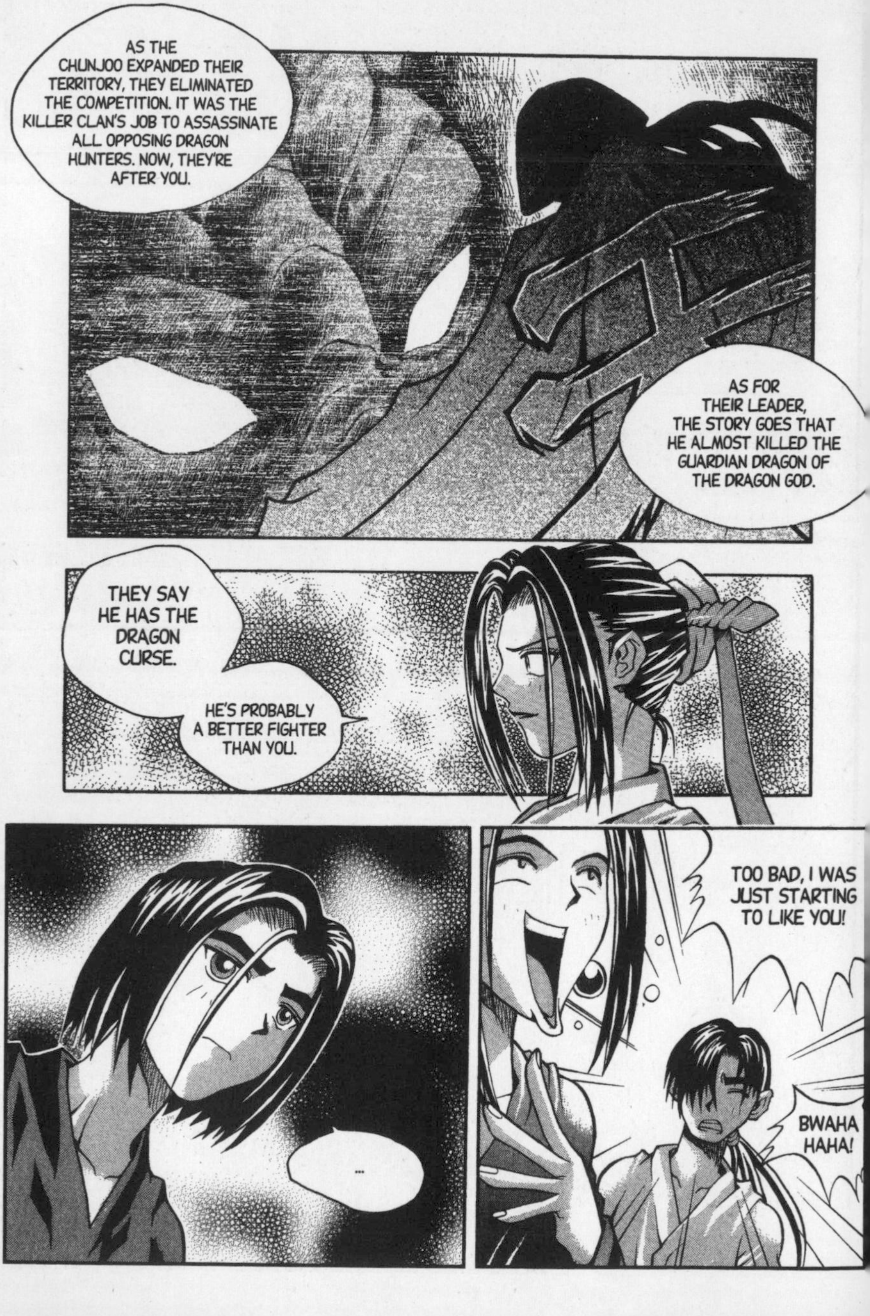
AS THE CHUNJOO EXPANDED THEIR TERRITORY, THEY ELIMINATED THE COMPETITION. IT WAS THE KILLER CLAN'S JOB TO ASSASSINATE ALL OPPOSING DRAGON HUNTERS. NOW, THEY'RE AFTER YOU.
AS FOR THEIR LEADER, THE STORY GOES THAT HE ALMOST KILLED THE GUARDIAN DRAGON OF THE DRAGON GOD.
THEY SAY HE HAS THE DRAGON CURSE.
HE'S PROBABLY A BETTER FIGHTER THAN YOU.
...
TOO BAD, I WAS JUST STARTING TO LIKE YOU!
BWAHA HAHA!

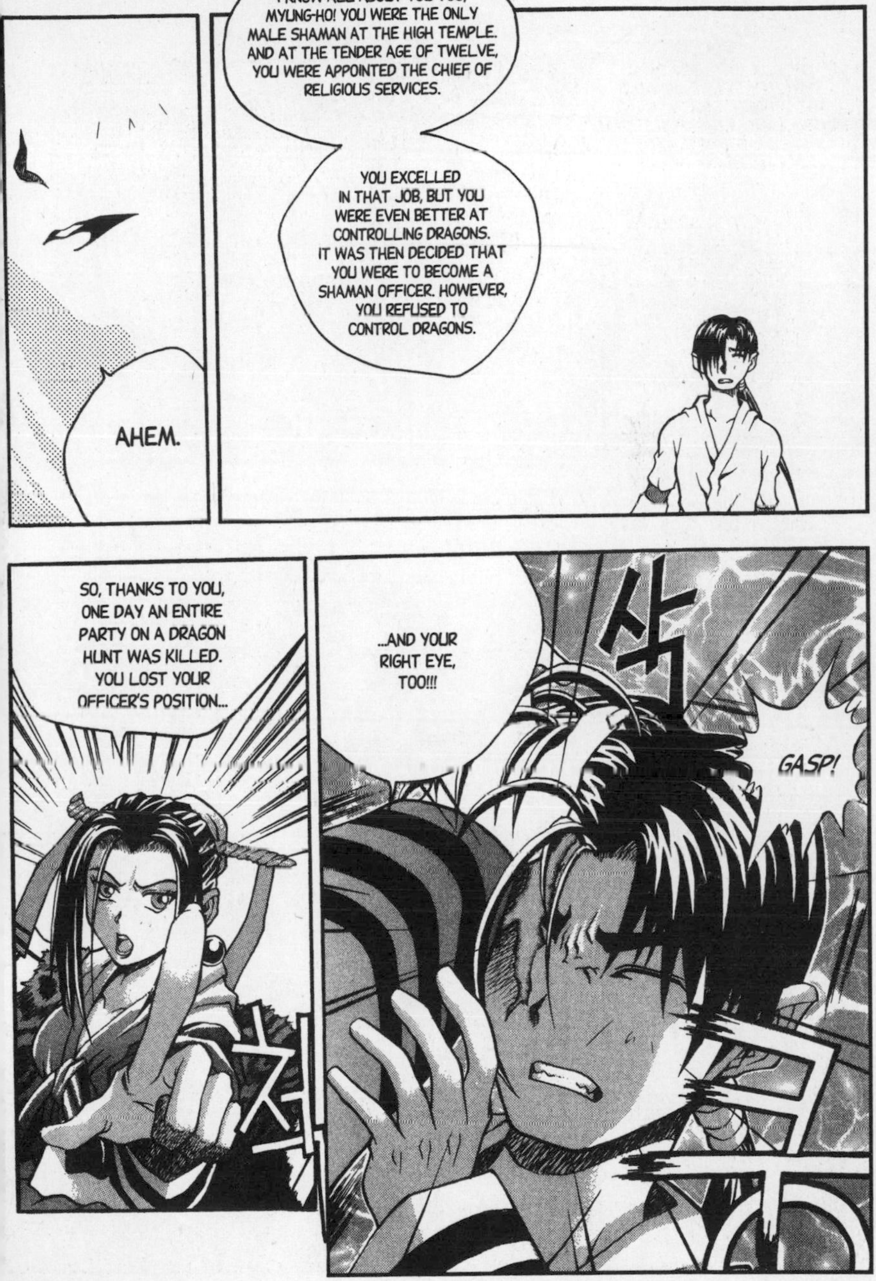
I KNOW ALL ABOUT YOU TOO, MYUNG-HO! YOU WERE THE ONLY MALE SHAMAN AT THE HIGH TEMPLE. AND AT THE TENDER AGE OF TWELVE, YOU WERE APPOINTED THE CHIEF OF RELIGIOUS SERVICES.
AHEM.
YOU EXCELLED IN THAT JOB, BUT YOU WERE EVEN BETTER AT CONTROLLING DRAGONS. IT WAS THEN DECIDED THAT YOU WERE TO BECOME A SHAMAN OFFICER. HOWEVER, YOU REFUSED TO CONTROL DRAGONS.
SO, THANKS TO YOU, ONE DAY AN ENTIRE PARTY ON A DRAGON HUNT WAS KILLED. YOU LOST YOUR OFFICER'S POSITION...
...AND YOUR RIGHT EYE, TOO!!!
GASP!

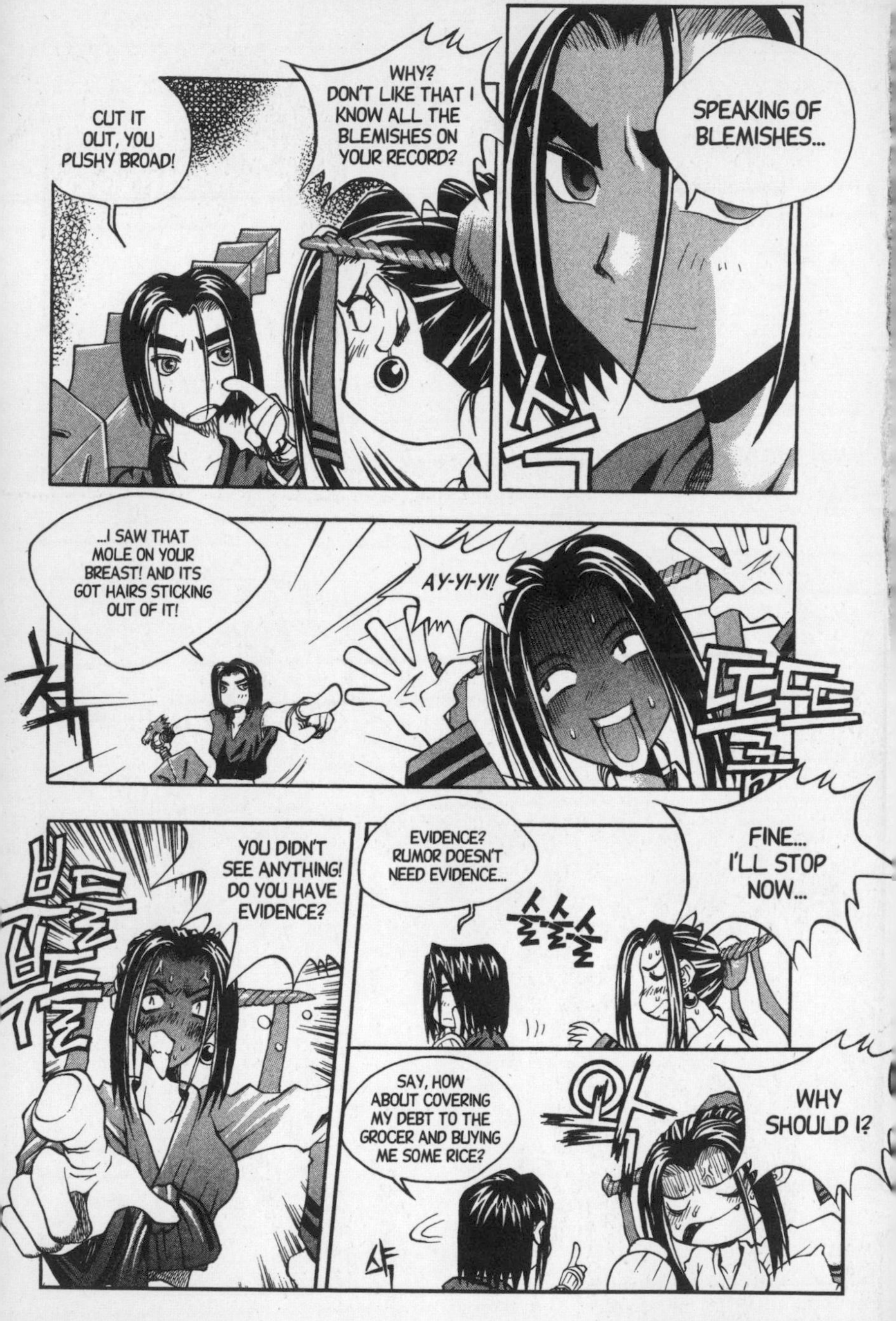
CUT IT OUT, YOU PUSHY BROAD!
WHY? DON'T LIKE THAT I KNOW ALL THE BLEMISHES ON YOUR RECORD?
SPEAKING OF BLEMISHES...
...I SAW THAT MOLE ON YOUR BREAST! AND ITS GOT HAIRS STICKING OUT OF IT!
AY-YI-YI!
YOU DIDN'T SEE ANYTHING! DO YOU HAVE EVIDENCE?
EVIDENCE? RUMOR DOESN'T NEED EVIDENCE...
FINE... I'LL STOP NOW...
SAY, HOW ABOUT COVERING MY DEBT TO THE GROCER AND BUYING ME SOME RICE?
WHY SHOULD I?

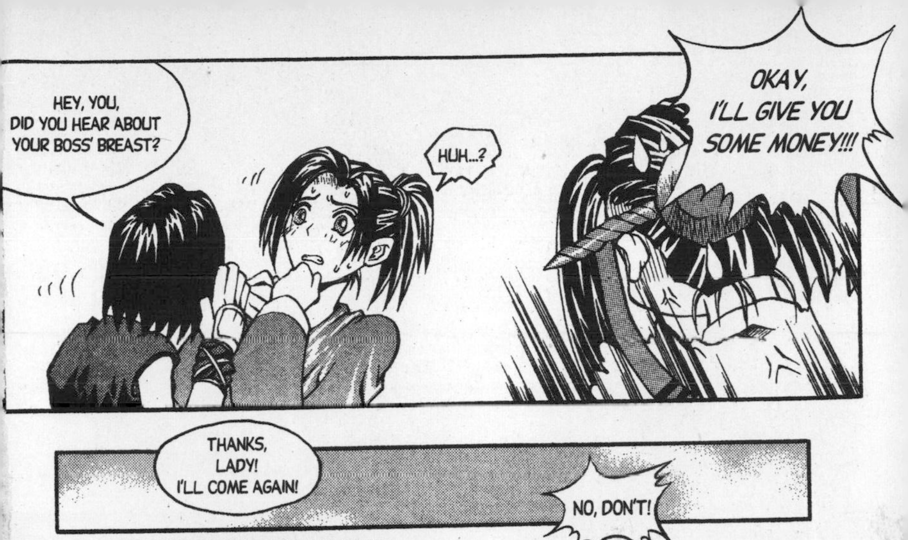
HEY, YOU,
DID YOU HEAR ABOUT
YOUR BOSS' BREAST?
HUH...?
OKAY,
I'LL GIVE YOU
SOME MONEY!!!
THANKS,
LADY!
I'LL COME AGAIN!
NO, DON'T!

NOTE: IT IS AN OLD KOREAN SUPERSTITION THAT SPREADING SALT ON THE DOORSTEP WILL KEEP A RUDE GUEST OR BAD PERSON FROM RETURNING TO YOUR HOME.

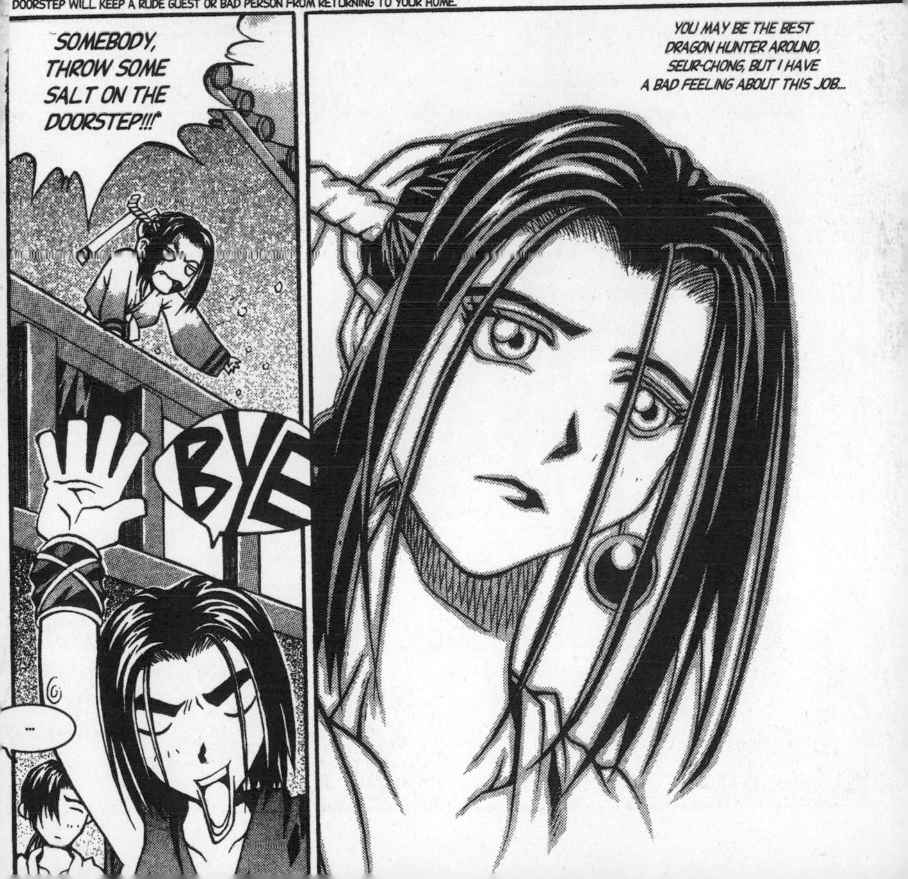
"SOMEBODY,
THROW SOME
SALT ON THE
DOORSTEP!!!"*
BYE
...
YOU MAY BE THE BEST
DRAGON HUNTER AROUND,
SEUR-CHONG, BUT I HAVE
A BAD FEELING ABOUT THIS JOB...

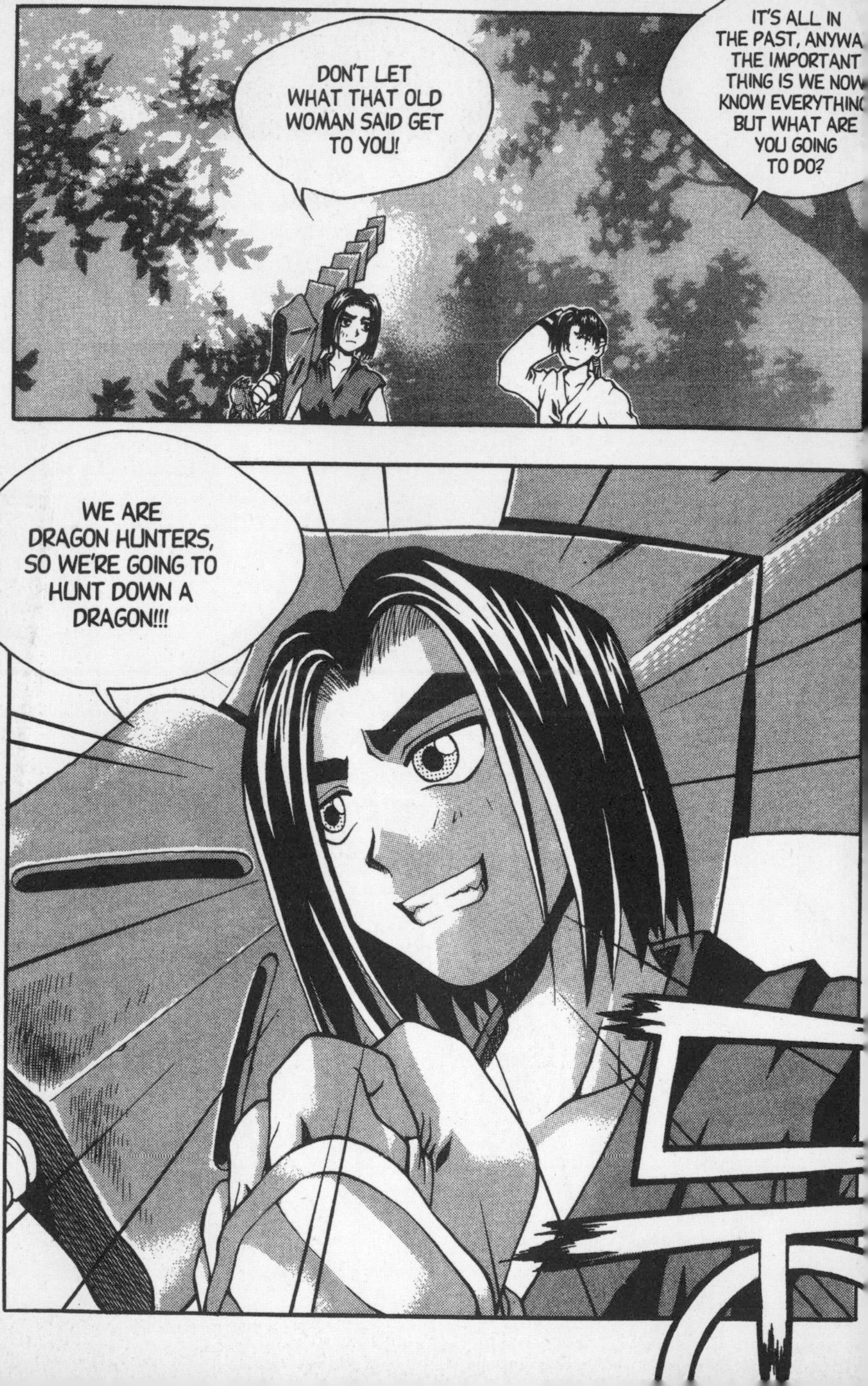
DON'T LET WHAT THAT OLD WOMAN SAID GET TO YOU!
IT'S ALL IN THE PAST, ANYWA THE IMPORTANT THING IS WE NOW KNOW EVERYTHIN BUT WHAT ARE YOU GOING TO DO?
WE ARE DRAGON HUNTERS, SO WE'RE GOING TO HUNT DOWN A DRAGON!!!

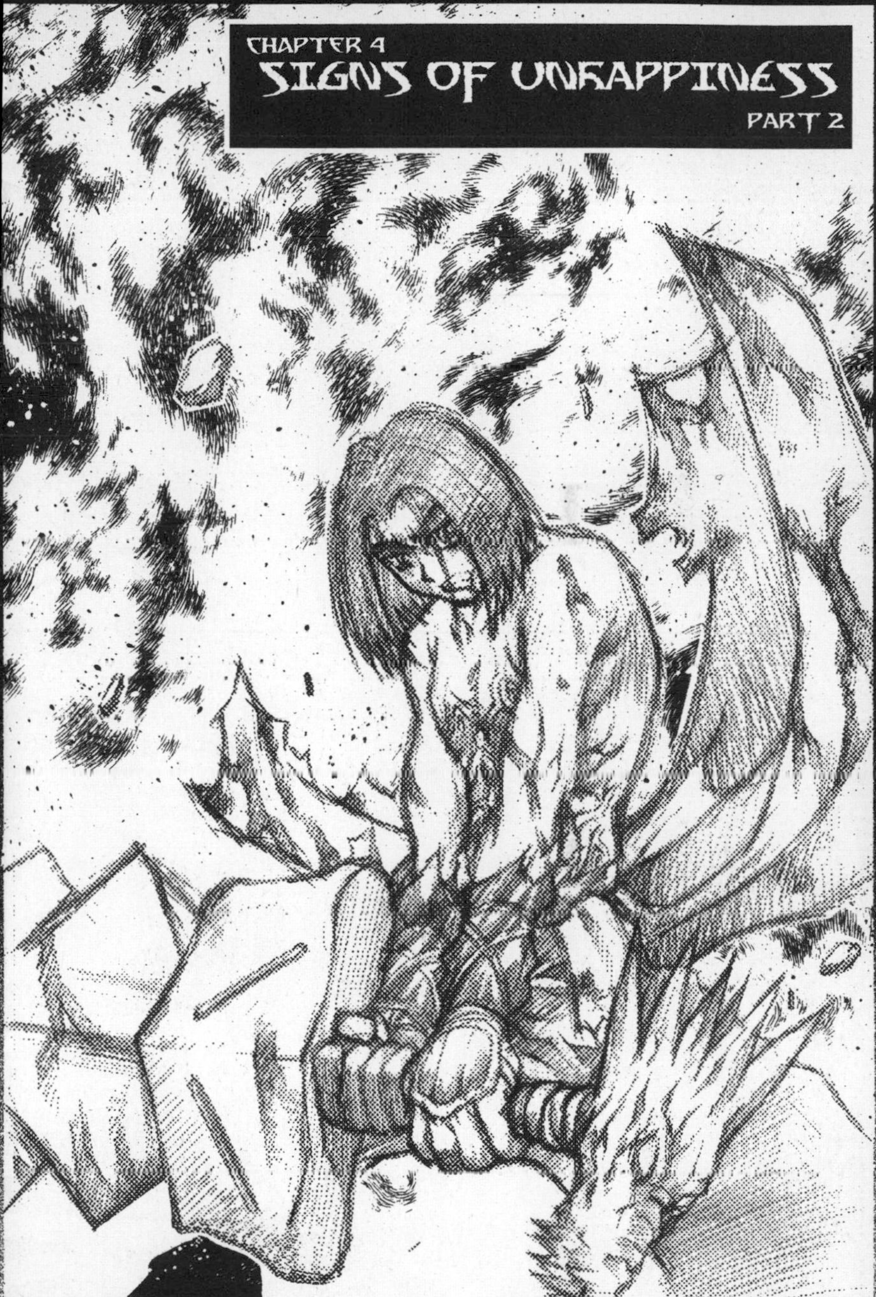
CHAPTER 4
SIGNS OF UNHAPPINESS
PART 2

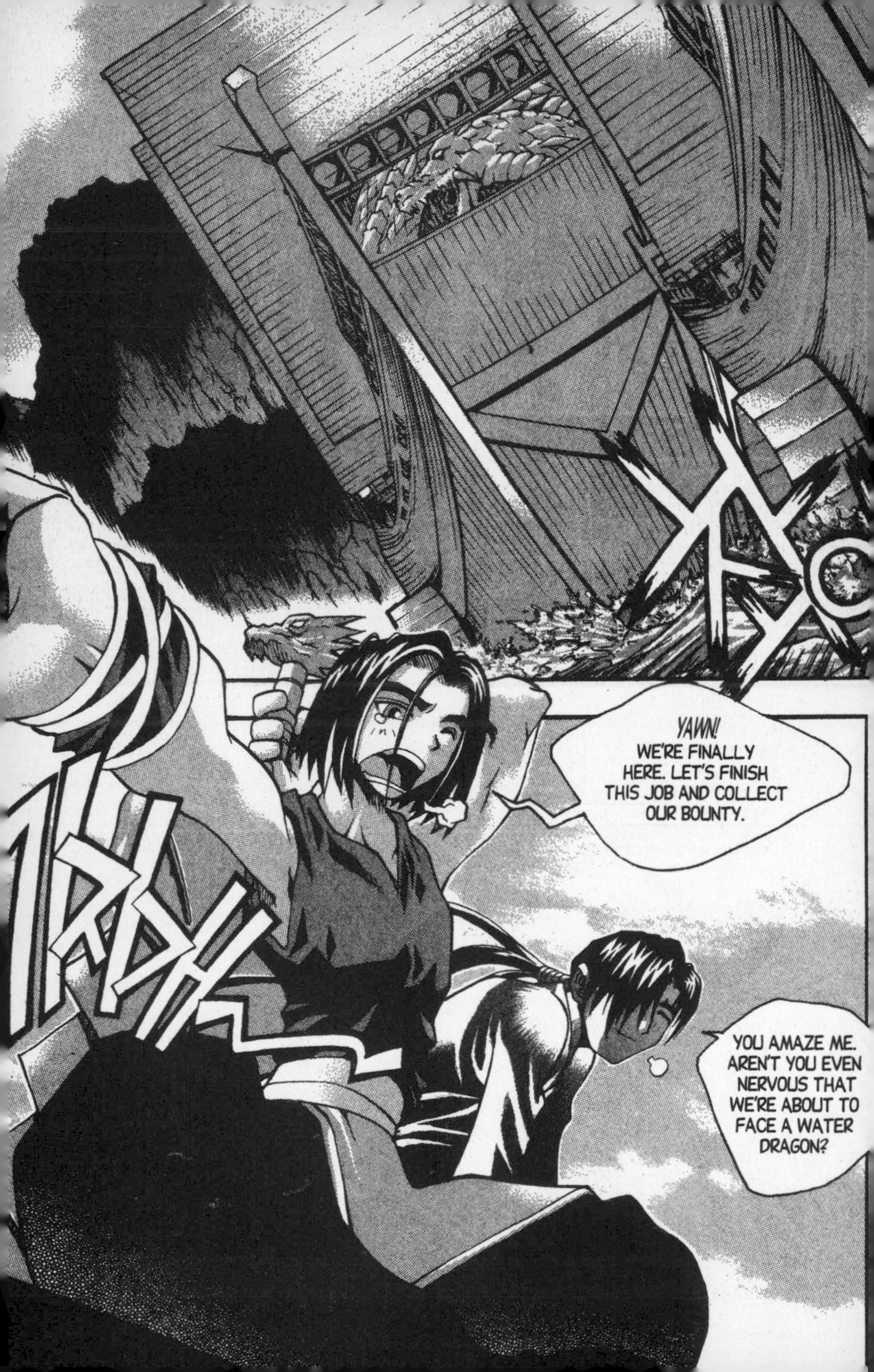
YAWN! WE'RE FINALLY HERE. LET'S FINISH THIS JOB AND COLLECT OUR BOUNTY.
YOU AMAZE ME. AREN'T YOU EVEN NERVOUS THAT WE'RE ABOUT TO FACE A WATER DRAGON?

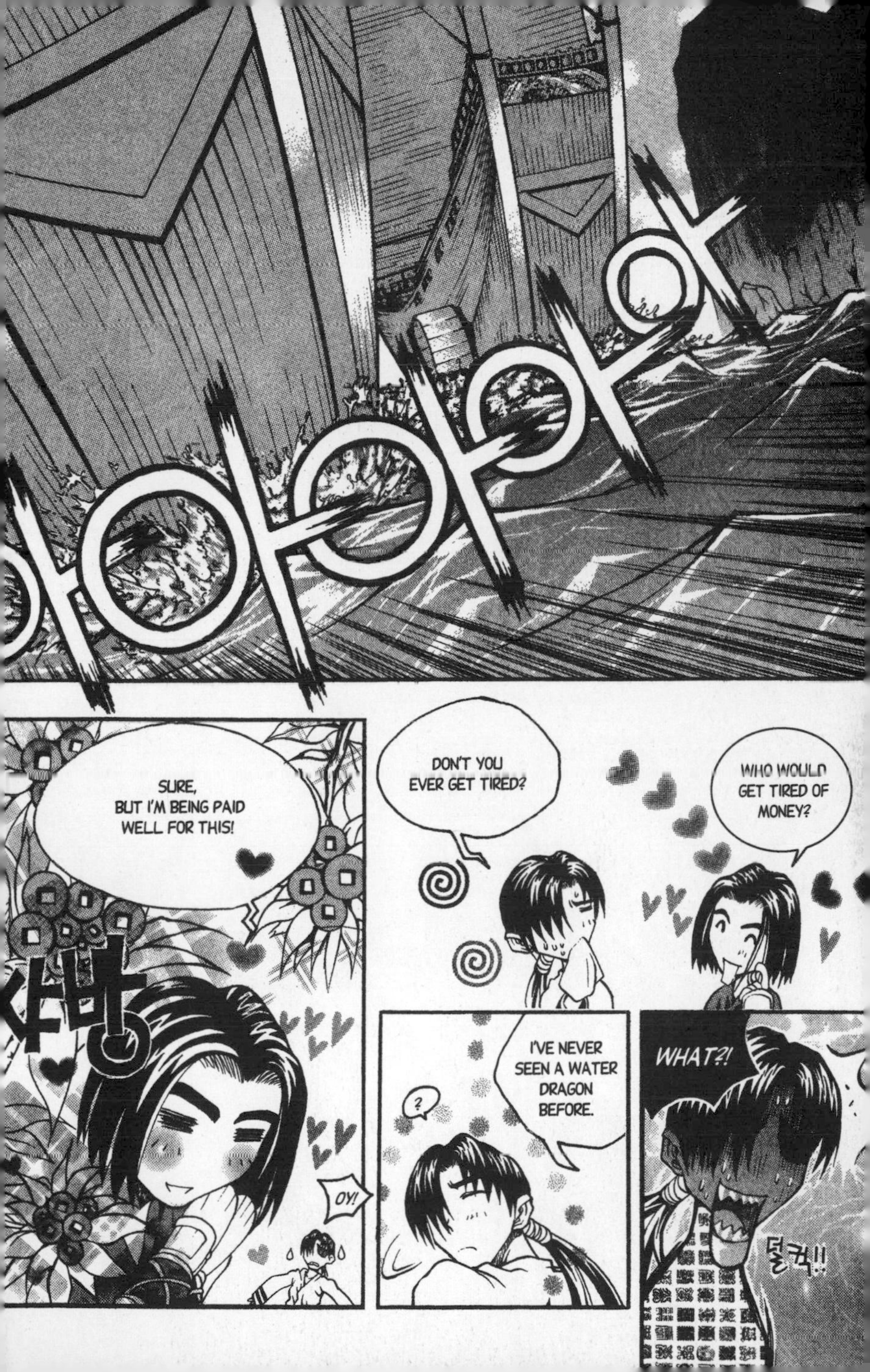
SURE, BUT I'M BEING PAID WELL FOR THIS!
OY!
DON'T YOU EVER GET TIRED?
WHO WOULD GET TIRED OF MONEY?
?
I'VE NEVER SEEN A WATER DRAGON BEFORE.
WHAT?!
덜컥!!

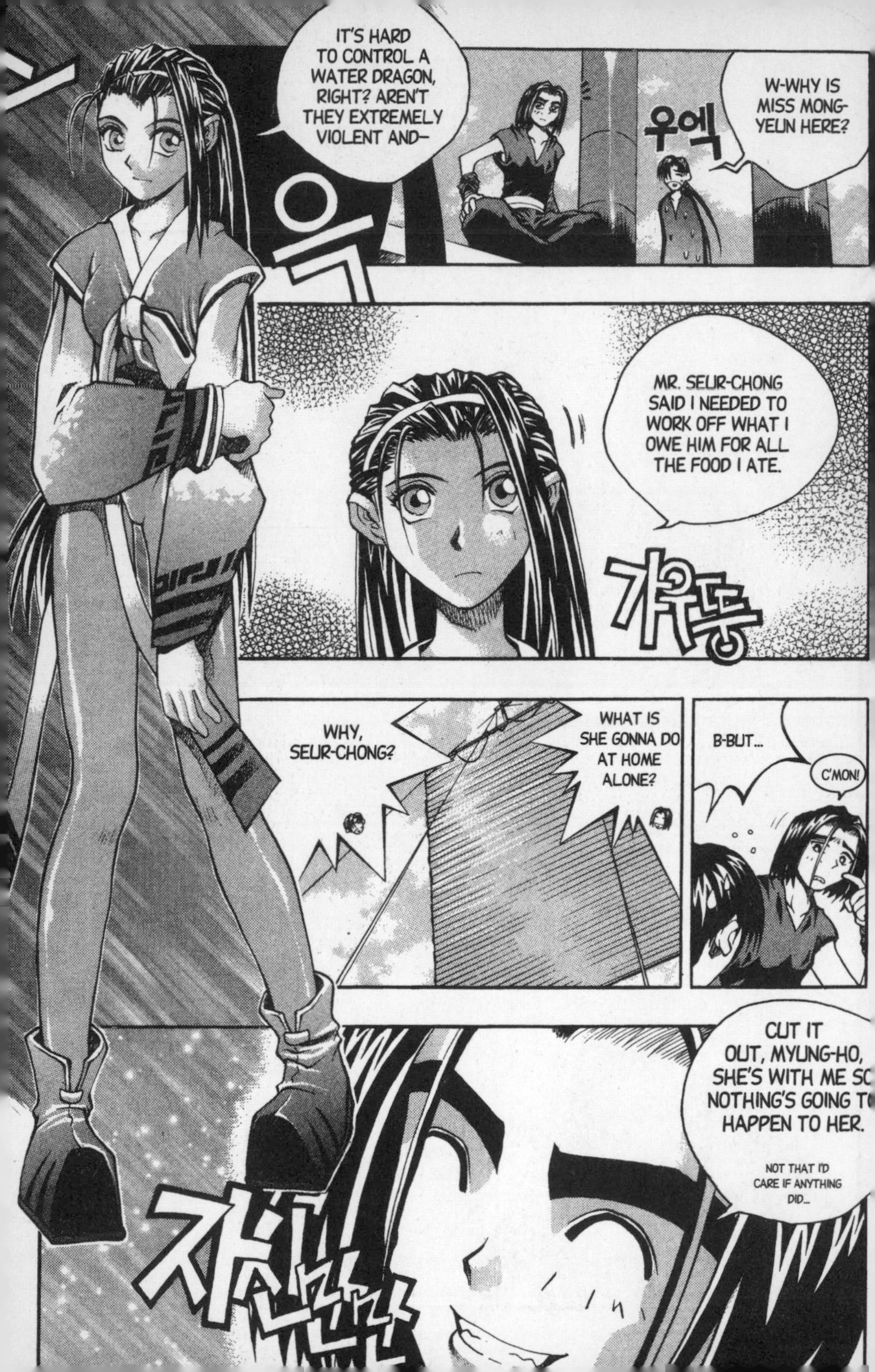
IT'S HARD TO CONTROL A WATER DRAGON, RIGHT? AREN'T THEY EXTREMELY VIOLENT AND–
우엑
W-WHY IS MISS MONG-YEUN HERE?
MR. SEUR-CHONG SAID I NEEDED TO WORK OFF WHAT I OWE HIM FOR ALL THE FOOD I ATE.
WHY, SEUR-CHONG?
WHAT IS SHE GONNA DO AT HOME ALONE?
B-BUT...
C'MON!
CUT IT OUT, MYUNG-HO, SHE'S WITH ME SO NOTHING'S GOING TO HAPPEN TO HER.
NOT THAT I'D CARE IF ANYTHING DID...

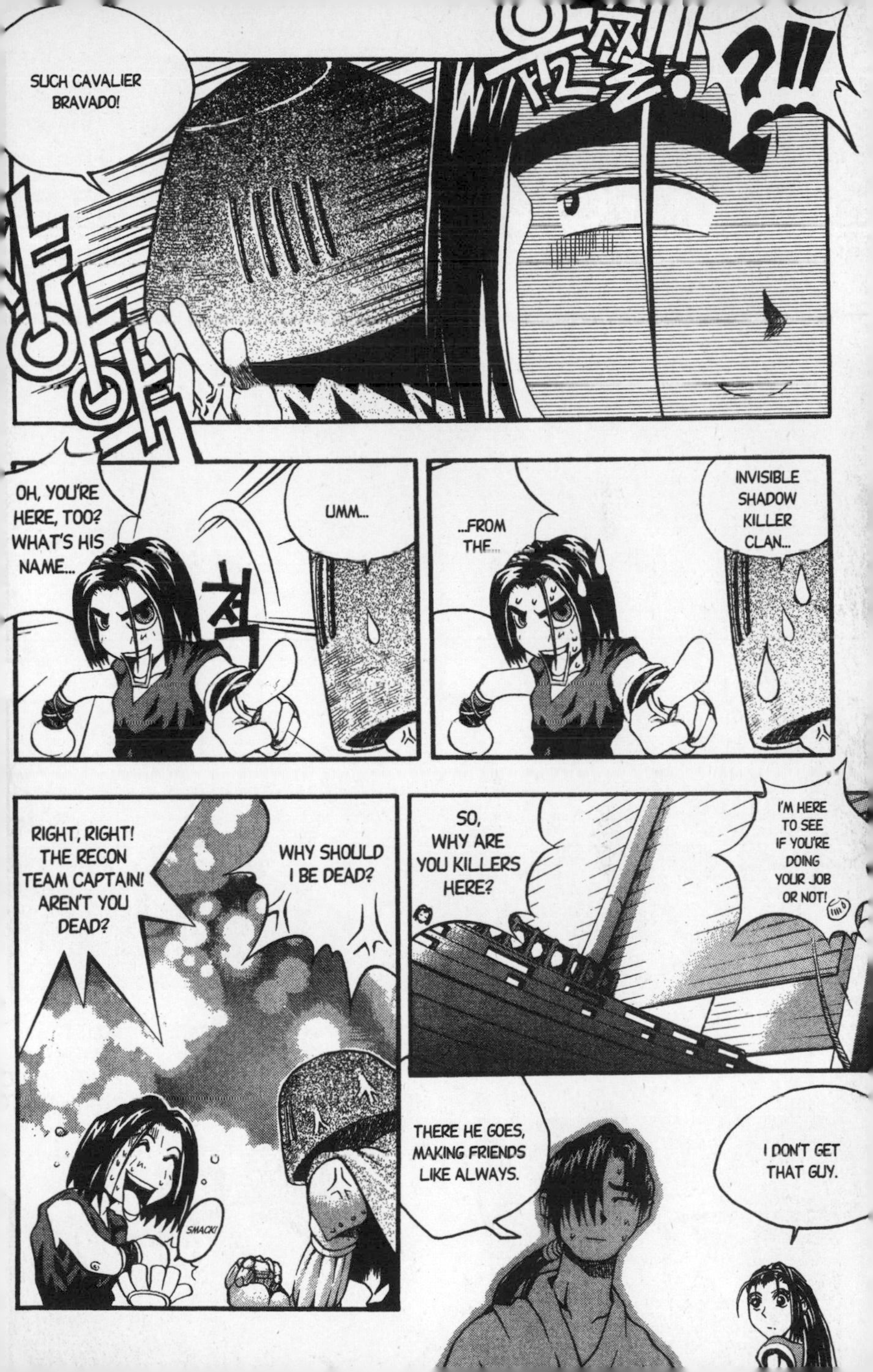
SUCH CAVALIER BRAVADO!
?!!
OH, YOU'RE HERE, TOO? WHAT'S HIS NAME...
UMM...
...FROM THE...
INVISIBLE SHADOW KILLER CLAN...
RIGHT, RIGHT! THE RECON TEAM CAPTAIN! AREN'T YOU DEAD?
WHY SHOULD I BE DEAD?
SMACK!
SO, WHY ARE YOU KILLERS HERE?
I'M HERE TO SEE IF YOU'RE DOING YOUR JOB OR NOT!
THERE HE GOES, MAKING FRIENDS LIKE ALWAYS.
I DON'T GET THAT GUY.

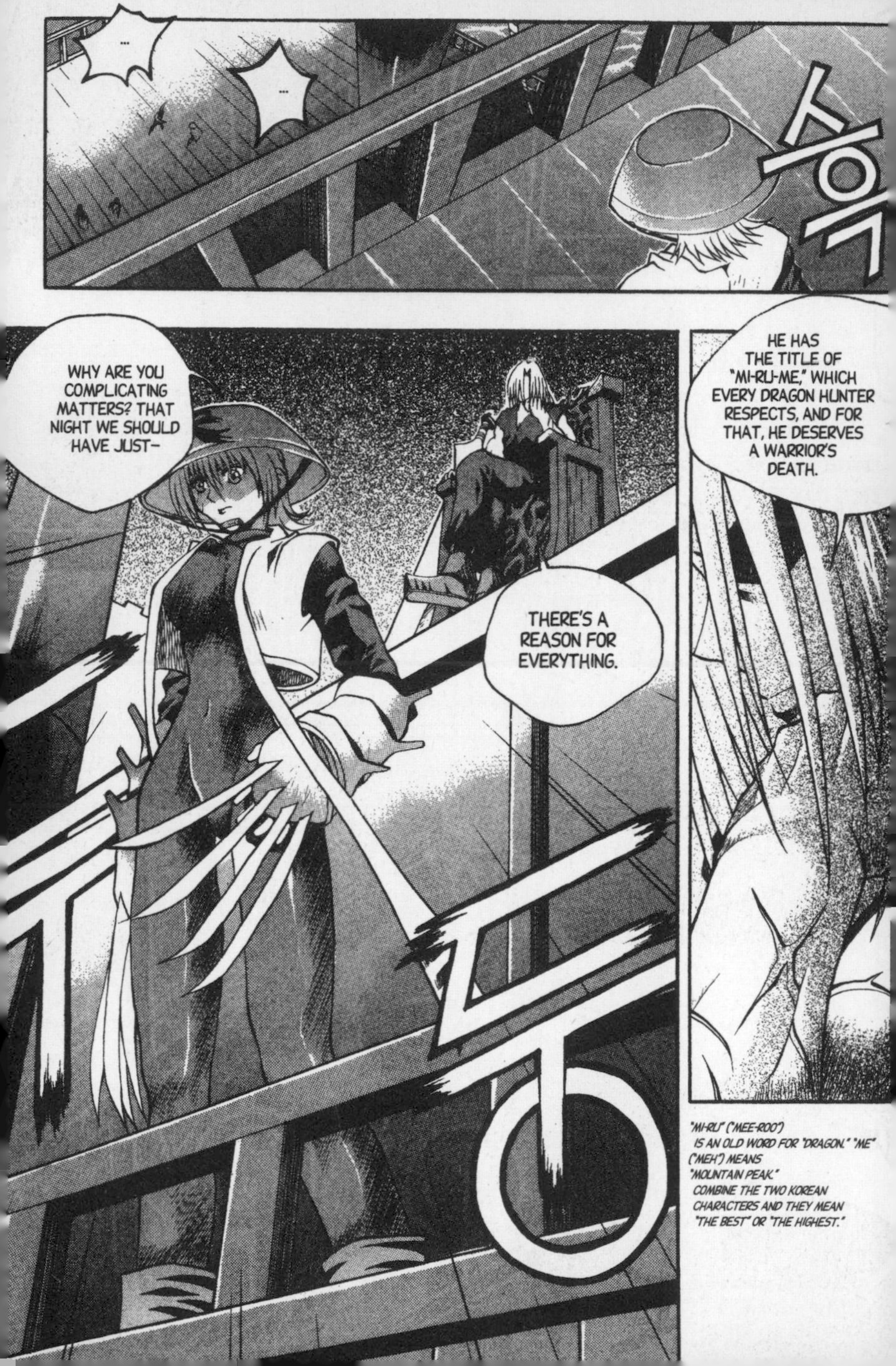
...
...
WHY ARE YOU COMPLICATING MATTERS? THAT NIGHT WE SHOULD HAVE JUST–
THERE'S A REASON FOR EVERYTHING.
HE HAS THE TITLE OF "MI-RU-ME," WHICH EVERY DRAGON HUNTER RESPECTS, AND FOR THAT, HE DESERVES A WARRIOR'S DEATH.

"MI-RU" ("MEE-ROO") IS AN OLD WORD FOR "DRAGON." "ME" ("MEH") MEANS "MOUNTAIN PEAK." COMBINE THE TWO KOREAN CHARACTERS AND THEY MEAN "THE BEST" OR "THE HIGHEST."

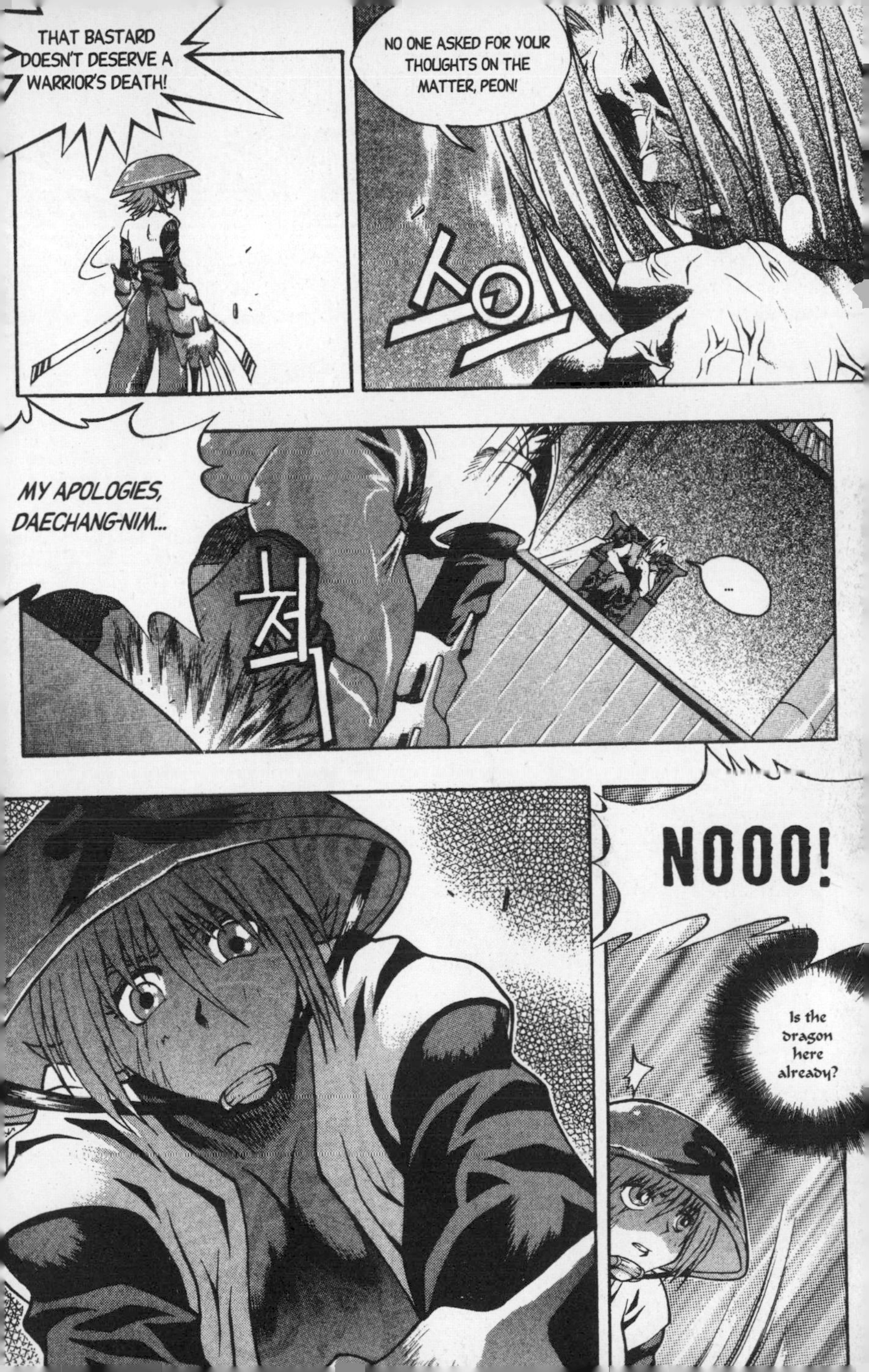
THAT BASTARD DOESN'T DESERVE A WARRIOR'S DEATH!
NO ONE ASKED FOR YOUR THOUGHTS ON THE MATTER, PEON!
MY APOLOGIES, DAECHANG-NIM...
...
NOOO!
Is the dragon here already?

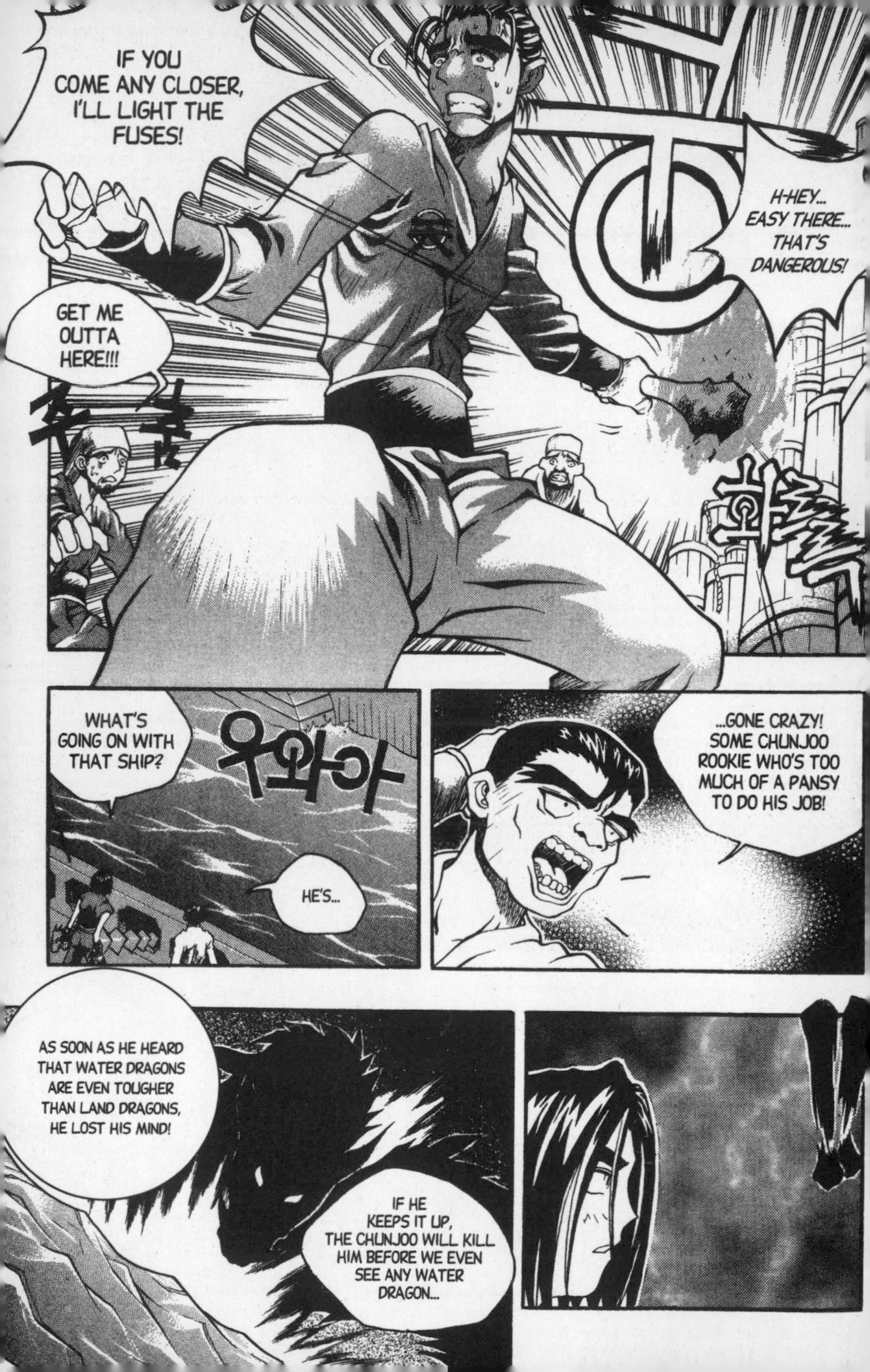
IF YOU COME ANY CLOSER, I'LL LIGHT THE FUSES!
H-HEY... EASY THERE... THAT'S DANGEROUS!
GET ME OUTTA HERE!!!
WHAT'S GOING ON WITH THAT SHIP?
HE'S...
...GONE CRAZY! SOME CHUNJOO ROOKIE WHO'S TOO MUCH OF A PANSY TO DO HIS JOB!
AS SOON AS HE HEARD THAT WATER DRAGONS ARE EVEN TOUGHER THAN LAND DRAGONS, HE LOST HIS MIND!
IF HE KEEPS IT UP, THE CHUNJOO WILL KILL HIM BEFORE WE EVEN SEE ANY WATER DRAGON...

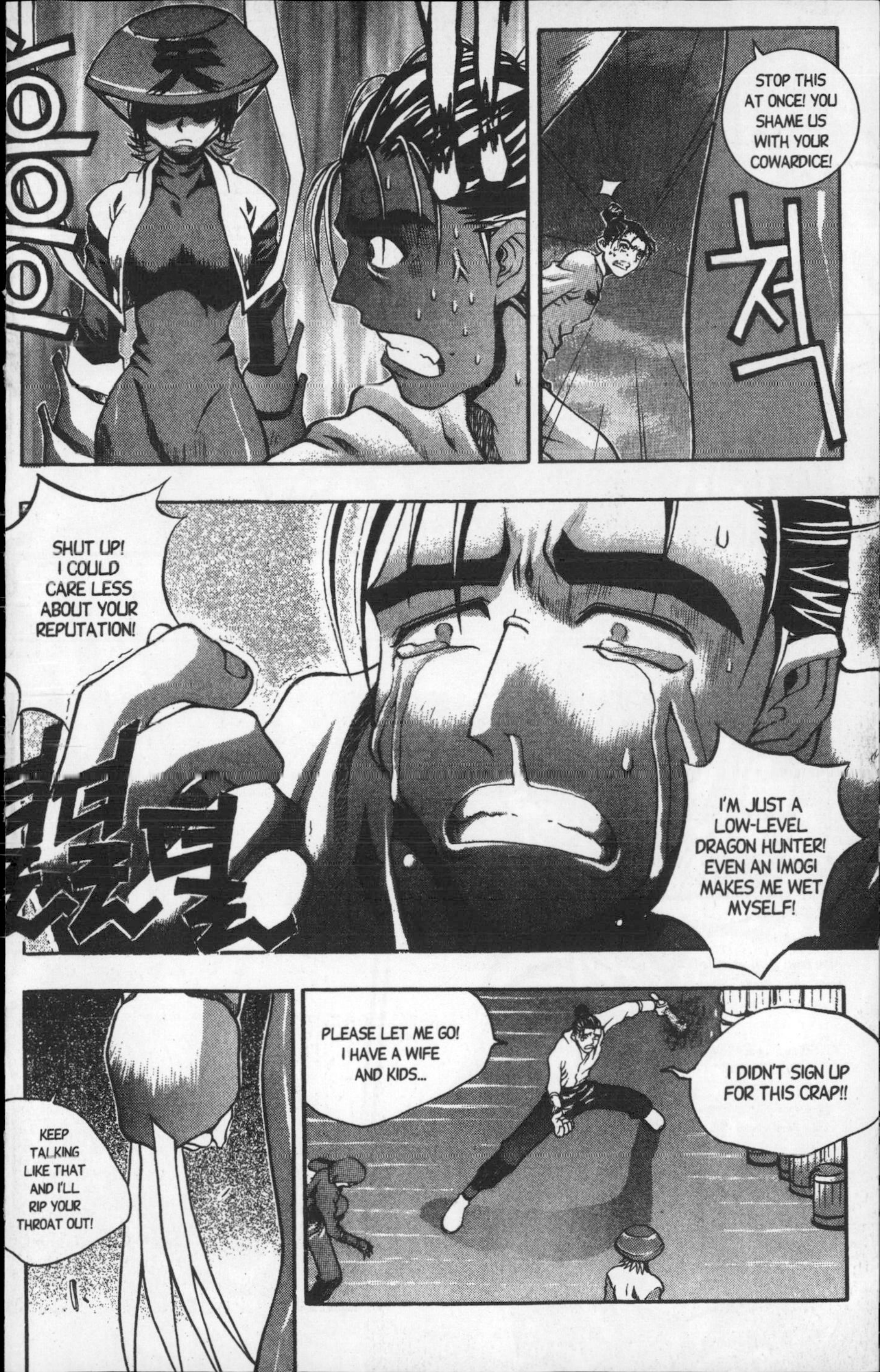
STOP THIS AT ONCE! YOU SHAME US WITH YOUR COWARDICE!
SHUT UP! I COULD CARE LESS ABOUT YOUR REPUTATION!
I'M JUST A LOW-LEVEL DRAGON HUNTER! EVEN AN IMOGI MAKES ME WET MYSELF!
KEEP TALKING LIKE THAT AND I'LL RIP YOUR THROAT OUT!
PLEASE LET ME GO! I HAVE A WIFE AND KIDS...
I DIDN'T SIGN UP FOR THIS CRAP!!

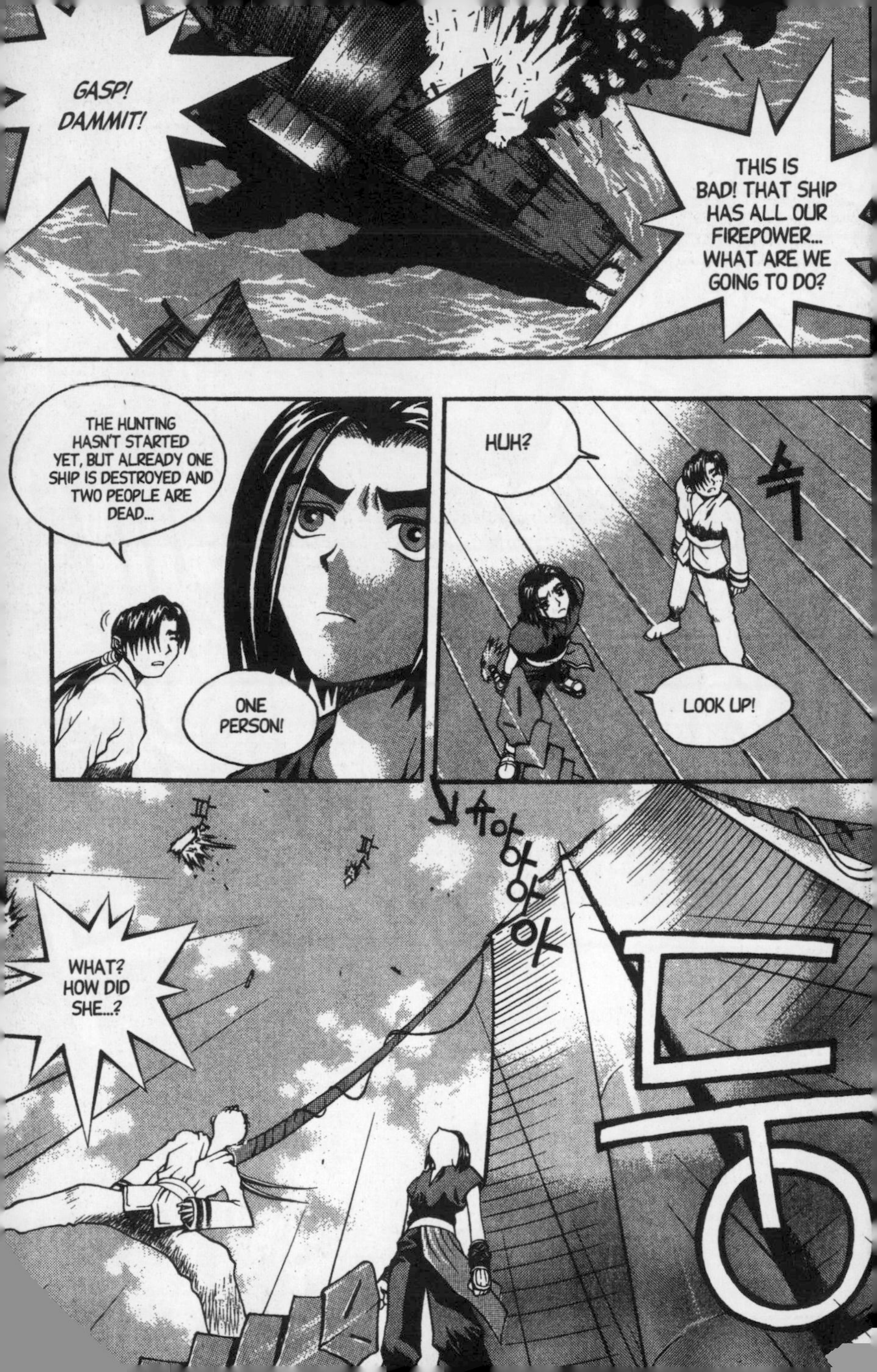
GASP! DAMMIT!
THIS IS BAD! THAT SHIP HAS ALL OUR FIREPOWER... WHAT ARE WE GOING TO DO?
THE HUNTING HASN'T STARTED YET, BUT ALREADY ONE SHIP IS DESTROYED AND TWO PEOPLE ARE DEAD...
ONE PERSON!
HUH?
LOOK UP!
WHAT? HOW DID SHE...?

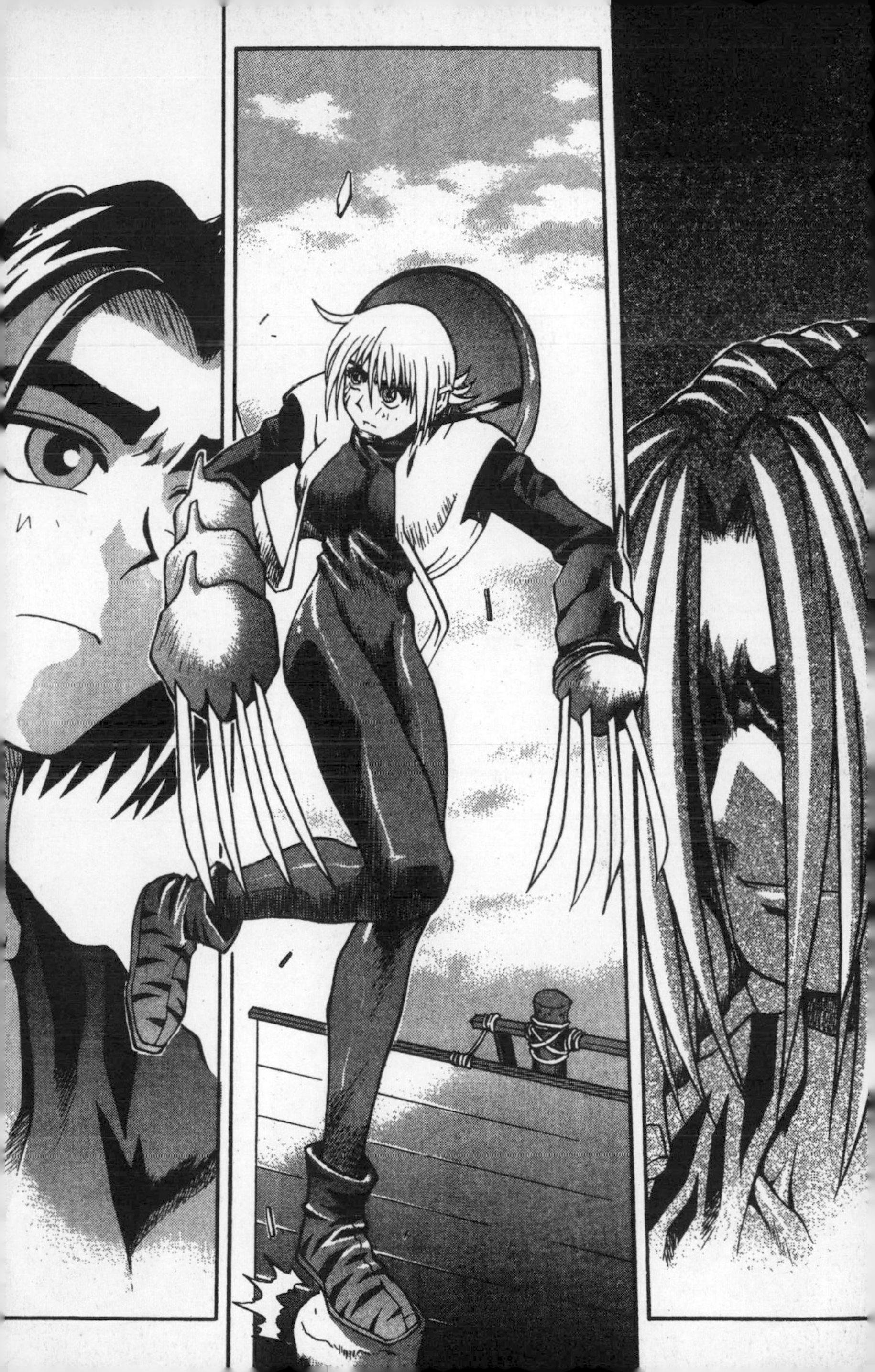

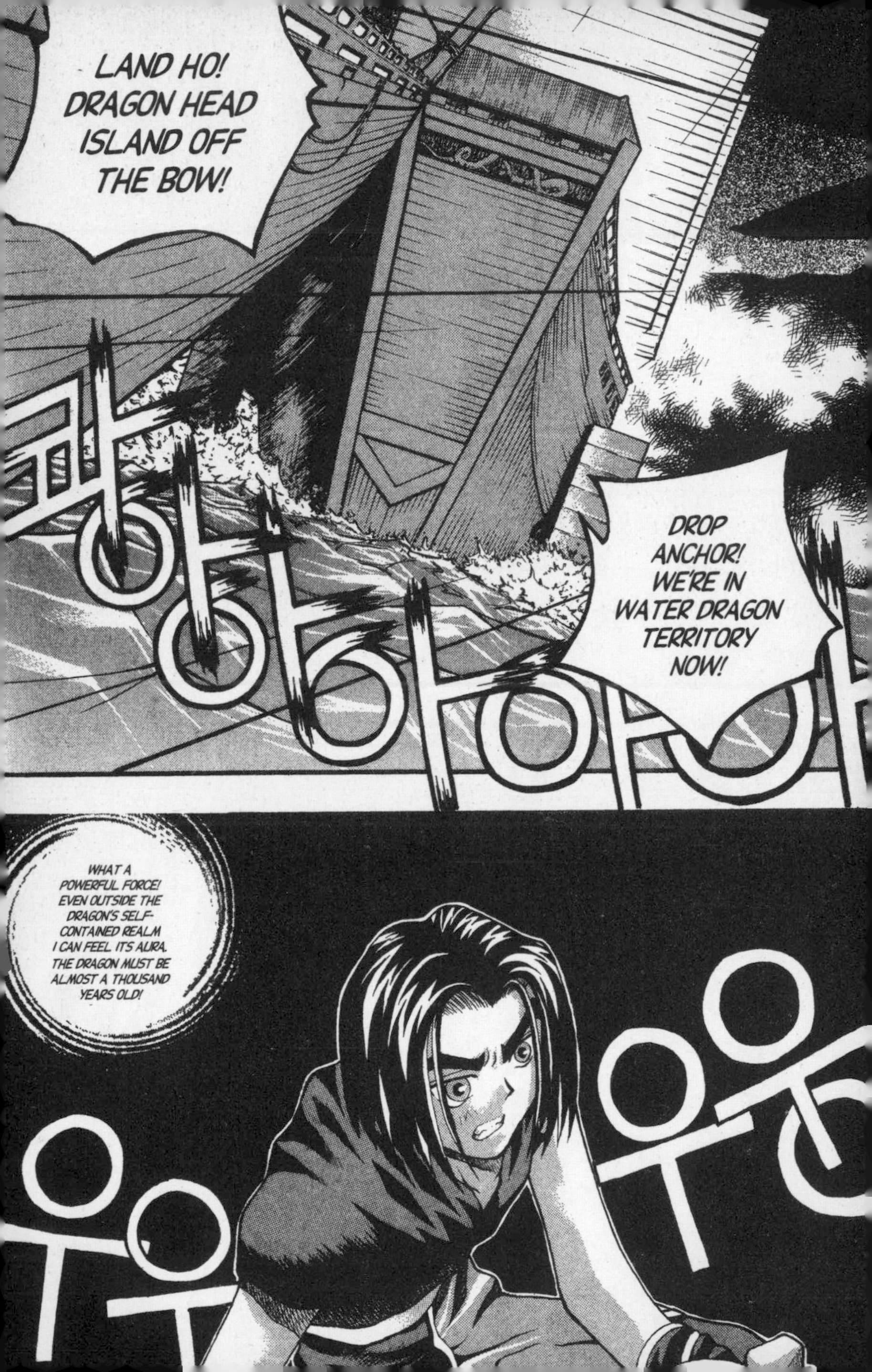
LAND HO! DRAGON HEAD ISLAND OFF THE BOW!
DROP ANCHOR! WE'RE IN WATER DRAGON TERRITORY NOW!
WHAT A POWERFUL FORCE! EVEN OUTSIDE THE DRAGON'S SELF-CONTAINED REALM I CAN FEEL ITS AURA. THE DRAGON MUST BE ALMOST A THOUSAND YEARS OLD!

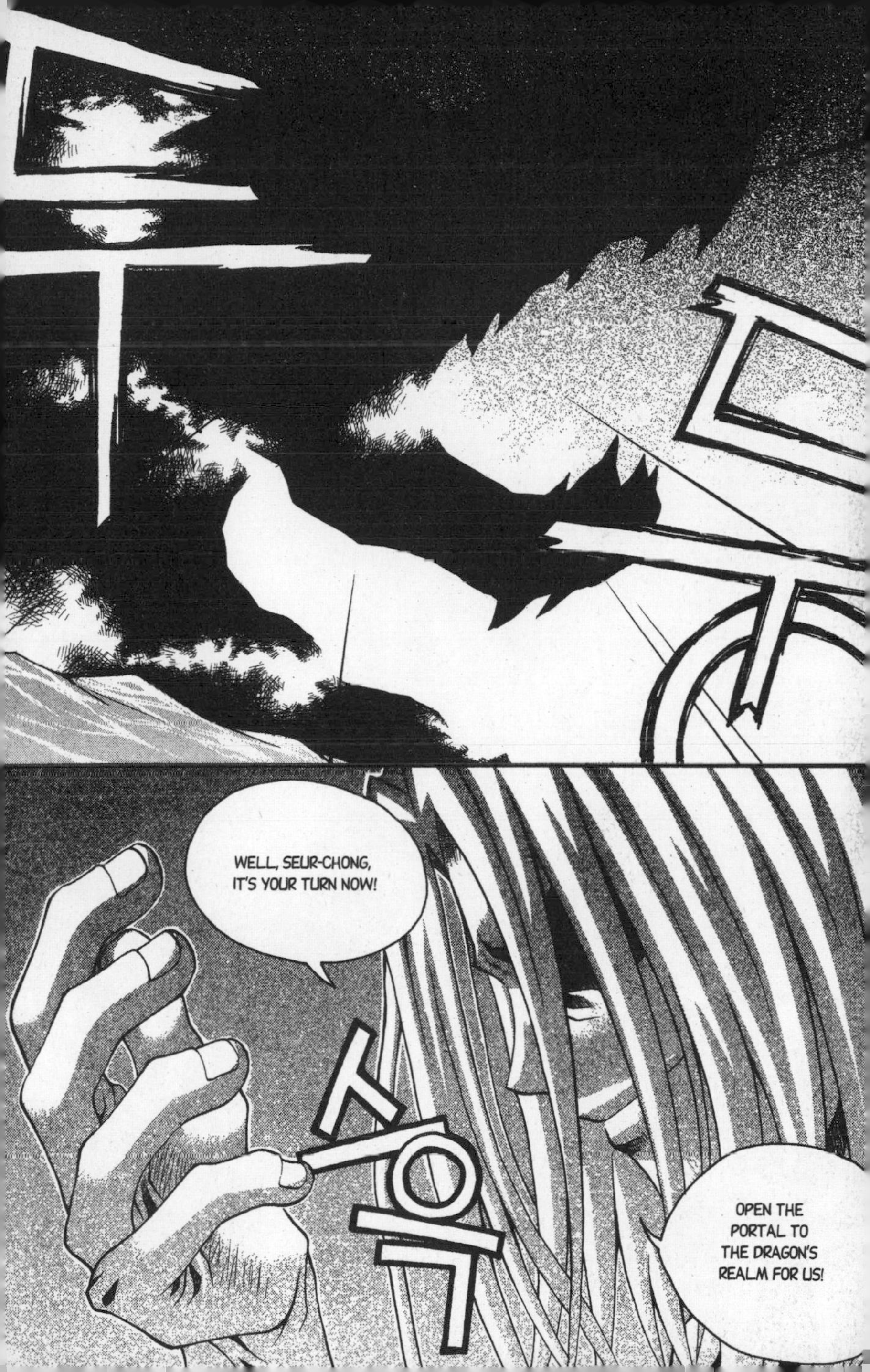
WELL, SEUR-CHONG, IT'S YOUR TURN NOW!
OPEN THE PORTAL TO THE DRAGON'S REALM FOR US!

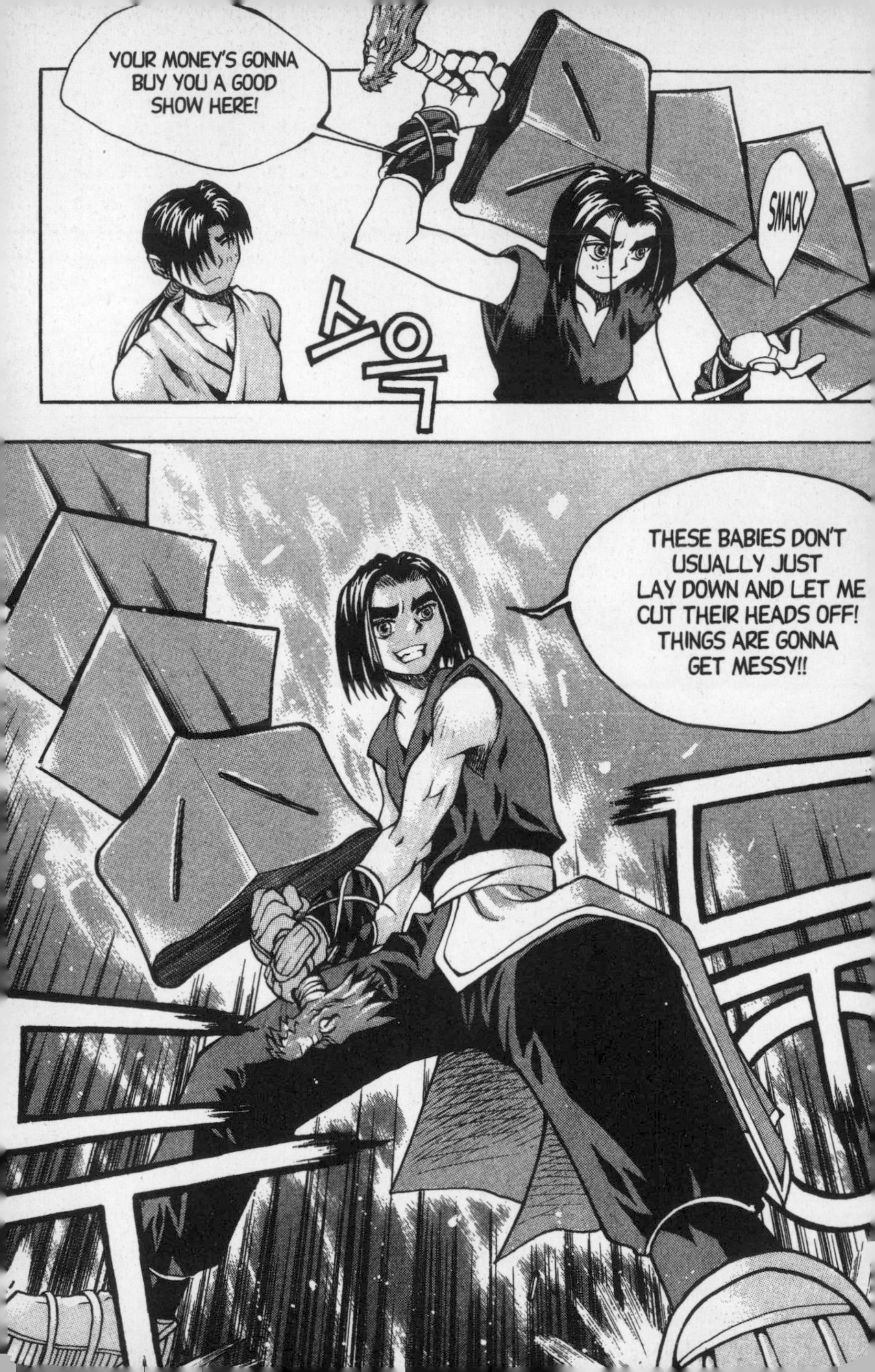
YOUR MONEY'S GONNA BUY YOU A GOOD SHOW HERE!
SMACK
THESE BABIES DON'T USUALLY JUST LAY DOWN AND LET ME CUT THEIR HEADS OFF! THINGS ARE GONNA GET MESSY!!

CHAPTER 4

SIGNS OF UNHAPPINESS

PART 3

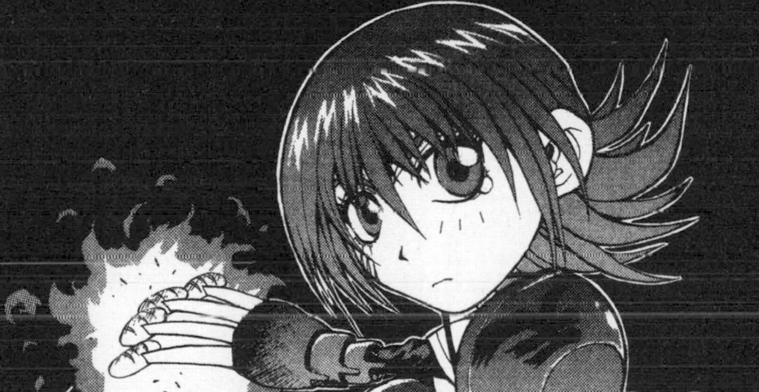

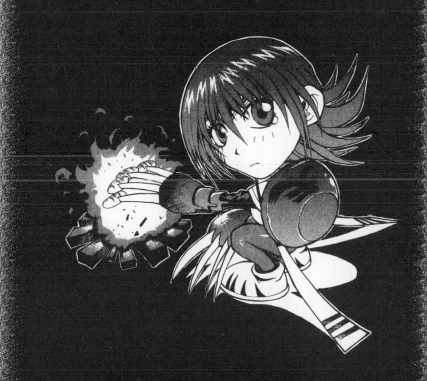

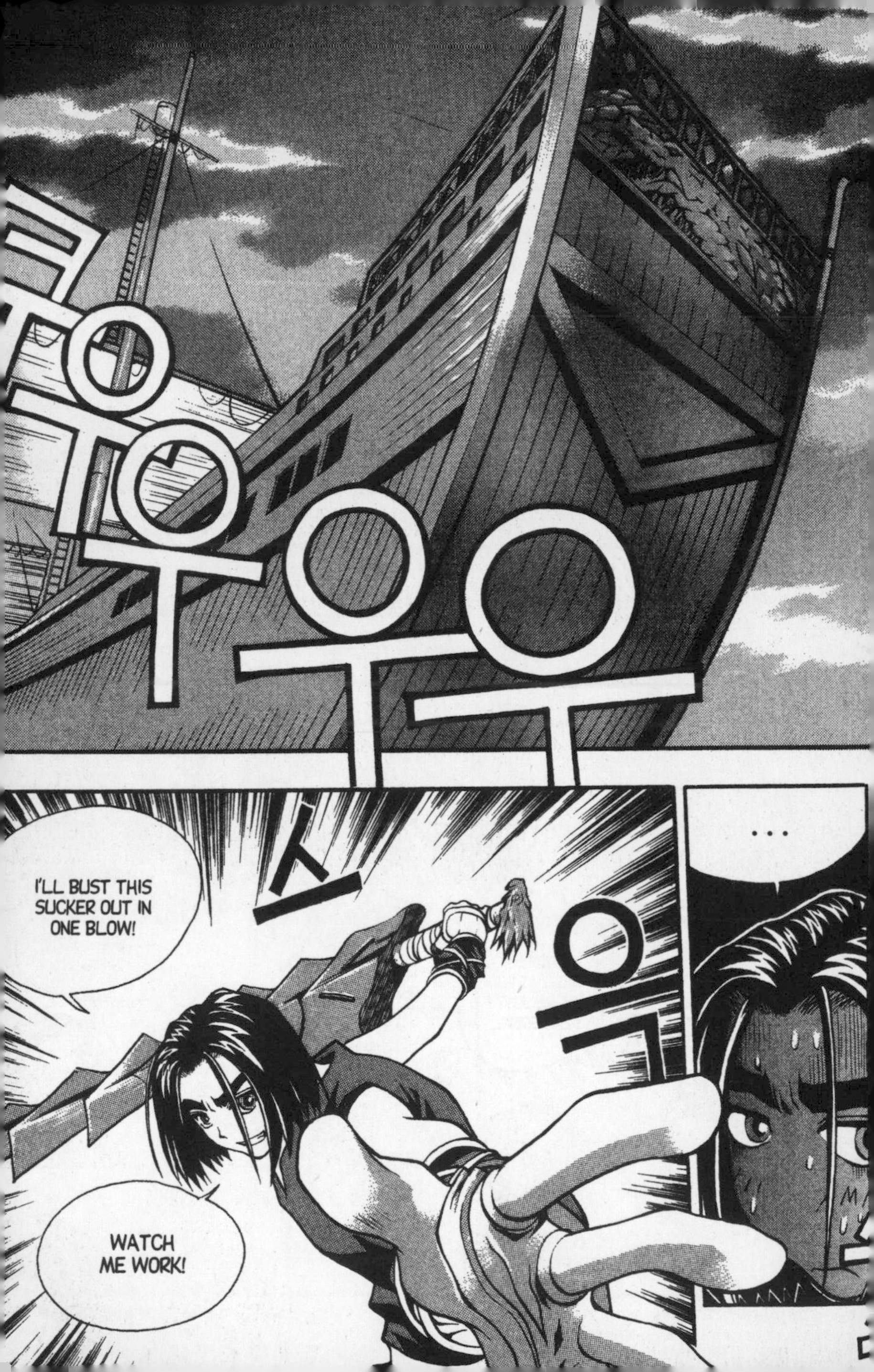
I'LL BUST THIS SUCKER OUT IN ONE BLOW!
WATCH ME WORK!
...

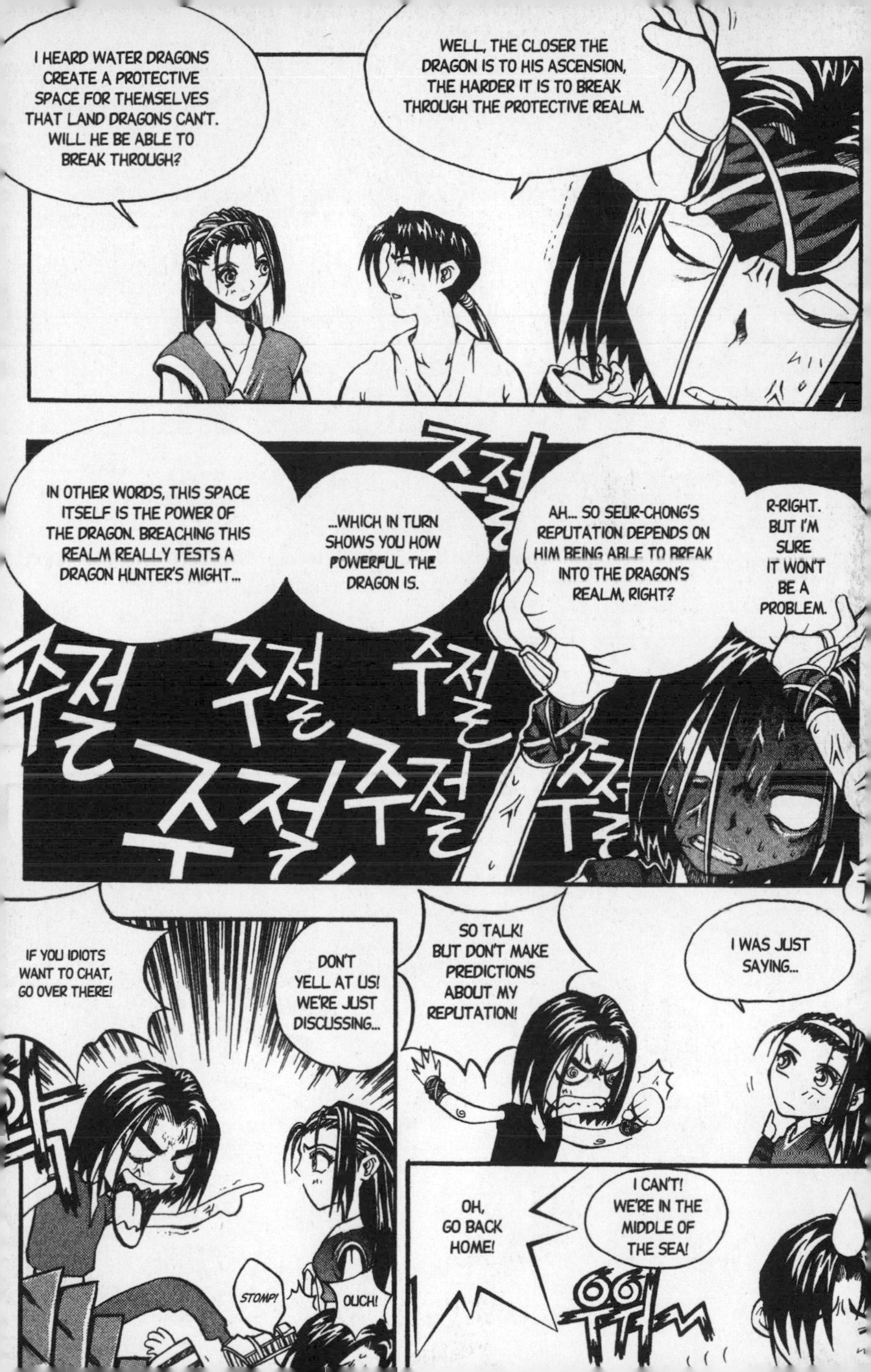

I HEARD WATER DRAGONS CREATE A PROTECTIVE SPACE FOR THEMSELVES THAT LAND DRAGONS CAN'T. WILL HE BE ABLE TO BREAK THROUGH?
WELL, THE CLOSER THE DRAGON IS TO HIS ASCENSION, THE HARDER IT IS TO BREAK THROUGH THE PROTECTIVE REALM.
IN OTHER WORDS, THIS SPACE ITSELF IS THE POWER OF THE DRAGON. BREACHING THIS REALM REALLY TESTS A DRAGON HUNTER'S MIGHT...
...WHICH IN TURN SHOWS YOU HOW POWERFUL THE DRAGON IS.
주절
AH... SO SEUR-CHONG'S REPUTATION DEPENDS ON HIM BEING ABLE TO BREAK INTO THE DRAGON'S REALM, RIGHT?
R-RIGHT. BUT I'M SURE IT WON'T BE A PROBLEM.
주절 주절 주절
주절 주절 주절
IF YOU IDIOTS WANT TO CHAT, GO OVER THERE!
DON'T YELL AT US! WE'RE JUST DISCUSSING...
STOMP!
OUCH!
SO TALK! BUT DON'T MAKE PREDICTIONS ABOUT MY REPUTATION!
I WAS JUST SAYING...
OH, GO BACK HOME!
I CAN'T! WE'RE IN THE MIDDLE OF THE SEA!

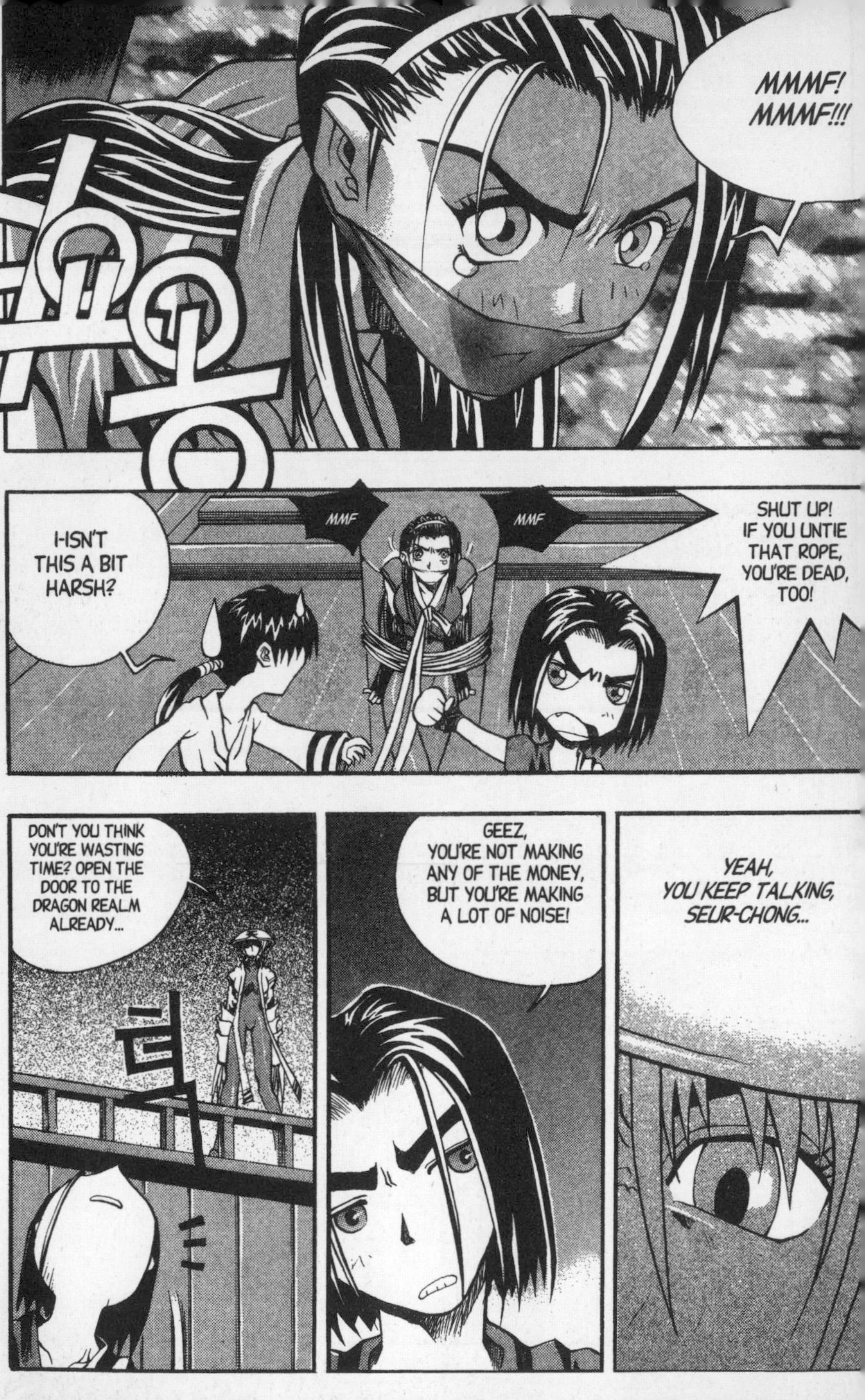
MMMF! MMMF!!!
I-ISN'T THIS A BIT HARSH?
MMF
MMF
SHUT UP! IF YOU UNTIE THAT ROPE, YOU'RE DEAD, TOO!
DON'T YOU THINK YOU'RE WASTING TIME? OPEN THE DOOR TO THE DRAGON REALM ALREADY...
GEEZ, YOU'RE NOT MAKING ANY OF THE MONEY, BUT YOU'RE MAKING A LOT OF NOISE!
YEAH, YOU KEEP TALKING, SEUR-CHONG...

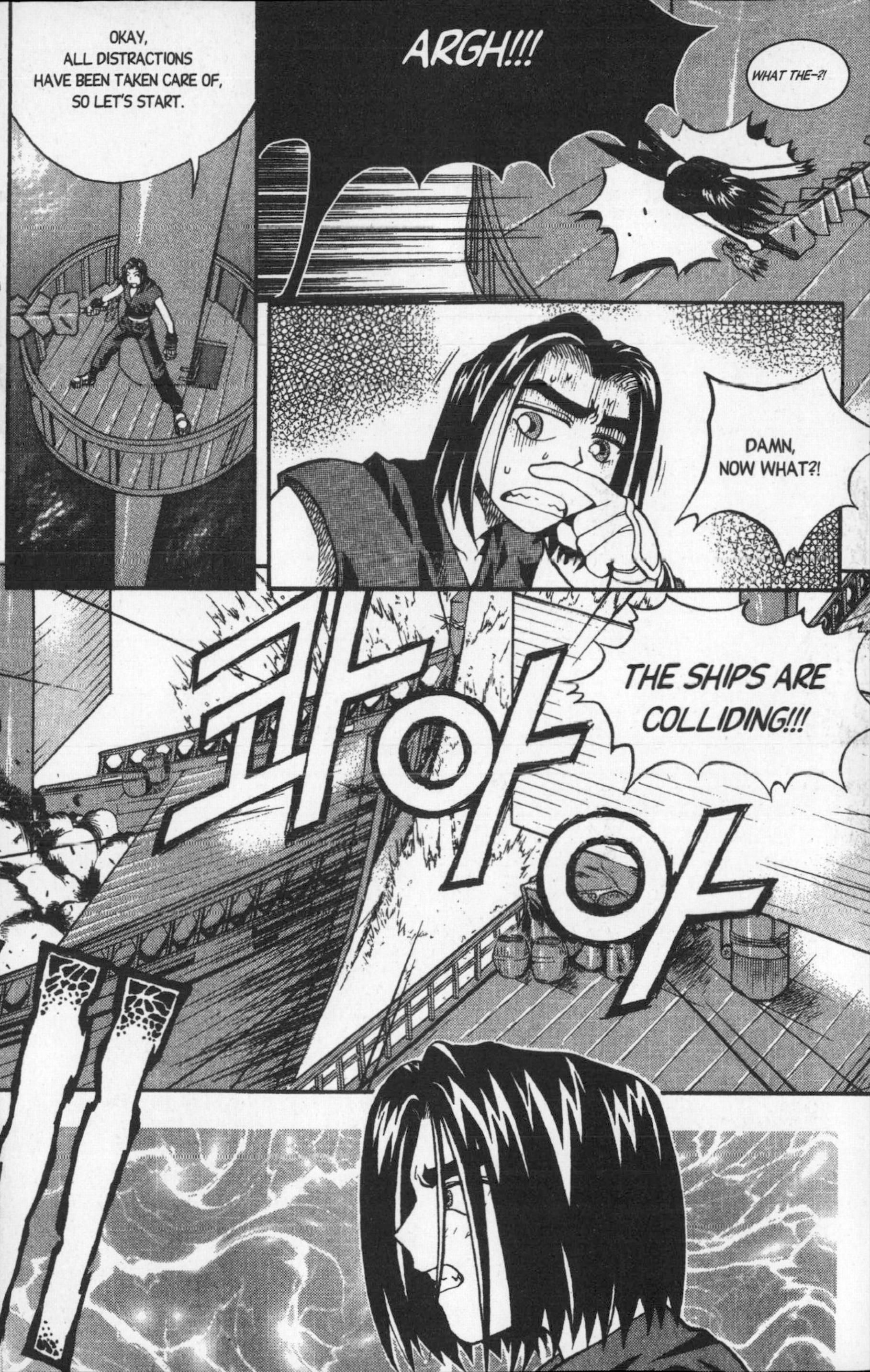
OKAY, ALL DISTRACTIONS HAVE BEEN TAKEN CARE OF, SO LET'S START.
ARGH!!!
WHAT THE–?!
DAMN, NOW WHAT?!
콰아아
THE SHIPS ARE COLLIDING!!!

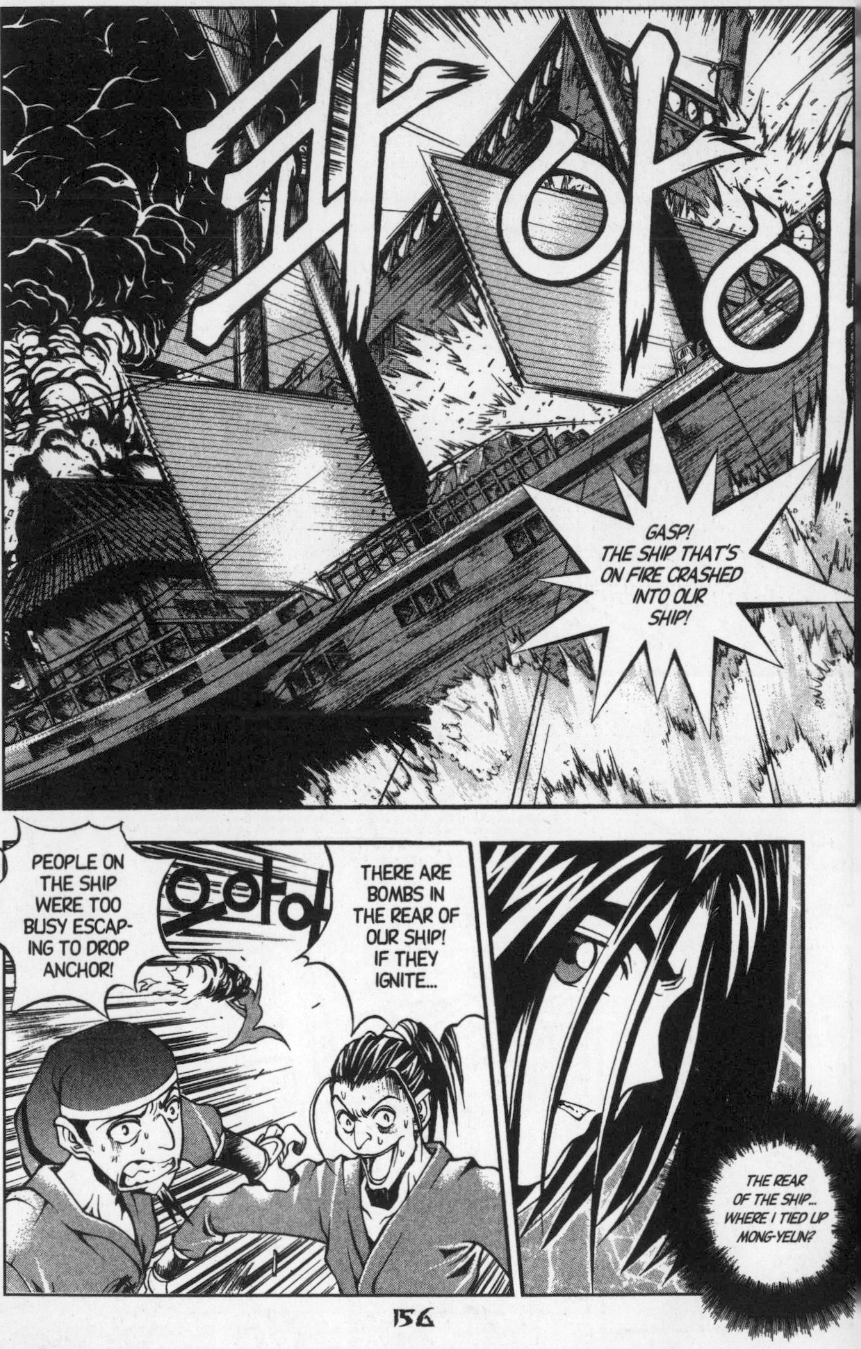
콰앙
GASP! THE SHIP THAT'S ON FIRE CRASHED INTO OUR SHIP!
PEOPLE ON THE SHIP WERE TOO BUSY ESCAP-ING TO DROP ANCHOR!
THERE ARE BOMBS IN THE REAR OF OUR SHIP! IF THEY IGNITE...
THE REAR OF THE SHIP... WHERE I TIED UP MONG-YEUN?

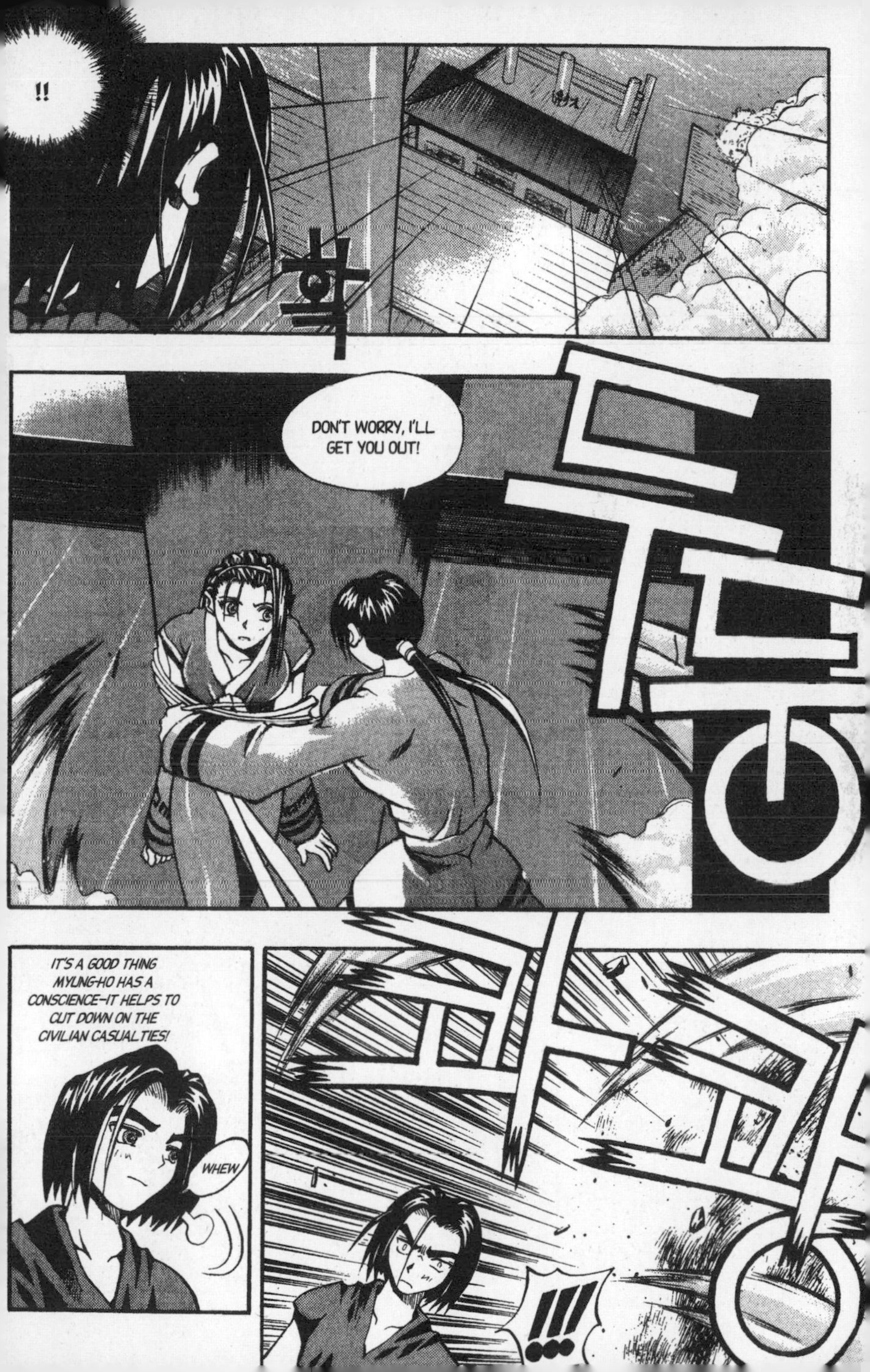
!!
DON'T WORRY, I'LL GET YOU OUT!
IT'S A GOOD THING MYUNG-HO HAS A CONSCIENCE--IT HELPS TO CUT DOWN ON THE CIVILIAN CASUALTIES!
WHEW
!!!

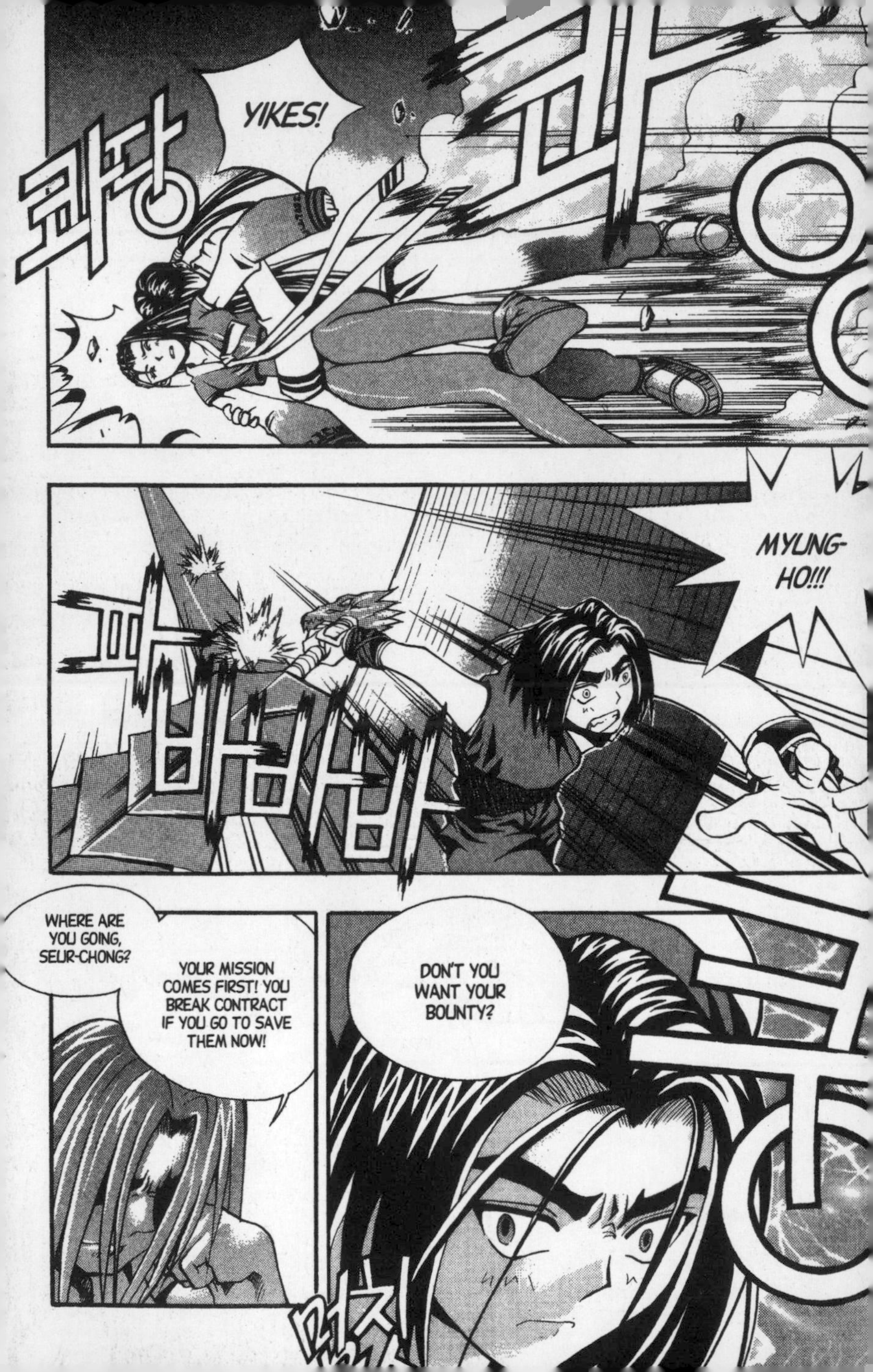
YIKES!
MYUNG-HO!!!
WHERE ARE YOU GOING, SEUR-CHONG?
YOUR MISSION COMES FIRST! YOU BREAK CONTRACT IF YOU GO TO SAVE THEM NOW!
DON'T YOU WANT YOUR BOUNTY?

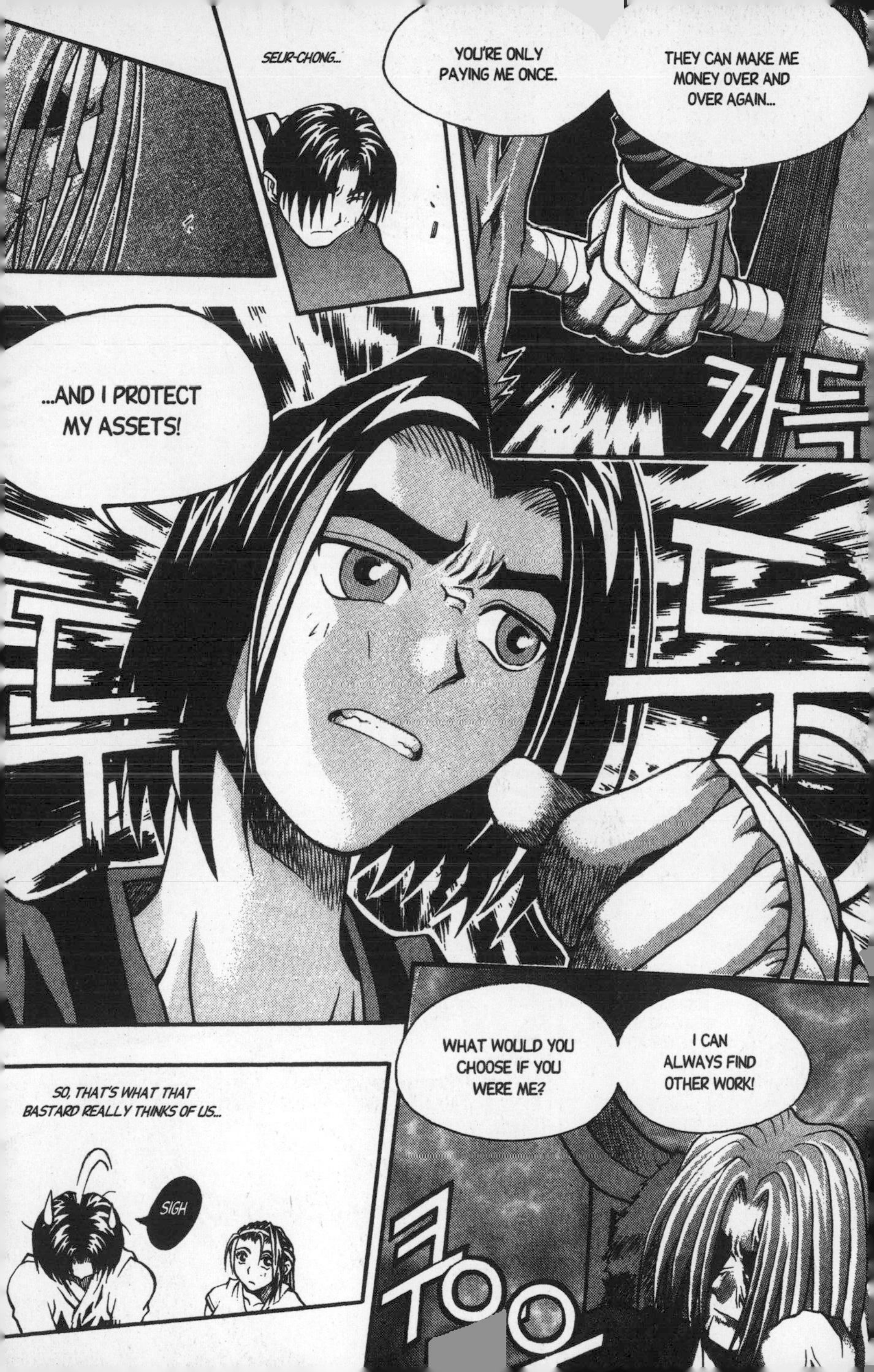
SEUR-CHONG...
YOU'RE ONLY PAYING ME ONCE.
THEY CAN MAKE ME MONEY OVER AND OVER AGAIN...
...AND I PROTECT MY ASSETS!
SO, THAT'S WHAT THAT BASTARD REALLY THINKS OF US...
SIGH
WHAT WOULD YOU CHOOSE IF YOU WERE ME?
I CAN ALWAYS FIND OTHER WORK!

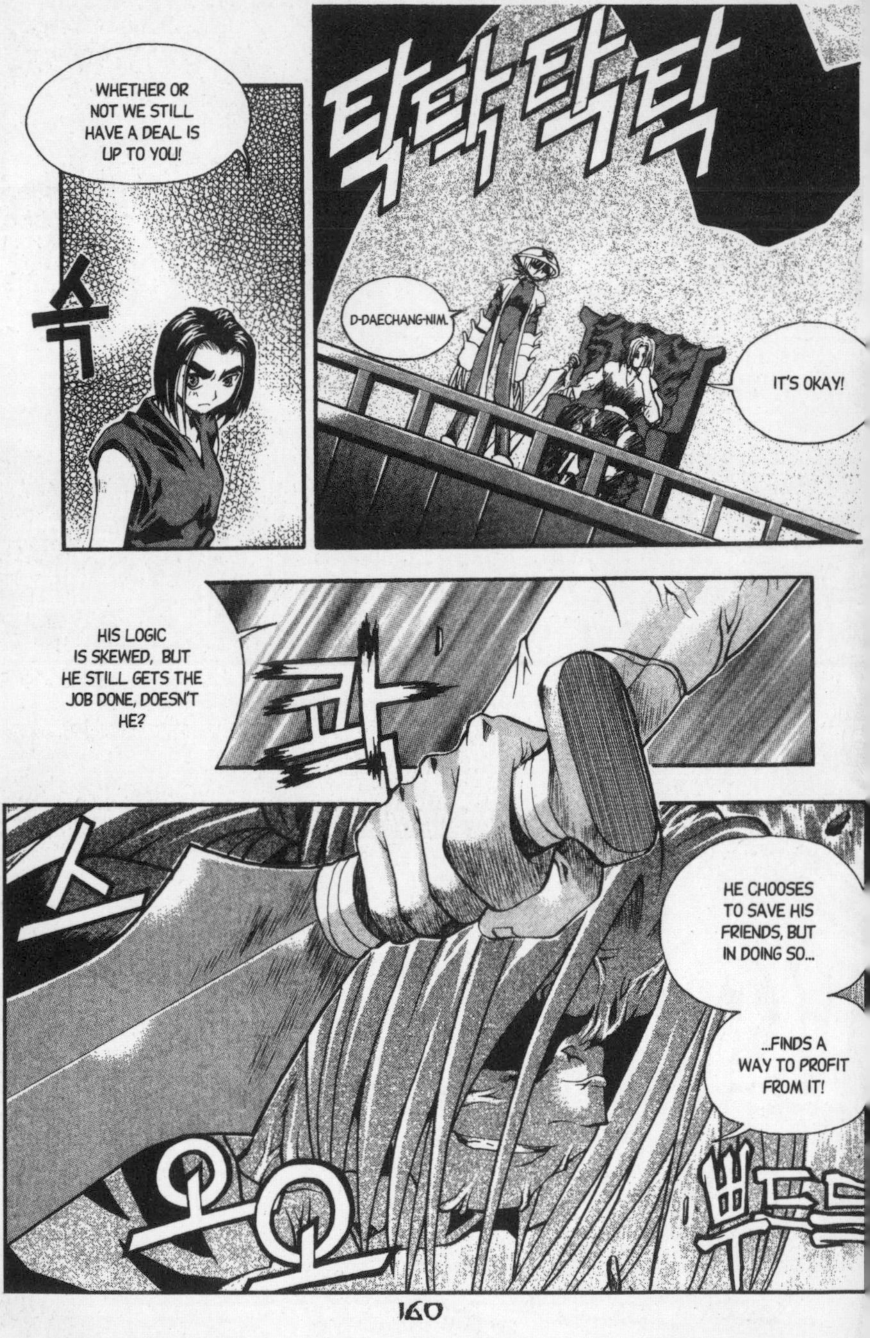
WHETHER OR NOT WE STILL HAVE A DEAL IS UP TO YOU!
슥
탁탁탁탁
D-DAECHANG-NIM.
IT'S OKAY!
HIS LOGIC IS SKEWED, BUT HE STILL GETS THE JOB DONE, DOESN'T HE?
콱
HE CHOOSES TO SAVE HIS FRIENDS, BUT IN DOING SO...
...FINDS A WAY TO PROFIT FROM IT!
뿌드득

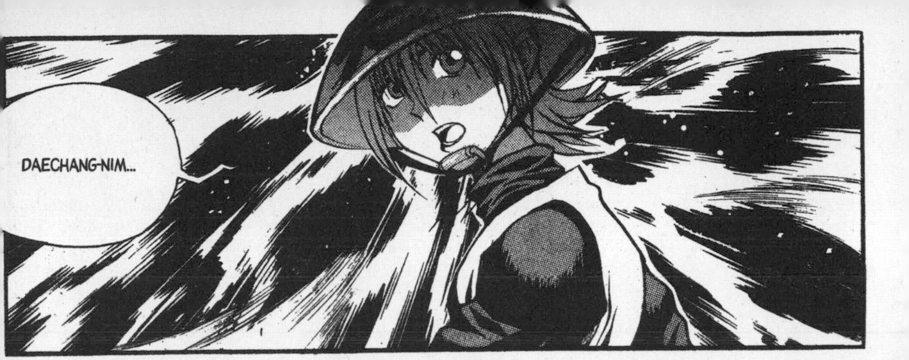
DAECHANG-NIM...

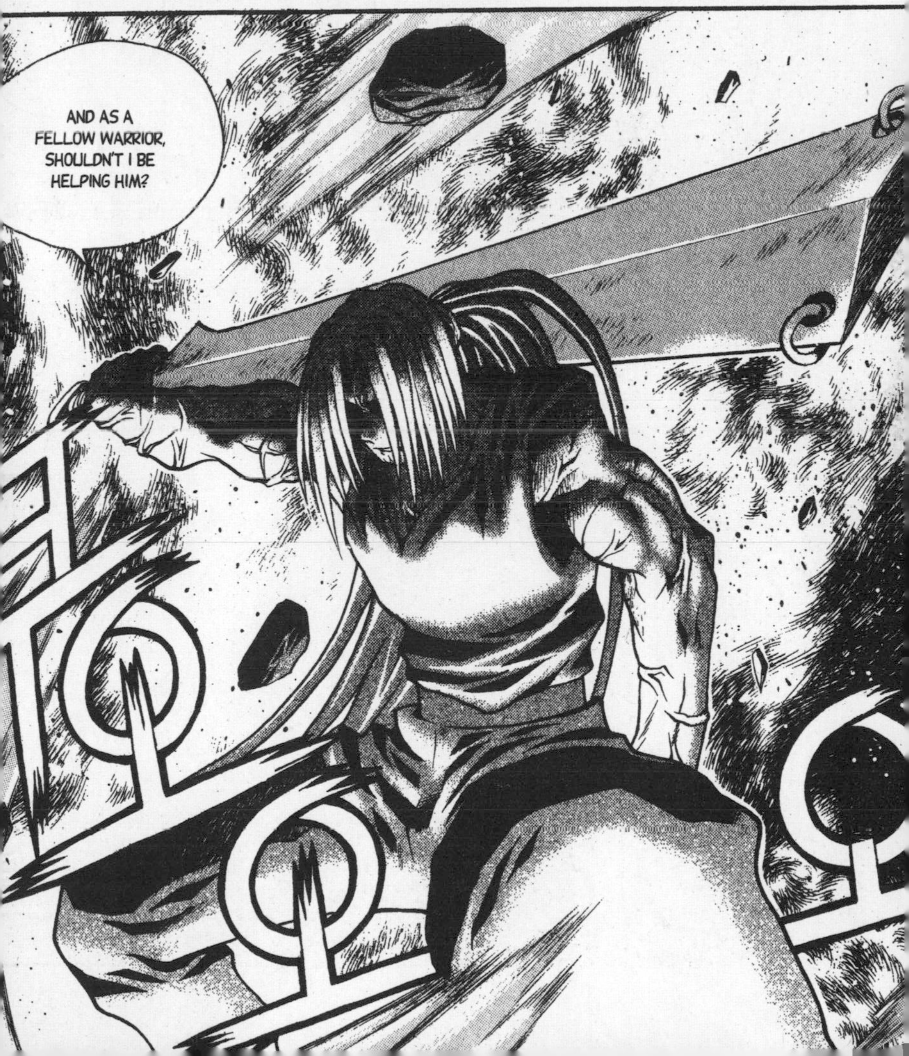
AND AS A FELLOW WARRIOR, SHOULDN'T I BE HELPING HIM?

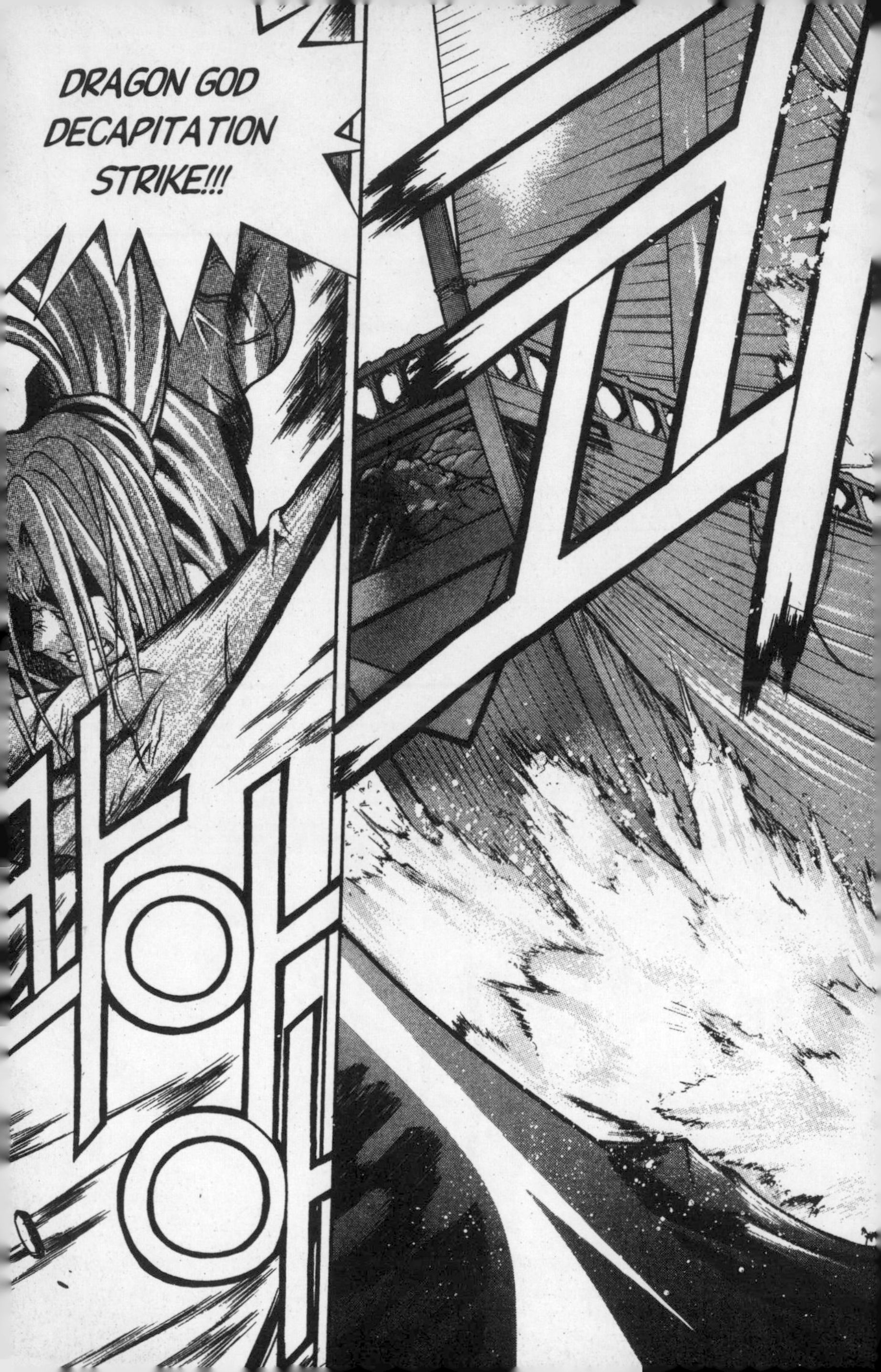
DRAGON GOD DECAPITATION STRIKE!!!

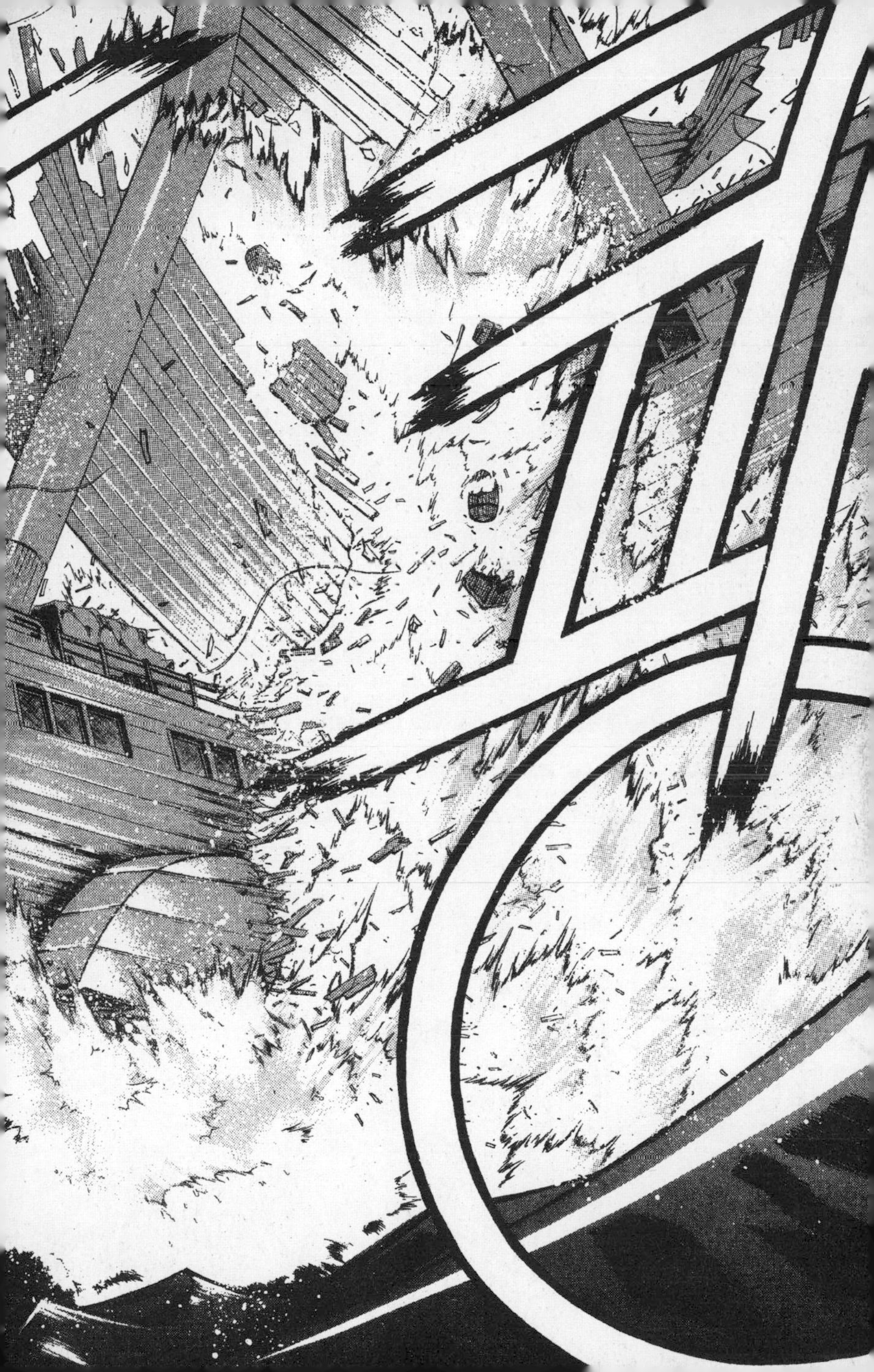

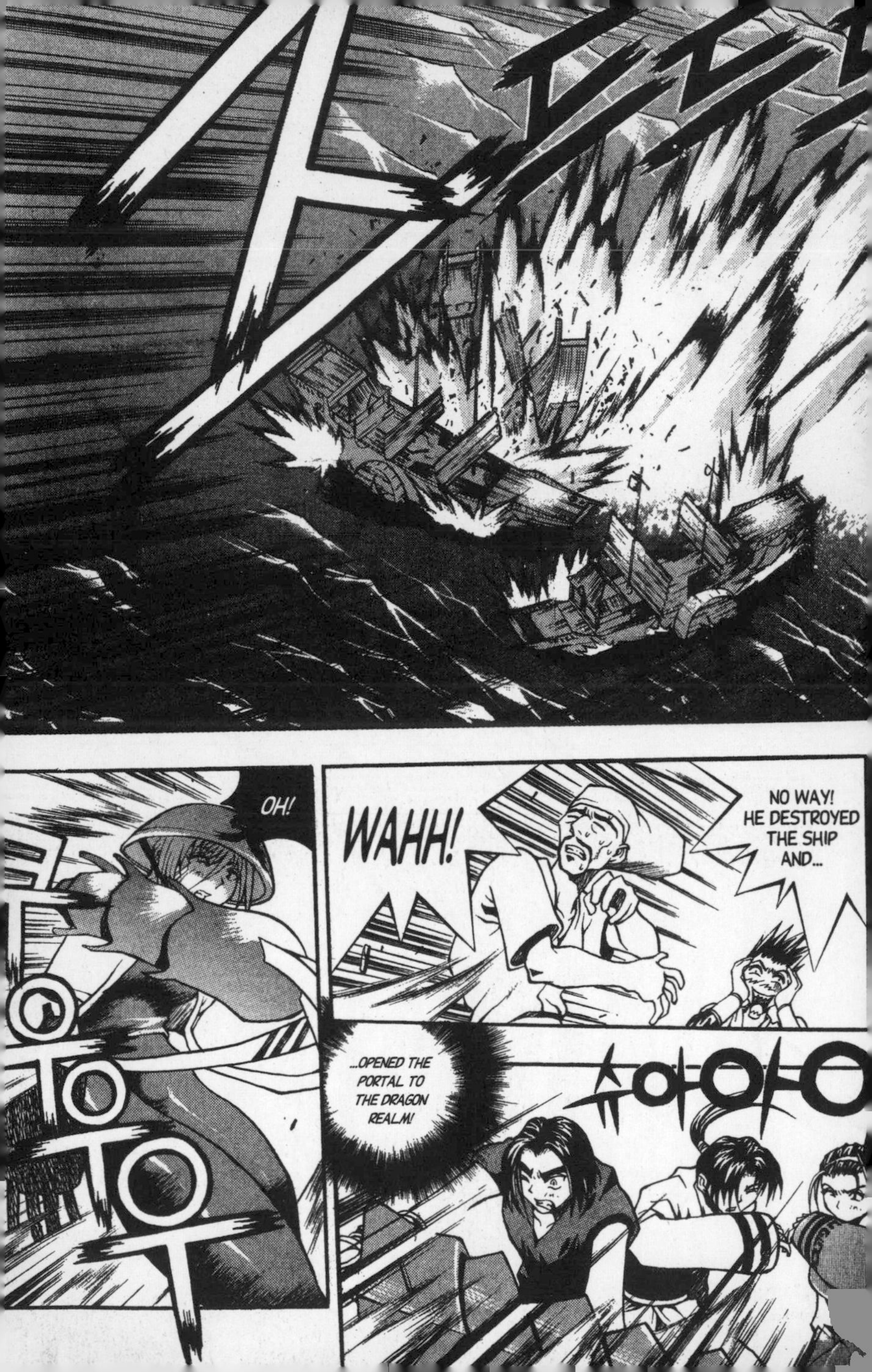
OH!
WAHH!
NO WAY! HE DESTROYED THE SHIP AND...
...OPENED THE PORTAL TO THE DRAGON REALM!

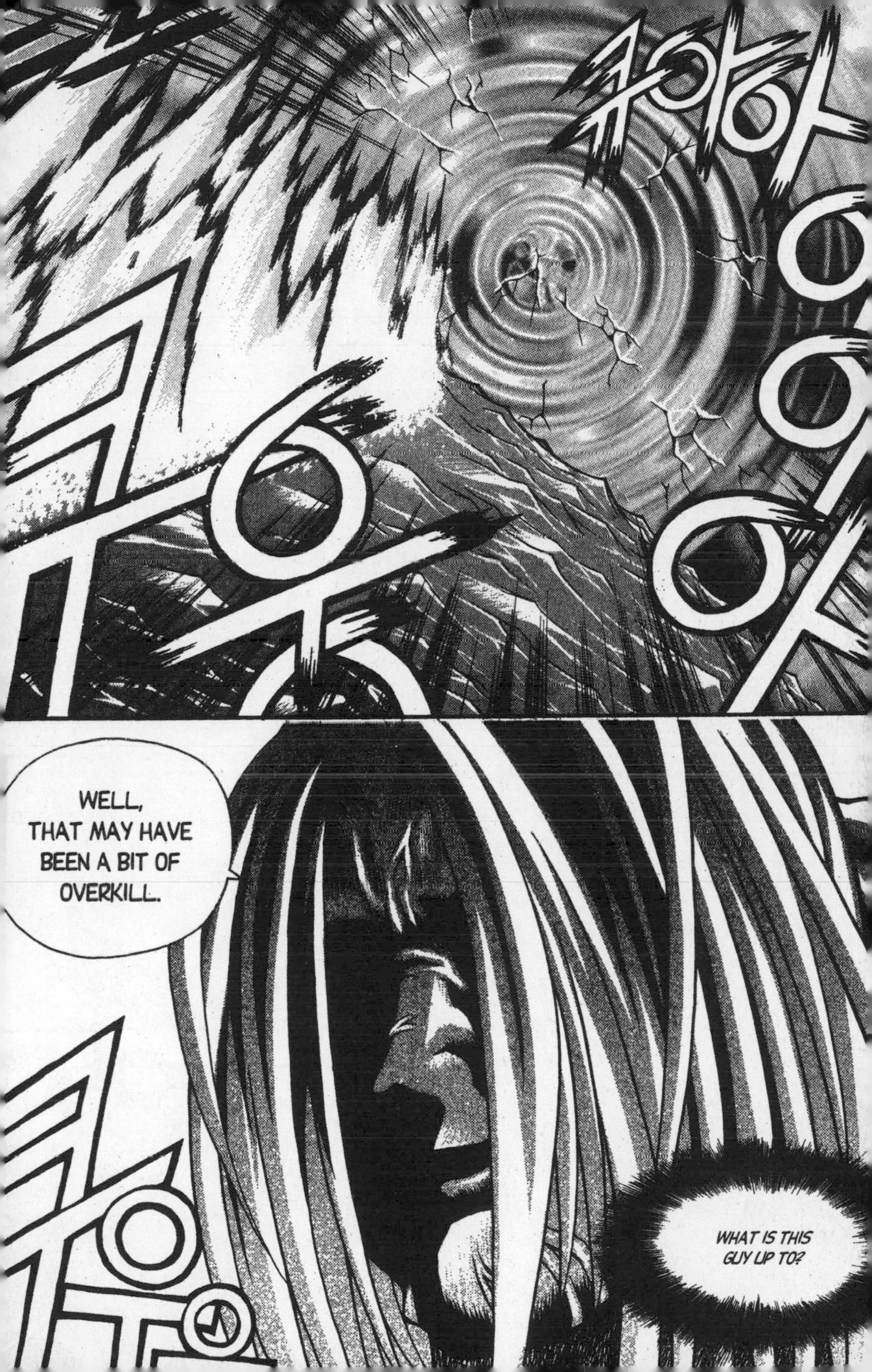
WELL, THAT MAY HAVE BEEN A BIT OF OVERKILL.
WHAT IS THIS GUY UP TO?

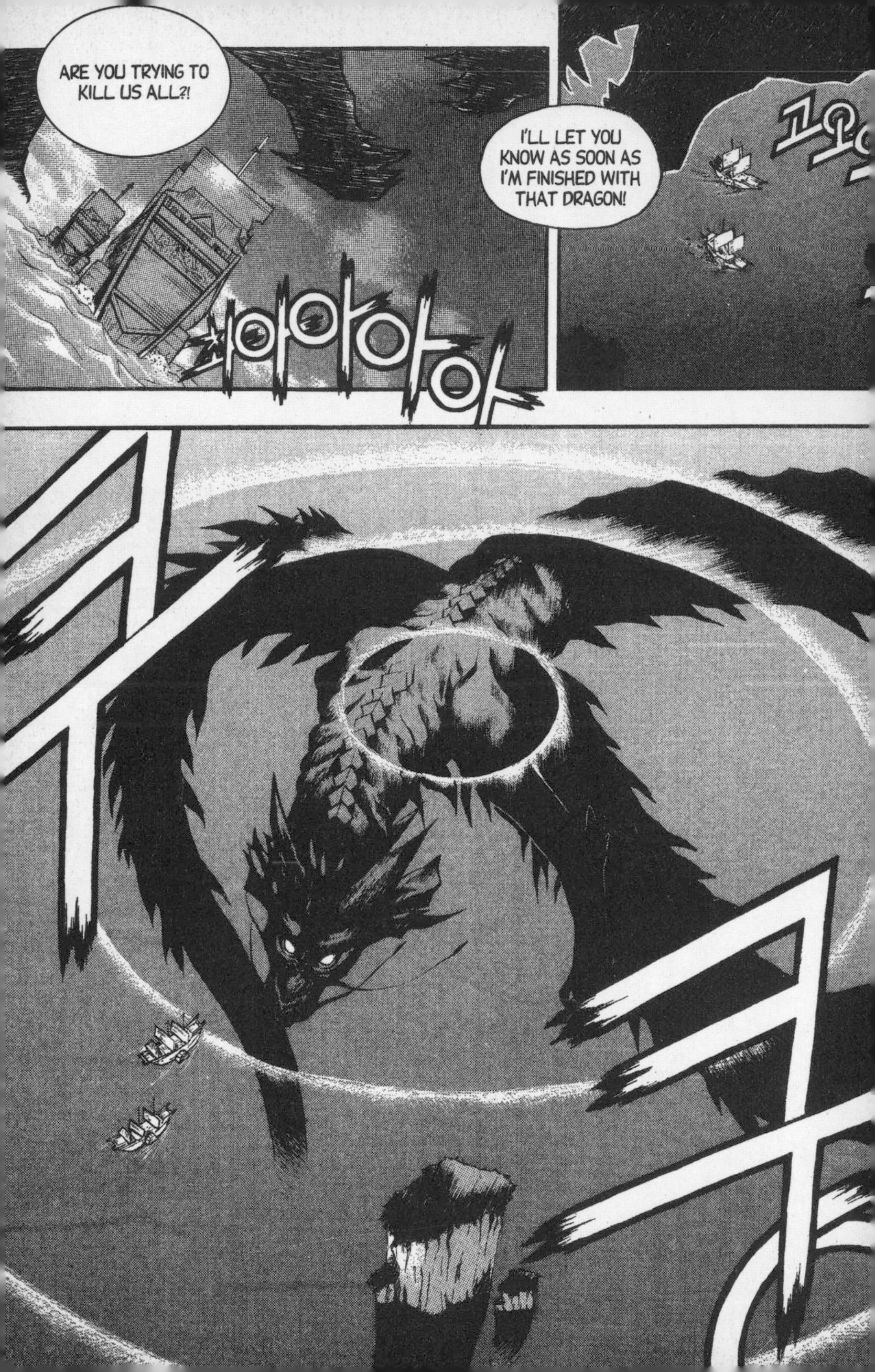
ARE YOU TRYING TO KILL US ALL?!
I'LL LET YOU KNOW AS SOON AS I'M FINISHED WITH THAT DRAGON!

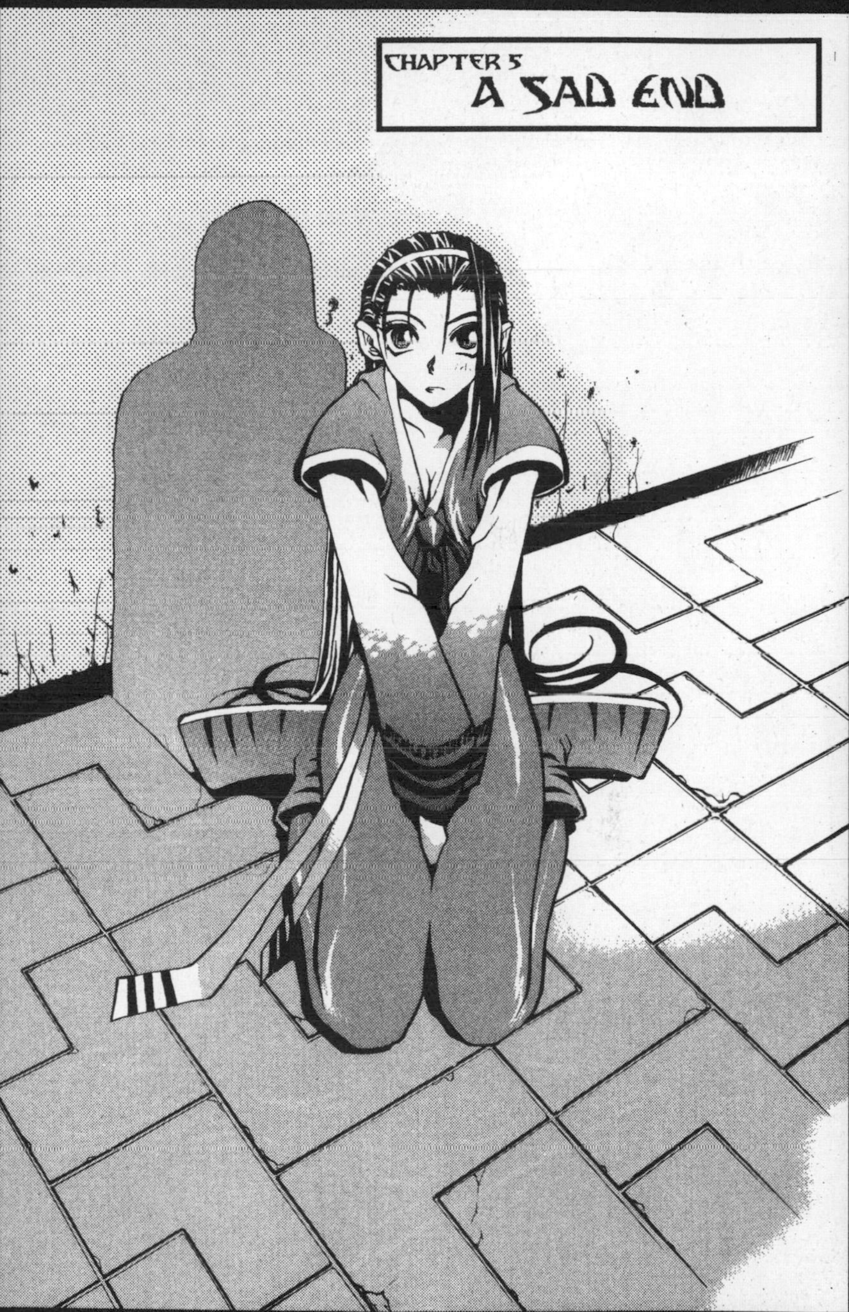
CHAPTER 5
A SAD END

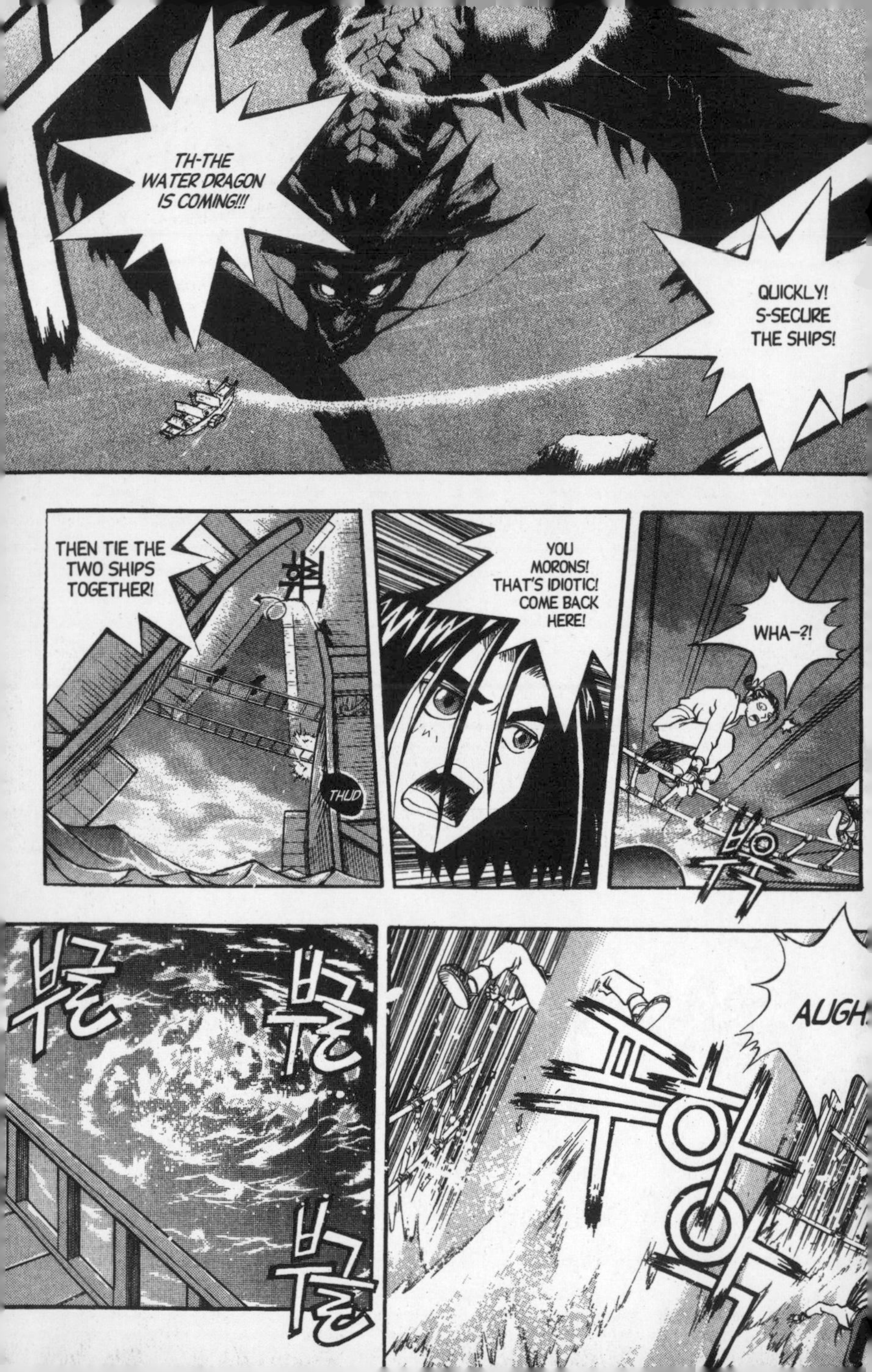
TH-THE WATER DRAGON IS COMING!!!
QUICKLY! S-SECURE THE SHIPS!
THEN TIE THE TWO SHIPS TOGETHER!
THUD
YOU MORONS! THAT'S IDIOTIC! COME BACK HERE!
WHA-?!
AUGH

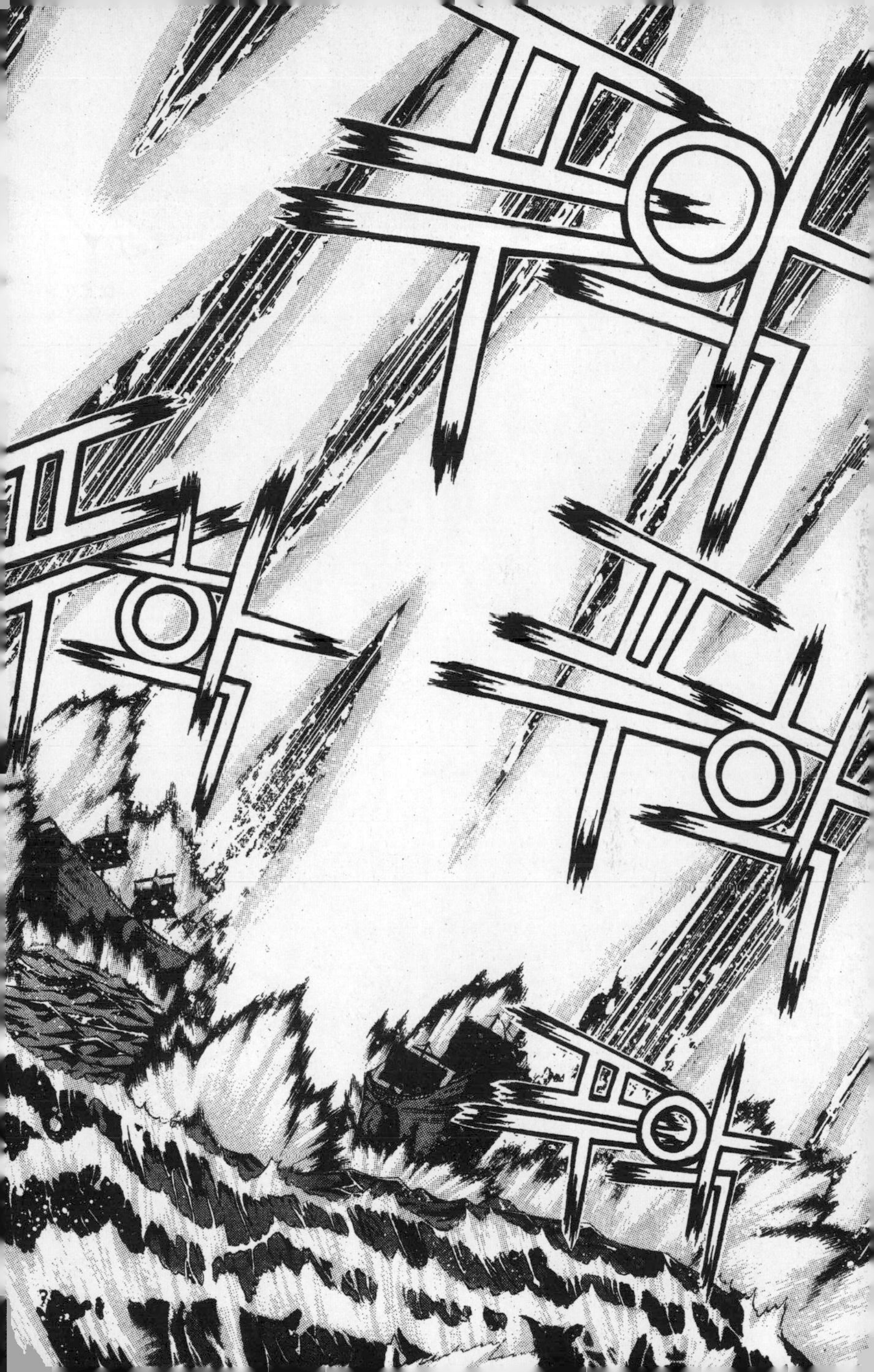

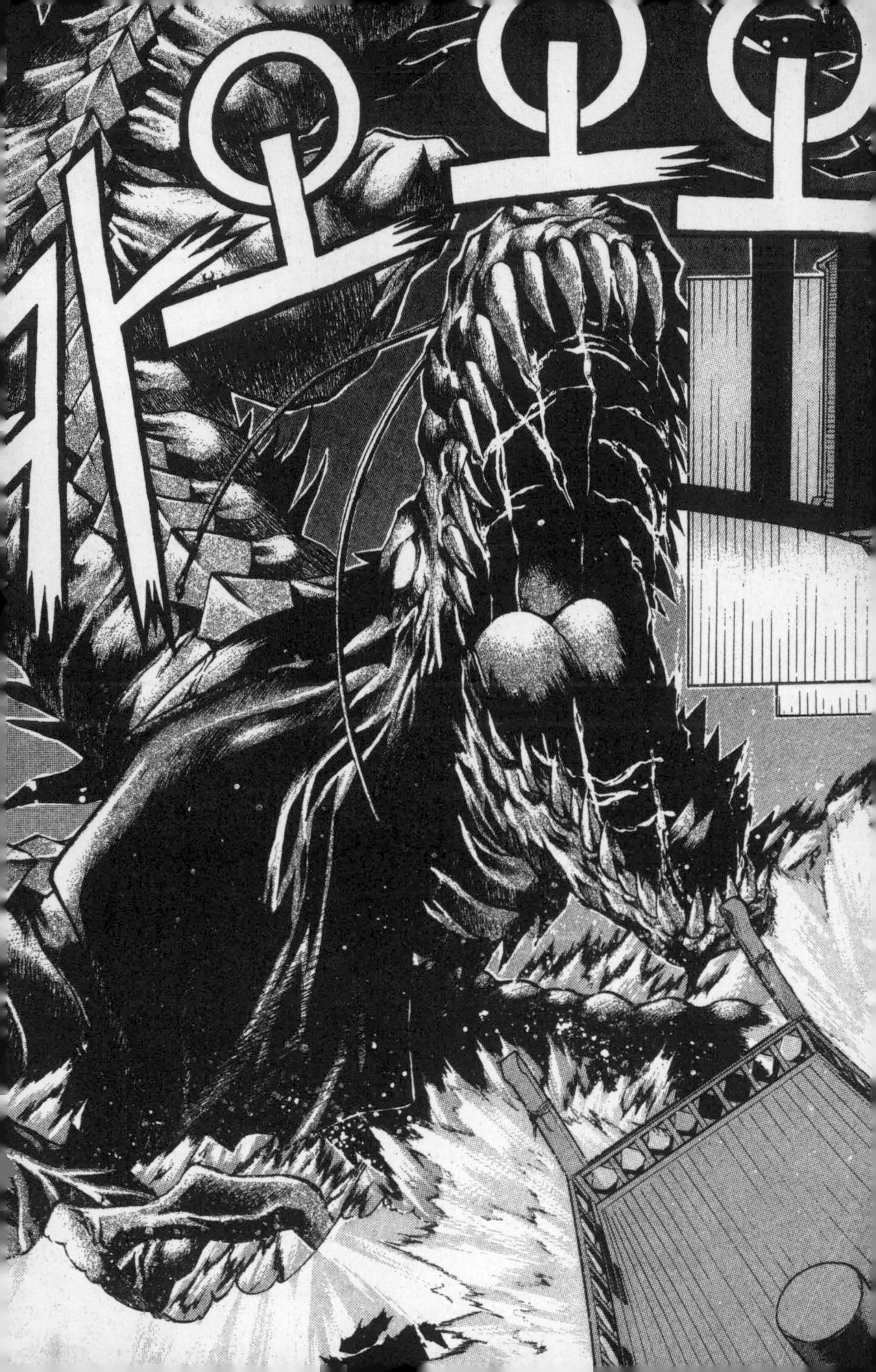

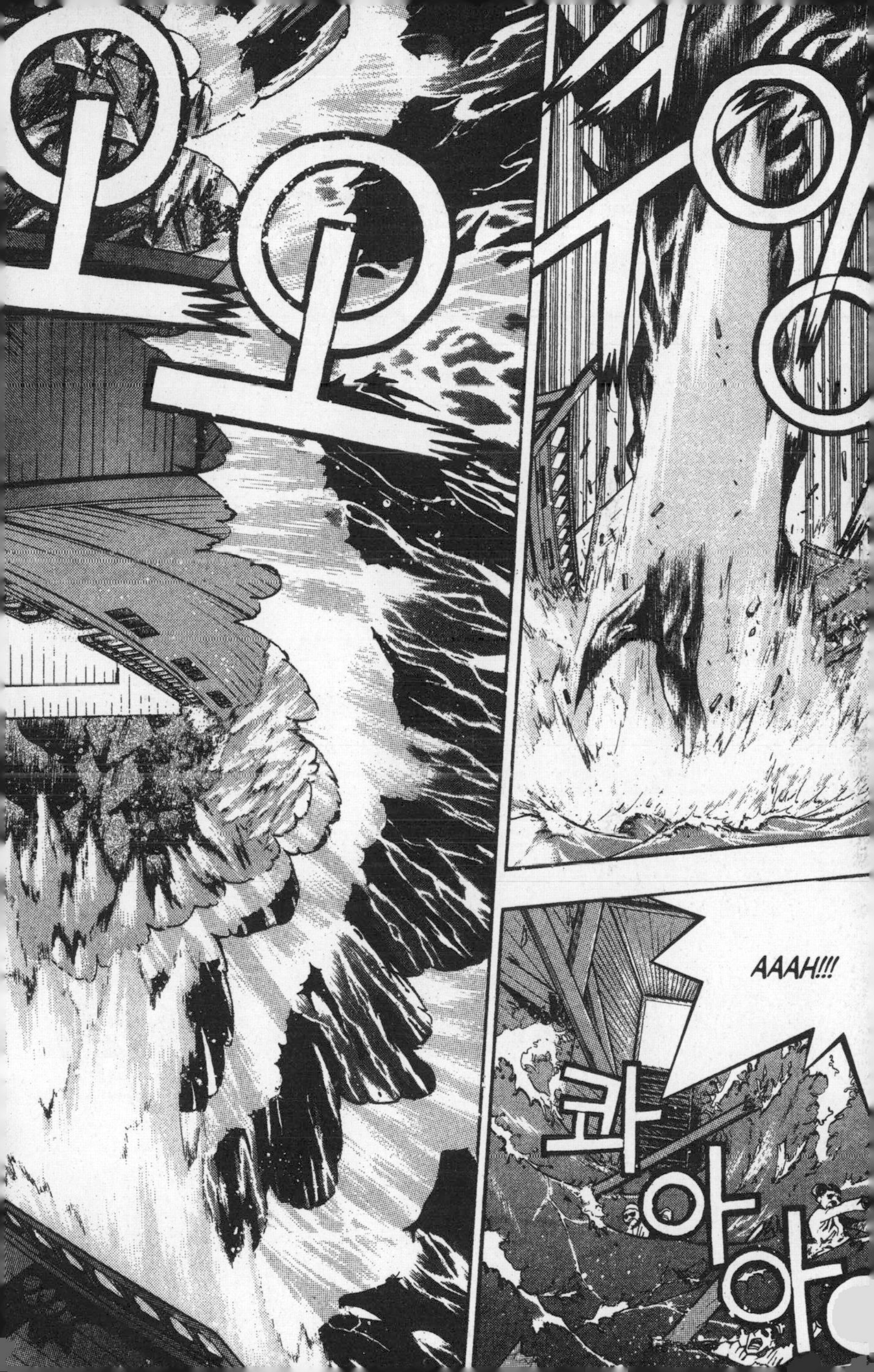
AAAH!!!
콰아아

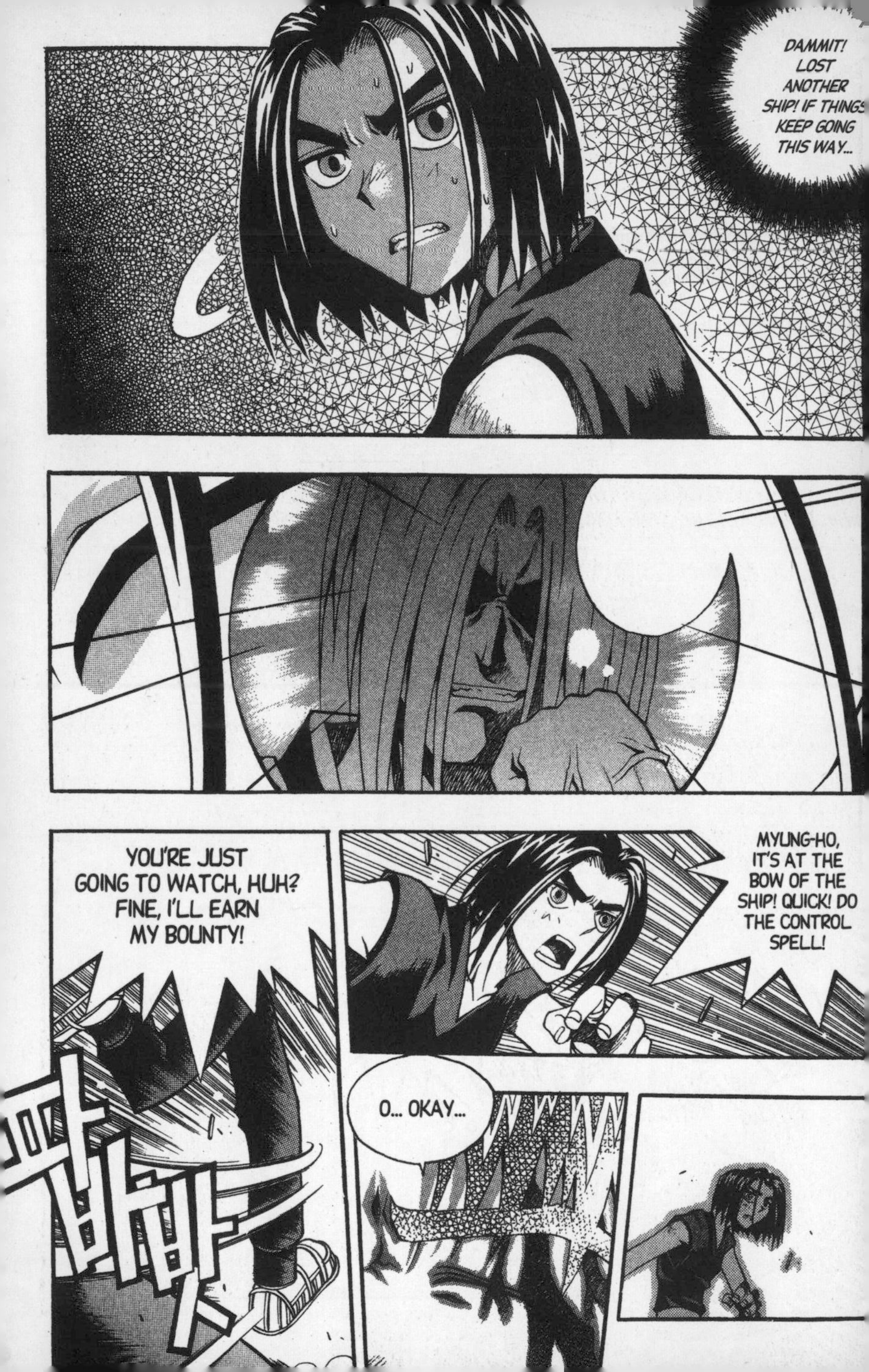
DAMMIT! LOST ANOTHER SHIP! IF THINGS KEEP GOING THIS WAY...
YOU'RE JUST GOING TO WATCH, HUH? FINE, I'LL EARN MY BOUNTY!
MYUNG-HO, IT'S AT THE BOW OF THE SHIP! QUICK! DO THE CONTROL SPELL!
O... OKAY...

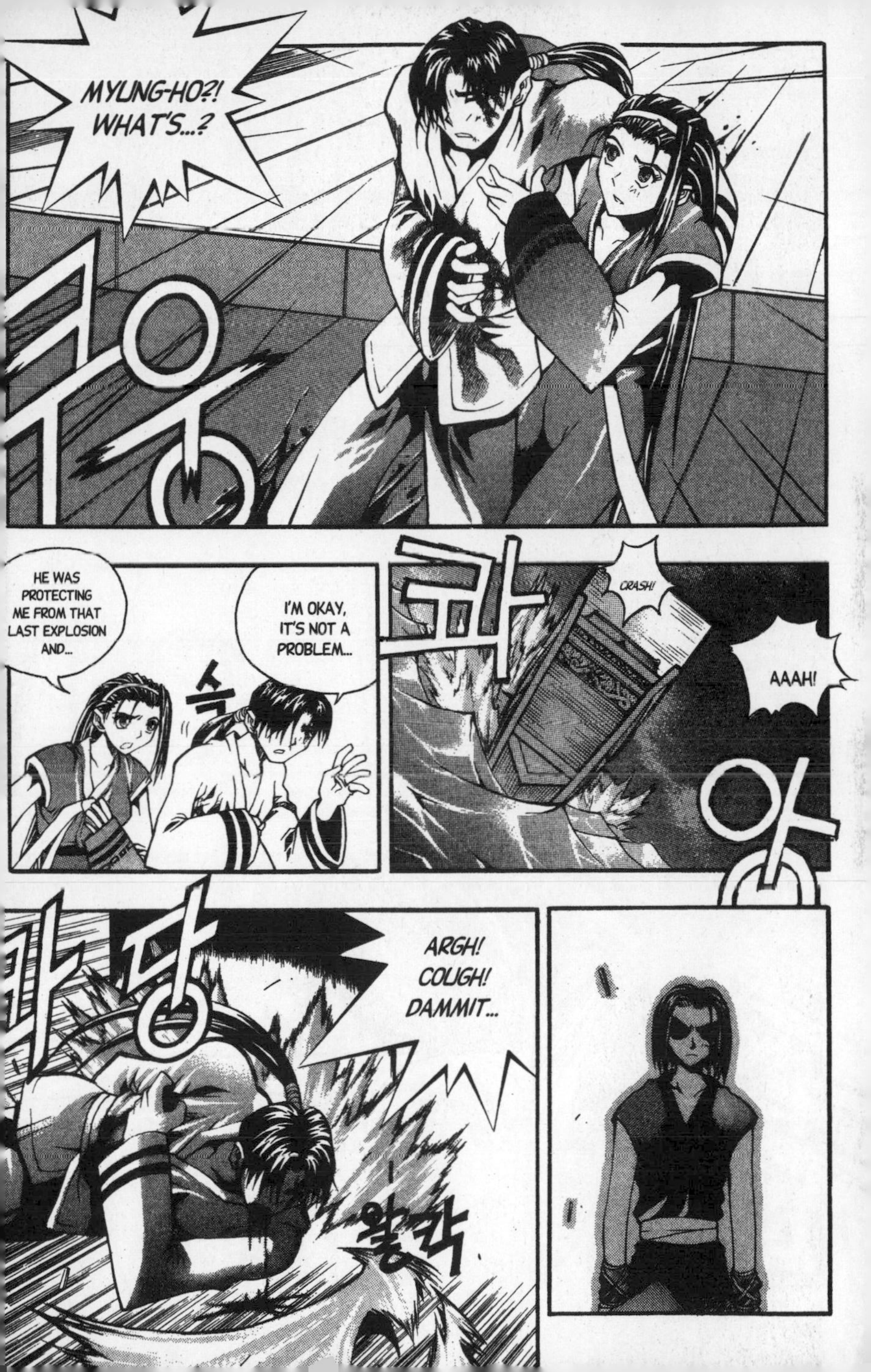
MYUNG-HO?! WHAT'S...?
HE WAS PROTECTING ME FROM THAT LAST EXPLOSION AND...
슥
I'M OKAY, IT'S NOT A PROBLEM...
CRASH!
AAAH!
ARGH! COUGH! DAMMIT...

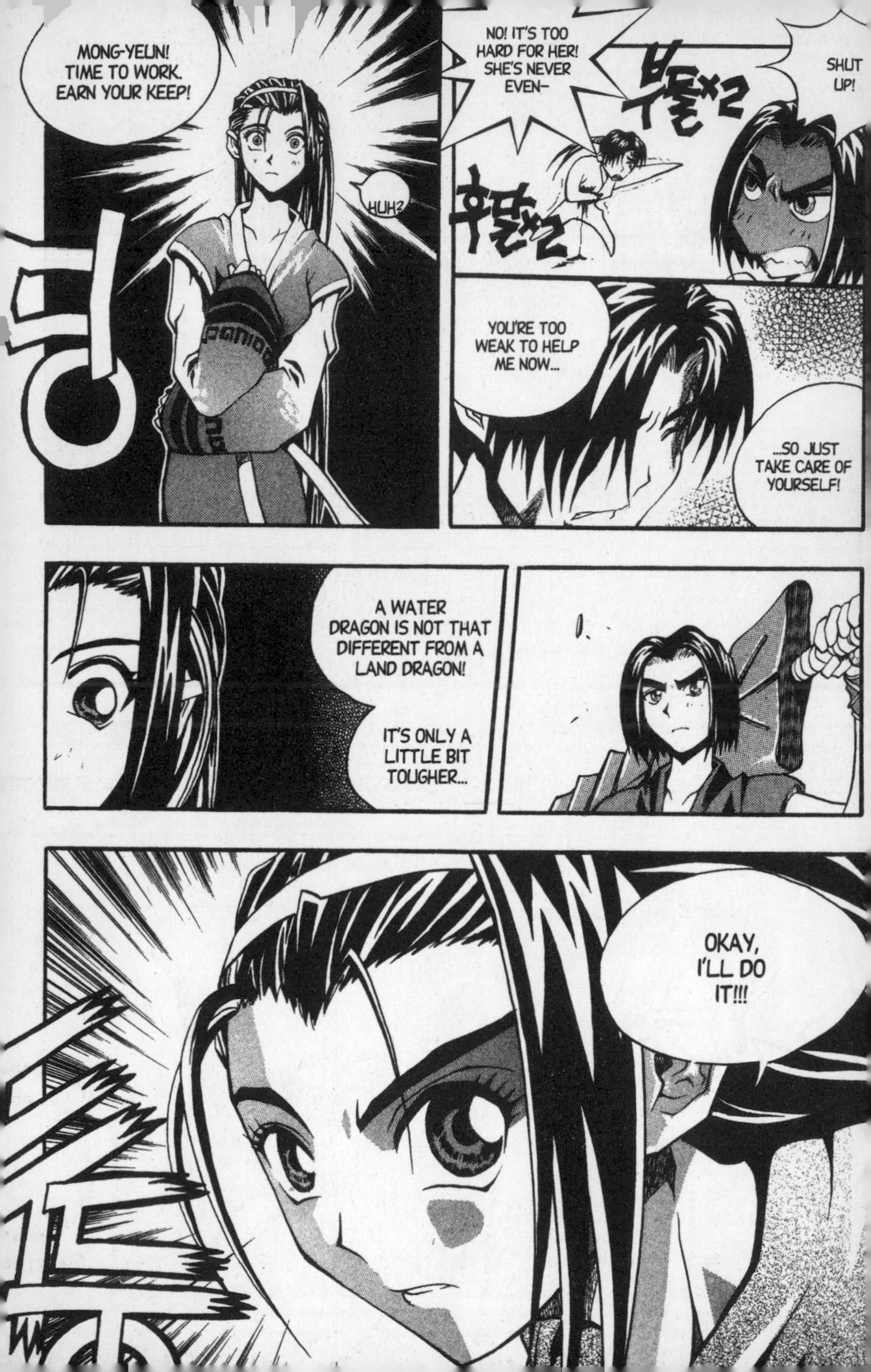
MONG-YEUN! TIME TO WORK. EARN YOUR KEEP!
HUH?
NO! IT'S TOO HARD FOR HER! SHE'S NEVER EVEN–
부들×2
SHUT UP!
후들×2
YOU'RE TOO WEAK TO HELP ME NOW...
...SO JUST TAKE CARE OF YOURSELF!
A WATER DRAGON IS NOT THAT DIFFERENT FROM A LAND DRAGON!
IT'S ONLY A LITTLE BIT TOUGHER...
OKAY, I'LL DO IT!!!

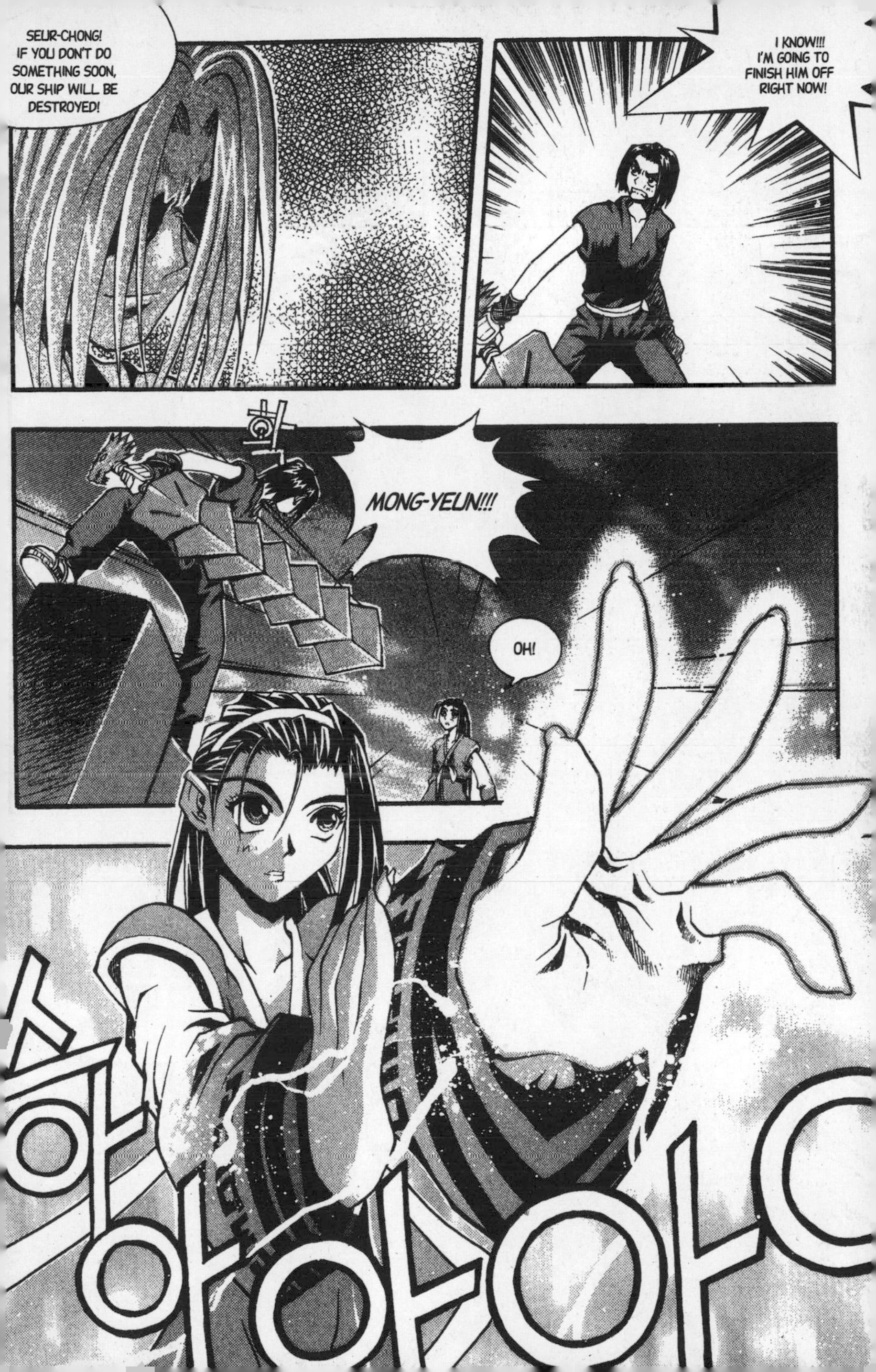
SEUR-CHONG! IF YOU DON'T DO SOMETHING SOON, OUR SHIP WILL BE DESTROYED!
I KNOW!!! I'M GOING TO FINISH HIM OFF RIGHT NOW!
MONG-YEUN!!!
OH!

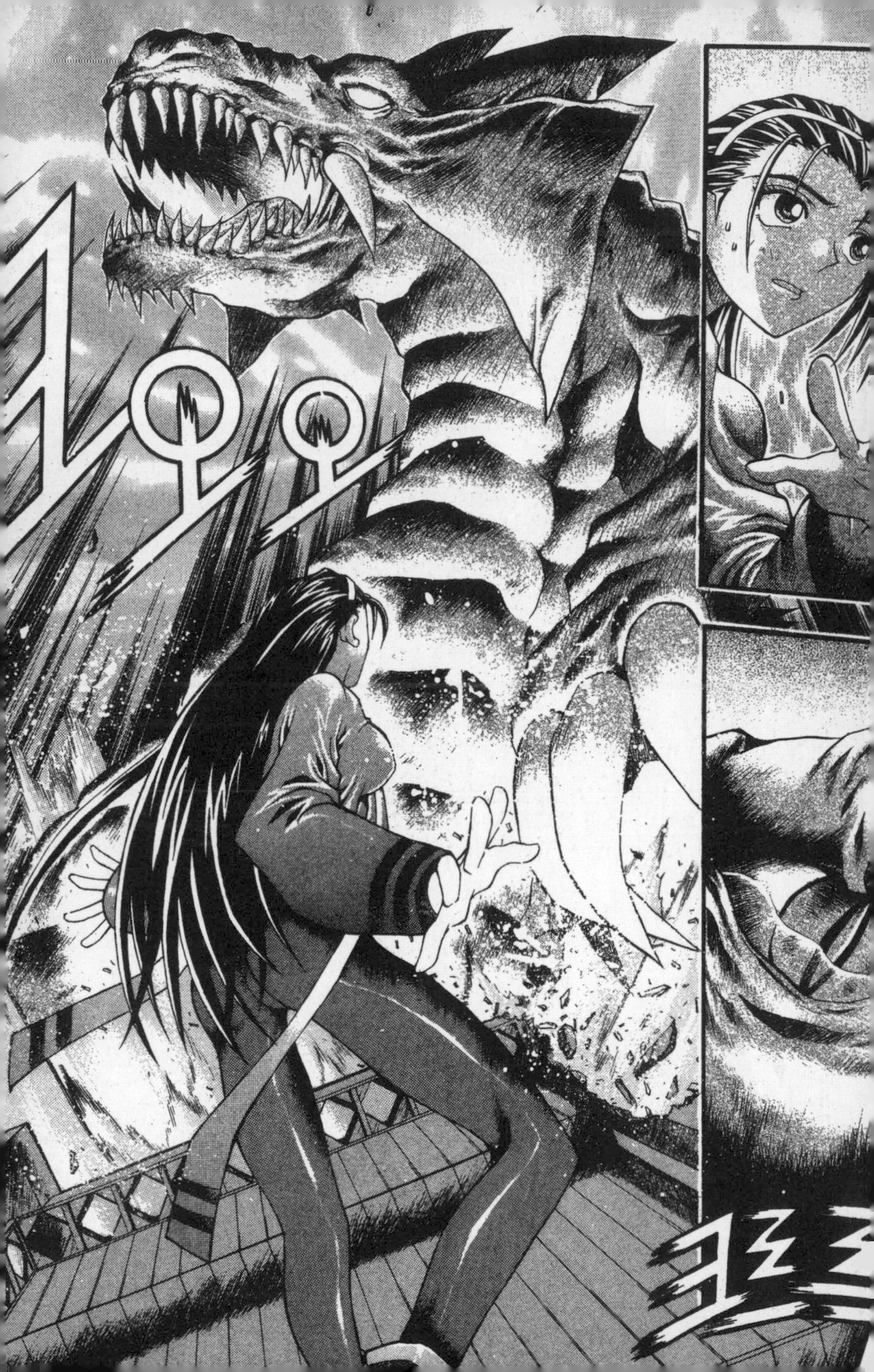

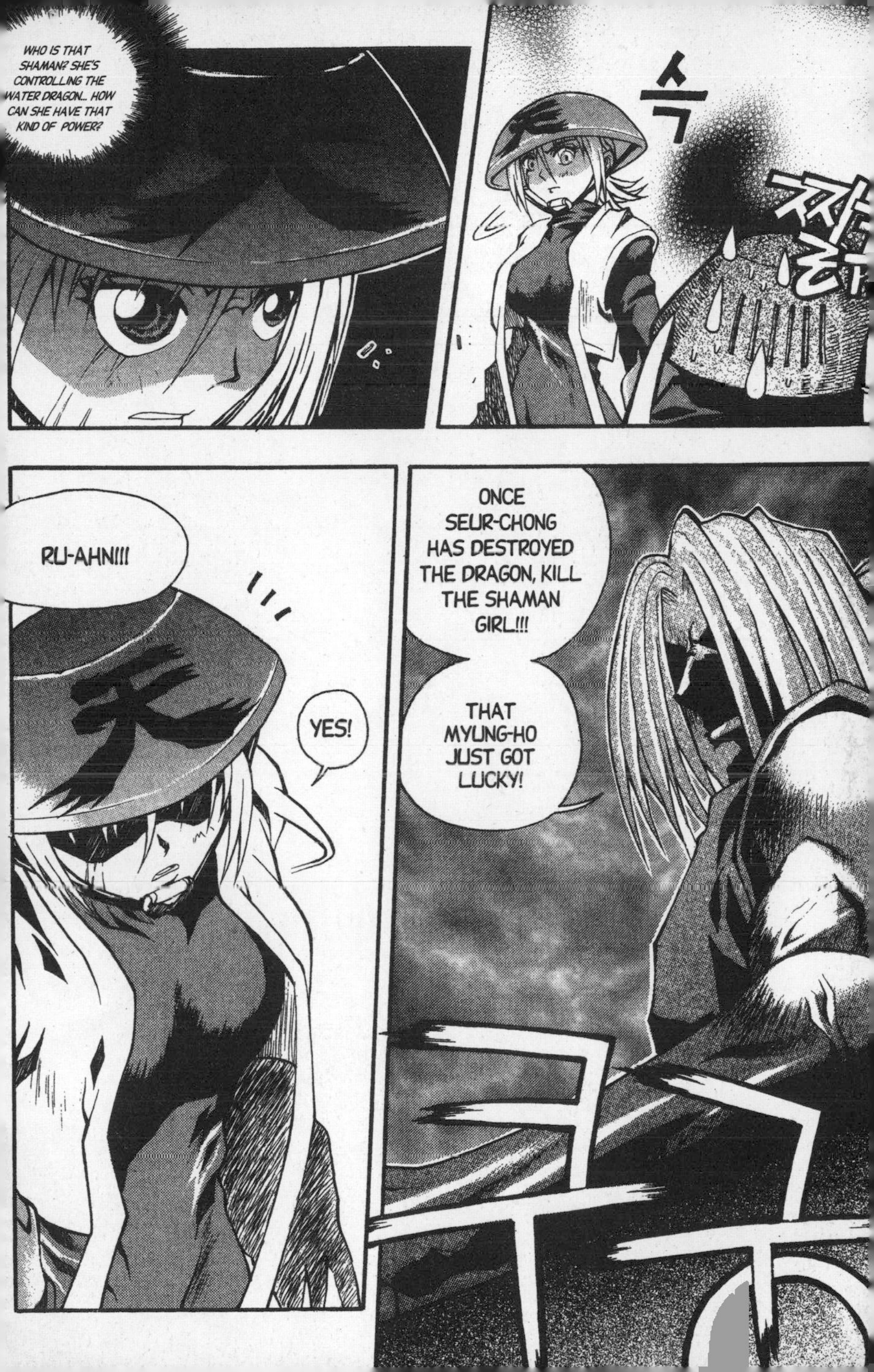
WHO IS THAT SHAMAN? SHE'S CONTROLLING THE WATER DRAGON... HOW CAN SHE HAVE THAT KIND OF POWER?
RU-AHN!!!
YES!
ONCE SEUR-CHONG HAS DESTROYED THE DRAGON, KILL THE SHAMAN GIRL!!!
THAT MYUNG-HO JUST GOT LUCKY!

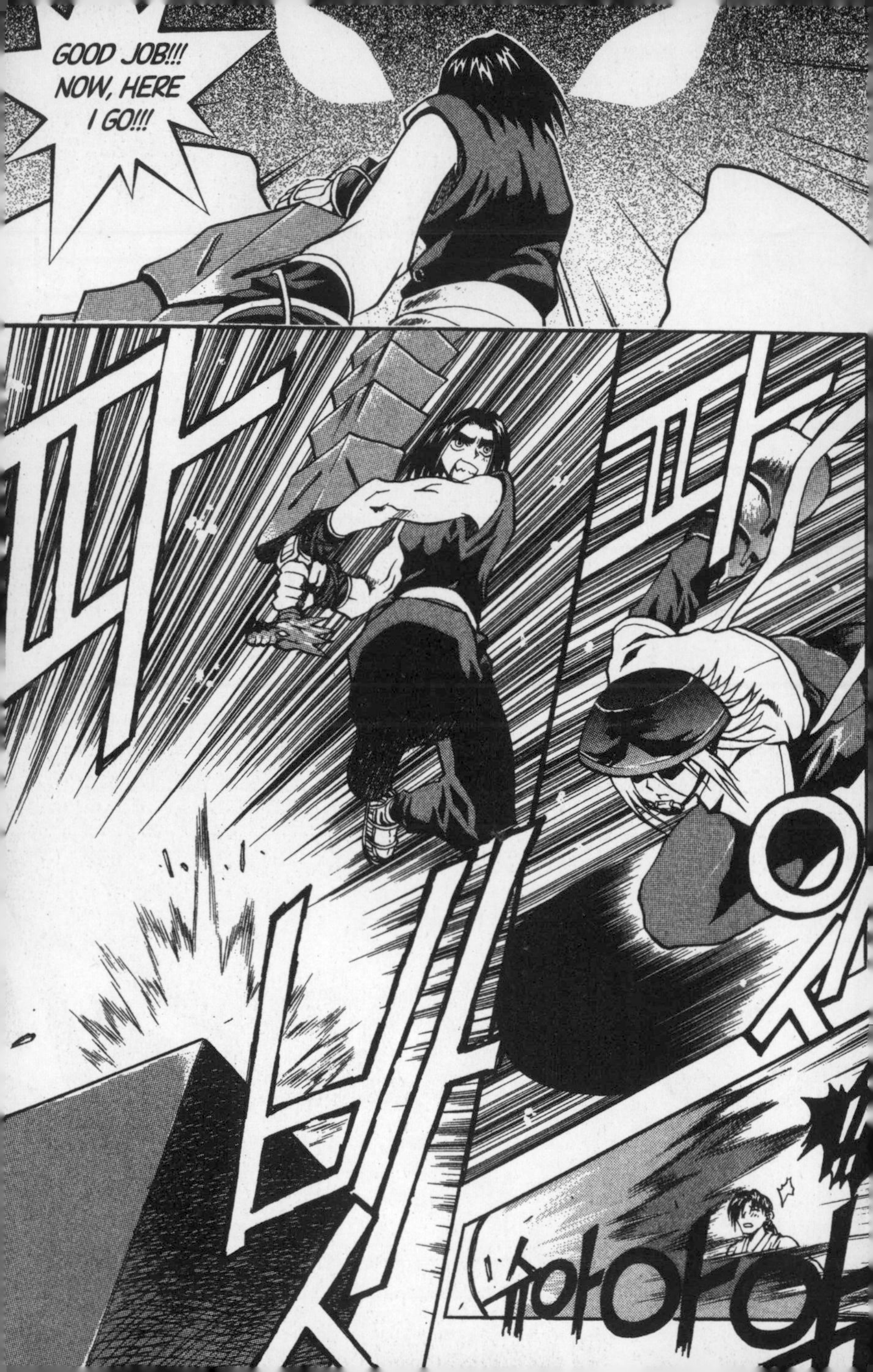
GOOD JOB!!! NOW, HERE I GO!!!

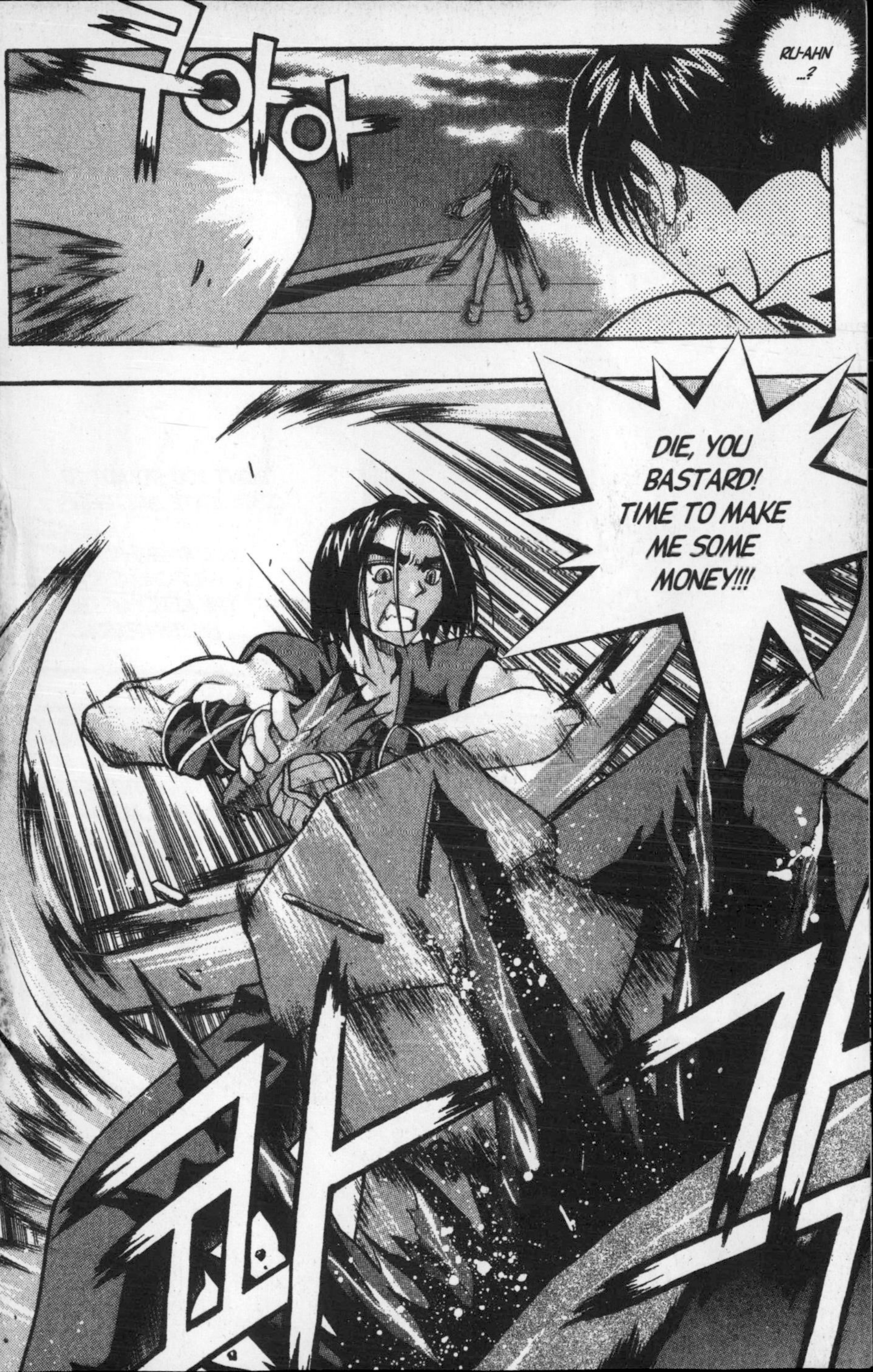
RU-AHN ...?
DIE, YOU BASTARD! TIME TO MAKE ME SOME MONEY!!!

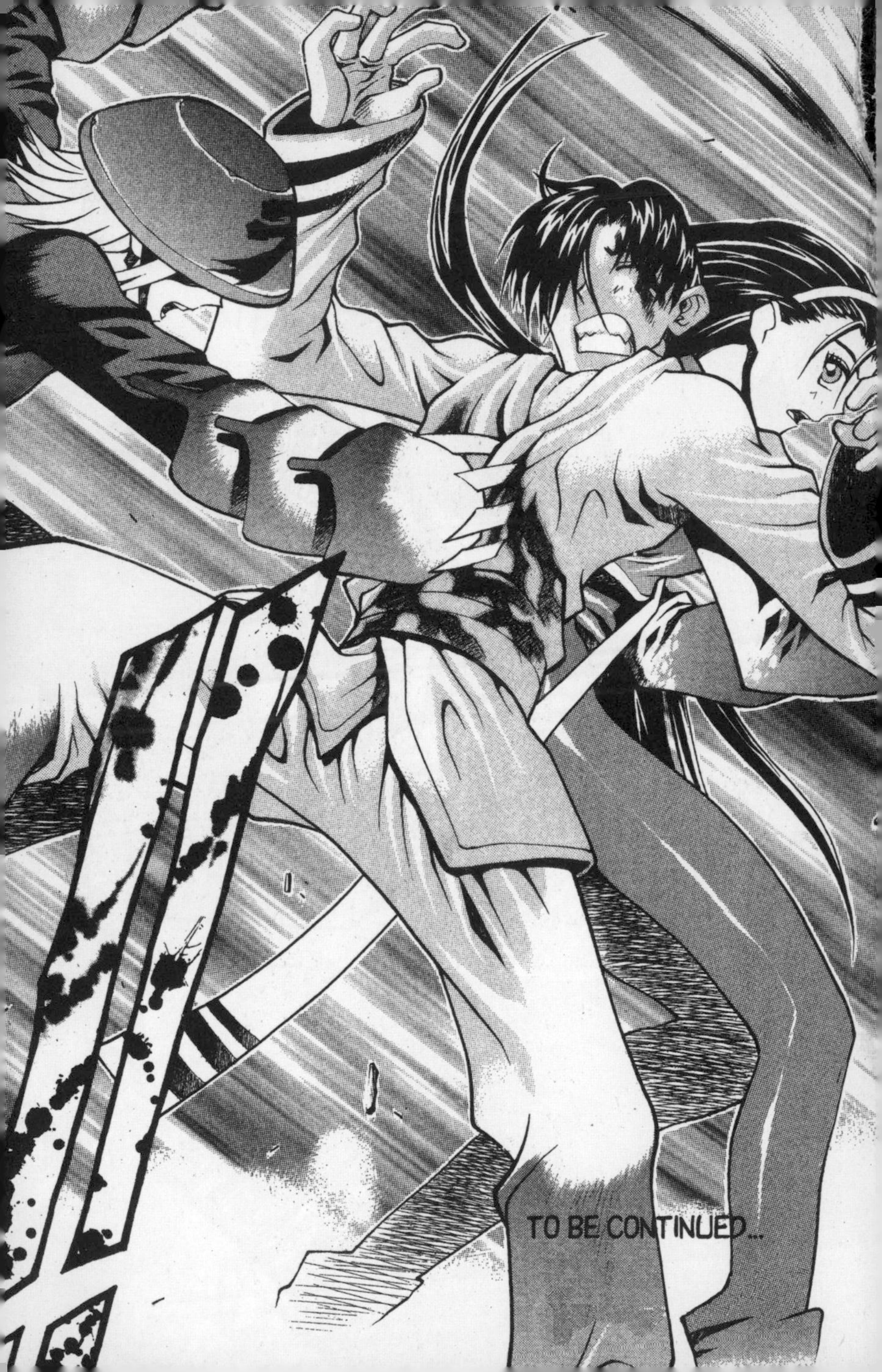
TO BE CONTINUED...

THE STUDIO REDSTONE STORY (CHAPTER 1)

Hello, this is Hong-Seock of Studio Redstone! I don't know how many of these I'm going to do, but here goes the first one anyway. This is going to be about my personal life... so consider it like a footnote.

Recently, Studio Redstone has been busy. First, we have been concentrating on the production of *Dragon Hunter* for a weekly magazine. We are also editing the *Dragon Hunter* trade paperback. These are only two things, but it's a lot of work for us! Friends who helped me with my previous comic book (*Cho In Jin*) all had to go do their military service, so I recruited a new team, but we're still learning how to work together. We're also learning how to color comic books and are still just "playing around." I use the expression "playing" because that's the most we can do right now. I hope our skills improve soon so we can stop playing around! Focus!

Speaking of playing, Studio Redstone also loves to surf the Net, but right now we only have a dial-up connection. Our studio is located in the city of Sangloksu in the Ansan prefecture. This area doesn't have high speed landline service yet; however, we badly wanted a faster connection, so we found a satellite service. We installed all the equipment and used the Internet (mainly for downloading), but it ended up being too expensive. We were told a high speed service was coming to the area soon, so we cancelled the satellite service. But as I write this, we still don't have a connection. I am so disappointed. But we hope we will have a high speed service someday, so we'll use the dial-up for now.

Finally, I resisted buying a PlayStation 2 for the longest time (I was actually saving money to buy a Sega Dreamcast, but I ended up making an impulse purchase of a PS2). I bought the PS2 mainly for the game *D.O.L. (Dead Or Live)*. I had high expectations for this game. However, I played it once, was disappointed, and never played it again. We just play *Strong Fist Tag* sometimes and hope that there will be better PS2 games in the future. We know it's stupid, but we're thinking of buying a Dreamcast because we love the *Street Fighter 2D* game. But PS2's DVD capability is fantastic...

Anyway, enjoy *Dragon Hunter*. I'll see you in Volume 2!

CREATING THE CHARACTERS

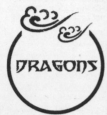

DRAGONS

Dragons exist in this world. They have much greater power than humans. They have abilities such as controlling lightning and thunder. With their abilities, they can also create their own realms, (spaces in which they can live). Dragons live infinitely, but they can ascend to heaven when their dragon stone is a thousand years old and transforms into a yoh-e-ju (dragon gem). Dragon scale is very strong, so people use it for making armor. The size of one dragon scale is four times the height of a man and its thickness is half a chuk (15.1515 cm). Seur-Chong's Mi-Ru-Do (dragon sword) is made from dragon scales.

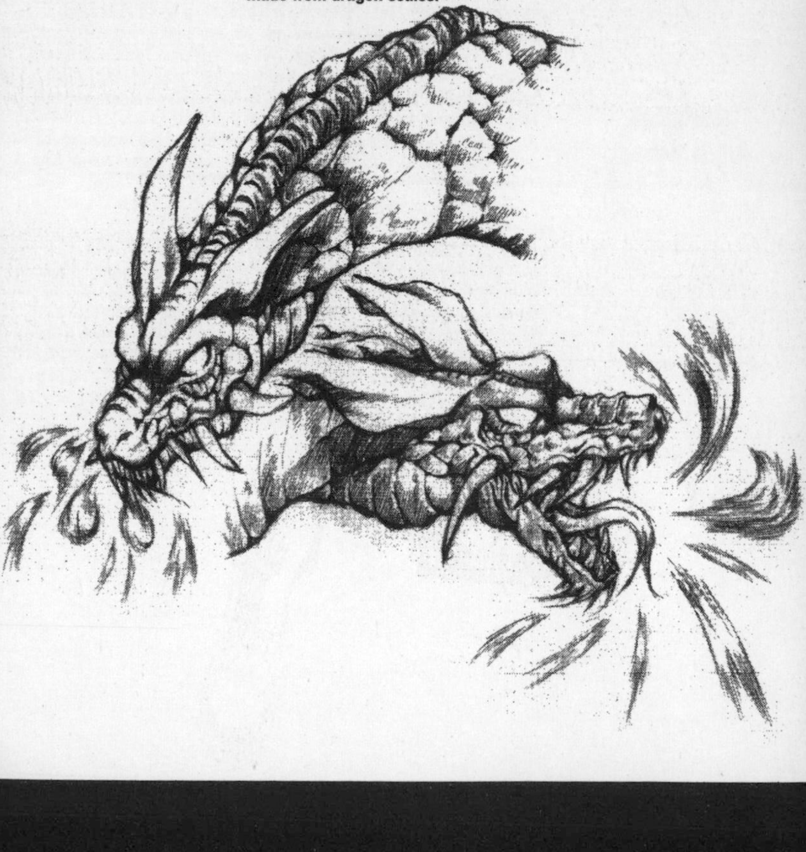

SEUR-CHONG

He is a reckless dragon hunter who loves making money. He hunts dragons with great abilities for the sole purpose of making money. His body is turning to stone because of a curse from a Guardian Dragon of the Dragon God. However, Seur-Chong does not care about the curse, and keeps hunting dragons to make money. People say Seur-Chong is similar to the author in that they both love money—which I cannot deny. Seur-Chong appears in almost every scene in this comic book, so it is not necessary to explain much more about him.

Backstory: When I first created Seur-Chong, he had a long ponytail. However, he looked like an honest person in that design, so his appearance was changed to the present design, which is more humorous. See end of this section for the original design.

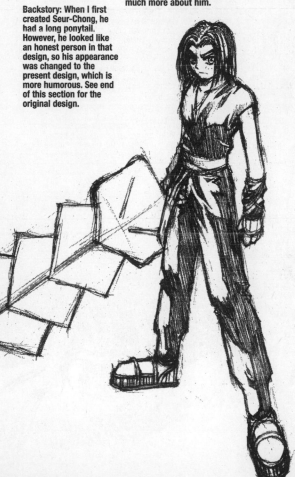

MYUNG-HO

Since Seur-Chong loves money and gambling, Myung-Ho was created to compliment him. His life was once saved by Seur-Chong, so I wanted to give the impression that Myung-Ho was reluctantly dragged into things. But Myung-Ho is also a shaman with great power and the ability to control dragons. He has been considered a nice guy and I am satisfied with that.

Backstory: Myung-Ho was supposed to die for Mong-Yeun in the 10th episode. However, he became so popular that the character survived. That is why Ahranseur's part became smaller than I originally planned. Does that make Myung-Ho a bad brother?

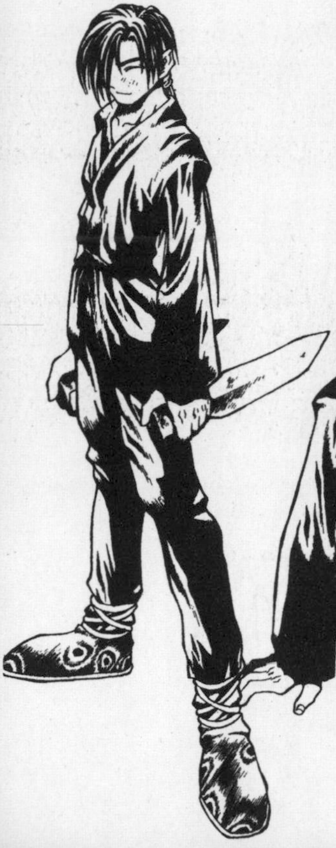

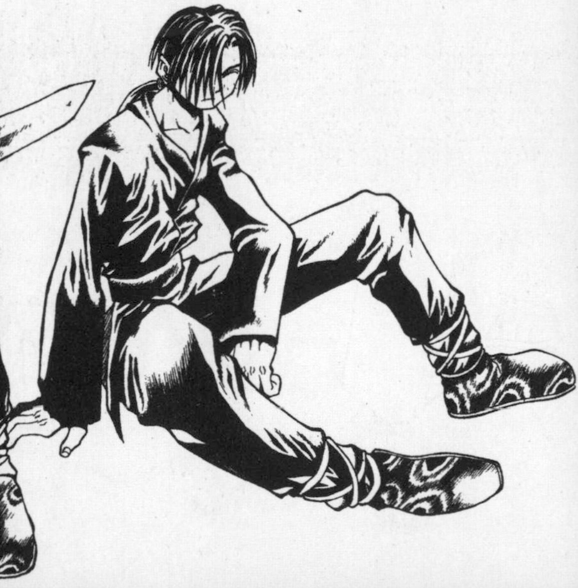

MONG-YEUN

She is a mysterious character, always has a poker face and does not make any sense when she talks. She is a female shaman. Upon joining Seur-Chong's company, she argued with him about almost everything. Mong-Yeun is not a main character at the beginning, but I believe her part will be bigger as a heroine soon. Personally, she is my favorite character, although her personality is...

ARANSEUR

She is Myung-Ho's little sister. She could have been a female shaman because her brother was a shaman who served at a temple. Aranseur does not like that her brother has a dangerous job as a dragon hunter. That's why she hates Seur-Chong. Her parents died when she was young and Myung-Ho raised her, so she is a tomboy. She was supposed to be a heroine after Myung-Ho's death. However, Aranseur's role as a heroine went to Mong-Yeun because of the change in plot. I feel sorry for her.

DAECHANG-NIM

(meaning "leader" or "boss")

I spent so much time creating this character and choosing a name for him, but his part ended up small. He has many secrets and his role will be very important, even in future stories. Please wait for his comeback. He will bring the "wind of blood." He has a name, but it is too early to reveal it.

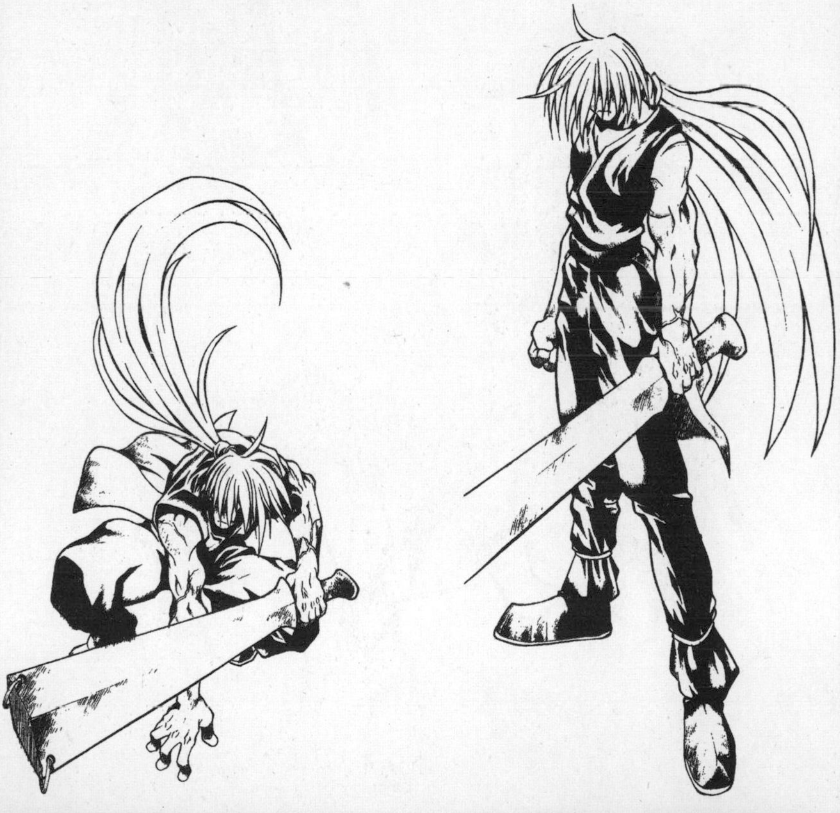

SO-CHUN

This character is so lucky. She started as an extra and became an important character. Her character supports Seur-Chong. She has a lot of personality. She is my second favorite character after Mong-Yeun. There will be a story of what happened between So-Chun and Mong-Yeun in future episodes. Please stay tuned for it!

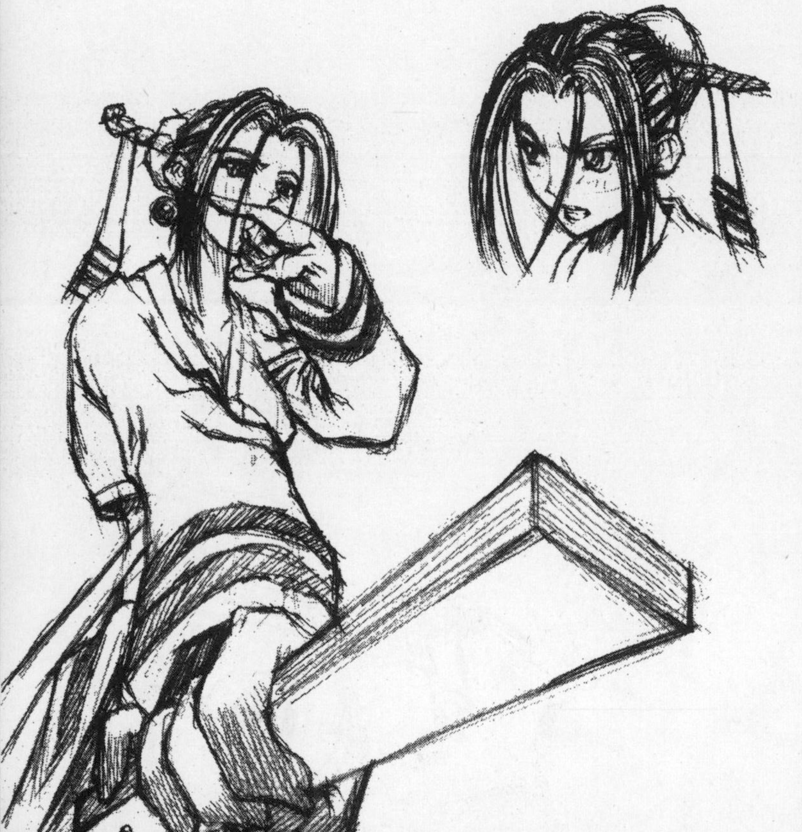

MOBILE UNIT

The mobile unit is made for hunting dragons. It is mostly made of wood, so it is fast but easy to destroy. It operates on a steam-powered engine that is made of bronze on the inside and wood on the outside. Some people who have higher social status have mobile units that are iron-plated on the outside for added protection.

SEUR-CHONG

This is one of the original designs for Seur-Chong. He has a thin body and long ponytail that makes him look like a Japanese samurai, so I threw out this design. I was somewhat disappointed that I spent so much time on an unused design...